# PETE SAMPRAS

## GREATNESS REVISITED

### STEVE FLINK

Foreword by
Chris Evert

New Chapter Press

# PETE SAMPRAS

## GREATNESS REVISITED

"Pete Sampras: Greatness Revisited" is published by New Chapter Press (www.NewChapterMedia. com) and is distributed by the Independent Publishers Group (www.IPGBook.com).

ISBN: 978-1937559946

For more information on this title or New Chapter Press contact:

Randy Walker
Managing Partner
New Chapter Press
1175 York Ave Suite #3s New York, NY 10065
Rwalker@NewChapterMedia.com

Photos are courtesy of Cynthia Lum, except the photo of young Pete Sampras on page 7 which is courtesy of Mark Winters and Cynthia Lum, the PowerShares Series photo of Sampras which is courtesy of the Invesco Series QQQ and InsideOut Sports & Entertainment, the 1990 U.S. Open trophy photo and the front cover which is courtesy of Alamy and the photo of Sampras with Bud Collins and Rod Laver which is courtesy of Anita Ruthling Klaussen.

# Dedication

To my inexhaustible father and mentor, Stanley Flink, who sparked my interest in tennis and has taught me many lasting and crucial lessons about my craft.

# Table of Contents

# ACKNOWLEDGMENTS

Where to start? Having worked happily as a tennis writer full time since 1974, I am indebted to a wide range of people who have played critical roles in the evolution of my career. Gladys M. Heldman—the founder of *World Tennis Magazine* and one of the sport's most indispensable leaders—was one of my biggest boosters. The affable Ron Bookman hired me to work at that prestigious publication 46 years ago and guided me generously. Both Gladys and Ron—who have both passed away—gave me the benefit of their considerable wisdom and helped me to gain a foothold in the sport as a journalist. The late Gene Scott gave me an important forum writing for his esteemed *Tennis Week* magazine from 1992-2007.

No one did more in my formative journalistic years to point me in the right direction than Bud Collins. I met him in 1969 at Wimbledon when I was 17. In 1972, he brought me aboard his professional ship as a statistician and "aide-de-camp" on his NBC and CBS telecasts at Wimbledon and the U.S. Open. Working for Bud gave me credibility in the tennis world and through my association with him innumerable prominent figures in tennis reporting circles got to know me. When Bud passed away in 2016, we lost one of our most revered figures. My friend John Barrett—widely admired for his work as an outstanding BBC commentator—has been a staunch ally and the late Herbert Warren Wind of *The New Yorker* believed in me more than I believed in myself. The late Ted Tinling taught me more about the inner workings of tennis than anyone else and his generosity of spirit enhanced my life more than he ever knew. S.L. Price of *Sports Illustrated* has long been one of my most trusted colleagues and a friend unlike any other, and Joel Drucker has shared his considerable wit and wisdom with me through the many years of our friendship.

Italy's inimitable Ubaldo Scanagatta has been an unwavering and outstanding colleague. The remarkable historian Andras Ruszanov is always generous in sharing his overview of the game with me. And the venerable Canadian journalist Tom Tebbutt is often by my side at the sport's major venues when the biggest matches are played. Brad Falkner spent a decade working for Tennis Channel and has always gone out of his way to champion my cause. Ken Solomon is CEO of Tennis Channel and he has incessantly been on my side of the net over the past twelve years. My longtime friend Greg Sharko of the ATP was invaluable in helping me reach some key players and coaches for the book.

I am indebted to all of the aforementioned people, and also grateful to those who agreed to be interviewed for this book. Many thanks to Rod Laver, Mats Wilander, Stefan Edberg, Jim Courier, Michael Chang, Todd Martin, Patrick Rafter, Goran Ivanisevic, Greg Rusedski, Martina Navratilova, Billie Jean King, Monica Seles, Mary Carillo, Robert Lansdorp, Tom Gullikson, Paul Annacone, Tracy Austin, John Austin, Ivan Lendl, John McEnroe, Brad Gilbert, Darren Cahill, and Novak Djokovic. Their recollections and observations about Pete Sampras were essential in providing a sharper view of what made him such a distinctive champion.

Let me single out a few others outside of the tennis universe who have influenced me significantly. The songwriter Burt Bacharach's soaring melodies have enriched my entire life and lifted my spirits ceaselessly—even while I am working. No writer has inspired me more than the lyrical Pete Hamill. I have been reading his extraordinary body of work ever since 1971, the year Pete Sampras was born.

I am deeply appreciative for the unbending loyalty of my wife, Frances, my son, Jonathan, and my daughter, Amanda. Jonathan's wife, Kasia, has also been very supportive, as has my sister, Wendy Levey. All of these family members have understood my tennis obsession, and their backing was reassuring as I was writing this biography.

In closing, I offer my gratitude to Pete Sampras for the countless hours he spent conversing with me so thoughtfully across the better part of a year. This book would not have been born without his incalculable contribution.

—Steve Flink
Katonah, New York
October, 2019

# FOREWORD

Whenever I think about Pete Sampras and how he shined as a tennis player, I remember that incredible combination of brute force and the amazing smoothness he always showed us. He was like silk on the court the way he covered it. His placid temperament stands out as well. Nothing seemed to bother him too much. His game was aggressive, but not his personality.

I could relate to his temperament, of course, because I was also known for keeping my cool. So I was annoyed when I heard him called boring by some people. They said that about me as well. I was protective of Pete when I heard that because he came along in the era of Andre Agassi, while Jimmy Connors and John McEnroe were finishing up their careers. Jim Courier, Boris Becker and other charismatic players were competing at the same time as Pete. But Pete wasn't boring at all.

When I would hear some fans say, 'Why doesn't he show more emotion or get mad or show some personality?' I thought that was unfair. Very much like Roger Federer, his tennis had beauty in itself. I liked watching him because he was the opposite of how I played—powerful, smooth and aggressive. It was a different style for me to watch. I was fascinated by it.

His standards were very high as a person and a player. Pete was admired for the dynamic way he played and the creativity, power and touch he brought to tennis. His sportsmanship was outstanding. He had so much respect for the game.

Pete had a great rivalry with Agassi that reminded me of mine with Martina Navratilova. It was very similar in some ways with the contrasting personalities. Andre was more charismatic and aggressive with his personality and Pete was more subdued. His rivalry with Andre had it all—serve-and-volleyer versus baseliner; power attacking player versus counter puncher; different builds; different backgrounds. Those contrasts made for an interesting rivalry and when I watched them play I found it very relatable.

Everyone talks about this incredible era in men's tennis with Federer, Rafael Nadal and Novak Djokovic, but Pete's era was great as well with himself, Agassi, Courier, Michael Chang, Boris Becker, Stefan Edberg and others. Pete brought a new brand of tennis to the scene. I keep coming back to that smoothness, which was unlike anything I had ever seen. He mastered the game like Federer has done. Pete had all the shots with his potent groundstrokes, superb volleying skills and a ferocious serve. He had the whole package.

I have only seen two players master the game and show that they have every shot in the book—Pete Sampras and Roger Federer. They mastered it temperament-wise and game-wise. We should never forget that about Pete. He brought a lot of kids into the game who emulated him, appreciated his good manners and wanted to play like him.

At the end of the day, Pete was not controversial, on or off the court. He just went his quiet way and did things on the tennis court that few people have. They called him "Gentleman Pete" and that is who he was. Sometimes the bad guys get the press. He is one of the good guys.

Steve Flink started his career around the same time I started mine, in the early 1970's. He is a tennis journalist who thinks more like a player and knows the game the way few people do. His career biography here on Sampras is an important reminder to all of us about what Pete meant to the sport and how beautifully he played it. Steve is a great writer and historian and in this book he puts Pete's career fully into perspective. I am sure you will enjoy reading this enlightening and comprehensive account about Pete Sampras, a very graceful champion and one of the greatest players any of us will ever see.

Chris Evert
Boca Raton, Florida

# INTRODUCTION

In many ways, I have been writing this book from the latter stages of Pete Sampras's career right up until today. As a reporter watching his career unfold and observing him competing with an equanimity few players have ever matched, I always held him in the highest regard. In my view, he won and lost as honorably as it could be done. He built a reputation as a straight-shooting athlete who had little or no interest in the showmanship that was so prevalent in his craft. This was his business and he took his life on the battlefield very seriously.

It impressed me immensely over the span of his 15-year professional career that his notion of what he wanted to achieve—and how he went about pursuing the highest honors the sport had to offer—was absolutely clear. I don't believe I have seen another tennis player in nearly five decades as a journalist who has been truer to his convictions or more willing to chase his aspirations with such grace and professionalism. Pete Sampras knew what he wanted and came to understand what it would take to realize his largest dreams and turn them time and again into reality. He was the ultimate professional of his era and a champion nonpareil who lived for nothing more than to play the game of tennis as well as it could be done. He intrinsically believed that as long as he remained totally immersed in what he was doing and did not deviate from his aims and agenda, no one could deny him when he was at the height of his powers in his kind of setting.

I became immersed in tennis when I was closing in on my 13th birthday, going to Wimbledon for the first time in June of 1965, being taken out to the shrine of the sport by my father. He had moved to London that summer and loved tennis, primarily as an avid club player. He wanted me to see a tournament that he knew transcended the game, to soak in the cultural experience, to attend a sporting event unlike any other.

Little did my father know that I would become immediately addicted to tennis. From that day forward, my mornings would start by perusing the sports pages in the newspaper searching for tournament results. I would attend Wimbledon and the U.S. Championships at Forest Hills day after day, summer after summer. By the time I was 15, my goal in life was to become a tennis reporter.

In the early 1970's, I established a foothold of sorts professionally, working behind the scenes with Bud Collins as a statistician on his CBS and NBC telecasts, helping him with his columns for the *Boston Globe* as well. In 1974, I was hired by the highly-regarded *World Tennis Magazine* as a writer and editor. I worked there happily for 17 years, moved on to *Tennis Week* magazine from 1992-2007 and have been writing regularly for *Tennis Channel* and tennis.com ever since. Over the last couple of decades, I wrote a couple of books on the history of the game and co-authored an instructional book with renowned coach and former American No. 1 Dennis Ralston.

Through my more than five decades in and around the game and nearly half a century of reporting on it, I have had the good fortune to witness a cavalcade of great players, from Rod Laver and Roy Emerson in my youth, to Arthur Ashe and Jimmy Connors, Bjorn Borg and John McEnroe, and all the way up to today's icons Roger Federer, Rafael Nadal and Novak Djokovic. I saw Billie Jean King in her prime, watched Chrissie Evert all across her two decades of supreme consistency in the 1970's and 1980's, marveled at the brilliance of Monica Seles and Steffi Graf and have witnessed the enduring eminence of the Williams sisters.

But no champion in my lifetime—first as a fan and ever since as a journalist—has impressed me more comprehensively than Pete Sampras. I watched him periodically in his first couple of pro seasons in 1988 and 1989. But it was when he won the 1990 U.S. Open at 19 in such startling fashion that I really stood up and took notice. I was convinced then that he would be a serious force in his field and I liked the way he conducted himself in such a no-nonsense manner. It struck me then that Sampras had the right set of priorities on a tennis court—fight hard, play fair, respect your peers, treat it all seriously and make it the most important thing in your life. Never surrender your integrity. Always play by the rules. Remember it is a sport and not just an occupation. Stay true to yourself.

The way I looked at it, Sampras unfailingly maintained those high standards and clear values for the rest of his career. He knew who he was and recognized how he should conduct himself out in the arena no matter how much was at stake or how often he was surrounded by stress. Tennis meant the world to Pete Sampras. He lived to make his mark in that undertaking. And as a writer who loved the sport as much as life itself, I chronicled his career very closely from that 1990 U.S. Open on. I felt in some ways that I understood him better than most of my colleagues. I believed that he represented the game exceedingly well and felt that he was not always portrayed fairly or accurately by many in my profession. To be sure, he was deeply respected by the media but too often the articles written on him were superficial. He was shy and reserved. He was also a multi-dimensional individual with deep sensitivity, a fine sense of humor and a sharp wit.

I first interviewed Sampras in 1992 and had several more sessions with him over the next couple of years. We did not meet in person until 1995, but thereafter I did many interviews with him both in person and over the phone. I felt that we had an extraordinary rapport based fundamentally on mutual respect. We spoke regularly through the rest of his career, but I continued doing the interviews long after he played his last official tournament, going out in style at the 2002 U.S. Open. Over the next decade and beyond, right up until the emergence of this book, I would talk once or twice a year with Sampras to get his impressions on his senior tennis events and on what was happening in the current men's game, writing lengthy columns on those topics.

Over the past year, from the fall of 2018 into the summer of 2019, I interviewed Sampras on countless occasions for this book. He was very generous with his time and willing to address a wide range of subjects. The timing of our discussions could not have been better because Sampras had transitioned in his life from a champion of the highest order obsessed with hitting tall targets in the field of competition to a husband and father with a different outlook on life, no longer consumed as all leading athletes are by personal goals. Now he is a family man enjoying his life as a parent and concerned largely with being a good husband and a compassionate and devoted father.

For me, writing this book has been a pleasure. In my head, I had mapped it out for a long while. I have drawn on my knowledge of his career and my sense of the person he is and the player he was. In my view, Pete Sampras at his best on hard courts, indoors or on grass is better than anyone who has ever lifted a racket. He was the consummate big match player with an incomparable champion's mentality. As for Pete Sampras the human being, in my view he is highly commendable, fundamentally decent and a fellow who speaks quietly yet forcefully about what he believes in. Speaking with Pete in our many sessions for this book, I was reminded of what it was I admired about him in the first place. There is a consistency to his character. He has always been quietly confident, clear in his convictions and an enemy of artificiality. In his late forties, Sampras is at his core the same unpretentious fellow he has always been.

I hope you enjoy reading this career biography about Pete Sampras as much as I enjoyed writing it.

Steve Flink
Katonah, New York

# CHAPTER 1

# THE GROOMING OF A FUTURE CHAMPION

As a new decade dawned in 1990, Pete Sampras, a gifted young player destined to establish himself as the greatest American ever to lift a racket, started making history of a high order at the tail end of his teens as the world of men's professional tennis was in the process of a reshuffling in the upper regions of the sport. In that memorable season, Sampras first came into view for many sports observers and displayed his athletic excellence and wide ranging skills as a tennis player of a rare ilk who could turn the court into his canvas and masterfully take apart formidable adversaries as if it was second nature to him. In many ways, he declared his greatness across an extraordinary New York fortnight with a U.S. Open triumph few had foreseen. Many learned fans witnessed his breakthrough and saw it as the birth of his eminence.

"Open Tennis" had commenced in 1968 only three years before Sampras was born and fittingly "The Rocket" Rod Laver—a hero to the young Sampras and a role model for players all over the globe—won his second Grand Slam the following year, affirming why he was an authentic candidate to be considered the best player of all time. The 1970's witnessed the emergence of renowned players including Sweden's implacable Bjorn Borg, who took eight of his eleven majors in that span, and the demonstrative American Jimmy Connors, who spent five consecutive years as the No. 1 ranked player in the sport.

Over the course of the 1980's, John McEnroe and Ivan Lendl achieved with extraordinary regularity when it counted the most. McEnroe, of course, had established himself with sweeping authority in the late seventies, taking his first Grand Slam singles title as a rambunctious 20-year-old in 1979. But the bulk of his best work as an artist unlike anyone the game had yet seen was done in the 1980's, when he spent four years in a row (1981-84) as the top ranked player in tennis. Lendl was the master of consistency in the eighties, claiming seven of his eight majors in that stretch.

But as the nineties commenced, it was apparent that the men's game was ready to be realigned in many ways. To be sure, great players like Sweden's Stefan Edberg and Germany's Boris Becker remained in the forefront of the sport, as did Lendl. And yet, it was apparent that the younger generation was moving swiftly toward the upper levels of the game, most notably a foursome from the United States who would turn the nineties into their showcase.

These Americans included the charismatic yet often confounding Andre Agassi, the industrious Jim Courier, the indefatigable Michael Chang, and, last but not least, the singularly versatile Sampras. All four had made their mark at the end of the 1980's, with Agassi rising strikingly to No. 3 in the world at 18 in 1988, and Chang becoming the first of the group to get on the board at a Grand Slam event, becoming the youngest man ever to rule at Roland Garros when he was 17 in 1989.

That cast of commendable young players formed the nucleus of what came to be regarded as "The Greatest Generation" ever in American tennis. They all would realize gigantic accomplishments. Each would land eventually in the shrine at the International Tennis Hall of Fame. Three of the four would reside at No. 1 in the world, while Chang narrowly missed a chance to make it to the top, achieving his best ranking at No. 2. They were backed up by other formidable American players including Todd Martin and Mal Washington. The imposing 6'6" Martin climbed to No. 4 in the world and took his place in two major finals.

Yet no one realized as 1990 unfolded that it would be Sampras who would move inexorably past his contemporaries from the U.S. to carve out a place for himself among the enduring luminaries of tennis. It would be Sampras who would —through force of will, depth of dedication and sheer talent— produce a record so lofty and unassailable that authorities from every corner of the globe would regard him as the greatest American ever to lift a racket—not to mention one of the very best, if not the greatest of all time, from any country.

But to understand the emergence of Sampras and why he established himself as a central figure in the history of his sport, to recognize how he became one of the most revered champions in the history of tennis, to put his inspiring and extraordinary life story as an American sporting icon into perspective, it is essential to go back to his roots. Pete Sampras was born in Potomac, Maryland on August 12, 1971. Sampras's father, Sam, was of Greek heritage, but was raised in the United States. Pete's mother, Georgia, grew up in Greece, but came to the U.S. when she was in her twenties after living in Canada briefly. His parents met in Washington where Sam was working and courtship led to marriage. Pete had three siblings. His brother, Gus, was four years older. His sister Stella—also a tennis player—was two years older. And his sister, Marion, was the youngest of the Sampras kids. The family was close-knit, and Pete Sampras got along with all of his siblings, but the shared love of and dedication to tennis brought him closest in some ways to Stella.

Both parents influenced Pete immensely, but in different ways. As he said in an interview for this book when asked how his mother and father rubbed off on him, "I see a lot of myself in my Mom with her toughness and internalizing. She was an

3

immigrant who came to Canada, made ends meet and didn't speak a word of English. Then she met my Dad and became a U.S. citizen. She was about hard work and that tough Greek mentality. I just see so much of my Mom in me with that Spartan toughness."

Shifting his attention to his father, Sampras said, "He was a hard worker who worked two jobs to support us. He talked more than my Mom. He would say, 'How are you doing, Pete? How are you feeling? How is your body?' We would go to the tournaments in the juniors and he always asked those questions. When I was 12 as a junior, I played a 16 and under tournament and beat the best 15 year old in Shreveport, Louisiana. I felt like I had won Wimbledon. A writer interviewed me right there on the court. The next day, I lost to Mal Washington 6-0, 6-1 and I am sitting there on the side of the court. My Dad comes up to me and that same writer was interviewing Mal. Dad said, 'You see what is going on? He is talking to Mal today.' He was telling me you are only as good as your last win. It was a tough lesson to learn, but that is how my Dad saw it. He was always a little pessimistic or a little negative, but I understood how he thought about things. As my career went on and I won Wimbledon, I would be thinking 'You have got to do it again.' Or 'You lose a couple of matches and you are not the toast of the town anymore.'"

His father's philosophy on life and tennis clearly left an indelible impression on Sampras in his junior days and well beyond. He said, "It's interesting because I used to fly privately when I was in my mid-twenties but when I lost I never felt like I deserved to be on that private plane. That was how I was thinking. I went through a couple of years of that, really taking my losses hard and not feeling I belonged on that charted plane. I think I got some of that practicality from my Dad. He was more talkative than my Mom. She was a little more to herself. But there is always one parent you can go to when you want to talk about something. I went to my Mom because she was easier to talk to in a way. I felt more comfortable confiding in my mother."

As a young boy growing up in Maryland, Pete Sampras started hitting tennis balls against a garage wall in Maryland, began playing casually on courts in a public park and had a clear affinity for the game. When Pete was seven, his father moved the family to Southern California and that altered his life forever. Now the sport was available to this boy year round. While most of his contemporaries were preoccupied with how they fared in the juniors—placing considerable stock in those events, measuring their self-worth largely on their results— Sampras was of another ilk.

He was guided in his junior days by Dr. Pete Fischer, who took over essentially as the captain of his coaching ship. Despite being an astute student of the game, Fischer was more a bizarre tennis mastermind than a tennis coach, but he found the right people to help assemble the pieces of Sampras's game and shape it into it something substantial and cohesive. Fischer turned to the highly regarded Robert Lansdorp to oversee Sampras's ground game, most notably the signature forehand side. Dell Little handled footwork and balance. Larry Easley worked largely on the volley. Fischer himself played a critical role in the development of Sampras's serve, emphasizing the benefits of serving with different spins to varying locations using the same toss.

Fischer was an atypical coach. Two-time U.S. Open champion Tracy Austin was a Californian who was coached by Lansdorp. Tracy trained a bit at the Jack Kramer Club where Sampras was a fixture. She does not remember precisely when she first saw Sampras, but believes he was about eight years old.

"The one thing I do remember," Austin recalled in an interview for this book, "was I had won the U.S. Open and I came back to the club and was hitting some balls. Pete looked at me and said, 'I am going to be more famous than you are.' And I was like, 'Okay, kid.' Here was this little skinny kid who was obviously very talented and I was like, 'Whatever.' I feel like he kind of knew where he was going."

Austin laughed at that recollection, but then addressed the role of Fischer more seriously. "Pete Fischer has to be given the credit for giving Pete Sampras the big picture and the dream that he could play like Rod Laver and win Wimbledon," she said. "When you have somebody behind you feeding you this belief and giving you confidence, I think it was very helpful to Pete Sampras. I would come close to calling Pete Fischer a genius. I didn't have a big picture plan. From an early age, Pete Fischer seemed to instill in Sampras's parents that their kid had the talent and told him this is what we are going to do—this is the big picture plan."

"Pete Fischer was not a good tennis player," Austin elaborated. "He possibly had the worst strokes I have seen in my life and here he was working with Pete Sampras and finding all of these other coaches as well. But Fischer was passionate about the game and obviously a brilliant man. If you ever saw Pete Fischer hit a serve, you would laugh that he could ever have had anything to do with Sampras's serve. What was amazing was the tennis mind that he had."

Sampras is essentially in accord with Austin, but shed additional light on Fischer's crucial role in his evolution as a player. "He made a big contribution to my game, especially when it came to my junior years," said Sampras. "On my serve, we would practice two or three days a week. He did one drill with me where the last second before I would hit the serve, he would tell me where to go with it. That helped me a lot to disguise my serve. Just before I hit it, he would tell me to go wide or go down the middle, but I would have the same toss for every serve and he would be standing there directing me. We would hit volleys and do the split-step. He was like the conductor saying, 'I am going to show you how to play' and, God, it just went from there."

Upon reflection, Sampras believed that how it all worked out so improbably with Fischer despite the unconventional approach to his development as a player was "like a perfect storm. Everything just landed perfectly and it was almost like divine intervention," he said. "I don't believe in holistic stuff,

Pete Sampras sits with his coach Pete Fischer (right) and USTA Junior Davis Cup Team Coach Mark Winters

but I look back and wonder how this all worked out with Pete Fischer who couldn't play tennis but taught me how to play. And I am serving-and-volleying at 14 with a one-handed backhand and 15 years later I had won seven Wimbledons. It doesn't completely make sense to me. It is like a diamond in the rough and lightning in a bottle. But he deserves a lot of credit in seeing what I might be able to do."

Yet working with Fischer was not simply a joyous experience for the young Pete Sampras. Not by any means. Fischer could carry his task master toughness too far. His idiosyncrasies were simultaneously his strength and weakness. He was obstinate, ornery and often insensitive in guiding his pupil through the minefields of the junior game.

"When I was a kid, he was very critical when he was coaching me," "said Sampras. "He was very smart and a genius with a 190 IQ, but he didn't quite understand what it takes to be out there in terms of the emotional side of the game. He saw me doing what I was doing and was immediately critical of me."

Fischer did not work with Sampras out on the professional tour, but they kept the lines of communication open. Fischer would weigh in from time to time and express his strongly stated views on how Sampras was playing. And then in 1997, long after he had stopped working with Fischer, Sampras was astonished to learn that his former coach had been charged with child molestation. Fischer had been accused by some of the parents of his patients in medical practice. Eventually, Fischer would take a plea deal and served several years in jail.

"I was shocked and disappointed," said Sampras of when he found out about the accusations. "I did not know what to think of it. I was a little confused. I remembered that he used to take kids on ski trips and I was one of those kids. None of us felt threatened. I didn't and my parents didn't feel threatened. So I guess when it came out, it showed that even when you have spent a lot of time with someone you may not really know them. After the news came out with the allegations, we had lunch and I was trying to support him. We had some heart to heart talks but he took the plea deal of three years because he didn't trust a jury that he thought would give him 15 years."

"This happened in the middle of my career, right in the heart of it," Sampras said in 2019. "He went to prison and he watched me play a bit during that time. He wrote me a couple of long letters in his very bad hand writing that I could barely read. He was very critical of my game and I was thinking 'He is not in a position to be criticizing me about anything.' So I was taken aback and didn't know what to make of what happened to him. I moved on with my life and career. I do remember when he was going to prison he found Jesus after being an atheist. I was just amazed by that. I just moved on and he is not in my life anymore."

Sampras was saddened by what happened to someone who had been such a central figure in his tennis life. It was a lot for a young man in his mid-twenties to sort out as he reflected on a man he had once revered and a coach who had been a crucial guiding force.

"He was very close to my family and he used to come over every Friday night for dinner when I was in the juniors," he said. "He really was a big part of the Sampras's, not just me but my parents and siblings. He helped my brother with some tutoring and me with some math homework. I trusted him and my parents trusted him with my tennis. It was one of the most unorthodox situations in all of tennis."

Lansdorp, meanwhile, was a pivotal figure among the Sampras coaches and a genius in his own right who worked over the years with Austin, Lindsay Davenport, Maria Sharapova, Eliot Teltscher and many other standout competitors. Lansdorp was most revered for his devotion to the formation of sound ground strokes among all of his players and it was in that area of the game where he was most helpful to Sampras.

In an interview for this book, he recalled his years of assisting Sampras on the courts and what he observed in his young pupil. "Pete developed what I called the reverse forehand, meaning he would follow through on the right side of his body," said Lansdorp. "I had a tape of Pete as a kid doing a drill with me where I fed him the ball really hard and it skidded on the line. And I was yelling, 'Pete, what is the matter with you? Move your feet and get in position.' And he said, 'Robert, the ball skidded on the line, okay?' He really could hit those reverse forehands on the run with a short follow through. His follow through was like Nadal. He really had a great running forehand, but most of the time it was not a regular follow through around the body like other players. People would always say, 'Oh My God, look at how his ball curves in the court' because he would come around the outside of the ball when he went down the line. But he could also angle it really well crosscourt. That was an interesting part of it."

The "reverse forehand" Lansdorp described was hit largely down the line, but, of course, Sampras would later became much better known for his running forehand crosscourt.

Sampras was being groomed as an attacking player through and through, but not one who was anything less than a major force from the backcourt as well. When Sampras was 14, however, he made a transformational switch in his game that was designed entirely to engender success much later on in the pro ranks. He shifted from what had been a stellar two-handed backhand to a one-handed shot off that side, realizing that this move would make transitioning to the net and punching one-handed backhand volleys a much easier task.

Sampras's prodigious record of winning 14 major championships speaks for itself and he believes unequivocally that going to the one-handed backhand was a chief reason why he celebrated such a sterling career and became one of the sport's most complete players.

And yet, his old junior and career long rival Michael Chang always wondered if Sampras might have been better off with the two-hander. In an interview for this book, Chang reflected, "When Pete made that move, I was like everybody else. I was thinking, 'You have got to be joking.' Pete had one of the best two-handed backhands. It was powerful, straight and flat. To be honest, I had no idea why he changed. Had he not changed to a one-hander he could have kept his one-handed slice with the ability to chip and charge and stuff like that. I think his backhand could still have been a great weapon that way."

Chang was asked about the emergence of Mats Wilander in the 1980's and his propensity to enhance his two-handed backhand with an effective one-handed slice off that side. He felt that would have been a productive option for Sampras if Pete had gone that route. "If you talked to anybody in the juniors back then, they would tell you Pete's two-handed backhand was a weapon," Chang said. "So when Pete went to the one-handed backhand, it was such a weakness for him at that time. For probably a year-and-a-half, he couldn't get a whole lot on it. People were picking on his backhand time and again. And even in his professional years, Pete definitely had a good one-handed backhand which allowed him to stay neutral in the point but he didn't hit it to the point where it was like Stan Wawrinka or Richard Gasquet, who could really rip you on that side. When Pete had the two-hander, he could also rip you on that side."

On how Wilander succeeded with his combination of the two-hander along with the one-handed slice, Chang added, "When Mats went to the slice while keeping his two-hander, that was a new thing. That combination had not really picked up momentum yet. Had Pete thought about that, he could have still had that unbelievable two-handed backhand of his along with the ability to hit the one-handed slice, changing it up and still chipping and charging like he did when he won the 1990 U.S. Open. Obviously Pete went on to have a great career, so you can't say the change to the one-handed backhand was a bad change. There is no way he would have been able to win as many Slams as he did. But there is always that question in my mind. I think he changed because he wanted the reach and the flexibility the one-hander gave him, but it would have been interesting had he not changed and instead added the one-handed slice to the two-hander."

Lansdorp shared essentially the same viewpoint as Chang on the Sampras two-hander. "I don't think I would have changed his backhand from two hands to one," he said. "That was not me. He had a great two-hander and even at 12 or a little older he could serve-and-volley unbelievably while he still had the two-hander. I really don't think I ever would have changed it. I don't think it would have hampered his winning all of those Wimbledon titles, plus I believe he would have won the French Open for sure."

Sampras understood why people like Chang and Lansdorp believe he could have stayed with the two-hander, but is convinced his game benefitted immeasurably from moving from two hands back to one. "It was similar to Andre Agassi's or Michael's," he said of his two-handed backhand. "It was solid and it wasn't a hole by any means. Why Pete Fischer changed me I don't really know. I will say: I wonder if I would have had a career like Andre's and won some majors as very much a counter-attacker if I had kept the two-hander. But no way would I have won Wimbledon as many times as I did. Here is the thing: I am an athlete and switching to the one-hander worked out because it matched my game and my movement. I was a good mover at the net and a good athlete and that is why I did so well at Wimbledon. I had the athletic ability to serve-and-volley. With a two-handed backhand I don't think I would have utilized my athletic ability the same way."

And yet, Sampras came to believe his junior career might have been different. "I would have done better," he said in 2019, "and I think I would have won Orange Bowls, Easter Bowls and all of those big junior tournaments. But would I have had the serve or the volley that I later had if I had stayed with the two-handed backhand? I have no idea. If I had stayed with the two-hander, maybe I would have played like Djokovic. Would I have won the French? That is a fascinating question and it is difficult to answer. But I just don't think I would have had the same career if I stayed with the two-handed backhand. I just don't. Sure, you give up a little bit with the one-handed backhand on the high backhand return, but you get way more of an advantage with the one-hander overall if you have my sort of game. I just felt like everyone was at the mercy of how the match would go because basically it was on my racket."

At the time, however, such an immense alteration in his game made Sampras pause for thought in the early stages of that evolution. "Man, it was a struggle for a couple of years and I had second thoughts about it," he said. "I thought it might have been a bad decision. My barometer was always Michael Chang. I beat him with the two-hander, but then lost to him with the one-handed backhand. But Pete Fischer was always saying it was about the big picture. It is not what you do in the juniors that matters but what you do as a pro. Big picture. Big picture. That is what he always told me. Everyone thought I was nuts when I made the switch. They thought Pete Fischer was nuts. The pro at the Jack Kramer Club where I played thought I was nuts. But I went along with it and just trusted Pete and trusted my Dad. They all were on the same page, so I did what I was told."

Part of that big picture mentality was envisioning a future that would take him to the loftiest levels of the game. Fischer was an unabashed admirer of the great Australians

Laver and Ken Rosewall and that rubbed off enormously on Sampras. "Pete Fischer would say things when I was a kid that were a little over the top," said Sampras. "He would say that my competition was going to be Laver. And there I am as a 14-year-old kid eating my dinner. He had this confidence in what he was doing, like going to the one-handed backhand. Pete's point of view was that no great serve-and-volleyer had played with the two-handed backhand. He was such a big fan of Laver and Rosewall and loved the serve-and-volley game. He tried to instill that in me."

Although Fischer wanted Sampras to develop a formidable serve that he could package cohesively with the volley, Sampras was never known as a big server as a junior and that would not come into view until the end of his teens when he was on the pro tour. Lansdorp nonetheless saw that potential early on during the junior days. "He had that serve [motion] when he came to me," Landsdorp mused. "His follow through was high, a little like Boris Becker. Even at 10 or 11, his elbow stayed up very high. I have to say, I have never had another kid that served with the motion Sampras had. Isn't that weird? I have tried to teach them, yet they could not do it. I never got one kid to stick with it. They all tried a little bit, but I never have had another who could serve like Pete did. You just don't see anybody serve like that. His shoulders were so loose and that led to his huge serve that he hit with such ease. The toss was always perfect with the left arm way extended. It was so effortless. He would come through that serve with no noise, nothing. That serve was just a thing of beauty from the time he was so young."

Chang was always around back then, competing against Sampras in their junior days, developing into a front line player. They also hung out together at times because of their devotion to tennis. Chang vividly recollected one day when they practiced with each other in California. The Changs invited Sampras to have a meal with them, cooked by Michael's mother Betty. "We were training in Palm Springs and we would have a morning practice and my Mom would have a fresh pasta waiting for us when we got back," Chang said in 2019. "She would cook the noodles and have a homemade sauce for lunch. So my Mom said, 'Pete, when you are done showering, come back and we will have lunch.' And Pete would come back and my Mom would make this incredible spaghetti with meat sauce, fresh tomatoes, fresh mushrooms, everything. And Pete looked at her and said, 'Mrs. Chang, if it's all the same to you, do you have any simple sauce?' She said, 'Pete, this is homemade and fresh.' And he would say, 'I know, and it's all great Mrs. Chang, but if it's all the same to you, if you have some regular Ragu I would be really happy with that.' Pete was just very straightforward and simple and I always appreciated that about him. I always got along with him and he comes from a great family. I have the utmost respect` for Pete Sampras."

Sampras readily recollected that pasta meal which symbolized his clear sense of self, what he wanted and how important it was for him to stick to his own routines and be steadfast in his beliefs. "I do remember saying I wanted the Ragu to Michael's mother," he said in 2019. "I liked things a certain way. I must have been 15 or 16. I have always been like that, and even today I eat the same foods and listen to the same music. It calms me down. When I played, I was very neurotic when it came to my sleep and my food and even the temperature in the room. I very much wanted things to be a certain way and if things were not going to feel a certain way I felt some anxiety. I checked into a hotel once in Paris and they didn't have air conditioning. I can't sleep in the heat so I was looking around Paris that year for a hotel with air conditioning. I had to have it that way."

Sampras was set in his ways from his junior days on. He knew himself well from the outset and would not be swayed from what he felt would carry him forward successfully. "In my career I was neurotic about my equipment and my rackets, my stringing and grip size," he said. "I hired Nate Ferguson full time so I didn't have to worry about stringing. I was crazy about my shoes and the way they fit and wearing two pairs of socks or one. I wanted the same length clothes, the same

14

color. It is fascinating looking back on that. I was in tune with everything around me and what I wanted. I didn't want a lot of people around me and just wanted to keep things simple in every aspect of my life. So I guess that story of the pasta with the Changs is a little symbolic. I knew what I wanted."

That precise way of looking at himself and examining his aims in life was an essential part of Sampras. Despite a self-effacing nature that would define who he was, where he would go and how he wanted to conduct himself as an athlete, Sampras saw himself unequivocally from the beginning as someone who was bound to succeed on a tennis court. As he wrote in his autobiography, *A Champion's Mind* in 2008, "I knew, I knew, almost from day one, that I was born to play tennis.... By the time I reached my teens, I assumed that I was going to win Wimbledon and the U.S. Open, which was a real reach."

Wanting to hear him expound on that pronouncement in an interview conducted toward the end of 2018, I mentioned to Sampras that he has always been exceedingly modest but wondered if this was simply a quiet belief and part of his makeup. He replied, "I was a very shy kid and even when I turned pro I was shy. I was just trying to find my own way, but on the court I was very competitive. I wanted to win, but as a kid I downplayed everything. I was one of the better athletes in my high school but I never talked about it. The football players had their jerseys on. I was a tennis player and people knew about me, but I didn't want to show off. I didn't want to call any attention to myself. I just tried to be very humble about it. I was almost uncomfortable about being a junior tennis player when I was in high school. But I always had this ability when I competed; that is where my ego came in."

Yet Sampras realized that it would take time for his game to gel and years of supreme dedication to become the illustrious player that he would be. That was why he did not dwell on his junior results. Only once did he reach the final of a national junior singles event in any of the age groups and that was in his last year of the 18s in 1987. He garnered a No. 14 ranking in the 14-and-under division in 1983, was No. 37 among 16-and-under players the following year, and rose to No. 20 in that division in 1985.

Moving on to the 18s, he was No. 56 in the nation for the 1986 season but closed out his junior career with his best season yet in the junior American game at No. 6 in the country in 1987. He had always played "up" in the juniors, facing older adversaries with more competitive experience. He did reasonably well, but Sampras was far from a dominant force. Yet always he had an extraordinary sense of self as he gazed into the future. In an interview for this book, he put into perspective his philosophy on why he relished the isolation of a tennis player determining his own destiny. No matter how many expert coaches he had or how much guidance he would get from others, it was, ultimately, all up to him.

"It really was up to me," he said, "and that is one of the beauties of tennis. There is not a parent, or a coach or a psychologist that is going to tell you how it should be. I think you are born with it. I really do. You are born with will, born with a tough mind and a tough heart. I don't think you can teach someone a will to win. You get in a situation and some players fold. Some players don't put in the effort. And there are some players that have the talent and do put in the work like myself or Roger Federer or Rafael Nadal. Tennis is such an individual character sport, like boxing. When a boxer is tired and getting beat, there is only one person that can get them out of it. It is the same way in tennis. And that is not easy. You are relying on yourself every time you go out there and that can take its toll."

Sampras turned professional in the spring of 1988 at Indian Wells in his home state of California. It was already a very prestigious event then and now is regarded by most players and authorities as one of the top five or six tournaments in tennis. Sampras was still about five months shy of his 17th birthday, mature in some ways beyond his years, but still living in the land of self-discovery as a player commencing a career but not entirely clear in his mind about what it would take to reap the largest rewards.

In that tournament on the hard courts, Sampras cut down India's stylish Ramesh Krishnan in the opening round, prevailing in a final set tie-breaker over the world No. 37. Next on the agenda for Sampras was world No. 25 Eliot Teltscher, a fellow Californian who had reached a career high in 1982 of No. 6 in the world. Sampras was victorious again. Although he lost to Spain's industrious Emilio Sanchez—then stationed at No. 18 in the world—in the round of 16, Sampras had clearly made an impression on his fellow players and the tennis cognoscenti. He turned professional right then and there.

That critical career move also meant that Sampras would not finish high school. He turned pro during his junior year and his days in the classroom were over. "I just felt I was ready to turn pro," he recollected. "It had been the consensus in my family that I was probably going to turn pro and not go to college. It was a leap of faith and a little scary when I did turn pro, but I just felt I could play with these guys. It wasn't like I was overmatched. I felt like I was just teetering on being able to play with these guys and those wins I had at Indian Wells gave me the confidence that this was as good a time as ever. So off I went. In a short time Andre, Jim and Michael all turned pro without going to college, which was normal back then."

Even a few years earlier, Sampras sensed he could hold his own with established pro players. "I remember hitting with Teltscher when I was like 15," he said, "and I was right there with him. I could hit with Eliot and play points and win baseline rallies and he was No. 11 in the world. And things happened pretty fast for me as a pro because I didn't have to play any satellites and got to the top 100 in eight or ten months. It did take me some time after that to really break through but I never had any regrets about not finishing high school and not going to college."

The rest of that 1988 campaign was unexceptional for Sampras, who finished the season with a 10-10 match record. He was still somewhat scrawny, not yet able to regularly overpower some of his older and more experienced adversaries and trying—often in vain—to discover what it took to succeed in the vast corridors of the men's game. He would have good days when his game was flowing and victory was an inevitability, but he could just as easily suffer through off days and lose matches he might have won.

For a chunk of that 1988 rookie pro season, John Austin—the older brother of Tracy Austin who won the Wimbledon mixed doubles crown in 1980 with his sister—was out on the road coaching Sampras. They were at the Rye Brook Open in Rye Brook, New York, right before the U.S. Open. Sampras had recently celebrated his 17th birthday. In the first round of that hard court event, Sampras eclipsed world No. 39 Michiel Schapers but then he fell in the next round to world No. 92 Jeremy Bates of Great Britain.

Austin was bewildered. "Pete did not show a lot of heart against Bates," he clearly remembered almost thirty years later. "He had carved up Schapers. So I said, 'Pete, you are so talented. You can't do that. You are so up and down!' I went off on him for about 45 minutes and he said, "Hey, I am Greek. I am a lover and not a fighter. What do you want from me?' So I went back to my old job at PGA West and walked away and Joe Brandi came in to coach Pete. Pete was talented but immature at that time. But I remember a few years later he came over to my house after winning the U.S. Open and he was just a different person. It was great to see."

In 2018, Sampras was reminded of his exchange with Austin at the Rye Brook Open in 1988, and laughed heartily. "When I first turned pro I was not always hard on myself," he said. "I would always say it is a learning experience. I think John wanted a little more out of me, wanted more fight out of me. At that stage, at 17, I didn't dig deep enough, wasn't mature enough and didn't want it enough. I remember him going off on me. I just had this talent and was good, but when you get into the heat of the moment at 17, you are still a kid and it is okay to lose. You know you will learn and you feel like you have all the time in the world. I certainly didn't feel that way when I hit my twenties. Maybe John saw something that alarmed him, but athletes need time and you have either got it or you don't. For me, it clicked a few years later."

All in all, however, his rookie year as a professional was not unproductive. He had an impressive win over world No. 8 Tim Mayotte in Detroit and concluded that 1988 season as the No. 97 ranked player in the world. That was nothing to be ashamed about, even for someone with large dreams of lofty destinations.

The 1989 season was a better one for Sampras as he widened his competitive world and gained valuable experience all year long. To be sure, he took his lumps over the course of that campaign, losing his first career appointment against Agassi on the clay courts of Rome by scores of 6-2, 6-1 in the second round. Moreover, he was taken apart 6-1, 6-1, 6-1 by the eventual champion Chang in the second round at Roland Garros. Yet Sampras kept moving forward, toppling 1985 Wimbledon finalist Kevin Curren on the grass courts at the Queen's Club on his way to the round of 16, losing there to his future coach Paul Annacone.

His level was decidedly higher than the year before. At the U.S. Open, appearing in only the fifth Grand Slam tournament of his career, still an unfamiliar figure to much of the sporting public, Sampras made a spirited run to the round of 16. In his previous four appearances at the majors, he had won only one match, but this time around in New York he came alive and performed with verve and a sparkle that would endear him to the American fans.

In the second round of that Open, Sampras collided with the defending champion Mats Wilander in a hotly contested duel under the lights in Louis Armstrong Stadium. Wilander had struggled inordinately through most of the year after taking three of the four majors in 1988, but the fact remained that the Swede fully expected to handle the American in such a setting. Wilander had burst into prominence in 1982 when he became the youngest man ever to rule at Roland Garros. In a spectacular fortnight, he had upended Ivan Lendl, Vitas Gerulaitis, Jose Luis Clerc and Guillermo Vilas for that title. That was no mean feat. Lendl would one day win the French Open three times and he had been a finalist the year before, falling in five sets against Bjorn Borg. Gerulaitis had been the runner-up to Borg in 1980. Clerc reached the Roland Garros semifinals in 1981. And Vilas was one of the stalwart clay court players of the era; he took the French Open title in 1977.

Wilander had demonstrated irrefutably that his run through that fortnight was not a fluke. He captured the Australian Open in 1983 and 1984, took the French Open again in 1985, advanced to two major finals in 1987 and then celebrated his magnificent 1988 campaign. The deep thinking Swede had hit something of an emotional wall in 1989, but he was seeded fifth at the U.S. Open and his status as a front line player was indisputable.

Sampras did not approach that meeting with pessimism, but he did not see victory coming either. Yet the 18-year-old American celebrated the most significant win of his young career, striking down a disbelieving Wilander in five sets, coming through 5-7, 6-3, 1-6, 6-1, 6-4. Sampras was unrelentingly aggressive, approaching the net no fewer than 175 times during the stern battle, winning 100 of those points. After Wilander broke back for 4-4 in the fifth set, Sampras refused to surrender, breaking in the ninth game and fending off four break points in the last game to close it out.

Speaking about that match in my December 2018 interview with him, Wilander said, "I was just completely wrong about Pete and how great he would be. I felt that it was not a great performance by me in terms of my mental attitude. I fought through without playing well and I was carrying some good, positive baggage from being the defending champion. I just couldn't believe that I could lose to him then. I remember in the press conference they were asking me if I thought Pete was really good and so on, and I was like, 'No, man, you can't play tennis like that with a big serve for a skinny guy. You have no idea whether he is going to hit the ball into the court or into the stands.'"

Wilander paused to collect his thoughts, amused that he could be so far off in his initial assessment of Sampras. He continued, "I was just a little upset after the match. Obviously I saw the fighter in him. But it was hard to see it all. I did see that he had this certain talent, but he was the kind of player who did not care about me as an opponent in terms of what I was doing. It was more like, 'This is the way I play, and if it works, it works. And it it doesn't work, this is just the way I play.' Boris Becker was maybe the first guy to play that way, but Pete had more finesse. I just wasn't in the right frame of mind to make a judgment on Pete back then."

Sampras recalled how uneasy he felt walking out on court to face Wilander and yet he was not totally in awe of the situation, nor was he afraid of confronting a percentage player like Wilander. "That was my introduction to the Center Court at the U.S. Open," said Sampras. "I was a bit intimidated and a little nervous and I was the major underdog playing Mats, who had won many majors. But I started believing more as the match went on. I was still so young and green and my game was still developing, even though I did have my weapons on the serve and forehand. I was just a young 18, trying to figure out my game, to figure out the tour. Mats wasn't maybe at the top of his game and he wasn't like an Ivan Lendl who could blow me off the court at that time. So I was just trying to serve-and-volley, get to the net as much as possible and put some pressure on Mats. That was the biggest win of my career at that time and a huge step in the right direction. It was a great feeling as the crowd got behind me that night. That was the start of something pretty big at the Open, but things got more serious the next year."

He would bow out in the round of 16 of that 1989 U.S. Open against compatriot Jay Berger, who was simply too solid on a Sunday afternoon from the backcourt. Yet that showing—his best yet at a major—was not insignificant. His match record for the year of 18-19 reflected some understandable inconsistency, but the fact remained that Pete Sampras was setting the stage for something substantial, building his reputation brick by brick and establishing himself indisputably as a player to be reckoned with.

He concluded 1989 ranked No. 81 in the world. Sampras was still very much a work in progress, but he knew his time would come. He did not realize that a landmark accomplishment was not far off on the horizon. He would find himself in the spotlight of the game sooner than he could ever have envisioned.

# CHAPTER 2

# UNEXPECTEDLY CAPTURING
# HIS FIRST MAJOR

During the early stages of the 1990 season, Sampras displayed signs of significant growth as a match player. His level of consistency far exceeded anything he had exhibited before. His self assurance was growing. His game was not fully formed but he was putting the pieces together. He was learning how to win.

The soft spoken American commenced the year with a quarterfinal showing in Sydney, losing to Wilander there. He then moved into the round of 16 at the Australian Open, toppling world No. 12 Mayotte 12-10 in the fifth set before removing Jordi Arrese and the Australian Todd Woodbridge. Sampras lost to 1983 French Open champion Yannick Noah in a four-set, round-of-16 appointment. He then advanced to the semifinals in Milan before losing to Lendl 3-6, 6-0, 6-3.

Not long after that, he won his first ATP World Tour singles title at the U.S. Pro Indoor event in Philadelphia. It was an early career milestone for the American. After splitting the first two sets with Agassi in the round of 16, his fellow American had to retire. Thereafter, Sampras ousted Mayotte and Mark Kratzmann to set up a final round meeting against the stylish, left-handed Ecuadorian Andres Gomez, who would secure the French Open crown about four months later. Sampras accounted for Gomez 7-6, 7-5, 6-2.

Over the next few months, Sampras was unable to find the same level of match-playing consistency. He did not play the French Open, but in June garnered his second singles title of the year on the grass courts of Manchester, prevailing in a two-tiebreak final over Israel's southpaw Gilad Bloom. That was his first taste of success on a surface he would master just a few years later. But the Manchester formula did not lead to what he wanted at Wimbledon; Sampras was beaten in the first round at the All England Club by Christo Van Rensburg of South Africa, bowing out 7-6, 7-5, 7-6.

But then, on the summer hard court swing in the United States, Sampras recovered his confidence and got back into a better groove with his game. In Toronto, confronting John McEnroe for the first time, Sampras upended the New Yorker in a three-set clash. He was beaten in the penultimate round by Chang, losing narrowly 3-6, 7-6, 7-5. Appearing next in Los Angeles, Sampras went once more to the semifinals before Stefan Edberg eclipsed him. After losing to Chang again in the round of 16 at Cincinnati, Sampras was a quarterfinalist in both Indianapolis and Long Island.

That run of reliability put Sampras in good stead for the U.S. Open and his third appearance at his country's Grand Slam tournament. He had pushed his ranking up into the top 15 on the ATP computer for the first time, earning a No. 12 seeding in New York. He was in a good frame of mind. He had made serious inroads as a player all through the season. But no one, not even Sampras himself, was remotely prepared for what he was about to put on display at the last major of the 1990 season.

Stefan Edberg was the top seed and the favorite at Flushing Meadows. But the taciturn Swede—victorious at Wimbledon for the second time earlier in the summer, where he fought fiercely to oust Becker in a tumultuous five set final – was ushered out in the first round of the Open by the Russian left-hander Alexander Volkov. Yet the other leading contenders for the last major of the season all went deep in the draw.

Sampras, meanwhile, largely unnoticed, tending to his knitting, taking it match by match, swept through the first three rounds comfortably. When asked in 2018 about his outlook heading into and through the early rounds of the 1990 Open, he replied, "I wasn't even thinking about winning the tournament. My goal was to just get to the second week. That is where I felt my game was. If I would have gotten to the round of 16 or quarterfinals, I would have felt pretty good about my Open. I was getting better as a player then which is why I was seeded 12th, but I didn't have any thought about winning the Open. That was the last thing on my mind."

He cast aside former Stanford University standout Dan Goldie 6-1, 7-5, 6-1 in the first round. He did not have an exceptional serving day, connecting with only 48% of his first serves. But he faced only one break point and saved it. Moreover, he was in utter command on both deliveries, taking 79% of his first serve points and a healthy 60% on his second.

Next up on the agenda for Sampras was a 25-year-old Swede named Peter Lundgren. Lundgren had floated around the top 100 in the world for many seasons, peaking at No. 25 in 1985. He would win three singles titles over the course of his career on the ATP World Tour. After retiring, he would coach the gifted Marcelo Rios of Chile, Hall of Famer Marat Safin, and most notably Roger Federer. He also worked with Grigor Dimitrov and Stan Wawrinka.

The previous autumn in 1989, Lundgren had toppled Sampras indoors at Stockholm in straight sets. But now he came upon a decidedly improved version of the same player. The 1990 Sampras was gaining ground, increasingly sure of himself, honing his attacking game and gathering strength and diversity. He picked Lundgren apart comprehensively, winning 6-4, 6-3, 6-3. In this encounter, Sampras was broken only once, in the fifth game of the first set. But from 2-4 down he captured four games in a row to seal the set and never looked back.

Now it was time for Sampras to confront Switzerland's stylish Jakob Hlasek, a 26-year-old who had reached a career high at No. 7 in the world in the spring of 1989. At the 1988 Masters tournament—now known as the ATP Finals—Hlasek had beaten both Lendl and Agassi on his way to the semifinals at the prestigious year-end event reserved for only the top eight players in the world. Hlasek could bother the best players in the world more than sporadically; he would finish with a 2-3 career record against Jimmy Connors and was 3-4 versus John McEnroe.

The Swiss stylist would defeat Sampras only once in seven career confrontations, but he tested him often. Nonetheless, in an afternoon skirmish on Louis Armstrong Stadium at the 1990 Open, Sampras came through without much stress, claiming a 6-3, 6-4, 6-1 triumph. Hlasek displayed good feel on his returns. His finesse was impressive. But Sampras erased seven of the eight break points he faced in the entertaining contest.

And so the stage was set for the first serious test for Sampras in the round of 16. He faced the unflagging left-handed Austrian Thomas Muster, the No. 6 seed and as rugged a fighter as could be found in the field. No one in tennis tried harder or got more out of his game. Muster's serve was not up to the level of most accomplished southpaws. His wide slice in the ad court was effective yet not wicked. Off the ground, he could stay in rallies steadfastly, but mainly because of his extraordinary court coverage and consistency rather than a potent strength off either side. He was a workhorse through and through and a top of the line competitor. He did not overflow with natural ability but his heart was second to none and his grit and gumption were twin virtues.

A year earlier, Muster had been the victim of a freakish accident that could easily have ended a lesser man's career. He had reached the final of the Miami Masters 1000 tournament, and would have taken on Lendl for the title on Sunday afternoon. But after his spectacular recovery on Friday evening in the semifinals against Yannick Noah when he rescued himself from two sets to love down and halted the Frenchman in five,

Muster had gone out to dinner and while walking was hit by a drunk driver. He was trapped briefly under the car, severing ligaments in his left knee.

Muster had to default the Miami final to Lendl and was gone for six months from tournament tennis, yet he still finished the year at No. 21 in the world. Being seeded sixth at the U.S. Open was a testament to his supreme physical and mental toughness. He played Sampras under the lights and the Austrian's industriousness and alacrity around the court— coupled with some surprisingly well struck second serve returns—made life exceedingly difficult for the composed yet concerned American. The conditions were difficult with a swirling wind and the sound of storms in the distance.

From the outset, Sampras had to deal with some dipping returns and deadly accurate passing shots from a typically unwavering Muster, who was awfully confident in the early stages of an intriguing battle. Sampras had not yet found his range off the ground and his play at the net was not as efficient as he would have liked it to be. The wind did not help matters, nor did Muster's almost tangible willpower. This was a bruising and taxing battle and Sampras was being asked to define his mettle, perspicacity and durability by an opponent who was seeded six places above him.

Comforting Sampras, however, was the fact that he liked the matchup with Muster. He felt it was essentially in his hands and that he could control his own destiny. As he reflected on the Muster showdown nearly 30 years after he played the Austrian, Sampras said, "I felt pretty comfortable against him. I could dictate and I was trying to serve-and-volley. He was standing way back on his returns so I felt I could kind of manipulate how the match would go. It was on my shoulders. He wasn't someone that was going to blow me off the court. At the time, my game was getting better. I would not have beaten him at 18, but at 19 I felt I was a little better than him. He was a tough competitor but I felt he was going to let me play."

And yet, a pendulum-swinging opening set with fluctuating fortunes on both sides of the net ultimately did not go Sampras's way. Muster served for it at 5-4, moved unhesitatingly to 40-15, and was up double set point on his own delivery. Sampras responded with situational urgency, releasing a forehand return winner down the line and then a backhand down the line passing shot into the clear. He was back to deuce. He collected the next two points with more clutch play, gaining level ground at 5-5.

The set was settled in a tie-break and Sampras served an ace down the T in the deuce court to take a 6-3 lead. He had three set points at his disposal. But Muster tenaciously stood his ground, coaxing a forehand volley error from Sampras and taking advantage of an unforced error off the forehand from the backcourt by Sampras. Now Sampras served at 6-5 with his third set point opportunity, but, after a convincing serve-and-volley combination, the American netted a high forehand volley from close range.

Muster swiftly put the next two points in his pocket. From triple set point down, he had swept five consecutive points, inconceivably taking the set away from his adversary. By the narrow margin of eight points to six in the tie-break, Muster was the first set victor. He had put himself in an enviable position.

Nonetheless, Sampras hit his stride and seemed to have the second set well within his grasp. He established a 5-1 lead and with his outstanding serve and all court acumen, it was unimaginable that he could lose from where he stood. Sampras twice served for that set, but he lost focus and intensity at the worst possible time. At 5-2, he was broken when Muster laced a forehand return winner past a fast charging Sampras, who was coming in behind a heavy kicking first serve at 30-40. At 5-4, Sampras was broken at 30, double faulting twice in that game. After Muster held for 6-5, Sampras was two points from losing the set in the twelfth game, but he aced the Austrian down the T and took the next point to move into a tie-break.

The pressure was almost entirely on Sampras. Muster had a set in hand. His physicality was one of his finest traits. No one wanted to find themselves down two sets against a man who was such an unwavering competitor. Sampras fully understood his predicament. But surviving in this sequence was a daunting task for the American, who found himself serving at 4-5, two points away from conceding the set.

True to his character, Sampras made no concessions with his back almost to the wall. A solid serve-and-volley behind a first delivery was too much for Muster; the Austrian lost that point on an errant passing shot. It was 5-5. On the next point, Sampras uncorked a crackling and unstoppable first serve down the T. He had given himself a set point, but Muster was serving at 5-6. Sampras played the point conservatively and was rewarded as Muster missed a forehand down-the-line approach shot, driving it long.

On a run of three crucial points, Sampras had rallied to take the tie-break seven points to five. After an hour and 42 minutes, he was back to one set all and breathing freely again. Although he had a brief letdown at the start of the third set—dropping his serve in the opening game on a forehand volley that flew off his racket and landed long—there was no reason for the teenager to be unduly worried. He would recover from 0-2 to 2-2. They went to 3-3 and then 4-4.

Unsurprisingly, Muster was not willing to surrender. He was going to make Sampras beat him. Sampras proceeded to do just that. In the ninth game, an ace down the T, his 13th of the match, took Sampras to 30-15. He held at 15 for 5-4 and then assiduously looked to secure a break that would make him virtually impossible to contain. At deuce in that critical tenth game, Sampras made a delayed approach off the forehand, rushing Muster into a backhand passing shot error. Now at set point, Sampras unleashed a running forehand crosscourt. Muster ran around his backhand and went for an inside out forehand, sending that shot into the net.

The American crowd erupted after that point. Sampras had put himself ahead two sets to one. His determination was strikingly evident and he could almost taste the flavor of victory now as he closed in on it. In his first two service games of the fourth set, Sampras conceded only a single point. A neatly executed chip-and-charge led to a netted running forehand pass from a beleaguered Muster. To 3-1 went Sampras. He promptly held at love for 4-1. From there, Muster could make no impression. In his last two service games, Sampras dropped only two more points. He crossed the finish line with a 6-7 (6), 7-6 (5), 6-4, 6-3 win over the ever combative Muster, moving into his first quarterfinal at a Grand Slam event. Sampras had succeeded with an unrelenting brand of attacking tennis, serving and volleying on almost every first delivery, approaching whenever possible on short balls. He came in no fewer than 142 times, winning 82 of those points. That 58% success rate was fundamentally the difference between the two players.

"The crowd was spurring me on," Sampras recalled in 2018. "I wasn't intimidated by Thomas. When he would grunt and then hit the ball, you could be thinking to yourself, 'Wow!' I respected him but liked being in that situation. That was an important win for me. I was dictating more as the match went on and felt good about that."

Sampras was right where he wanted to be, immersed in the second week at a major, one of the last eight men vying for the U.S. Open crown, relaxed about what he was doing and where he might be going. But one thing was certain: he was not looking beyond Ivan Lendl, the ultimate professional, the man who had finished four of the previous five years as the No. 1 ranked player in the world on the official ATP computer. Moreover, Lendl had won his eighth and last major earlier in the season at the Australian Open and had set a modern "Open Era" men's record by reaching eight consecutive U.S. Open singles finals, taking the title three times in that sterling span from 1982-89.

In other words, Lendl was a U.S. Open institution. He lived in nearby Greenwich, Connecticut and had installed a Decoturf II court at his home to replicate the hard court conditions at the U.S. Open. Lendl had been a singularly transformational figure in tennis, taking off court training to a new level in the gym, shaping his game to control matches with a devastatingly potent inside out forehand, a powerfully driven one-handed topspin backhand down the line, and a big serve designed to set up his forehand and dictate from the backcourt.

Lendl was the No. 3 seed at the Open, placed behind Edberg and Boris Becker. Sampras had only played Lendl once before, losing 3-6, 6-0, 6-3 in the semifinals indoors at Milan earlier in the season. But he had trained at Lendl's house a few years earlier during the Masters tournament. Michael Chang believes that the time spent in Connecticut with Lendl was invaluable for Sampras in terms of mentality and development.

"I think he learned a lot from Ivan at that time," said Chang in 2018. "He was basically seeing how hard guys have to work to become one of the best in the world. There are not going to be too many guys training harder than Ivan. You can't pull out the long marathon matches that Pete did through his career unless you put the work in."

Lendl well-remembered the young Sampras coming to his home for those training sessions. "I believe Pete was 15 or 16," Lendl told me in December of 2018. "It is my recollection that he already had a big serve and he was very talented, but you need to know what is in their heart to see how good they are going to be. I didn't know yet how well he performed under pressure, but obviously in the long term he performed quite well."

As for how he performed in his 1990 U.S. Open quarterfinal against Lendl, Sampras clearly lifted his game considerably from the level he had reached against Muster. He had no alternative but to do just that. Lendl was at his best on hard courts, backing up his serve with bullets off the forehand, setting the tempo from the backcourt with his immense power, and wearing down his opponents with both his will and his capacity to bear down hard on the biggest points.

"Before playing the match," Sampras recollected in 2019, "I knew Ivan and had practiced with him. I felt I could hold my own. He was one of my idols growing up. I looked up to him a lot and he was a powerful player, but going into our Open match in 1990 I felt reasonably comfortable about how my game matched up with his. He didn't like guys coming in and serving and volleying. So I just came in and was serving quite well and dictating play the first couple of sets. Ivan was maybe lacking a little bit of confidence and was just past his prime. His results over that year were a little suspect so I felt he was a little vulnerable."

Locked at 4-4 in the first set, Sampras was pressed hard by Lendl in a hard fought ninth game. Lendl reached deuce on the Sampras serve, backing up the American with a down the line topspin lob. Sampras could not get enough on a backhand overhead, allowing Lendl to crush a forehand passing shot winner down the line. But with the stakes high, Sampras was unswerving. His first serve elicited a backhand return error from Lendl and then he did some stellar work at the net, punching a forehand volley down the line, leaping for an acrobatic overhead and finishing the point with a forehand drop volley winner.

Sampras had dealt capably with a tense situation in that critical ninth game of the opening set. He held on. Serving to stay in the set at 4-5, Lendl had a couple of game points before saving a set point as a chipped backhand return from Sampras landed inches long. Lendl earned a third game point but Sampras obstinately refused to give that game away. After a fourth deuce, Sampras made it to set point for the second time, and sealed it on his own terms. He came forward to punch a crisp backhand volley crosscourt, pulling Lendl well off the court. Lendl went for the down the line passing shot but missed it. Sampras had secured the all-important opening set 6-4 and Lendl was distressed by that outcome.

At 4-4 in the second set, after both men had held across the first eight games, Lendl made his move. For the first time in the match, he broke the big serving 19-year-old. Sampras saved one break point in that ninth game but Lendl gave himself a second chance, sending a hard hit topspin backhand return at the feet of the incoming Sampras, who had no chance to answer it. Down break point for the second time, Sampras was unable to respond. Lendl's down-the-middle return drew a forehand error from Sampras.

Lendl had the break for 5-4 and was serving for the set, a game away from one set all. But he played the tenth game entirely too negatively, opening with a glaring forehand down the line mistake, then double faulting for 0-30. Sampras patiently probed on the following point before approaching behind a forehand inside in. Lendl missed the passing shot: 0-40. Although he made it back to 15-40, Lendl was broken at 15 for 5-5 as Sampras clipped the baseline with a forehand approach, drawing an error with that shot. Nevertheless, Lendl had four break points in the eleventh game but could not convert. In closing out that game, Sampras made one of his patented leaping overheads that would become a personal trademark in the years to come, putting it away athletically, leaving Lendl dumbfounded. Sampras was exuberant about the hold for 6-5.

Three times in the twelfth game, Lendl was precariously perched at set point down. Sampras netted a forehand pass with a good opening down the line; chipped a backhand second serve return wide; and netted a forehand second serve return when running around his backhand. Lendl held on for 6-6.

Fittingly, the set was resolved in a tie-break. Sampras opened the sequence with an ace out wide for 1-0. He got the mini-break for 2-1 and followed with a pair of service winners for 4-1. Lendl took the next two points on his serve but Sampras was giving away nothing on his own delivery. Two first rate serve-and-volley packages took him to 6-3 and he closed it out 7-4 with a forehand down the line passing-shot winner. Sampras did not lose a point on serve in that tie-break, advancing to a two-set lead. In the latter stages of both the first and second sets, when the chips were down and he could have surrendered his authority, Sampras was unflinching.

"Those first couple of sets," said Sampras, "I was emotional. I was fired up and ready to go and then I had a letdown. But tennis is not like basketball where you run out the clock. You still need to close him out. I relaxed a little bit after winning the second set and he kept fighting. That was maybe a little inexperience and then he raised it up and I dropped a little bit. I knew he was fit and was not going to give in. It was a sign of me letting up when Ivan won the third and fourth sets."

The third got away from Sampras in a hurry. Lendl surged to 3-0 and held all the way through the set, mostly with comfort. Sampras was missing much more from the baseline and Lendl found rhythm and range. Serving for the third set at 5-3, Lendl held at love with sharp efficiency.

It was apparent that the essential color of the match was changing. Over the first four games of the fourth set, Lendl won 16 of 22 points and roared to 4-0. Sampras served one double fault in losing his opening service game and two more in the third game. His intensity had dropped decidedly. Lendl was now setting the tempo. A competitive role reversal had taken place.

But Sampras wisely did not let the set go tamely. He held in a four-deuce game with his 18th ace for 1-4, broke Lendl in the sixth game and held in another long game for 3-4 with his 20th ace. After Lendl held at love for 5-3, Sampras wiped away a set point against him in the ninth game with a forehand volley winner and made one last push when Lendl served for the set at 5-4. Sampras had a 15-40 opening to get back on serve, but Lendl fended him off, winning the set 6-4, leveling the contest at two sets all.

Many in the sport's cognoscenti liked Lendl's chances at this stage. He was poised to impose himself physically, to exploit his significant gap in experience over Sampras, to put himself one match away from a ninth U.S. Open final in a row. But Sampras was undaunted. As he recalled, "I regrouped and tightened up my game in the fifth set and played with more sense of urgency. I found that emotion again. I always had the serve to be able to close it out and rely on and in that match my serve kind of got me through it because I did feel like I was getting tired. We were playing some long rallies and I didn't like the way it was going."

At the start of the fifth set, Sampras did indeed reapply himself and, perhaps knowing that the finish line was in sight, played with renewed vigor. Not by accident, his best serving set was surely in the fifth. He recognized the magnitude of the moment. He knew what was at stake. Sampras realized that he could still get the job done as long as he took matters back into his own hands and served with the purpose, power and precision that would show the world the kind of athlete and tennis player he was—and the incomparable champion he would one day become.

The first game of that final set was critical. Sampras held at 15, commencing that game with a gorgeous backhand stab volley winner, going to 40-15 with a neatly executed forehand half volley winner off a low return down the middle from Lendl, and getting the hold with a service winner. Lendl answered with a love hold for 1-1 but an unshakable Sampras held at 30 for 2-1 despite missing four of six first serves. His dexterity at the net was the difference in that game.

Serving at 1-2, Lendl was under siege. He double faulted to fall behind 30-40, got out of that jam and had two game points, but Sampras would not let go of his quest to get the break right then and there. After three deuces, Sampras garnered a second break point, and this one he converted with a terrific return setting up a forehand inside in winner. Sampras was back on the ascendancy, ahead 3-1 and surging with self conviction. Buoyed by two aces and only one missed first serve, Sampras held at love for 4-1.

Champions like Lendl do not bow out without a spirited stand. He held at love in the sixth game and then had Sampras at 0-30 in the seventh. But Sampras met that moment with the same kind of composure he would demonstrate over and over again across his career. He aced Lendl down the T, releasing his 24th untouchable delivery of the match. Sampras moved to 40-30 but a resolute Lendl took the next two points.

Lendl thus had a break point in this critical seventh game of the fifth and final set. Sampras proceeded to put in a first serve deep to the backhand and Lendl chipped his backhand return into the net. Sampras followed with his 25th ace, this one down the T. At game point for 5-2, he did not falter, following his second serve in and drawing a netted chip return from Lendl.

Lendl had made a strong push to turn the match back in his favor, but his effort went unrewarded, mainly because Sampras had played like a veteran in his mid-twenties rather than a fellow stationed at the end of his teens. Serving to stay in the match, Lendl seemed out of inspiration and ideas. He trailed 15-40, double match point, served an ace, but missed his first serve at 30-40. Sampras took a forehand second serve return and came in behind it. Lendl's passing shot was well produced but Sampras made a low forehand volley down the line. All Lendl could do was throw up a lob and Sampras put away an overhead with certitude, thus completing a stunning 6-4, 7-6 (4), 3-6, 4-6, 6-2 triumph over a renowned adversary.

Lendl was understandably disappointed by an unfulfilled comeback. "Pete played well and served well in that match," said Lendl in an interview for this book late in 2018. "I thought once I clawed my way back into the match, I could take him on conditioning, but he served so big it didn't matter. That was the disappointing thing for me. I thought after the third and fourth sets I could win the match. He just kept serving so big throughout the match and even in the fifth he served big. That was the difference that day and in most matches Pete played."

Lendl is the last one to speak hyperbolically, so, listening to him praise Sampras effusively, it was hard to ignore the seriousness or authenticity of what he was saying. "I know that Pete is by far the best player I ever played," asserted this all-time great who competed against other luminaries including John McEnroe, Jimmy Connors and Bjorn Borg over the course of a storied career. "He had the best serve I ever faced. No doubt about it. Not only could he back it up so you could not just put the return back in play and say 'Okay, I am in the point' but his serve crumbled on your racket. It had not only pace but spin as well, so you couldn't just block it back. He was one of the very first players, it not the first, to use the second serve as a weapon and he started hitting it really hard at times."

Lendl paused for a moment, and then continued, "He was also the best athlete of all the guys I played. There were numerous times I played against Pete and I won my share [Sampras took their career series 5-3]. I would hit a good topspin lob against him and he didn't even back up. He just jumped up and put it away."

Sampras examined that Open win over Lendl and his fifth set heroics differently. He felt he could win. He was not giving up on himself. "The way I always played," he said in 2019, "I might struggle a bit but I am able to turn it on. I broke him in the fifth and then broke him again at the end of that set. I managed at times to sense what could be the turning point of a match and I did that in the fifth set against Ivan."

Asked why he served his best in the fifth set, he replied, "That can happen. I lost some energy in the third and fourth, but near the end I felt some adrenaline and the crowd was into it. You come out with more speed on your serve and I remember picking it up a bit. He kind of played the same the whole match, and I felt I just raised my game enough in the fifth to close it out. But a part of me was thinking when it was over, 'What the hell just happened?'"

Understandably after such a big win on a monumental stage, after making it to the final weekend at a major for the first time and toppling a player of such extraordinary stature, Sampras was astonished.

"I was shocked," he said. "Walking into the press conference into a full room —that had quite honestly never happened to me in my life. Beating Ivan at the U.S. Open and being a 19-year-old kid, just walking into that conference, was a little intimidating for me at first. So to talk about it and get my thoughts on the front page of the *New York Times* sports section was surreal. It was eerie. It was as if maybe I had arrived. But I was not fully comfortable with it. Nineteen is pretty damned young. I look at a lot of these young players today and I don't think we will ever see a teenager win a Grand Slam tournament again. I realized how young I was and how young it is to win one of these majors as a teenager."

While Sampras was on this stirring run in New York, commentator Mary Carillo was following it all with a sense of amazement and admiration. As she watched him perform on the premier stage in American tennis in front of an American sports audience unlike any other, she could not help but be reminded of the character Hermie in the movie "Summer of 42." The film was released in 1971, the year Sampras was born. Hermie was a shy teenager with the mannerisms, earnestness and an unmistakable decency strikingly reminiscent of Sampras. In that summer of 1942 film, Hermie poignantly loses his virginity with an older woman and his world is sweepingly altered. In the summer of 1990 at the U.S. Open, Sampras was declaring his manhood as a tennis player by striking down one big name after another across a fortnight that would change his life irrevocably.

Carillo said in an interview for this book, "Pete was Hermie. He was just a kid, still a teenager and he had that sort of gangly, ropey looseness to him. But you could tell that he still took himself very seriously and that was what was so cool about him. When he beat Lendl, he didn't seem surprised. He knew what he was trying to do and knew he was capable of doing it. He didn't act overwhelmed. I guess it would be fair to say that even back then there was this air of inevitability about Pete Sampras. He owned everything he did. He acted like he belonged."

As Sampras made that journey through an extraordinary New York fortnight, he was coached by a fellow named Joe Brandi, with whom he had joined forces at the Bollettieri IMG Academy. Brandi had the good sense to let Sampras figure things out largely by himself, although he still offered some words of wisdom when he had something of substance to convey.

As Sampras said decades after the fact, "I had been looking for a coach and had moved to Florida. I became good friends with Jim Courier, who was like a big brother to me then. He was working with Sergio Cruz. Joe was one of the pros at Bollettieri's and I was looking for someone full time. We got along quite well. He was a pretty mellow guy who didn't say too much, but at the Open he was a big help on what I was trying to do out there with my strategy. I knew how Muster, Lendl, John and Andre played. Still, he gave me the right hints. I just liked his personality. He was very low key and mellow. He didn't make a big deal out of things. I liked that sort of tempo."

Courier remembered that stretch leading up to the 1990 U.S. Open very well because he had developed a nice friendship with Sampras over the previous couple of years. "Pete came across from California and hadn't been a high school student at Nick's like I had been, so I knew the ropes there a lot more than he did," said Courier. "We turned pro at the same time so we were both in the same boat, trying to make our way up to the top 100 from there and using coaches from Bollettieri's. I was with Sergio Cruz and he was with Joe Brandi so it was just a matter of getting Pete comfortable in that environment and helping him get acclimated to Florida as well. He wasn't that familiar with it and he didn't have his family there. It was more my environment than his, so I was a big brother there. Out on the tour we played doubles a lot in our first couple of seasons before singles became a priority. So I certainly felt that vibe very much and was happy to be there for him. We did a lot of on and off court training together. It was a great time in our lives."

Sampras and Brandi roomed together during that 1990 Open at a New York hotel. As Sampras remembered it, "I was trying to save a few bucks on hotel rooms. It worked out well. I slept like a baby those whole two weeks and Joe was very supportive. He didn't say too much and when you are competing as I was and playing well there is not much you really need. Joe recognized that and he wasn't going to tell me a bunch of things that might be confusing. I was playing great and getting better as the tournament went on. I was finding my game. So he just sort of stayed out of the way."

After his big win over Lendl, Sampras fully understood that making the semifinals was a long way from winning the title. He was still not thinking about winning the tournament.

That would have been premature. His next opponent would be John McEnroe, who won the U.S. Open four times between 1979 and 1984. He had been revitalized over the course of this 1990 New York fortnight, most persuasively in a five set, round of 16 victory over the Spanish workhorse Emilio Sanchez. He had backed up that win with a straight set dissection of the young American David Wheaton.

In an interview with McEnroe for this book, he candidly expressed his optimistic feelings heading into that 1990 Open semifinal with Sampras. "Pete was obviously as a tennis player mature way beyond his years in a way that I didn't realize," said McEnroe. "Pete had come off beating Lendl, but I thought this was a good matchup for me because you have got a guy in Pete who will probably come down a little bit and not necessarily be able to stay at that level at that young of an age. I think I miscalculated my strategy because I sort of said to myself, 'This guy is going to beat himself so I can be a little more conservative.' I wasn't as aggressive and wasn't coming in as much as I probably in my mind should have been."

McEnroe was reflecting on what went wrong from his standpoint without shortchanging Sampras. He continued, "Pete had a lot of pop on his serve and forehand, but I thought it would be a little more hit and miss from him. I was playing tentative and tight, maybe realizing this might be one of my last chances to win the Open."

Sampras was feeling upbeat about his chances after having toppled McEnroe not long before. He said in one of our 2018 interview sessions, "Honestly, I felt pretty good going into that match with John. I liked my matchup with him and felt I had time to play against him. He didn't like playing a big serve-and-volley player. He liked to be the one dictating. His game was obviously tremendous, but I had some time to return against him. I felt comfortable serving-and-volleying, just doing my thing. I served out wide to his backhand, which he didn't like. I had beaten John in Toronto before the Open over the summer. I don't want to say I overpowered him, but my weight of shot compared to his was an advantage. I knew what was coming from John. I knew his tendencies. And I just remember that my backhand returns were clicking. I kind of got in the zone. I felt I was really moving well that day and John, like Ivan, was just a little past his prime at 31, not as dominant as he had been and maybe a little vulnerable."

Here was Sampras, walking out onto the Saturday afternoon New York stage, unintimidated by taking on one of the most renowned athletes of his time, composing himself as if he had lived amidst these surroundings all of his life. He comported himself as if he was made for such an occasion.

McEnroe opened the proceedings with gusto, holding serve in the opening game at 15 with consecutive aces and then taking Sampras to two deuces in the second game. But Sampras shook off any mild apprehension that might have been inside him. He broke McEnroe in the third game. After McEnroe rallied from 0-40 to 30-40, Sampras strikingly displayed his swiftness afoot. He drove a backhand pass down the line and McEnroe retaliated with a drop volley. Sampras scampered forward with uncanny quickness and angled a backhand pass crosscourt low and into the clear. He had the break for 2-1 and consolidated it quickly with a love hold, closing out that game commandingly with a forehand volley winner and an impeccably crafted overhead.

McEnroe released four aces in the fifth game and managed to hold on, but he was still pushed to deuce. Yet Sampras was unflustered, holding at love for 4-2 without missing a first serve. The younger American was very much at home now in the field of competition, thoroughly controlling the climate of the match. With McEnroe serving at 30-30 in the seventh game, Sampras struck a forehand return winner off a second serve. On the following point, Sampras sent a flat forehand approach down the line with interest and McEnroe erred on the passing shot. It was 5-2 for Sampras. He followed with another love hold to seal the set. He had not conceded a point in his last three service games of the set.

Having taken a shellacking in that first set, the prideful McEnroe wanted to immediately start making amends. He aced

Sampras out wide in the deuce court to hold at 15 for 1-0 in the second set and the magnificent left-hander boosted his morale in the process. Sampras answered with two aces on his way to 1-1, prompting CBS commentator Pat Summerall to perceptively say, "He [Sampras] plays with such an air of confidence—not arrogance."

McEnroe was clearly not as confident as his opponent, but he was driven as always by an absolute obsession to win. He served his way to a 3-2 lead and then had three break points in the sixth game. Sampras remained implacable, saving the first two with excellent first serves, erasing the third when a McEnroe lob landed long. Back to 3-3 came the determined and purposeful Sampras. Having emerged unscathed from that corner, Sampras pounced, making one scintillating passing shot off the forehand, another off the backhand, and then getting good pace on a backhand return that coaxed an error on the volley from McEnroe.

Sampras had broken for 4-3. He had a game point for 5-3 but McEnroe connected with a backhand return winner past the charging Sampras. McEnroe was now looking to exploit his attacking instincts ceaselessly. He took the next point and broke Sampras for the first time, following his return in and executing a backhand drop volley immaculately. McEnroe was back in the set at 4-4, serving with new balls and brimming with confidence.

But Sampras was imperturbable. After McEnroe double faulted to make it 15-15 in the ninth game, Sampras made a terrific backhand return that was too much for McEnroe to handle on the volley and then a low return forced McEnroe to dig out a half volley. Sampras passed him easily off the forehand. Down 15-40, McEnroe saved one break point, but then he double faulted into the net. Perhaps the quality of Sampras's returns earlier in that game had created added anxiety in McEnroe but, be that as it may, Sampras was in the driver's seat, ready to serve for a two-set lead, ahead 5-4.

And yet, McEnroe was fighting forthrightly to keep himself in the set. He played spectacular tennis to reach break point, pressing forward as only he could, showing off his great hands at the net. But Sampras always trusted himself on serve, unblinkingly meeting every challenge head on. The crowd was sensing a chance for a closer match and a possible McEnroe revival, but Sampras, as he recalled, was "in my own world out there." He saved the break point with a second serve into the body, drawing an errant backhand return from McEnroe. A service winner down the T took Sampras to set point and his superb serve-and-volley combination wrapped it up.

From the danger of break point, Sampras had played three clutch points in a row to establish a two-sets-to-love lead. Through the first seven games of the third set, both men held serve without facing any break points. But Sampras double faulted at 30-30 in the eighth game, and, at 30-40, McEnroe made the most of it, angling a backhand crosscourt, pulling Sampras out of position and then driving a forehand crosscourt for a winner. Serving for the set at 5-3, McEnroe held at the cost of only one point, easily putting away a high first volley at 40-15.

The New York audience was exhilarated by McEnroe's third-set triumph. McEnroe himself was buoyed by the progress he had made. But both players recognized that Sampras remained in an advantageous position. As Sampras said in 2019, "Even though I lost that third set and the crowd really got behind John—which obviously happens in that situation—I never felt at all like I was going to lose. As a young player, when you get confident and you see you can do it, and you have beaten him three weeks before, it gives you a sense of security. If I had never played John and didn't know him I might have frozen. But I was comfortable on the court with him."

McEnroe reflected in late 2018, "I became more aggressive in that third set and had some success to win it. But I had put myself in a big hole. It is hard to come back from two sets down against anyone, and certainly against Pete."

Sampras demonstrated in the opening game of the fourth set that he wasn't going anywhere, that he was controlling his own destiny, that this match was still in his hands. He held at love, starting with an ace down the T, closing out the hold with an elegant serve-volley one-two punch that set up a winning overhead.

McEnroe was unbending as well, holding at love for 1-1 with an ace down the T. They stayed on serve until McEnroe served in the sixth game. He fought as hard as he could to hold on through three deuces and saved three break points. He had rallied from 15-40 down, but Sampras fully recognized the value of this moment and the importance of denying McEnroe the opportunity to stay in the match. On his one game point, McEnroe double faulted into the net. His first volley on the following point lacked sting and Sampras exploited that opening with a scorching forehand passing shot. Now at break point for the fourth time, Sampras majestically rolled a backhand return crosscourt for an outright winner.

Prevailing in that game left Sampras in excellent shape. He held at love for 5-2 before McEnroe took the eighth game without the loss of a point. Sampras then served for the match at 5-3. This was where Sampras thrived; there has been no better closer on serve in the history of tennis. A brilliant backhand passing shot down the line lifted Sampras to 15-0. A blockbuster of a second serve that stifled McEnroe made it 30-0, followed by an ace down the T for 40-0. McEnroe saved one match point but, at 40-15, Sampras fittingly ended it all with his 17th and last ace of the contest, sent exquisitely down the T.

Sampras had come through commandingly, eclipsing McEnroe 6-2, 6-4, 3-6, 6-3. "I wasn't intimidated out there," Sampras said nearly 30 years later. "As much as the crowd was rooting for John and while they were not in awe of me, they did seem surprised by me. It was a combination of those two things that helped me to win."

McEnroe knew he was up against a player who would reshape the future of tennis. Sizing it up nearly 30 years later, McEnroe said, "Pete's firepower was incredible. I noticed it with Boris Becker when he was young. They could take the racket out of your hand. If you asked me one player I didn't like playing, it was Pete more than any other person because I wasn't able to do my thing as much as I wanted to. Normally I would be the guy to make people uncomfortable, attacking them, putting pressure on them, not letting them relax."

McEnroe had more of substance to say about Sampras, adding, "He was winning or losing points on his terms all the time. You could hold easily, but you did not feel like you were making an impact on his head. Pete also had that great second serve, which was very important and not talked about enough. And he covered the court more quickly than many realized, which sort of shocked me a little bit, not only in that Open match but the other couple of matches we played. He was so quick to move forward and even at the baseline he moved incredibly. He was just a tremendous athlete, even more athletic than I had realized going into that U.S. Open match."

After beating McEnroe, Sampras was now aware of what he was on the verge of achieving. Reaching the final of the U.S. Open was beyond his wildest dreams, but he was taking it in stride and not getting ahead of himself. As he said in 2018, "Up until that point, I didn't know what it meant to win the Open, or what was at stake. So, after beating McEnroe, maybe that calmed me down. If I had been 30 years old and this was my last Open, maybe I would have been a little tighter and more sensitive [to the situation] but at that point I was free-wheeling, having fun, popping aces and hitting backhand return winners. It was almost in slow motion for me. That is what it felt like."

His opponent in the final on September 9, 1990 was none other than Andre Agassi, his stylistic opposite and charismatic adversary. Tracy Austin reflected in 2018 on this great American rivalry between Sampras and Agassi and what it would become, "We were lucky as fans to see one of the best returners in the game against one of the best serve and volleyers, so the contrast in styles was fun. We are missing that in today's era. Pete and Andre's personalities were so different as well, with the coolness of Pete against the swashbuckling Andre. You could not find two more different personalities."

Sampras would not quarrel with that assessment. As he said in 2019, "The 1990 Open was our first real big match.

We always got along well and made efforts with one another. I remember when I first saw him in our junior days and he had earrings and long blonde hair. My first impression was that you don't see this every day. He was from Vegas and he would come with his Dad in this big Lincoln car. I was supposed to play him at one of the junior tournaments and he did not show up. Then he got to No. 3 in the world in 88' and I was ranked about 90 then. We saw each other around in those years but didn't talk that much. We respected each other but our personalities were just very different."

Agassi had played one of his finest matches to knock out the defending champion Becker in a come-from-behind, four-set semifinal. Although this was his first Open final in 1990, he had been in the semifinals the previous two years, losing on both occasions to Lendl. Earlier in 1990, he had been in his first major final at the French Open and was heavily favored to defeat Andres Gomez, the left-handed Ecuadorian who was ten years his senior. But Gomez upended the American in four sets on the clay.

Back in New York on the hard courts, the incomparable ground striker from Las Vegas with spectacular returns off both sides and a mastery of control, power and precision from the baseline was a clear favorite to beat Sampras in the title round clash. Sampras did not mind that in the least, knowing deep down that he had the game to startle Agassi if all went according to plan. But the fact remained—Sampras was the underdog. Unmistakably.

"No doubt about it," said Sampras when he was in his late forties. "I knew Andre was the heavy favorite at that 90' Open. As far as our games at that point, he was a much better player who had been ranked No. 3 in the world. He had been around and was much more established than I was. I basically came out of nowhere, the young American trying to make a few bucks and see what I could do. And I felt like not having a day off between the semis and the final really helped me at that point, because I just went to sleep that night, woke up and just played another tennis match. If I had a day off to think about it and walked into the Open, doing a press conference or interviews or signing autographs, everything would have stopped and I would have thought about it. Who knows what would have happened?"

Instead, Sampras stayed in sync. "I just had my same routine, had my warmup and went out and played Andre at 4 pm. I just kind of went from John to Andre and I felt sort of similar. They were different players obviously, but I felt I could play against Andre. He wasn't going to blow me off the court. I think he was surprised that I came into that final playing as well as I did. Once I came in firm and strong and imposing my game, I think he got tight. He was like, 'Oh my God, I am supposed to win the Open. This is a great opportunity to play Pete. He is not that good at this point.' And I think he felt uncomfortable. I capitalized on that and was hitting my groundstrokes well and moving well, doing everything I wanted to do. Andre had a sense of panic once he saw what I was doing."

From the outset of the Sampras-Agassi confrontation, Sampras was primed for this appointment. He was blazing from the opening bell on, relaxed and almost oblivious to what was at stake, going for his shots as if it was a first round match in some remote corner of the world. But this was the U.S. Open final and the historical consequences were immense. Lesser men would have been severely compromised by the importance of the occasion, by knowing that a vast worldwide audience was watching on television and nearly 20,000 spectators were gathered at Flushing Meadows to witness it in person. Sampras, however, was undaunted by what he was doing, remaining in his own bubble, ignoring all the outside distractions.

Agassi seemed apprehensive as soon as the battle unfolded, as if he sensed that he had stepped into the arena against an unconsciously soaring opponent who was not going to pay any attention to him. Agassi could sense from the beginning that Sampras would not stop going boldly for his shots. It was understandably unnerving. He had dealt magnificently with Becker the day before, playing that match largely on his own terms from the backcourt, out-dueling the

German in the fast paced rallies with better ball control and greater baseline versatility.

But the Sampras meeting had an entirely different look and feel to it. Agassi quickly seemed shell-shocked by the barrage of brilliance and sheer creativity that was being thrown at him relentlessly from the poised fellow on the other side of the net. At 1-1 in the first set, Sampras seized the initiative. After a couple of deuces, Sampras took his tennis to a level Agassi could not answer. He drove a topspin backhand cleanly down the line, got the short ball he wanted, and came in behind a flat forehand down the line. A harried Agassi netted a backhand passing shot. Overwrought by the pressure he had faced all through that game, Agassi drove a forehand long off a return from Sampras that was not deep. Sampras had the break for 2-1.

Sampras proceeded to flex his athletic muscles, to showcase his supreme talent for the fans to relish, to burst into another gear. He opened the fourth game with a serve-and-volley gem, putting away a backhand first volley down the line. He took the next three points all with aces, sending each of them down the T. In a flash, Sampras had reached 3-1. Agassi kept his teeth in the tussle, holding on tenuously from deuce in the fifth game. But Sampras served-and-volleyed as well as it can be done to reach 4-2, holding with the loss of only one point.

Agassi was backing up his serve with some hard hit balls off both wings, getting good depth on his shots. He held on for 3-4 at 15 and then got to 30-30 on the Sampras serve in the eighth game. Sampras then released his fifth ace, out wide in the deuce court. At 40-30, he unleashed one of his big first serves to the Agassi backhand, eliciting a netted return. To 5-3 went Sampras. Agassi then played one of his best service games to hold at 15 in the ninth game, forcing Sampras to serve out the set.

Sampras was more than up to that task. He moved to 15-0 by serve-volleying to the forehand side and forcing Agassi into a return mistake. An ace out wide, his sixth of the set, gave Sampras 30-0. A crackling service winner down the T to the

Agassi backhand made it 40-0 and Sampras held at love when Agassi netted a forehand return off a kicker from Sampras. In five service games across the opening set, Sampras had won 20 of 23 points against the best returner in tennis.

Agassi had acquitted himself well, holding serve all but one time in that first set, fighting hard to stay with Sampras, hoping to find some chink in his opponent's armor. But he had nowhere to go on this occasion. Sampras was untouchable on serve, volleying soundly with extraordinary feel and putting on a virtuoso display from the baseline. Agassi's only hope was that Sampras would wake up from this dreamlike state and realize what he was doing. But that was not going to happen.

Nonetheless, Agassi did all he could to avoid getting blasted off the court. He had a couple of very tough holds in the early stages of the second set, advancing to 2-1 after saving three break points in the third game. The unflappable Sampras took no notice, holding at 15 for 2-2 with his ninth ace and then going full force after a service break in the fifth game.

Agassi saved one break point but then Sampras laced a forehand down the line return with too much mustard on it. At break point for the second time in that game, Sampras played one of his most remarkable points of the entire encounter, approaching down the line off the forehand, reading Agassi's crosscourt pass, punching a backhand volley down the line, and keeping it low. On the run, Agassi went crosscourt with his forehand pass, but Sampras was camped out on top of the net, crushing a forehand volley down the line into an open court. The crowd erupted. Sampras walked to his chair at the changeover, gratified by what he had just done. Agassi went to his chair like a boxer who had taken too many right hooks to the head.

Down 15-30 in the next game, Sampras was the epitome of the unruffled competitor. He came to the net on two of the next three points, winning them confidently, holding at 30 for 4-2. Agassi admirably refused to drift into despondency, holding at love in the seventh game before Sampras responded by holding at 15 for 5-3. Serving to stay in the set, Agassi commenced the ninth game with a double fault. He got to 30-30 but Sampras attacked from a deep position to draw an error from Agassi and then came over a backhand return and sent it down the line for a spectacular winner. Set to a clear-eyed Sampras, 6-3.

In the opening game of the third set, Sampras missed seven out of ten first serves and faced his first two break points of the match. But an unswerving Sampras held on for 1-0, staying on the attack, making Agassi come up with his best brand of counter-attacking play. After Agassi held from 15-30 for 1-1, Sampras had first serve problems again, missing five of eight. He faced a break point in that game as well, but saved it impressively with a backhand volley winner crosscourt off a forehand passing shot from Agassi. Sampras had anticipated that shot uncannily.

Agassi held on for 2-2 at love, but he would not win any more games. Sampras held at 30 for 3-2, serving his eleventh ace of the match in that game. He broke for 4-2 at love with a backhand winner down the line off an inside-out forehand from Agassi. Agassi's forehand corner was wide open and Sampras found it. Sampras knew he was closing in on a monumental achievement. He held at love for 5-2 with a forehand volley winner after a fine pickup, a service winner and back to back aces, raising his total to 13 for the match and 100 across the tournament.

Sampras had won 12 of 14 points and eight in a row to put Agassi in a dire predicament. The Las Vegas native was serving at 2-5 in the third, down two sets, one game away from elimination. He made a go of it in a two deuce game, but Sampras kept his foot on the accelerator, taking the last two points to close out an unimaginably flawless performance in his first major final against a formidable adversary. Agassi tamely netted a forehand off a short backhand return on match point: 6-4, 6-3, 6-2 Sampras. In three nearly immaculate sets, Sampras was not broken, putting 53% of his first serves in play, winning 35 of 38 points first serve points (92%). Moreover, Sampras double faulted only once.

At 19 years and 28 days old, Sampras had made history of the highest order by establishing himself as the youngest man ever to win the championships of his country. That was no mean feat. Moreover, this was his first ever tournament triumph on a hard court in his professional career. He had never even been to a final on the ATP Tour held on hard courts until his riveting Flushing Meadows fortnight. He had cut down the No. 6 seed Muster, three-time champion Lendl, four-time victor McEnroe and the No. 4 seed Agassi in succession. With each and every match, Sampras had improved markedly, raising his game round by round, playing the kind of tennis that was seemingly two to three years away from him. It was nothing less than stupendous.

Reminiscing about that seminal 1990 victory 28 years after it happened, Sampras said, "God, I can't explain how I played that day against Andre. I had never played that well in my life, even in practice. I was serving incredibly well, hitting my ground strokes the way I wanted, coming in and dictating. I was moving great. I guess it had always been there. But to do that in the finals of the U.S. Open is hard because nerves can come in. I woke up that day feeling no nerves and he did. To this day, I wish I could give a better answer about why it happened. I just continued where I left off from my match with John and went in with the same attitude, but with my game even better against Andre. And he just felt the weight of it and lost his game. He sort of panicked. I have seen highlights of that match and he looked like a deer in the headlights at times because of what I was doing. That is when it all came out for me as a player. Quite honestly I didn't expect it."

Agassi was still somewhat dazed when it was over. He had been trounced and it was understandably difficult for him to come to terms with such a devastatingly one-sided defeat in the final of a major he had surely expected to win.

In his autobiography, *Open*, published in 2009, Agassi, writing in the present tense throughout the book, reflects on that loss to Sampras. He mentions his initial career meeting with Sampras in the spring of 1989 when he won so easily in Rome, and thought that Sampras would never be a front line player. In his account of the 1990 Open final, Agassi writes, "There's simply no way I can lose to Pete, that hapless kid I watched with sympathy last year, that poor klutz who couldn't keep the ball in the court. Then a different Pete shows up. A Pete who doesn't miss. We're playing long points, demanding points, and he's flawless. He's reaching everything, hitting everything, bounding back and forth like a gazelle. He's serving bombs, flying to the net, bringing his game right to me. He's laying wood on my serve. I'm angry. I'm helpless.... When it's all over I tell reporters that Pete gave me a good old fashioned New York street mugging. An imperfect metaphor. Yes, I was robbed. Yes, something that belonged to me was taken away. But I can't fill out a police report, and there is no hope of justice, and everyone will blame the victim."

That was a somewhat convoluted explanation for why he lost that match. Agassi was fundamentally and inescapably outplayed across the board. Nothing was taken away from him. Sampras played with absolute purity, rose to the occasion, produced sublime tennis, and was the decidedly better player. To be sure, Sampras stunned Agassi with the quality of his performance and his sustained brilliance. It was a straightforward, well-deserved, first-rate piece of business from a worthy champion. That was the bottom line.

Carillo was in the broadcast booth for many of Sampras's most significant matches over the course of his career, including the 1990 Open final against Agassi.

"Andre was supposed to win that match," she recalled in 2018. "This was all new territory for Pete. Andre had been around and was a known quantity. I remember we had a shot of Andre on television and I said, 'His eyes look scared.' The director took a close-up shot of Andre and there seemed to be tears in his eyes. He was just overwhelmed by the fact that Pete was hitting him off the court."

When he got close to victory, was Sampras apprehensive or suddenly too aware of where he was? "No. It was automatic," he said. "I was just playing. I did not think about what was at

A star was born when Pete Sampras rolled to the U.S. Open title in 1990 at age 19

stake. It was just about me playing Andre and the Open wasn't even on my mind. It was just a tennis match. I did feel differently as I got older and I sometimes felt the anxiety. I remember one year at Wimbledon thinking at a changeover, 'You have to hold your serve three more times and you can have your Wimbledon.' But at that Open final in 1990, I was just playing him. It was what I wanted to do and it was very matter of fact. I wasn't thinking too much and sometimes I play my best when I don't think. It is all reactionary. And he was off. He felt some pressure. It was like the perfect storm."

The way Sampras was playing that day, no one in the world could have stopped him. He had moved beyond himself a few years before he was ready to turn in displays like that more regularly, before he was ready to understand what it all meant and what it would take to live up to the excellence he had exhibited.

As Lendl said for this book, "Beating the three of us—myself, McEnroe and Agassi—back to back to back was a tall order for anyone, never mind a 19-year-old. We saw what was in his heart. The moment Pete did that and won the U.S. Open that way, it was quite obvious that he was something special as a player."

Because he was so young and his 1990 run was extraordinarily unexpected, Sampras needed to take stock and come to terms with his newfound status as a winner of an everlasting prize. "I wasn't ready for the responsibility," he mused in 2019. "I remember my agent that night I won the 90' Open says, 'Okay, tomorrow we have Good Morning America, The Today Show, CBS Morning News, Charlie Rose...' and I was like, 'What?' So to wake up the next morning with almost no sleep and talk about what just happened wasn't easy for me. I had done like two interviews my whole life and it was surreal. I felt like a deer in the headlights. I was not ready for it. I went from being nobody to winning one of the biggest tournaments in the world, to being the youngest U.S. Open champion ever. You look at other sports and people like Jordan Spieth and Tiger Woods were more groomed for their moment. I wasn't groomed. I was thrown into the lion's den, not that it is bad. It just happened too quickly. I felt it the next day and for the next six months. The reality hit home. I had to figure some things out game-wise and with just being who I was. Nineteen is young. You have a lot of maturing to do."

That maturation would come, yet it would take some time for a great player who had dreamed of towering achievements—but had never envisioned himself as a celebrity—to get more comfortable with his altered status. He was navigating new territory. There were some inevitable obstacles ahead. But Pete Sampras had demonstrated over an astounding New York fortnight that he was here to stay.

# CHAPTER 3

# GROWING PAINS LEADS TO
# GREATER GAINS

After his startling run at the U.S. Open, Sampras, still
trying to digest what had happened to him, did not fare that
well in his next three tournaments. In his first appearance at the
season-ending ATP World Tour Championships in Germany—
an elite event reserved for only the top eight players in the
sport—he lost two of his three matches and did not make the
semifinal cut. But he concluded the year on a high note by
capturing the Grand Slam Cup crown in Munich, Germany,
toppling the towering left-hander Goran Ivanisevic, Chang and
Brad Gilbert for that title.

He opened 1991 well enough by reaching the final at
the U.S. Pro Indoor in Philadelphia, but a disciplined Lendl
prevented the American from defending his title, prevailing in
five sets. Sampras struggled through the first half of the year
and was beaten soundly 6-3, 6-1, 6-1 at the French Open by
Thierry Champion of France in the second round.

Not long after, he started finding his form, reaching
the final of Manchester on the grass. He was beaten by the big
southpaw serving of Ivanisevic in straight sets. Sampras was
ousted at Wimbledon in the second round by the dangerous

Derrick Rostagno, the same man who had nearly upended Boris Becker two years earlier at the U.S. Open. Rostagno had two match points in that second round skirmish before Becker—the beneficiary of a very lucky forehand passing shot that clipped the net cord and flew over the racket of Rostagno on one of the match points—went on to win his only U.S. Open title.

Leaving the Rostagno disappointment behind him, Sampras went to work purposefully on the hard courts across the summer of 1991, playing with growing self-assurance. He won the tournament in Los Angeles, stopping Gilbert in the final on the hard courts there. At the Masters 1000 tournament in Cincinnati, he removed Edberg and Courier before losing to the left-handed Frenchman Guy Forget—a superb server in his own right—in the final. He then won Indianapolis, cutting down Courier before halting Becker in the final.

Following that spirited run over the summer, he looked entirely capable of holding on to his U.S. Open title. No one leading up to the proceedings in New York had played better on the hard courts. But, having turned 20 not long before the Open, still growing into his talent, uncomfortable about living up to what he had done a year earlier, he was knocked out in the quarterfinals by a first rate Courier 6-2, 7-6 (4), 7-6 (5).

In many ways, Sampras was relieved. He had known how arduous a task it would be to defend that Open title. "It's kind of like the monkey is off my back," he said at the time. That comment was met with disdain from Connors, who did not understand that Sampras at 20 was still in the process of discovering the competitive commitment it took to succeed at the highest levels of the game. Not until he was 21 did Connors secure his first major. Perhaps he had lost sight of where he stood at 20, and of what it took to grow into the champion he would one day become.

Sampras buckled down during the autumn indoors, winning Lyon, reaching the final at Paris, and securing the prestigious ATP World Tour Championships for the first time, defeating Courier in a four-set final. That was an important breakthrough to prevail at what was arguably the fifth most prestigious tournament in all of tennis. Thus he came to the end of his tournament year and it was a fitting way to proclaim that ahead of him would be a golden stretch. He did suffer a pair of hard defeats away from home against the left-handed Frenchmen Henri Leconte and Guy Forget indoors in France at the Davis Cup Final. Forget's win was his third in a row against Sampras over the course of that 1991 season, including two final round victories in that span. No one else pulled off that remarkable feat against Sampras during his career within a calendar year.

But the fact remained that Sampras had by and large closed the 1991 season powerfully and productively. He had made it abundantly clear that the 1990 season and, most importantly, the U.S. Open triumph, was neither an accident nor an anomaly. He belonged among the elite. Sampras soon knew where he was headed, understood what he wanted and was willing to sacrifice almost everything in pursuit of his tallest goals. And as 1991 ended, he had formed a crucial partnership with a new coach who would shape who he was and make some subtle adjustments in his game, playing a crucial role in allowing Sampras to start making the most of his vast potential. This coach was a remarkable man who had peaked at No. 15 in the world and reached the Wimbledon doubles final with his twin brother, Tom, in the 1980's. His name was Tim Gullikson.

After finishing his impressive career as a player, Tim Gullikson turned to coaching and found he was even better suited to that line of work. Among the star pupils he counseled was none other than Martina Navratilova. Gullikson was a superb student of the game and an unfailingly upbeat fellow beloved by just about everyone in the sport for his decency, integrity and, above all else, congeniality.

In the autumn of 1991, Sampras was looking for a new coach. His agent, Ivan Blumberg, called Tom Gullikson because Sampras was interested in having him serve as his new coach. Tom Gullikson had also established an excellent reputation for himself as a coach working with Jennifer Capriati among others, proving to those in his world that he knew what he was doing. He would serve as an outstanding U.S. Davis Cup captain starting in 1994 through the rest of the nineties.

Gullikson was asked in the fall of 1991 to visit with Sampras at the Nick Bollettieri Tennis Academy-now renamed the IMG Academy—in Florida. Tom Gullikson did just that. As he recalled in a 2019 interview for this book, "I drove down there and Pete and I practiced and worked out a bit and then we had, I would say, a two-and-a-half to three hour lunch. We just talked about his game and his goals and what kind of coach he was looking for. I was very impressed with how mature he was, and how focused he was on his career. You could almost hear the inner drive in his voice. It was a very intense, very engaging conversation. At the end of the day, Pete and I got along well and the whole experience was pretty positive."

But Gullikson had just signed a coaching deal with the USTA. He said, "Pete, if this was a little different timing, I would be absolutely thrilled and honored to work with you. I think you are a very nice young man and obviously tennis wise you have got a tremendous game and a massive upside. I see only green arrows pointing up for you. But right now I am committed and I just renewed my contract with the USTA. But there is a guy that looks like me and talks like me and is a lot of fun. Why don't you have my [twin] brother Tim come down and talk to you?"

That, of course, is precisely what happened. Tim Gullikson and Sampras hit it off well and soon started working together. As Tom Gullikson said, "Pete loved Timmy, loved what he had to say about his game and their partnership was formed. One of the things that Pete always said is that Tim not only made him a champion on the court but made him a champion off the court as well. Tim was everybody's best friend and he taught Pete how to be a real guy."

Sampras, of course, had not yet won Wimbledon, or, for that matter, come even close. Tom Gullikson watched at the very end of 1991 when Sampras made his debut for the United States in the aforementioned final against France, and was outmaneuvered by the wily left-handers Forget and

Leconte. As Tom Gullikson explained, "Pete lost those matches because he couldn't return their serves. Tim saw the backhand return especially as a glaring hole in Pete's game. Tim was a good right-hander and I was a left-hander and he played me every day of his life. Tim had a rock solid backhand return and a good understanding of positioning and how to deal with the whole leftiness stuff. He worked with Pete on how to hit a blocked backhand return, how to hit a really firm chip like an abbreviated backhand volley, and when Pete was driving through the backhand return how to get the racket head going through the ball rather than coming straight up on the ball. So it was about positioning and patterns, where to stand on the returns and the angles. After Tim started working with Pete, Pete's record against lefties was incredible."

Jim Courier backed up Tom Gullikson's analysis of what made Tim Gullikson such an outstanding coach for Sampras. Having grown up in the juniors with Sampras—and playing some doubles together with his friend early in their pro careers—Courier observed how much of a difference Gullikson made in shaping the Sampras game at a momentous time. In an interview for this book, the stalwart American Davis Cup player and captain put that contribution into perspective.

"Pete's forehand was a bit of a problem early on in his career," Courier said. "It was certainly a big weapon but it was erratic. He didn't really have the running forehand yet that would be his signature shot other than the serve. Tim also really solidified Pete's backhand and gave him a lot more options with the slice. Pete became very good at putting people like me under pressure by making returns and having the athletic ability to get into the net at his own discretion and wreak havoc on the server. There were a lot of places you could go and feel safe in Pete's game before Tim got a hold of him. They got shored up pretty quickly."

In 1992, Sampras flourished in a multitude of ways under the guidance of Gullikson, gaining a greater understanding of what he could accomplish. The combination of Sampras's innate greatness and Gullikson's uncluttered view of how to bring out the best in his charge was fully apparent over the course of the 1992 season.

Sampras did not win a major, nor did he quite reach the pinnacle of No. 1. But his record and level of play were stellar across the board. He won 72 of 91 matches, the most by far that he had ever played. He collected five titles. He went to the quarterfinals of the French Open for the first time, made it to the penultimate round of Wimbledon for the first time, and advanced to the final of the U.S. Open.

It was an outstanding campaign in almost every way. His record was diversified and he achieved significantly in a variety of conditions, winning tournaments indoors at Philadelphia, on clay at Kitzbuhel, twice outdoors on hard courts during the summer, and again indoors during the autumn. His overall standards were exceedingly high all year long.

The only lingering frustrations were his losses at Wimbledon and the U.S. Open. At Wimbledon, he had beaten defending champion Michael Stich convincingly in a straight-set quarterfinal and then took on Ivanisevic in the semifinals. Their contest was played on Court 1 rather than the Centre Court because incessant rain had put the tournament behind schedule. Agassi and John McEnroe were pitted against each other simultaneously on the Centre Court. Sampras took the first set in a tie-break from the 6'4" Croatian southpaw, but then dropped the second.

Discouraged by dropping that critical second set, he did not do himself justice in the last two sets, falling 6-7 (4), 7-6 (5), 6-4, 6-2. He did not give up, but in some ways he gave in and part of the reason for his resignation was his disillusionment about dealing with the fearsome Ivanisevic serve—the most burdensome one he would face all through his career.

Sampras felt helpless watching 36 aces fly past him at alarming speeds that afternoon. Tim Gullikson helped Sampras recognize what was going on and how to put it in better perspective. As Tom Gullikson remembered Tim saying, "Pete, why would you get disappointed getting served off the court? What do you think you do to everybody? That is what you do to other players. But when somebody else does it to you, it is not okay? You have got to learn to deal with this.'"

Sampras took that advice in the right light. He realized that Gullikson was right, understanding that Ivanisevic's recipe for succeeding was somewhat like his own. Ivanisevic went ahead 3-2 in his rivalry with Sampras when he won that semifinal at Wimbledon in 1992 and he extended his lead to 5-2 the following year, but Sampras carved out a number of critical victories over his rival thereafter and eventually won their head to head series handily 12-6, taking ten of their last eleven clashes.

In any event, that Wimbledon loss disturbed Sampras deeply, but not nearly as much as his defeat at the hands of Stefan Edberg in the U.S. Open final later in the summer. Sampras had not been feeling well at the end of his four-set semifinal win over Courier the previous day and had IV treatment afterwards. He had a tough night trying to recover and get back to full force. The word was that he did not get to sleep until 3 am and then he woke up at 8 am still not feeling like himself.

That afternoon, he began auspiciously against the Swede, winning the first set. Edberg took the second but Sampras served for the pivotal third set and was poised to take control of the match. But, uncharacteristically, he did not close out that set as was his custom. He served two double faults at 5-4 in the third and eventually lost the set in a tie-break. As Sampras faded mentally in the fourth set, Edberg coasted home comfortably, winning 3-6, 6-4, 7-6 (5), 6-2. Had he prevailed in that encounter, Sampras would have secured the No. 1 world ranking in the process.

Sampras was convinced then, and had the same feeling as he moved into his late forties, that he did not lose to Edberg because of lingering physical difficulties after the Courier match carrying over into the final. He believed he was beaten by Edberg because he did not fight with the required ferocity. It was a life-altering experience, one that changed him irrevocably as a competitor.

As he said to me in a 2018 interview, "For those couple of years from the 1990 Open that I won until I lost the Edberg final in 1992, I just wasn't sure what I wanted out of the game. I wanted to win, but how much will did I have? How much heart did I have? For those two years I am not sure if I was one hundred percent willing to sacrifice. I got into that final against Edberg and woke up feeling good. I was happy to be in that final. I was not nervous. He didn't really play that well and I certainly didn't play all that well. I lost that third set in the tie-break and something popped. My energy in the fourth set completely went away. I did not dig deep and I felt like I went through the motions. I knew the truth of that. For weeks and months after that, I looked myself in the mirror and really asked myself what I wanted."

Sampras realized he had not lived up to the competitive standards he was demanding from himself. He understood that he had wilted at the end when he should have been battling with all of his heart for survival. As he said, "Nobody really cares who comes in second and that was a tough lesson I learned. Stefan was not playing that well and knowing I could have beaten him stung me a lot. I would not use the word quitting, but I did not fight hard enough in the fourth set. I didn't fight the way I should have to the very end. That bothered me for weeks and months and for the rest of my career. The feeling that I did not give it my all bothered me more than anything."

Expanding on that point, Sampras said, "From '92 to '92 there was this uncertainty in me, but the way I lost that Edberg final, I couldn't have been more clear after that about what I wanted to do. My outlook on my tennis and my life completely shifted after kind of packing it in when I played that fourth set against Edberg. That 30 minutes changed the next 10 years for me. For the rest of my career, from that point forward, I didn't win every major final, but I felt like I at least fought hard. Maybe I would have learned that lesson in another way later in my career if it hadn't happened the way it did against Stefan, but that was where the rubber hit the road and it all shifted for me."

In an interview for this book, Edberg—who came from a break down in the fifth set against Richard Krajicek, Lendl and Chang en route to his title-round meeting with Sampras—recollected his impressions of that 1992 Open final against Sampras. He said, "I have read about how Pete felt. We all have turning points in our careers. Sometimes you feel there are matches you should have won, or something you did wrong, or something you wanted to do different. That was obviously quite a tough final for both of us. He had a tough semifinal that went into Saturday night and I had that long second week playing a lot of hours. I don't think either one of us felt very good going into the final. Once you are in the final, you give everything you have and maybe you reach some point of exhaustion, either physically or mentally. Winning that third set when it is one set all is very crucial, especially if you are tired. You get the momentum and you feel stronger. If you lose the third set like Pete did, you may feel it is a long way back."

Sampras was permanently altered by that bruising setback against Edberg on September 13, 1992. He finished 1992 stationed at No. 3 in the world, ranked behind Courier and Edberg. But Sampras had made serious inroads. The Ivanisevic Wimbledon setback and, more significantly, the Edberg experience at the Open, were career defining moments. He was figuring out what it took to be a top of the line champion. He was on the verge of something substantial. The following year, he would start marrying his talent to his goals. He would make his presence known when it counted the most. He would move past anything he had ever done before.

# CHAPTER 4

# THE BEST IN HIS PROFESSION

Commencing his 1993 campaign, Sampras displayed a level of consistency that was impressive. His form was more reliable than ever, week in and week out, surface to surface, everywhere he went. He took his opening tournament of the season in Sydney on the hard courts in Australia, handling Thomas Muster without losing a set in the final. At the Australian Open, he seemed ready to claim the title, but, once more, Edberg beat him on a big occasion, prevailing 7-6 (5), 6-3, 7-6 (3) in the semifinals. Sampras led 4-0 in the first set and 5-2 in the third but could not exploit those openings.

Across the spring, Sampras hit his stride, capturing three consecutive hard court tournaments. He took the Masters 1000 title in Miami over countryman Mal Washington, upended Gilbert in the final of Tokyo and then edged Courier 6-3, 6-7 (1), 7-6 (6) in Hong Kong. That trio of triumphs lifted Sampras up to No. 1 in the official ATP Rankings for the first time in his career on April 12, 1993. He had worked hard to get there and wearing that label suited him well.

In an interview I did with Sampras for *Tennis Week Magazine* the week after he took over at No. 1, he said, "I knew at the start of this year that if I had a really good first three or four months, I could possibly get to the top. I didn't have many points coming off the computer, but I also knew I would have to win some tournaments. I guess reaching No. 1 has happened sooner than I thought it would, but I am very happy it has happened."

Elaborating on his achievement and addressing the fact that that he had not played Davis Cup for the United States the previous month because he was so committed to moving up to No. 1, he said, "I made a personal goal for this year to try to be No. 1 and that was a big incentive of mine. I felt that going around the world a week after Miami and playing on grass in Davis Cup would have jeopardized my goal. I wanted to concentrate on achieving something that not many people had done. I knew I was going to be criticized for not playing Davis Cup, but being the best player in the world was very important to me. It was a tough decision, but, as it turned out, it really worked out for me."

Buoyed by that breakthrough and comfortable wearing that No. 1 robe, Sampras maintained a commendable level of consistency, reaching two semifinals on clay at Atlanta and Rome, and making it to the quarterfinals of the French Open for the second year in a row, only to lose a hard-fought, four-set duel with clay-court specialist Sergi Bruguera. The wily Spaniard went on to win the tournament over Courier, and defended his crown the following year.

A few weeks later, Sampras was back at the All England Club for his fifth attempt at winning the tournament that mattered more than any other in the game of tennis. Sampras had won only one match in his first three years before his journey to the semifinals in 1992. Now, proud to be the No. 1 player in the world, eager to assert himself on the lawns, knowing he was better than anyone else in the world of grass court tennis, Sampras came in as the top seed for the first time. He realized that a big opportunity awaited him over the fortnight and wanted to succeed there for two chief reasons: it had been his primary goal ever since switching to the one-handed backhand as a 14-year-old to rule on the lawns at Wimbledon and Sampras had not won a major since the 1990 U.S. Open. He sorely wanted to add another of the premier prizes to his collection.

And yet, Sampras had another obstacle to overcome this time around—a nagging shoulder injury that was worrisome even before the tournament started. It could have kept him out altogether, but he was able to get treatments for inflamed tendons and proceeded into the event. His first round match against Neil Borwick of Australia was no facile task, but he came from behind to defeat the world No. 121 6-7 (10), 6-3, 7-6 (3), 6-3. He knocked out another Australian, Jamie Morgan (No 58 in the world), in the second round 6-4, 7-6 (5), 6-4 and then accounted for Byron Black of Zimbabwe 6-4, 6-1, 6-1. In the round of 16, Sampras clipped Great Britain's Andrew Foster 6-1, 6-2, 7-6 (6).

That smooth passage through the first four rounds took Sampras into a quarterfinal confrontation against the defending champion Agassi. In 1992, Agassi had startled himself and the entire tennis community with the way he adapted to the grass on only his third visit to the shrine of the sport. To be sure, he had been a quarterfinalist in 1991 and had nearly moved into the semifinals before bowing against compatriot David Wheaton in five sets.

But, in 1992, he had been obliterated by Courier in the semifinals of the French Open and had hardly touched a racket for two weeks after that. He might not have played any tennis at all in that stretch. Despite poor preparation and not really knowing what to expect from himself, Agassi's magnificent returning and his remarkable capacity to control rallies on the grass and dominate from the backcourt had carried him to a string of victories over three-time champion Boris Becker in five sets, three-time victor John McEnroe in a straight sets semifinal and then another five-set triumph over the ever-intimidating Ivanisevic in a memorable five-set final.

In 1993, Agassi was seeded only No. 8 but he had overcome both Patrick Rafter (the 2000 and 2001 finalist) and Richard Krajicek (1996 champion) to arrive in the last eight. The Sampras-Agassi contest was eagerly anticipated by everyone in the know. It was still a young rivalry. Agassi led 4-3 in their head-to-head series but they had not played since he had surpassed Sampras at the French Open on the clay in the quarterfinals the previous year. This was their first appointment on a grass court. And despite the fact that Agassi had taken the title the year before, Sampras was the prohibitive favorite to succeed on the Centre Court against his countryman.

In the early portions of the match, Sampras was confounding Agassi with his tactical acuity. It was among his most cerebral performances. Rather than trying to simply outhit and overpower his opponent in Agassi's service games, he mixed up soft backhand slices with potent yet purposeful forehands. He did not come over the backhand very often, nor did he overplay the forehand. This was disciplined, probing, finely calculated, well-conceived tennis. Meanwhile, Sampras was serving tremendously, finding the corners regularly, keeping Agassi guessing and moving his delivery around impeccably.

Over the course of the first two sets, employing his imaginative game plan, executing soundly, bearing down hard and making the game look easy, Sampras faced only one break point—erasing it with an ace. He broke Agassi four times in that span, disrupted his opponent's rhythm almost incessantly and was masterful in every aspect of the game. He dropped only four games in establishing a convincing two-set lead.

But the complexion of the contest changed decidedly early in the third set. Serving in the second game, Sampras rallied from 0-40 to 30-40 but a persistent Agassi gained the break for 2-0 on the next point with a low forehand return on the stretch provoking a backhand half volley error from Sampras. Agassi had discovered some daylight at last.

He made that break count, holding serve four times from there without facing a break point. He had found his range and raised his game significantly. Agassi took that third set 6-3 and was back in the match.

At the beginning of the fourth set, he broke Sampras again. With Sampras serving at 30-40 in the first game, Agassi unleashed a stinging forehand return down the middle, rushing

Sampras into a mistake on the backhand volley. Agassi was now backing up his serve ably. He had found his timing and was hitting through the court rhythmically. Sampras was no longer harming Agassi from the baseline and his serve location was slightly off. At 3-5, serving to stay in the set, hoping to at least start serving the fifth and final set, Sampras was stymied by the brilliancy of his opponent's returns. He saved one set point but, after double faulting, was beaten by a perfectly orchestrated one-two punch from Agassi, who went down the middle on his return again and set up a winning backhand passing shot down the line.

Agassi had claimed the fourth set 6-3. He had the momentum going his way again. Sampras, who had seemed somewhat preoccupied by his right shoulder acting up, was rubbing the shoulder now. Yet he got right back to work. His returns and overall ground game were outstanding in the opening game of the fifth set, but two break point opportunities eluded him. Agassi held on for 1-0. Sampras then applied himself ably, holding on in the second game. He managed a service break in the third game after Agassi double faulted at 30-30. On the following point, Sampras returned to his first set recipe, chipping a backhand return and inviting Agassi to drive a two-hander long down the line.

Sampras seemed to have restored order on his side of the net. But serving at 30-40 in the following game, he double faulted, allowing Agassi back to 2-2. That could have been a jarring and debilitating blow for a champion who seldom would lose his serve from a break up in a final set. But Sampras played the fifth game beautifully. He opened with a topspin lob winner and took the next point with an aggressive approach off the backhand. After Agassi reached 15-30, Sampras went on the attack once more, making a forehand volley winner. Covering the court with astounding alacrity, Sampras broke at 15 for 3-2 by looping a backhand crosscourt and coaxing Agassi into an errant backhand.

Pumping his fist, thoroughly exhilarated, delighted about where he stood in the score-line, Sampras was back out in front 3-2 in the fifth. He proceeded to take his next two service games at the cost of only two points. Serving to stay in the match at 3-5, Agassi fended off two match points, surprisingly serve-volleying on both. He held on in that ninth game. This meant that Sampras would have to serve out the match in the tenth game.

Here is what happened: An ace out wide for 15-0; an ace down the T, 30-0; another ace out wide for 40-0. Then Agassi missed a second serve return off the forehand. Sampras had held at love to complete a 6-2, 6-2, 3-6, 3-6, 6-4 victory. Sampras had served 23 aces, pouring in 66% of his first serves in the match and winning 85% of those points. It was in many ways the most fascinating contest of their entire head-to-head series. Sampras had looked capable of a decisive straight-set win. Agassi had seemed poised for a spectacular five-set comeback. But, in the end, Sampras had managed his inner emotions exceedingly well and his fifth-set showing was outstanding. The way he served in the final game was symbolic of his whole career and emblematic of what separated him from the rest of the pack.

"I remember slicing and dicing him those first two sets," said Sampras in 2018. "I knew he was defending the title so I felt, 'Okay, he has got the pressure on him to defend.' He picked up his game and started hitting his great returns. I felt this match was similar in a way to playing Lendl at the 1990 Open, when he came back to win the third and fourth sets. I let Andre back in the third set, just as I had done with Lendl at the Open. But like I felt with Lendl, I had a sense of urgency in the fifth. The weight of my game can sometimes make the difference and the pressure I put on some opponents can make them tight. Then, boom, the match can switch. I was relieved when I won that match."

Facing Boris Becker in the semifinals, Sampras was primed. The burly German had turned Wimbledon upside down as a teenager in 1985 and 1986. In '85, he became the youngest man ever to win the sport's most coveted title at 17. An overpowering physical force who knocked the cover off the ball on both sides and served mightily, Becker earned the nickname "Boom-Boom" for the speed and explosiveness of his serve.

He won the title again in 1989. Becker was a player born for grass-court tennis and no doubt a Wimbledon fixture. He had been in six finals altogether and at this Wimbledon of 1993 he had reversed the result of his 1991 title-round meeting with Michael Stich, overcoming his countryman in five high quality sets.

Becker was playing so well that the incomparable coach and strategic genius Pancho Segura had told a friend outside the Gloucester Hotel in London, "Becker is a cinch for the title. Cinch!" But Segura and a few other experts—including the South African doubles wizard and prominent commentator Frew McMillan—were underestimating Sampras as a big-match player coming into his own. This was his first confrontation with Becker at a place they both cherished. They were locked at 3-3 in their rivalry but had never faced each other at any of the majors.

Becker was far more experienced on prominent stages at the majors than Sampras and he had garnered five of his six career majors by then. But Sampras believed he was the better player. "We played similar games," he said in 2018, "but I just felt I was a little better mover. In some areas, you could see that on grass. I felt if I could get the ball down low against Boris I would have an edge."

This one came down largely to the outcome of the first set. Becker needed that set more than Sampras. Neither man lost serve in that opening set, although Becker was on the brink at 5-6. Consecutive double faults put him set point down, but he emerged from that predicament unscathed. In the ensuing tie-break, Sampras went ahead 4-3 with a chipped backhand return eliciting a backhand volley error. That gave him the crucial mini-break. He did not lose a point on his serve all through the sequence. Sampras came out on top seven points to five.

Becker was clearly deflated after giving his all in that first set. At 1-1 in the second set, he double faulted three times and was broken at love. Sampras sedulously protected that break for the rest of the set but he was challenged forthrightly by Becker at the end. Serving at 4-3, Sampras saved a break point with a backhand first volley executed with sidespin that skidded away for a winner. He held on for 5-3 but, two games later, was made to work inordinately hard again for the hold.

At 5-4, Sampras trailed 15-40 after double faulting long. But his serve-and-volley was too good on the next point and then his magnificent forehand first volley crosscourt landed safely in the corner for a winner. Two more fine first serves backed up by stellar volleying gave Sampras the set 6-4 and put him ahead two sets to love.

Becker had raised his return game significantly at the end of the second set, but to no avail. Sampras again broke early in the third set and was unyielding on his own serve. Serving for the match at 5-4, he saved two break points. On the penultimate point of the match, he made an outstanding backhand half volley pickup. Becker blasted a passing shot but Sampras at full stretch pulled off an astonishing forehand drop volley winner at a nearly impossible angle parallel to the net. At match point now, he punched a backhand volley into the clear: 7-6 (3), 6-4, 6-4 Sampras. The two best grass court players of their respective eras had collided on the Centre Court and Sampras had been too good for Becker.

And so, for the first time, Sampras advanced to a Wimbledon final. He wanted this tournament very badly. But to win it, he would have to topple his old friend and fierce rival Jim Courier, who was enjoying the most productive period of his career. This was his third major final in a row across 1993. He had taken the French Open in 1991 and 1992 before moving within striking distance of a third crown in a row on the Paris clay—more precisely known as terre battue. Courier was leading Bruguera 2-0 in the fifth set before his bid for the "hat trick" fell short.

Moreover, Courier had won the Australian Open in both 1992 and 1993. He had four Grand Slam singles titles in his collection, three more than Sampras. He was ranked No. 2 in the world—right behind Sampras—but his experience on the most consequential stages was greater than that of his opponent.

Until then, Courier did not have as much faith in his game on grass as he did on hard or clay courts and that was understandable. His extreme western grip on the forehand made it harder to exploit that central shot in his repertoire. The lower bounces did not suit his unorthodox two-handed backhand that resembled a baseball swing. In his four previous appearances at Wimbledon, he had only once made it to the quarterfinals, advancing to that round in 1991.

But Courier had been impressed when Agassi won Wimbledon the year before. Since Agassi was a fellow baseliner with some striking stylistic similarities—as well as some unmistakable differences—Courier understandably was encouraged by what his old colleague from the Nick Bollettieri Tennis Academy had done.

Tom Gullikson had been friendly with Courier for many years. Gullikson was aligned with the Player's Club in Palm Coast, Florida. There were two grass courts at that facility. Gullikson invited Courier to train with him for ten days after the end of Roland Garros and, of course, before Wimbledon.

As Gullikson recollected, "Agassi's Wimbledon of 1992 definitely inspired Jim. He felt like 'I may be more of a baseline player but I can play on grass.' So Jim kind of went into that Wimbledon of 1993 pretty loose, with a mindset of 'If I can keep my head together and don't get annoyed with bad bounces and the unrhythm of grass-court tennis if you will, then I could do well.' Jim and I had a very good relationship from the time he was 17. So it was kind of ironic that Sampras and Courier ended up meeting in the Wimbledon final because Timmy was calling me every day while working with Pete and asking how Jim was doing on the grass. I watched their final from right behind the player's box and was trying to just enjoy the tennis and be neutral, knowing an American was going to win the title either way. I liked both guys a lot."

Courier easily recollected that period up to and including his meeting with Sampras. He said in 2019, "Prior to Andre winning Wimbledon in '92, I hadn't seen a baseline player win Wimbledon in men's tennis. I felt rather helpless at the baseline trying to stay back and do what I was comfortable doing, especially with my grips, which were a little more extreme than some other players. The lower bouncing grass at the time was pretty challenging for me and I felt I had to serve-and-volley to succeed there. That was really hard for me to make an adjustment. Once I saw Agassi stay back and be successful in '92, I just made the determination that I would stay back in '93."

But Courier did not conduct his business entirely from the backcourt. He said in 2019, "It is funny because my recollection until about two years ago was that I served and stayed back all the time, but I happened to be on a plane a couple of years ago and they were playing my final with Pete in '93 on ESPN Classic. And I couldn't believe how much I served-and-volleyed."

Sampras had never been more nervous before a tennis match. He explained in 2018, "I was very nervous for a couple of reasons. One was thinking about how I felt after losing the '92 Open final. And the second was that playing Jim was different from playing anyone else in the world at that time. He and I were friends. We had been doubles partners. We had stayed together at Bollettieri's. So I just felt a lot of anxiety and didn't sleep well the night before. You go to bed and wake up at 2 am. You go back to sleep and wake up at 4 am. You just can't settle down. I just had this fear of losing and the fear of how I would feel if I did not win. I wasn't eating well either. I just felt the weight of winning the Open in '90 to kind of giving up at the Open in '92, to this match with Jim in '93. I was thinking, 'This is it.' All those things were on my mind. It was very clear that I had learned the hard way the difference between winning and losing these major finals. It is a tough business we are in."

Sampras valued the friendship he had enjoyed with Courier and recognized the difficulty of remaining as close as they had once been at this stage of their careers, with one man stationed at No. 1 in the world and the other residing at No.

2. Naturally, while the two men remained highly respectful of each other and appreciative of the history they had shared as competitors and pals in a one on one sport, Sampras clearly felt it was inevitable that they would keep a certain distance while fighting so ferociously for the same prestigious prizes.

He said in 2019, "It was not just tricky but impossible. I strongly believe you can't be the kind of friends that are going out to dinner, checking in and talking on the phone or playing golf. When you are the best in the world competing for majors, it is not that we didn't like each other, but you needed a little separation to focus. You just can't let someone in that wants to be in your life when you are trying to take something away from him. Jim and I handled it as well as we could and that was true also with the others like Andre and Michael. You are happy for them when they win, but at the same time envious. Jim and I were very close and had spent a lot of time together. He was like a big brother to me as I turned pro and he made his break and I made mine. We hit the pinnacle with that Wimbledon final in 1993 but it slowly diffuses and I went to my camp and he went to his. That is just the way it is."

Sampras clarified, "Jim is a very competitive guy in an outward way and I was competitive but more internally. Slowly we went our separate ways. It is just impossible to keep the relationship the same as it was. You just can't do it. Jim, Andre, Michael and I all had great careers and we came out of it reasonably friendly and respectful. Jim and I to this day stay in touch. He is someone I have had a nice history with and Jim is a good guy, but certainly when we were competing for majors we just accepted how it was going to be and we were okay with that."

The final took place on a stiflingly hot day, meaning that the conditions were better suited to Courier, who was a workhorse unlike any other in tennis and a man who did not really mind dealing with soaring temperatures. Sampras— much like Novak Djokovic in later years—was uncomfortable in the extreme heat. He could play through it with his iron will and stout heart, but it was a tougher task. The heat complicated his challenge against Courier, a fighter through and through with astounding physicality.

Watching this match from his home nation in Serbia was the six-year-old Djokovic, a kid with a large imagination and even a sense of destiny about his future in the sport. In an interview for this book done in August of 2019, Djokovic recalled where he was when Sampras collided with Courier on the London grass and the impact it had on him as a youngster dreaming about a place of prominence in a game he was embracing with all of his heart. Sampras had limitless appeal to the young Djokovic.

As Djokovic remembered when he spoke to me for this book in the summer of 2019, "I was six and watching Pete play this Wimbledon final on the television in a mountain called Kopaonik in Serbia where I grew up and started playing tennis maybe a year-and-a-half before I actually first saw Pete on the television. My parents were running a restaurant as a family business and they were building three tennis courts in front of the restaurant. I was born and raised in Belgrade which is the capital of Serbia, but this was the summer and I was spending a lot of time on the mountain because my parents had their restaurant there. I would go on every school break to the mountain. I fell in love with the sport. I had no tradition of tennis in my family but I would hit for hours against the wall and my parents saw my passion for the game. They bought me a racket and supported me."

Djokovic attended tennis camps on those three courts in the Serbian mountain town. So by the time Sampras and Courier moved into the boy's view from afar at Wimbledon, Djokovic's enthusiasm for the sport was unbridled. As he recalled, "I started following tennis on television but the first video image of a professional tennis match that I actually saw was Pete winning his final in '93. I was so amazed with his skills and his composure and with the whole setting of watching him play on the most sacred Centre Court of the sport. I just fell in love with everything. When you are that young you believe in everything. You live through your dreams and your dreams are your reality. You have that moment of, let's say, a revelation when you just know that one day it is going to be you on that court holding the trophy."

Elaborating on this theme, Djokovic said, "I really felt that day watching Pete that it was kind of like a higher power that was in a way instilled in me. I just kind of received that information from above. It is just one of those things that you can't explain. You just feel it and know it deep inside. But for me Pete was the guy. I was actually doing my impersonations from very early stages of my tennis career and by the time I was seven, a year after this match, I started impersonating the top players and taking the best shots from each one of the top guys. But with Pete, even though our tennis styles were quite different, I still looked at him as my idol. And what impressed me the most about him that day watching him in the Wimbledon '93 final—and later on—was his ability to stay present and stay calm at the most decisive moments, to be mentally tough when it matters the most. And that is what separates him as one of the greatest tennis players ever to hold a racket. It was just the way he coped with the pressure and came up with his best game when it was needed the most. And that is something I feel I have picked up from him in a way and kind of defines my career as well in the big moments, especially the most recent one in the Wimbledon [2019] final against Roger Federer."

Djokovic came away from observing Sampras in that Wimbledon final of 1993 with a lasting admiration for his hero. He explained, "I was his big fan and I remember that when my Dad and I would watch tennis, he was cheering for Agassi and Courier even though he liked Pete more at the time. That was because of me and my feelings. He was purposefully cheering for Agassi and Courier so he could provoke me and trigger me. In those early days especially, I was such an avid fan of Pete and I kept following his results. When I got the chance to hit a few balls for the first time with him at Indian Wells in 2010 it was amazing when I saw him coming my way because I felt a flashback of my entire childhood and all those moments of supporting him and looking up to him. Here was my idol coming up to me, shaking my hand and acknowledging what I have achieved."

And so, with the young Novak Djokovic sitting in front of a television screen watching, the two American warriors went out onto the Centre Court on this balmy afternoon of July 4, 1993 and both men were ready for the appointment. Courier was mixing up the serve-and-volley and staying back a lot as well, backing up his serve potently with explosive forehands and his two-hander was holding up well. Sampras was serving and volleying with extraordinary consistency. Neither man came close to a break point in the opening set.

By this stage of the tournament, the Centre Court grass played more like hard courts after a fortnight of fine and incessantly dry and hot weather. This was helpful to Courier, but the fact remained that he was in the sport's most fabled arena against a player who was going to turn it into his personal showcase in the years to come. Even in the debilitating heat with the courts playing largely to his liking, Courier recognized that he would probably need to play the fast court match of his life to win in this setting against a singularly formidable adversary.

While Courier had played a whale of a semifinal to devour Edberg in four sets with a barrage of remarkable returns, the Swede's standard serve was a heavy kick and it gave the American more time to set up winning returns off his backhand side. As Courier recalled, "I had a beat on Stefan's serving pattern by that point in our rivalry and knew that he liked to go to my backhand on big points. So I was just laying in wait for that kick serve to come to that spot and pummeling it with a good amount of success. He didn't shift away from that pattern so it kept working in my favor. I surprised myself more than anyone else in the room. I don't think many people would have given me much of a chance against Edberg and I certainly didn't give myself a whole lot of a chance because of the surface discrepancy. So beating Edberg on grass in the semifinals of Wimbledon was one of the biggest surprises in my career. That was quite unfathomable."

Sampras, however, was a much bigger and better server than Edberg. The Swede was a player who designed his game to close in tight behind his kick serve and take command with his phenomenal skills on the volley. Even after that uplifting victory over Edberg, Courier knew he would be hard pressed to stop Sampras, but he was not pessimistic. He said in 2019, "I was a big underdog against Pete the way I was against Edberg, but I thought, 'Look, I have a shot because Pete is going to be very difficult to break, but if I serve smart and at a high percentage I think I can be difficult to break as well.' And that is kind of how it played out."

Neither Courier nor Sampras was giving much away in the first set of their final. Courier mixed in the serve-and-volley to the Sampras backhand to keep his opponent off guard, while predominantly staying back. Sampras simply kept pressing forward in his usual fashion—relentlessly, persuasively and stylishly.

It was a remarkably well played set on each side of the net. Both players were executing their game plans almost impeccably. Leading up to the tie-break, Courier won 24 of 32 points on serve and Sampras replicated that feat, although Courier stood at only 50% on first serves leading up to the tie-break while Sampras was above 68%. In two different service games—at 2-2 and 5-5—Courier connected with only 20% of his first serves, missing four of five in both instances.

Yet Sampras was not able to get any traction on his second serve return points because Courier was so unerring from the backcourt and so intelligent about unexpectedly serving and volleying enough to keep Sampras honest—even on the second delivery. Moreover, Courier was cagey. He said, "I was a baseball pitcher as a kid, so I used that same philosophy of trying to keep hitting my spots and keeping my opponent guessing. The grass was much faster back then and it didn't rain for the entire fortnight. Within the sport, my spot serving was pretty well respected and I think I did a good job of hitting the corners against Pete that day."

Yet Sampras did not dwell on his returning; he just kept serving as only he could. At 4-5, he unloaded three aces in a quick hold at 15. At 5-6, he served another ace for 40-15 and advanced to 6-6 at the cost of only one point.

On the opening point of the tie-break, Sampras found an open space for a backhand down the line passing shot winner. An unstoppable first serve lifted Sampras to 2-0 and he surged to 3-0 with a familiar pattern, serving wide to the Courier forehand in the deuce court, sending a forehand volley down the line into the corner and drawing an errant lob off the backhand from a harried Courier.

Courier took two points in a row before Sampras released his sixth ace of the set out wide in the ad court, followed by an excellent wide slice serve to the forehand that Courier could not return: 5-2 Sampras. A heavy forehand crosscourt from Sampras was too much for Courier to handle and now it was 6-2. Courier saved one set point with a well-executed serve-and-volley, but Sampras then served down the T to set up a forehand first volley winner to the open court. Sampras had taken the tie-break 7-3 without losing a point on his delivery, missing only one first serve. Courier had not played badly by any means in that sequence, but Sampras had approached nearly every point with clarity and conviction.

The second set unfolded much like the first. In the second game, Courier was taken to deuce on his delivery for the first time, but he surprised Sampras with another serve-and-volley combination, volleying behind Sampras to win the point. He held on for 1-1. The two combatants held with ease until Courier served to stay in the set at 4-5. He led 40-0 but Sampras rallied to deuce. Courier was incensed when the umpire overruled on a Sampras forehand that had been called long. When they replayed the point, Sampras connected with a running backhand passing-shot winner.

That shot took Sampras to set point, but Courier's crackling inside-out forehand was too good and Sampras slipped while chasing it. Courier took the next two points, holding on gamely for 5-5. Serving in the eleventh game,

Sampras held at love with three aces. He had won 13 points on serve in a row and 24 of 27 service points in the set. Courier flirted with danger again in the twelfth game. He was down set point but saved it with a terrific topspin lob. He held on for 6-6. Another tie-break would decide the outcome of the second set and perhaps determine the victor in the match.

This one was much tighter. Sampras led 3-1 but Courier captured the next three points. Later, Sampras served at 5-6 and set point down. He served and volleyed on his second delivery, sending a first volley down the line off the forehand into the corner for a winner. But he did not punch that volley as he normally would. As Sampras recalled in 2019, "Jim was pissed because I pushed that volley and kind of hit the line. It was just a very tight volley that managed to drop in. I was definitely feeling the nerves on that point. You miss that one and it is one set all."

Courier said in 2019, "My recollection is I thought the ball was going out and I even thought that the linesman may have missed the call. But in hindsight, having seen that point on the plane, it looked like the ball did catch some powder. But that was a high tension moment and I am very emotionally invested in the outcome of that point, so I had to try and simmer down. You don't get too many chances against Pete on any surface, let alone grass. So that was a big chance and it vanished."

Instead, knowing he had been fortunate that his shaky volley had landed in, Sampras changed ends of the court relieved yet confident. He sent a deep second serve to the forehand of Courier, knowing he had much success with that play all match long. Courier missed a down-the-line return off that fine serve. With Courier serving now at 6-7 and set point down, Sampras patiently waited for his opening. On the 12th stroke of the exchange, he blasted one of his trademark forehands crosscourt on the run and Courier netted a forehand down the line under considerable duress. Sampras owned the tie-break 8-6. He led two sets to love.

Courier believed he was foolish on that set point against him. He said more than a quarter of a century after the match, "I made the fatal mistake of hitting a ball to his running forehand to lose it, which was just an idiotic move. You just shouldn't do that. He was so good at making it look like there was a hole there on his forehand side, but he just closed it and hit a winner crosscourt. Experience should have told me that there wasn't a hole there and to just keep going to his backhand."

Yet Courier remained determined and eager in the third set. Sampras double faulted at break point down to give Courier a 2-0 third-set lead, but secured eight of the next nine points to knot the score at 2-2. Serving at 3-4, 30-30, however, Sampras missed a high backhand volley. Then Courier made a first rate low return that created a big opening for a backhand down-the-line passing-shot winner: 5-3 Courier.

The No. 3 seed—Edberg had been placed above him based on his excellent record on grass over the years and his two tournament triumphs at Wimbledon—held at love in the following game, closing out the set cleanly with an ace. He now trailed two sets to one. Sampras realized how depleted he was at that stage of the match. He said in 2018, "I remember being low on fuel. It was hot and nervous energy burns a lot of energy out of you. Jim was a really fit guy and I was getting tired, plain and simple. I was fatigued. Some of it was the heat, but a lot of it was just that nervous energy. I just felt the weight of what was going on and I was flat out tired."

Yet Sampras was an abundantly disciplined athlete who knew how to deal with daunting physical difficulties by sharpening his focus, summoning all of his inner resources and raising his intensity. He started the fourth set with an excellent service game, opening and closing it with aces, holding at 15. Having lost his service twice in the third set when weariness set in and Courier elevated his game, Sampras was back in a very good rhythm. In establishing a 3-2 lead, he won 12 of 15 points on his delivery. Now he went full force after a break, pounding a forehand approach with force, drawing a passing shot error from Courier for 15-40. Courier climbed to 30-40 but Sampras outhit him from the baseline on the next point. On the 16th shot of a fierce exchange, he approached confidently down the line off the forehand, keeping the ball low. Courier was trapped too far back behind the baseline. He had no play to make a passing shot. On to 4-2 went a highly-charged Sampras with that timely break.

His 22nd ace of the match gave Sampras a 40-0 lead in the seventh game. Courier won the next two points but, at 40-30, Sampras directed a forehand first volley down the line to coax a topspin lob error from Courier. Sampras had moved to 5-2, just one game away from winning his first Wimbledon. Courier held on in the eighth game and so Sampras had to serve it out in the ninth. The opening point was spectacularly played by both players, ending with a netted diving forehand volley from Sampras. Sampras garnered the following two points for 30-15 but the anxiety was crowding in on him now.

He was hunched over, trying to stretch, wanting to end it all swiftly. A deep second serve drew a return error from Courier, and now Sampras was crouching again. He sent a second serve at 40-15 out wide to the forehand, sticking with a winning formula. But Courier laced a return down the line that Sampras could not handle on the half volley. At 40-30, Sampras made certain to get a first serve in down the middle and punched a backhand first volley crosscourt without overplaying it. The volley stayed low on the grass and Courier netted a backhand pass. Sampras raised his arms jubilantly. He had just won the most important tournament in all of tennis, overcoming the man who had finished the previous year as the No. 1 ranked player in the world, winning the final 7-6 (3), 7-6 (6), 3-6, 6-3. He had at long last collected a second major title, moving past his anxiety to reward himself handsomely with a hard earned triumph that would put him into a different sphere of the sport from that point forward.

Sampras spoke with clarity in 2019 about the deep inner tension he felt on that afternoon long ago. Talking about why he was hunched over at the end, he said, 'It was nerves. It was the moment. It was exhaustion. It was the accumulation of two days of stress. There was no coach and no parent that was going to tell me something to get me through that. It was up to me. I was not feeling great but I really wanted to win."

Courier felt he played awfully well. He said, "I couldn't have played a better grass court match. I just ran into a player in Pete who was at a different level on that surface."

Tom Gullikson spoke with Courier after the match. He said, "I remember speaking with Jim and I am a big stats guy. Sampras double faulted only four times in four sets and his average first serve speed was 119 mph and his average second serve speed was 109 mph. For the differential to be only ten mph is absurd. Not many players today can say they have a 10 mph differential between first and second serves. So when people talk about the Sampras serve, certainly he had one of the greatest first serves of all time. But Courier said to me, 'How can I compete with a guy who has two first serves every point?' I thought that was pretty funny, but true."

Putting this triumph into historical perspective, Sampras emphasized, "That first Wimbledon win was a big turning point in my career. I had that big win at the Open in 1990 and then went through two years of doing fine, but not being willing to get dirty. In that match with Jim, I got dirty. I dug deeper maybe than ever to win. I played the next number of years with a lot of relief because of what that win meant."

The significance was so large in Sampras's mind that he felt in retrospect winning that first Wimbledon was of even higher value than taking the U.S. Open in 1990. He said in 2019, "Beating Jim to win Wimbledon was more important than my first Open. The first Open was great. It was wonderful. It was a fairytale. But this one at Wimbledon in '93 was more about, 'Here I am and I am going to be around for a while. And I could very well dominate this sport for the next six or seven years.' I felt that in my heart and I felt I was just more comfortable as a man, more comfortable in the limelight, more comfortable being the best player in the world. It took me some time to get there, but everything just calmed down over the next six or seven years. That was a big one at Wimbledon."

It clearly was. As Courier put it, "In hindsight, it certainly was a line of demarcation for both of us. If I win that one, maybe he has doubts and doesn't go on to the success that

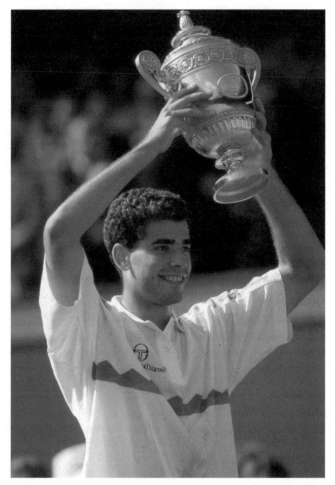

Pete Sampras won his second major singles title at Wimbledon in 1993

he has and that gives me more opportunities. He shut me down on many an occasion at a major. Who knows? You never really know. But I didn't go away from Wimbledon feeling like it was a failure of an event at all. I was certainly disappointed that I had come so close and I had lost that one as well as a close five-set final in Paris, but I certainly liked the way I was playing. In many ways it was probably a more pivotal match for Pete than it was for me."

That is surely the case. A loss there might have left a lasting mark on the Sampras psyche. He put an almost unbearable amount of pressure on himself to win that tournament, to fight uncompromisingly and find a path to victory. He had done just that. And he had upended in succession the defending champion Agassi, three-time former Wimbledon victor Becker and four-time major champion Courier. Knocking out that renowned ABC trio was a monumental achievement and a sweepingly impressive way to make a breakthrough on the lawns of the All England Club. He had captured his first major almost unconsciously, but in taking his second he was acutely aware of everything he was doing and what it all meant. Now Sampras was becoming what he always wanted to be. He was a different man made of tougher stock, obsessed with making the most of his potential, poised to take over tennis for some time to come.

# CHAPTER 5

# THE CLASS OF THE FIELD IN NEW YORK

Having realized such an overarching goal by winning Wimbledon, Sampras was never near peak efficiency during the summer on the hard court circuit leading up to the 1993 U.S. Open. But by no means was he that far from the top of his game. After losing early at the Masters 1000 tournament in Montreal, Sampras was a semifinalist in Los Angeles and Cincinnati and he reached the quarterfinals in Indianapolis. In those last three events, Sampras lost each time by the slimmest of margins, bowing out in final-set tie-breaks against a trio of top notch attacking players in Richard Krajicek, the ubiquitous Edberg and the young Patrick Rafter.

All of that match play was excellent preparation for the U.S. Open. The plan for him all along was to be at his zenith in New York, to prevail at the last major of the season and to start making a habit out of being the last man standing at the major championships. He was not content after his Wimbledon triumph. He was determined to succeed again when it counted.

Opening his U.S. Open campaign for the crown against France's inimitable Fabrice Santoro in New York, Sampras rolled to a 6-3, 6-1, 6-2 victory over a player who had earned the nickname of "The Magician." Santoro's two-fisted strokes were hard to read. His finesse was astounding. He could invent shots spontaneously and sprinkle the court with startling winners. When he was inspired, Santoro was, to the hilt, a crowd pleaser. His unconventional approach to the game and reliance on his instincts could make Santoro a nuisance for Sampras or anyone else to play and in their career series the American finished 4-3 versus the Frenchman. But on this occasion, it was no contest. Sampras won 95% of his first serve points, never faced a break point and was the far better player on the fast hard courts.

He did have a difficult clash with Daniel Vacek in the second round. This big server from the Czech Republic won three majors across his career in doubles, but his highest ranking ever in singles was No. 26. He lost all five of his career duels with Sampras, but this was his best performance ever against the American. Vacek served 24 aces, six more than Sampras. Sampras lost his serve only once but was pushed into a fourth set tie-break against his aggressive adversary, prevailing 6-4, 5-7, 6-2, 7-6 (3).

After crushing the Frenchman Arnaud Boetsch 6-4, 6-3, 6-1, Sampras then knocked out Sweden's future top ten player Thomas Enqvist 6-4, 6-4, 7-6 (4) to reach the quarterfinals. Enqvist—who had toppled Agassi over five sets in the first round—was a big ball striker who hit a very heavy ball, but he was outclassed. After conceding only 14 points in his first 14 service games, Sampras served for the match in the third set and did not close it there, but he finished it off with controlled aggression and sound percentage tactics in the tie-break.

The stage was set for Sampras to play an eagerly anticipated quarterfinal contest under the lights in Louis Armstrong Stadium against Michael Chang. Chang had solidified his place in the game since he had stepped forward to become the youngest French Open men's victor back in 1989 at 17. He took some hard knocks in 1990 but ended that season productively by joining Agassi to lead the Americans past Australia in the Davis Cup Final. In both 1990 and 1991, Chang finished at No. 15 in the world but in 1992 he climbed to No. 6

and was ever so close to a spot in the U.S. Open final. Facing Edberg in the penultimate round, Chang was ahead 4-2 in the fifth set but lost that match in a U.S. Open record-breaking five hours and 26 minutes to the taciturn Swede.

Chang's 1993 campaign had been impressive. He had taken titles in Jakarta, Indonesia and Osaka, Japan. He was a semifinalist at both Indian Wells and Rome. And, over the summer leading up to this meeting with Sampras in New York, Chang had been a finalist in Los Angeles and Long Island and had won Cincinnati over Agassi and Edberg.

Perhaps even more importantly, Chang still very much held the upper hand in his rivalry with Sampras. Not only did he have his long historical record of success against his fellow American going back to the juniors, but as professionals they had clashed on eight occasions and Chang had been the victor in six of those meetings. He had won the first five confrontations, dropped the next two, but had then had been the winner over Sampras in their previous head-to-head showdown at Miami on hard courts in the spring of 1992.

Examining that 1993 U.S. Open quarterfinal with Chang in an interview for this book, Sampras said, "It just goes back to the juniors with me and Michael. It was this kind of weird, eerie feeling that I might have been the best player in the world and, even if he was ranked 40, I would still feel those nerves. Michael always gave me problems and he was a fighter who made me play a lot of balls. He was one of the fastest guys on the tour and up until that point at the '93 Open I just struggled to close him out."

The first two sets of the Sampras-Chang contest were exceedingly hard fought on both sides of the net. Chang challenged his countryman audaciously, taking his second serve returns as early as possible, returning with authority and being as aggressive as possible in the baseline exchanges. Not a service break was to be found by either player in the opening set, but Chang was wide-eyed, hyper-focused and opportunistic in the tie-break. Sampras did not put a first serve in during the sequence and double faulted to fall behind 0-3. But the fact remained that Chang was letter perfect. He attacked every Sampras second serve, made all of his first serves and swept seven points in a row to sweep the tie-break unhesitatingly.

Chang broke Sampras for a 3-2 lead in the second set but Sampras rallied to 3-3, held easily for 4-3 and then broke again for 5-3 with a far-reaching demonstration of his talent. He laced a forehand crosscourt on the run, pulling Chang out of position. Now Sampras approached crosscourt off the backhand and then moved in nimbly for a nifty backhand drop-volley winner down the line executed with a shade of sidespin.

With that dazzling display, Sampras was poised to make it one set all. He had captured three games in a row convincingly. But Chang maintained his posture of ultra-aggression on second serve returns. He won the first point of the ninth game by going in behind a backhand return, reading Sampras's forehand down the line pass and succeeding with a backhand volley winner. With Sampras serving at 15-40, Chang's forehand down-the-line return was a winner. He had broken at 15 and soon Chang held on at 30 with an ace for 5-5.

Both players held easily to set up another tie-break. For Sampras, this one was critical. He could not afford to fall behind Chang two sets to love. From that juncture, it would have been a tall order to win three sets in a row with no margin for error against someone of Chang's durability. Sampras knew full well that he would need to impose himself and secure the second set tie-break without any wrinkles. He realized precisely what was at stake.

Fittingly, Sampras opened the tie-break with an ace down the T. Chang then missed on an approach shot. Sampras connected with a running forehand passing shot down the line. Then Sampras coaxed a return error from Chang and that gave him a 4-0 lead. Soon it was 5-2 and Sampras was serving. He took the next point and then sent a 125 mph first serve down the T that was unmanageable for Chang.

Sampras had been victorious seven points to two in the tie-break. He was back to one set all and it was as if a brand new, best-of-three-set battle was ahead. Chang held in the first game of the third set, but Sampras stunned his adversary by taking the next six games in succession. He was swinging so freely now and executing with such astonishing authority that Chang was blown off the court. Sampras had advanced to two sets to one in no time flat.

At the start of the fourth set, Sampras had a brief letdown, double faulting twice to trail 0-30 in the first game. But he recovered rapidly, taking four points in a row for the hold. At 40-30, Sampras had the crowd gasping when he angled a diving forehand finesse volley sharply crosscourt. The fleet-footed Chang chased it down but had no play. Sampras promptly broke at love for 2-0 when he hammered a forehand approach to elicit a passing shot error from Chang. Serving at 40-30 in the third game, Sampras missed his first delivery and Chang came in behind another backhand return. That tactic had worked well earlier in the confrontation, but not now. Stylishly unruffled, Sampras rolled a backhand passing-shot winner crosscourt to reach 3-0.

By now, Sampras was in a semi-unconscious state, guided by his keen instincts, free of inhibition, playing with sheer inspiration. Chang was befuddled. The No. 7 seed was trying to figure out how to win points rather than games. Sampras pieced together an impeccable return game, breaking at love for 4-0 and then, helped by two aces, holding at love for 5-0. He had won eleven games in a row. In the first five games of this fourth set, Sampras had taken no fewer than 20 of 25 points. Chang would hold once in the sixth game, but Sampras served it out at love to complete a remarkable 6-7 (0), 7-6 (2), 6-1, 6-1 triumph.

As Sampras said in 2019, "Those last two sets against Michael in that quarterfinal at the Open in '93, when I kind of dominated him, carried me on for the rest of my career against him. I felt I could overpower him, which I did those last two sets at the Open, but up until that point I was always uncomfortable in that matchup. I was a little surprised that maybe those first two sets took something out of him. He had been playing well and I was playing well, but maybe it was physically tougher for him to keep up that pace than for me. He might have gotten a little tired and the weight of my shots and my serve took its toll on him. By then I could dictate when I wanted to dictate. So those third and fourth sets of the 1993 quarterfinal were just a big two sets for me, not to just try to win that Open but because it was Michael and he had been a thorn in my side for all of those years. But after those first two sets, I think Michael felt, 'Well, Pete is better than me now.' And I felt I kind of figured him out. So that was a very big moment in my career as far as playing Michael."

Interestingly, Chang put that match entirely out of his mind. He said in 2018, "To be honest with you, I don't remember the '93 Open. Maybe I am too scarred from losing to Pete three years later at the U.S. Open in the final. There was a stretch there of about six years in a row where I lost to the eventual champion at the Open."

Surprisingly, Chang did not consider the 1993 Open loss to Sampras the turning point in their rivalry. He believed his defeat against his old rival three years earlier at the 1990 Grand Slam Cup was the pivotal one. Sampras took apart Chang 6-3, 6-4, 6-4 about three months after he had won the Open for the first time.

As Chang recollected, "I remember very specifically having a conversation with my brother Carl before that match at the 1990 Grand Slam Cup and I was a little arrogant and cocky about it. I was like, 'This is a great opportunity.' I was playing Pete and I was not afraid to play him. Granted, the Grand Slam Cup court was super fast, I still felt like I had Pete's number. But that match was the turning point. With the shots he was hitting, this was not the Pete Sampras I had grown up with. It was not the Pete Sampras I had played all of these years. This was a different Pete Sampras. His serve was more accurate and he was not serving anymore to the patterns I was used to him serving. He was now hitting all four corners properly and in the right spot. Before then, he could only hit one side on the deuce and one side on the ad court. He would go wide in the deuce court and down the T in the ad. I would give him the outside, and if he made one out of four or one out of five on the outside it didn't matter. I had enough looks on second serves to get into the points and get a break or two. That is how I had beaten him. But this was another Pete Sampras."

After pulling away inexorably against Chang in the 1993 Open quarters, Sampras had a semifinal meeting against Alexander Volkov. Sampras walked on court with clear notions of what he wanted to convey to his opponent from the opening bell. He served three consecutive aces in the first game. He would not face a break point over the course of the match, releasing 19 aces, making the low volleys look misleadingly easy. The Russian was seeded 14th and was at his career peak in the rankings. He had beaten Sampras on hard courts earlier in the season at Indian Wells. But Sampras was much too good for the left-hander on this occasion, moving swiftly into the final with a 6-4, 6-3, 6-2 victory.

Now Sampras was one match away from a second major title in a row as he took the court for the final on September 12, 1993. The only man standing between him and the crown was the Frenchman Cedric Pioline, an elegant shotmaker from France who was enjoying the finest fortnight of his life. The No. 15 seed had produced the upset of the tournament, toppling Jim Courier in the round of 16. Courier was the top seed at that Open because he had briefly recaptured the No. 1 position in the ATP rankings, but he was unable to contain the Frenchman, who found one opening after another to unleash flamboyant winners off his one-handed backhand while profiting from a subpar performance by the American.

Pioline had also ushered the 1988 champion Wilander out of that tournament. In the quarterfinals, he upended No. 8 seed Andrei Medvedev and, one round later, he accounted for the Australian Wally Masur. He had earned his place in the final at Flushing Meadows. But Pioline's apprehension about facing Sampras was abundantly evident. He had lost to him twice in his career to date, and would never defeat the American in nine appointments across the nineties.

Right out of the gates, Sampras made his move. He broke Pioline in the opening game, taking advantage of a double fault from the Frenchman that put the underdog behind 15-40. Then Pioline served and volleyed and Sampras wisely sent his return down the middle, keeping it as low as possible. Pioline punched a backhand first volley long. The American had achieved the immediate break for 1-0. Although Sampras missed every first serve in the second game, he still held at the cost of only one point.

The 22-year-old American nearly broke again in the third game but Pioline erased a break point. Unswerving, Sampras moved briskly to 3-1, again losing only one point on serve. Both men held easily until Pioline served at 2-4, when he served-volleyed his way out of another break point. But he was merely delaying the inevitable. Sampras held at 30 for 5-3. Serving for the set in the tenth game, Sampras started with an ace and held at love to seal the 6-4 set in 37 productive minutes. In five service games, Sampras had won 20 of 24 points, backing up his delivery skillfully, giving Pioline cause for consternation.

Sampras commenced the second set just as he had done in the first, gaining a service break, this one on a double fault from a beleaguered Pioline. Serving at 30-40 in the second game, Sampras was broken for the first time in the match, netting a forehand first volley off a chipped return from Pioline. It was 1-1.

They went to 3-3, but Sampras was eager to reassert his authority, and he did just that. Pioline double faulted long at 30-40, allowing Sampras to advance to 4-3. Sampras served his tenth ace to open the next game, holding quickly for 5-3. Serving for the set in the tenth game, Sampras refused to let his guard down. At 30-15, Pioline sent a sizzling forehand passing shot up the line, but Sampras had blanketed the net, showing off his underrated agility, punching a backhand volley crosscourt into the clear. Staying back on his second serve at 40-15, Sampras was patient and purposeful. Pioline erred off his much more vulnerable forehand wing. The 6-4 set belonged to Sampras.

The pattern continued. For the third set in a row, Pioline was broken in the first game, this time on consecutive double faults. But, as was the case in the second set, Sampras lost his serve from a break up, uncharacteristically double faulting twice as Pioline rallied to 1-1. It hardly mattered. That brief lapse was nothing more than that. Sampras resumed his mastery of the match briskly, breaking in the third game with consistently good returning off both sides.

Back ahead 2-1, Sampras was unstoppable the rest of the way. He took his next three service games with ease, winning 12 of 15 points in that span. Now Pioline was serving to stay in the match. The Frenchman saved one match point with a beautiful backhand stab finesse volley, but followed with a miss-hit backhand. Down match point for the second time, Pioline took himself out of his misery with a double fault. Sampras had forged a 6-4, 6-4, 6-3 victory for his third major title.

"I thought I played well," reflected Sampras 25 years after confronting the Frenchman in New York. "Cedric was a good player but not quite a Courier. He didn't play very well in that match against me at the Open. He was very talented but it was always windy out there in those days. Cedric had those big, long swings and he was shanking a couple of shots. I felt like I was on my game and I thought I was very efficient, serving well and doing what I do out there. My big win that year was over Michael. Volkov tended to throw in the towel every now and then. Against Cedric, I felt if I played well I should beat him and win the tournament and I was happy that happened."

Coming into 1993, Sampras had deep concerns after not winning a major the two previous seasons. But succeeding at Wimbledon and the U.S. Open sent him into a new phase of his career as the man to beat, as indisputably the best player in the world, as the pace setter of the sport. Taking his second U.S. Open title two months after claiming his first crown at Wimbledon was absolute proof of his supremacy. Now he was right where he wanted to be, supremely confident about what he had already done, driven with quiet ferocity to keep going strong.

Pete Sampras raised the U.S. trophy for a second time in 1993

After the Open in the fall of 1993, Sampras won a couple of tournaments in Lyon and Antwerp, defeating Pioline in the finals of the former and the semifinals of the latter. He also made it to the finals of the ATP World Tour Finals, losing a hard-fought contest with the gifted Michael Stich. In his last tournament of the year, he was beaten in a semifinal barnburner by Petr Korda 13-11 in the fifth set at the Grand Slam Cup. But the fact remained that this was his best year yet. He played and won more matches by far than he did in any other year of his sterling career, finishing with an 85-16 record, securing eight titles, taking two majors. He had gained considerable confidence from the way he had competed and the prizes he had accrued.

Heading into 1994, Sampras was well aware that his time had come. His goal was to maintain his winning ways, keep piling up one major after another and stay ahead of the pack. He knew that his best tennis was surely yet to come.

# CHAPTER 6

# BUILDING ON HIS SUCCESS

When the 1994 season commenced in January, Sampras was determined to stay at the top of the tennis mountain. His primary objective was to exploit every opportunity he had to put more majors into his victory column. That was his chief priority. His outlook had been sharply altered by the prizes he had secured in 1993. Now his view of himself had changed irrevocably.

Sampras wanted to make certain he was ready for the first Grand Slam tournament of the year at the Australian Open. Leaving nothing to chance, he entered two tournaments prior to the proceedings in Melbourne. In the first, he was upended by a gifted player with a wide range of skills named Karim Alami at Doha. The dashing 20-year-old from Morocco came from behind to beat Sampras in three sets.

But the world No. 1 moved right on to Sydney and took the title there, stopping the sporadically brilliant Korda in the semifinals before ousting Lendl in the final. He thus headed into Melbourne knowing he had a good chance to not only get a title there, but also to sweep his third major in a row. Those twin pursuits were in the forefront of his mind.

His opponent in the first round was Joshua Eagle, an Australian who excelled in doubles and later reached the top

20 in that capacity. Facing Sampras on his own, Eagle was outclassed 6-4, 6-0, 7-6 (5). On paper, Sampras's second-round assignment looked like a straightforward romp. He was up against the inexperienced and unproven Yevgeny Kafelnikov of Russia, the No. 60 ranked player in the world. Kafelnikov was closing in on his 20th birthday. This was only the second major tournament of his young career. He had never played the Australian Open men's event before.

Kafelnikov, of course, had seen Sampras play countless times and was more than familiar with the American's serve-and-volley strengths and his all-court craftiness. But Sampras hardly knew who Kafelnikov was at that stage. For him, this was just another second-round meeting at a major. He was taking nothing for granted but could never have envisioned what was about to unfold.

The Russian would later establish himself as a great player in every way. Before his career was over, he would win two majors in singles and four more in doubles, lead Russia to a Davis Cup triumph and reach No. 1 in the world. Kafelnikov was inducted at the International Tennis Hall of Fame in July of 2019. His stellar career results merited his inclusion at the shrine in Newport. Interestingly, despite taking Sampras down to the wire at Melbourne in 1994, he later detested the matchup against the American, losing their career series 11-2, achieving his only wins in a brief span on clay in the spring of 1996.

Sampras would come to have much respect for Kafelnikov in the years ahead, but this was his first look at the Russian. As he said in 2018, "It's always a little tricky against someone I hadn't seen play. So I was just feeling him out on the Rebound Ace court that was tricky for me. In every Grand Slam tournament there is always a match or two when you are not playing great. You just fight through it. This was one of those matches."

Elaborating on that Kafelnikov harrowing encounter, Sampras recalled, "I had heard of Yevgeny. When I played him at the '94 Australian I thought, 'This guy is good.' Yevgeny was up and coming but I could tell that he had a lot of ability."

The match started with the favorite in his familiar mode, serving-and-volleying forcefully on first serves, setting the tempo with his crackling flat forehand, daring Kafelnikov to find a way to prevent him from shaping the battle in his own image. In the first set, Kafelnikov did show his propensity for making solid returns time and again and he was adventuresome off the ground, driving winners from improbable positions.

Sampras broke Kafelnikov on a double fault to move ahead 3-1 in the first set. Serving for the set at 5-3, he rolled to 40-0 but the Russian was not compliant here, saving three set points on his way back to deuce. Sampras served an ace at deuce and put away a backhand volley into the open court to close it out 6-3 on his fourth set point. That last game of the first set did not seem particularly significant at the time, but in retrospect perhaps it was.

Kafelnikov broke Sampras for the first time to reach 2-0 in the second set. He advanced to leads of 3-0, 4-1 and 5-2. When Sampras served to stay in the set in the eighth game, Kafelnikov put his excellent two-handed backhand to good use, releasing three down the line winners off that side. That was his specialty, his signature shot. He got the insurance break, taking the set convincingly 6-2, proving that he had found his bearings.

Sampras got right back to work in the third set. He broke early, held on easily for 3-1 and then broke again in the fifth game. At 30-30, he blasted away with a flurry of scorching forehands that left Kafelnikov helpless and followed with a high trajectory topspin backhand return coaxing a netted forehand from Kafelnikov. Sampras had gone ahead 4-1 and soon held at love for 5-1.

But the set was not over. Kafelnikov held on in the seventh game and then broke Sampras with a beautifully struck backhand passing shot down the line. But Sampras stayed with his aggression, breaking Kafelnikov for the third time in the ninth game of the set, getting good pace on an inside-out forehand and drawing an errant backhand from Kafelnikov. Set to Sampras 6-3.

There was no time to celebrate having a two-sets-to-one lead. In a startling sequence, Kafelnikov took 12 of 15 points in establishing a 3-0 fourth-set lead, breaking twice in that span. It was in the third game that Kafelnikov shined most brightly, putting away a forehand volley confidently, connecting with a forehand passing-shot winner on the run, making a stupendous running forehand topspin lob winner and sealing the break with a backhand down the line passing shot winner. He held easily for 4-0. Now Kafelnikov had won 16 of 20 points to put the fourth set almost out of reach for Sampras. Serving at 1-5, Sampras did not win a point. He had astonishingly been broken three times in that set. Kafelnikov had returned with extraordinary consistency and had run away with the set, winning it 6-1.

And so this pendulum-swinging second-round collision was going into a fifth set and what a compelling conclusion it would be for the spectators. Sampras drew first blood in that final chapter of the skirmish, breaking serve to lead 2-1. He stretched his lead to 3-1 with a love hold—serving an ace and volleying superbly in that game—and, having won 12 of 14 points to gain the upper hand, seemed certain to find victory from there.

Serving in the fifth game, Kafelnikov was on the brink of elimination. Sampras was striving for the knockout punch. An immaculate backhand passing shot into the clear and a topspin lob winner gave the American break point for 4-1. But Kafelnikov rescued himself steadfastly. Sampras rolled a backhand pass low crosscourt, but the Russian half-volleyed with good depth. The American put up a topspin lob but Kafelnikov handled it well on the backhand overhead. Sampras followed with a cross-court passing shot off the forehand, but his adversary read it well, punching a forehand volley down the line. Sampras tossed up another lob but Kafelnikov was ready, putting away an overhead confidently.

Kafelnikov held on from there, not allowing Sampras to gain greater security. Nonetheless, Sampras served three aces en route to 4-2. In his next service game, however, Sampras was denied the hold he so dearly wanted. At 30-30, he serve-volleyed effectively behind a first delivery, but Kafelnikov was unimpressed, countering with a remarkable topspin lob winner. He took the next point by provoking an error from an off-balance Sampras.

Spectacularly, Kafelnikov rallied to 4-4. He swiftly advanced to 5-4, making his renowned opponent serve to stay in the match. Sampras had no margin for error left. He aced Kafelnikov down the T for a 30-0 lead in that tenth game of the final set, but soon was pushed to 30-30. The No. 1 seed was two points away from losing a confrontation he had seemed certain to win. Sampras missed his first serve and stayed back behind the second. He sent a backhand safely crosscourt and here at last Kafelnikov seemed to realize what he was the verge of accomplishing. He netted a backhand down the line, exposing his anxiety in the process. A first rate serve-and-volley combination from Sampras led to an errant forehand pass from Kafelnikov. It was 5-5. The Russian moved quickly to 6-5, forcing Sampras for the second time to either hold serve or head for the locker room in defeat.

Sampras met that moment ably. After a double fault put him three points from losing at 15-15, he collected the next three points with firm resolve, closing out that crucial game with a pair of unstoppable first serves. Having climbed to 6-6 with that clutch effort, he broke in a long game for 7-6, driving his trademark running forehand crosscourt with too much pace for Kafelnikov to handle.

And yet, much to the chagrin of his many boosters, decidedly against the odds, Sampras did not win a single point when he served for the match. Kafelnikov broke back at love, finishing off that admirable effort with two picture-perfect passing shots—one off each side. The tumultuous fifth set was now locked at 7-7. The following game went to deuce three times. Each man had openings. But Sampras secured the break with persistence.

At 8-7, he had a second chance to close out the account on serve. Once more, it was not easy for him to get across the finish line. Two timely aces and a service winner lifted the American to 40-15, with two match points at his disposal. It had been a long and excruciatingly close battle and Sampras had been extended to the edge of his competitive limits. He missed wildly off the forehand and then netted a forehand approach. Two match points had come and gone. An obstinate Kafelnikov was refusing to surrender. The score was locked at deuce. Sampras was reaching back with nearly all of his resources to forge a victory, playing the game with the full range of his emotional intensity, dealing with the adventuresome but unfamiliar Russian as best he could. But he was not yet at his destination.

At deuce, Sampras directed a second serve to the Kafelnikov forehand, drawing a netted crosscourt return. Having arrived at match point for the third time, Sampras came through this time as Kafelnikov finally blinked, driving his two-hander long down the line. Victory had been salvaged by Sampras 6-3, 2-6, 6-3, 1-6, 9-7. This was a prime example of his vastly underrated qualities as a competitor; he did not win this match with anything resembling his best stuff, but rather with the size of his heart, the depth of his determination and the strength of his mind.

Reflecting on that contest with Kafelnikov, Sampras asserted, "It was a dogfight. Yevgeny showed over his career that he is very talented. He returned well and had a pretty big first serve. Australia was always a dogfight for me, always a tough major. I never liked those Rebound Ace courts. I had to grind it out against Kafelnikov to get through that one. That match was a little bit scary, but when I got through it I felt I had a second life."

All great players meet those propitious moments forthrightly, move past them, and win largely by utterly refusing to lose. Bolstered by his narrow victory, Sampras handled the left-handed Frenchman Stephane Simian 7-5, 6-1, 1-6, 6-4 to earn a round of 16 appointment against Lendl. The former world No. 1 was now stationed at No. 17 in the world, but was still playing at a remarkably high level, extending Sampras to 7-6 (5), 6-2, 7-6

(4) in a hard-fought contest. On the biggest points, Sampras was the better player. He served no fewer than 19 aces.

Now in the quarters, Sampras encountered the kind of debilitating conditions that are not uncommon in the land "Down Under." Facing Sweden's Magnus Gustafsson—the No. 14 ranked player in the world—Sampras had to not only find a way past a capable opponent, but also overcome a hard set of circumstances. The air temperature was about 100 degrees. The wind was blowing ferociously, up to 36 mph. The heat reflecting off the hard court was measured at 126 degrees Fahrenheit.

As he did only on the very hottest days, Sampras wore a hat and tried to conserve energy. But the wind played havoc with his serve and Sampras had 17 double faults on the day. Nonetheless, he came through when it counted. As was the case against Lendl, he won a couple of tie-breaks and that was why he prevailed 7-6 (4), 2-6, 6-3, 7-6 (4).

Now the tournament favorite was into the penultimate round and he came upon none other than his old rival Jim Courier, the No. 3 seed. This one had the feeling of a final. Courier was in full pursuit of a third Australian Open crown in a row. He was a magnificent hard-court player. He seemed entirely comfortable on the Rebound Ace hard courts that had always given Sampras problems over the years.

The two Americans would be involved in many close encounters at all four of the majors through the years, but this was not one of those times when the outcome was ever much in doubt. Courier's game resembled Lendl's in some ways. He built his game around a relatively big first serve coupled with a devastatingly potent inside out forehand. Although his two-handed backhand was vulnerable at times and not a real weapon in the rallies, he made it awfully difficult for opponents to get to that side because his forehand was so overwhelmingly potent.

But, on this occasion, Courier was not at his best by any means, although he did not play badly. He was slightly below par, while Sampras played his finest tennis of the tournament by far. From the early stages, Sampras's sharpness and mindset were apparent. He broke for 3-1, employing a short backhand chipped return to draw Courier uncomfortably in, then sending a deceptive backhand pass whistling down the line for a winner. That was all he needed to seal that set 6-3. In his last three service games after the one break, Sampras won 12 of 15 points.

The second set went to 4-4. But Sampras raised his level in the ninth game, breaking at 15 with a searing forehand passing-shot winner down the line. Serving for the set at 5-4, Sampras opened with two aces and held at love. In his last three service games of the well-played second set, Sampras did not lose a point. He had a two-sets-to-love lead.

Courier did create an opening with Sampras serving at 1-2 in the third, reaching break point twice in that fourth game. But after two deuces, Sampras held on with an artistic play, whirling around athletically for a backhand volley winner on the stretch. He was inspired, highly charged and irresistibly on his game. Serving at 3-4 in that set, Sampras faced another break point, but a deep first serve to the backhand provoked a netted return from Courier. Sampras sternly held on for 4-4.

Now Sampras turned the tables on his countryman in the following game. With Courier serving at 30-30, Sampras dipped a backhand pass crosscourt to make Courier volley up and then ran around his backhand for a forehand inside-in passing shot winner. On break point, Sampras kept a forehand pass sufficiently low to elicit a netted forehand volley from Courier.

Courier tried when he could to take the net away from the multi-faceted Sampras, but he could only get so far with that strategic approach. Sampras now served for the match at 5-4 in the third. His play at the net in that last game was magnificent. On the first point he used a down-the-line backhand volley to set up a winning backhand volley crosscourt. He followed with a gorgeous low backhand volley down the line creating an opening for a forehand volley winner. He went on to hold on at love, winning the match decisively 6-3, 6-4, 6-4.

That clear-cut triumph was the right way for Sampras to head into his first Australian Open final on January 30, 1994 as he chased a third major championship in a row. He was fresh, eager and expecting a lot from himself. His opponent surprisingly was a good friend from the United States who was just coming into his own. This 23-year-old fellow was 6'6" and a first-rate serve-and-volley player with a wide wing span that made him very dangerous on his remarkably clean returns. Todd Martin was stepping into the spotlight for the first time and building a fine reputation for himself as not only a player but an unimpeachable sportsman.

Martin, who after his playing career became one of the sport's primary leaders as the CEO at the International Tennis Hall of Fame, was always a voice of reason and high intelligence. The 1994 Australian Open final he played against Pete Sampras was a seminal moment in his life and career. He had turned professional in 1990 after playing for Northwestern University. By the end of 1993, he had made his way up to No. 13 in the world, reaching the quarterfinals of Wimbledon that season, taking his first pro title on the ATP Tour at Coral Springs, Florida on clay.

Now, at the start of 1994, he was ready to operate in loftier territory than ever before. The No. 9 seed in Melbourne, he made an exhilarating turnaround to oust the No. 4 seed and two-time Australian Open victor Edberg. After dropping the first set against the Swede in the semifinals, Martin ran out the match on a string of three consecutive tie-breaks.

"I played a great match against Stefan," said Martin in an interview for this book done in late 2018. "I had every reason to be pretty confident against Pete. I matched up well with him previously and I was playing significantly better than I had when we played at the U.S. Open a couple of years before [Sampras won in five sets]. But I was just way too excited. The night before the final I had a horrible time eating. It was also Super Bowl Sunday, so my coach and I were trying to figure out where we would watch the Super Bowl after the final. Retrospectively, there was a horrific job done by me of managing my own world at that moment, although looking back on it, this does not surprise me. It was uncharted waters for me. The unfortunate part is that my game was ready for that final with Pete but my mind wasn't."

Sampras, of course, had a different point of view. He had a 2-0 record against Martin as they walked on court in Melbourne. He was a young man with clear convictions and a growing belief that no one in the world was going to stop him if he was anywhere near the top of his game. He was not only self-assured but also unshakable.

Talking about Martin and that 1994 Australian Open final in an interview for this book, Sampras said, "Todd had this big kick serve to my backhand which was always tough for me. And if you don't get your shots where you want them to go when Todd is not on the run, he would hit a big ball. He had given me some troubles but I always thought if I got into some rallies with him and got into the movement stuff, I could beat Todd. But he returned very well and he was a big guy."

Moreover, Sampras held Martin in high regard as a human being and as a man with whom he had much in common philosophically. As he explained in 2019, "Todd was just such a nice, low key guy. He and I hit it off from the beginning. We were similar in personality. Todd was a thoughtful guy that never wanted attention. He just developed into a top player and we got along well on and off the court. He was just an easy competitor to be around with no edge to him. He certainly gave me a lot of problems on the court but off court our personalities gelled well. He was kind of sarcastic like Tim Henman, just sort of easy going with a dry personality in the locker room who enjoyed being funny."

Looking at the matchup with Martin and the way he remembers the 1994 final in Australia, Sampras said, "I tried to add the body serve to my game against Todd to not let him dictate. Also, when he hit his second serve out to my backhand, I had to try to do something with it where I could get it deep to his backhand and then it was 'Let's go play a point.' But when he got it out to my backhand it was tough to hit on top of it and hard to chip it aggressively. So I made a conscious effort to do something with that shot. If you don't start off in a neutral spot and Todd was dictating, that is when you get into trouble."

Despite his considerable respect for Martin, Sampras felt very good about his chances going into that final. He said in 2018, "I felt I was the favorite. I was walking out there as the best player in the world. I felt I should win if I played well. Maybe it was my game. I just felt like it was on my racket and no one else's, against Todd or Andre or Michael or anyone. I felt at this stage I was the man to beat. As I got older, I felt more comfortable being the best player in the world and having that responsibility."

Martin fully understood the Sampras psyche and how his friend was approaching their title round meeting. He reflected in 2019, "Pete would have walked out there with an air of not disengaged or unconcerned confidence, but with that air that it was important for him to carry that presence he had with the expectation that he was going to win against everybody. You didn't see Pete walk on court with varying levels of focus or excitement or anything. He was just very, very calm. Always. And I think in spite of the fact that he probably game wise respected me a little bit more than some players—because I could take the racket out of his hand a little bit—I don't think that would have had any impact on how he felt walking on the court. Pete felt if he played well, the world was his oyster."

The first set of the Sampras-Martin skirmish was fought out purposefully on both sides of the net. Given that Sampras was the much more experienced competitor under these circumstances—this was his fifth major final while Martin was making his debut in such a setting—the opening set probably was an imperative for Martin and not necessarily for his opponent. But Sampras always came out for Grand Slam tournament finals determined to set the pace from the outset, secure the first set and impose himself with increasing force and persuasion from there.

Martin, however, acquitted himself honorably. Serving at 1-2 in that first set, he survived a four-deuce game, saving a break point with an excellent half volley digging him out of trouble and leading to a forehand volley winner. Until the set was locked at 3-3, Sampras had been untouchable on serve, taking 12 of 13 points. But Martin found his range on the return of serve in the seventh game. After Sampras double faulted on the first point, Martin sent a backhand down the line that landed for a winner and then Sampras missed a running forehand crosscourt.

This was right where Martin wanted to be, leading 0-40 on the Sampras serve, looking to gain that initial break of the match. But Sampras had an uncanny knack for raising the stakes when he was in apparent trouble on his serve. He proceeded to make three first serves in a row. Two of his serves—one into the body and one out wide—were unanswerable and Sampras erased the other break point with a serve-and-volley package that was just too good.

Nevertheless, he double faulted to give Martin a fourth break point. Once more, the world No. 1 displayed his customary poise under pressure, connecting with another first serve, following it in for a backhand half volley winner down the line. After four deuces and much tension, Sampras held on for 4-3. There were no breaks to be found by either player, but at 5-5 Sampras double faulted to fall into a 30-40 deficit.

If Martin could take this critical point, he would move into a very advantageous position, serving for the set and gaining a good foothold in the match. But the bigger the point, the better Sampras seemed to perform. He directed a first serve into Martin's body and the big man faltered on the return, sending it long. Sampras saved a second break point and held on to lead 6-5. Martin answered in kind to make it 6-6 and so they would settle the outcome of that set in a tie-break.

From 1-2 in that sequence, Sampras garnered five points in a row, starting with an ace for 2-2, followed by one of his slice serves out wide in the deuce court that lured Martin into a forehand down-the-line return wide. With Martin serving the next two points, Sampras made excellent low returns on both, forcing his adversary into a missed first volley on the former and coming through on the latter by taking the net away from Martin and producing a flat forehand winner down the line. Serving at 5-2, Sampras serve-volleyed immaculately, executing a backhand first volley down the line that was textbook perfect and then easily putting away his next volley.

Martin managed to save two set points, but Sampras was characteristically unshakable, passing Martin off the backhand for a set concluding winner. Sampras won that tie-break 7-4, missing only one first serve all the way through.

Speaking nearly 24 years after the match, Martin recollected his lost opportunities in that first set, lauding Sampras for his steadfastness when it counted. He said, "On one of the break points I hit a really good return at his feet from my backhand side and he hit not a shoestring but probably a sock high, backhand inside out volley, which I think caught the line. It was one of those volleys that if any of us were tense we could not execute like that. Where Pete was so dynamic was that whether he was serving or receiving, when the time came to play better, he did. Most of us when that time came hopefully would play better. But there was no such button to push as to say, 'Okay, now!" Pete had that button. Everybody saw his serve as the primary button pusher, but with Pete it was comprehensive. He did everything better when the stakes grew."

Addressing the setback in the tie-break, Martin realized that those elusive break points he did not convert had residual benefits for Sampras. He said, "Judged on the whole, I felt I had outplayed him in the first set. But if you miss those opportunities, there is a knock-on effect that in the latter parts of the set you are going to get Pete's best tennis."

Having withstood a barrage of big hitting and stellar returning from Martin in that first set, Sampras was predictably more at ease. He broke Martin for 2-1 in the second set in one of their longer exchanges, prevailing in a 21-stroke rally by cagily chipping a backhand down the line to make his tall opponent bend. Martin missed a forehand approach.

Sampras was free flowing now, holding at 15 for 3-1, and, after striking two return-of-serve winners, breaking at love for 4-1.

The top seed had a brief letdown, dropping the next two games. And yet, from 4-3, he put down the clamps as only he could. Serving in the eighth game, he lost only one point. After Martin saved a set point in the next game, Sampras served it out with cool authority, holding at 15, winning that set 6-4.

Sampras was returning with increasing consistency and variation off the backhand, finding his spots time and again on serve, and closing in on victory. With his chipped backhand return paying large dividends, he broke Martin in the first game of the third set, and then added an insurance break for 4-1. When Sampras held at love for 5-1, his triumph was all but assured. But Martin replicated his second-set pattern of recouping, collecting three games in a row.

Yet he was delaying the inevitable. Serving for the match a second time, Sampras dropped the first point, released two aces in a row, approached the net and elicited a passing shot error, and then placed an exclamation point on a highly-professional performance with an inside-out forehand winner. With that hold, Sampras had moved past Martin 7-6 (4), 6-4, 6-4. He had attained a third Grand Slam singles title in a row, a first Australian Open crown and a large measure of pride in starting a new season on such a celebratory note. As usual, he wore his success comfortably, showing gratitude about what he had done, refusing to celebrate ostentatiously. As usual, he was dignified, understated and classy.

Sampras had turned a corner in his career and was not looking back. He had won the last two majors of 1993 and now had stamped his authority at the first Grand Slam tournament of 1994. Never before had he collected three consecutive majors, and it was a feat he would not realize again. His fellow players recognized that Sampras, at 22, was exploring the boundaries of his diversified game, but still significantly shy of his zenith. He had set himself up for a magnificent year by getting on the board so early at a major. The rest of that 1994 campaign would be filled with many triumphs, a few disappointments and the

With his win at the 1994 Australian Open, Pete Sampras took his third straight major singles title

multitude of trials and tribulations all accomplished figures experience in their fields. Sampras could not pause for more than a few brief moments to fully appreciate his Australian Open win. He subscribed to the notion that a champion never rests on his laurels.

# CHAPTER 7

# ANOTHER TITLE RUN
# AT WIMBLEDON

Having come through to win the first major championship of 1994 at the Australian Open, the fact remained that Sampras remained fixated on the other Grand Slam tournaments. But that did not mean he was not fired up to compete at the week in and week out events on the ATP Tour. He took those tournaments very seriously and, like all players with high aspirations and a wide range of goals, he could not tolerate the taste of defeat.

In his first tournament after Melbourne, Sampras was knocked out in his opening match at Philadelphia by the Dutchman Jacco Eltingh, an outstanding doubles player who could be dangerous on his day in singles. But then Sampras went on a spectacular winning spree that demonstrably showcased he was not only the leading player in his profession but also a multi-faceted champion.

Leaving the Eltingh loss behind him in a hurry, Sampras won the Masters 1000 hard court tournament at Indian Wells, California with victories over Muster, Edberg and, in five sets, Korda. Next he went to Miami for the Masters 1000 event. In the final of that tournament, he was due to meet Agassi, but was suffering from a severe stomach ailment beforehand and was not feeling well enough to start at the scheduled time. But Agassi did not want to have a title handed to him that way. He generously let Sampras rest and recover until he was ready about an hour after the allotted time. Sampras was serving at 5-2 in the first set but lost five games in a row. But he came on strong to win the last two sets comfortably to claim the title with a 5-7, 6-3, 6-3 triumph.

Next on the agenda for Sampras was another hard court tournament in Osaka. He was victorious there. In Tokyo, he upended Chang in the final. And then he moved out onto the clay and crushed Becker in the final of the Italian Open in Rome, claiming that crown with a resounding 6-1, 6-2, 6-2 win over the German. To be sure, clay was Becker's worst surface but he had enjoyed a good run to the final and Sampras had destroyed him with a virtuoso performance.

Having won five tournaments in a row for the first and only time in his career, he won a couple of matches at the World Team Cup on clay before losing to Stich. Sampras had won a career high 29 matches in a row. So he came into Roland Garros with plenty of confidence and little reason to doubt himself. It seemed entirely possible that he would become the first man since Rod Laver in 1969 to take four majors in a row and the first since Laver to establish residence in the winner's circle at all four Grand Slam tournaments.

It was not to be. He made it to the quarterfinals of the French Open for the third consecutive year. Playing Courier, he split sets and was serving at 4-4, 40-15 in the third set. But his fellow American was an outstanding clay court player. Courier had not won the French Open in 1991 and 1992 or reached the final in 1993 by accident. He raised his game and took over from the backcourt, winning 6-4, 5-7, 6-4, 6-4.

Had Sampras found a way past Courier, he would have earned a rematch against Sergi Bruguera, the Spaniard who beat him the year before in four sets. If he had toppled Bruguera, Sampras would have garnered a final round meeting against another Spaniard named Alberto Berasategui. Retrospectively, Sampras could well have been the champion that year in Paris.

Having lost that chance, he went to Great Britain and reached the final of the ATP tournament at the Queen's Club in London. Todd Martin was at the top of his game that day, overcoming Sampras 7-6 (4), 7-6 (4). As Martin recalled, "I played two nearly flawless sets and two nearly flawless tie-breaks to do that. Playing on the grass made defending my own serve easier."

Sampras remained unflappable. He was well prepared for Wimbledon. It was his best-ever first half of any season. In that span leading up to the lawns of the All England Club, he had won seven of the eleven tournaments he had played. His game was flowing freely. His state of mind was strong. He was the clear favorite to retain his Wimbledon title.

He had something of a test in the first round at the All England Club from fellow American Jared Palmer, a pure serve-and-volleyer with a game well-suited to the grass. Sampras beat the world No. 57 by scores of 7-6 (4), 7-5, 6-3. In the second round, he met Richey Reneberg, a first-rate returner who excelled in doubles and was a Davis Cup teammate. Sampras took apart his countryman and world No. 35 6-3, 6-4, 6-2. Facing a third compatriot in a row, Sampras routed Chuck Adams, the world No. 72, 6-1, 6-2, 6-4.

In the round of 16, Sampras accounted for world No. 51 Daniel Vacek—a formidable fast-court player—6-4, 6-1, 7-6 (5). He cut down world No. 8 Chang 6-4, 6-1 6-3 to reach the semifinals. On the grass, Chang did not have the artillery to stay with his old adversary. In his semifinal-round contest, Sampras avenged his loss to Todd Martin at the Queen's Club, eclipsing his tall adversary 6-4, 6-4, 3-6, 6-3.

Near the end of that encounter, however, Sampras hurt his ankle. It remained problematic as he came into the final against his fiercest grass-court rival, the formidable left-hander Goran Ivanisevic. Two years earlier, it was Ivanisevic who prevented Sampras from reaching the final at Wimbledon, winning their semifinal in four sets.

This time around in Great Britain, Ivanisevic was in fine fiddle. The lanky southpaw had performed mightily over the fortnight. Standing 6'4" but somehow looking taller, weighing in at 180 pounds, deeply intense but prone to volatility as a competitor, Ivanisevic had served spectacularly all through the tournament. In six matches on his way to the title round against Sampras, Ivanisevic had blasted 142 aces and had been broken only four times. In the semifinals, he had been at his very best in sweeping past Becker without dropping a set.

Sampras held Ivanisevic in high regard, immensely respecting the Croatian's grass-court game and, particularly, his awesome serving. He regarded the Ivanisevic serve as the single most fearsome he ever faced. He realized that he had to sedulously protect his own serve and make that an even higher priority than usual because Ivanisevic was so tough to break.

As Sampras said late in 2018, "Playing Goran on grass was always uncomfortable. I felt like he could serve me off the court and you can't do much about it. I remember that was the last year that we played with the fast balls and his serve was so devastating. Early in that '94 final he hit a couple of serves that almost went over the tarp at the back of the court. And we were playing at 2 o'clock. Serving into that 2 o'clock sun was always something I would think about the night before the match. Serving around the sun was how I looked at it. I was dealing with that sun at that hour and looking into it. If you get broken one time against Goran, that could be the set."

Asked how he coped with it when the sun was at its worst and shining so brightly in his eyes, he replied, "I was praying for some cloud coverage and just using my experience to toss around it, but that doesn't make your serve any easier trying to adjust with the ball toss. And playing Goran you feel you are under the gun from the very beginning. I remember getting through that period between 2 and 3 o'clock. That was important."

Many fans were not enamored with the Sampras-Ivanisevic matchup on grass because the points were violent and short. There were no real rallies. The tennis was fast paced, revolving largely around the serve. Points were over almost before they started. But some of the spectators did not realize how much skill it took and how much pressure it created on the competitors to play that kind of tennis on the most fabled tennis court in the world with the outcome having such lasting implications for both players. The margins were unimaginably thin. Neither competitor could afford any carelessness or indecision.

Moreover, the grass was playing faster in those days so the conditions suited the attacking players much more than is the case today. Sampras mused in 2019, "People didn't always appreciate [what we were doing] because there weren't any rallies, but I was playing against one of the biggest weapons in the history of the game, trying to fend him off and trying to use my own weapon on the serve. If people just saw how fast the court was and you had two guys going toe to toe, and if someone had a hiccup, he was going to lose the match—[they would realize] that was really tough. You really had to stay on your toes, but I felt my intensity was there for that final and I was very focused. I remember throwing out a couple of screams [of joy] after big points that I won that day."

Sampras walked out onto the Centre Court for this July 3, 1994 final with Ivanisevic wearing a strap on the outside of his ankle and tape under his sock. It was indeed an exceedingly bright day and the Centre Court was bathed in bright sunshine. The temperature was right around the 100 degree mark.

Sampras served first on this scorching afternoon, uncorking one ace and holding at 15 despite missing four out of five first serves. Ivanisevic responded with three aces and a love hold for 1-1. Both players held with relative ease up until 3-3. By then, the towering southpaw had already released seven aces. In the seventh game, Sampras was stretched to deuce but at that stage he went to one of his bread and butter patterns, serving wide to the Ivanisevic two-handed backhand in the deuce court, opening the court for a forehand first volley winner down the line. That serve-and-volley, one-two punch gave Sampras game point and he held on for 4-3 with a deep first serve to the backhand drawing an errant return.

Now the American found an opening. He reached 15-40 on the Ivanisevic serve, giving himself two chances for a 5-3 lead. But the left-hander sent his eighth ace of the match down the T, and then his heavy second serve to the backhand provoked an error from Sampras. Ivanisevic finally held on for 4-4 after three deuces, connecting with his ninth ace, thundering that delivery down the T.

After Sampras held comfortably for 5-4, he returned skillfully again, reaching triple set point on the Croatian's serve at 0-40. But Ivanisevic proceeded to win five points in a row for 5-5, serving aces on four of them. His ace total for the set was up to 13. His determination was strikingly evident and that clutch serving display denied Sampras a chance to seal the set.

Other players—even some of the great ones—would have been preoccupied with the way their chance to win the critical opening set was taken away so explosively, but Sampras was a man with one of the largest hearts and toughest minds in the game. Too many observers failed to take stock of Sampras as a competitor and underestimated his ability to fight with quiet ferocity and move past even the most devastating of disappointments.

That is exactly what he did in the eleventh game. Serving at 30-40, the accuracy of his first delivery down the T was extraordinary. Ivanisevic missed his backhand return on the stretch. This long and nerve-wracking game featured four deuces, but Sampras ultimately held on with an athletically impressive move coming forward. Serving-and-volleying, he made a first-rate backhand half volley that caused Ivanisevic to miss a backhand pass. To 6-5 went Sampras, but Ivanisevic held on in the twelfth game at 30 with two more aces, raising his total for the set to 15.

Fittingly, the two great servers would settle this set in a tie-break. The first five points were taken by the server, but then Sampras made his move, rolling a backhand second-serve return down the line and drawing a backhand half volley long from his opponent. That made it 4-2 for Sampras. Once again, Ivanisevic missed his first serve and Sampras dealt effectively with the second. His down-the-line backhand passing shot was too much for Ivanisevic to handle.

Sampras had surged to 5-2 and was poised to serve out the tie-break from there. He did just that. First, he went in behind his second serve, digging out a low backhand first volley down the line, setting up a backhand crosscourt volley winner. On the following point, Sampras got the first serve in and Ivanisevic missed a backhand return. Sampras had won the tie-break seven points to two. Ivanisevic had served his 16th ace of the set in that sequence, but won only one other point. He did not take any points on the Sampras serve. The American's tunnel vision in the tie-break and some timely shotmaking had carried him deservedly to a one-set lead.

At 1-2 in the second set, Sampras was down break point, but saved it with another excellent down-the-line backhand volley that was both deep and unanswerable. He held on for 2-2. Otherwise, both players were holding convincingly until Ivanisevic served at 4-4. He had two double faults on his way to a 15-40 deficit, giving Sampras a look at two break points for the chance to serve for the set. But Ivanisevic volleyed behind Sampras and clipped the baseline for a winner. He then came up with his 23rd ace, followed by two more potent first serves. The big man had raised the stakes and advanced to 5-4.

Sampras was now serving to stay in the set. Ivanisevic passed him cleanly off the backhand to reach 30-30 in the tenth game. He was two points away from one set all. Sampras relished these moments, knowing that he had no reason to be fearful of the big points, trusting himself to make something substantial happen. He produced an ace for 40-30 and held on with another ace, placing both serves immaculately down the T. The American was back to 5-5. Ivanisevic then held at the cost of only two points before Sampras took his serve at love.

Another tie-break would determine the outcome of the second set. Sampras had the advantage of having a set in hand while Ivanisevic sorely needed to win this one and thus play his way back into the match. Until Ivanisevic served at 3-4, not a point had gone against the server. But Sampras took full advantage of a second serve to his backhand in the ad court, coming over that return and keeping it low. Ivanisevic could not clear the net on a difficult first volley.

Sampras had the mini-break for 5-3 but Ivanisevic took the next point on his serve. Sampras would serve the next two points with a chance to close out the tie-break. But he punched a backhand first volley wide as he went down the line. 5-5. He collected himself swiftly, swung his first serve out wide in the deuce court to the Ivanisevic backhand and made an impeccable backhand first volley winner crosscourt.

Ivanisevic now served at 5-6. His first serve was a thunderbolt down the T and should have been impossible to return. But Sampras made a magnificent forehand return down the middle. Ivanisevic was serve-volleying but had to chip his backhand half volley down the line meekly. Sampras moved in and sent his backhand passing shot down the line, forcing his adversary into a netted low backhand volley. Sampras had come through seven points to five in the tie-break to forge a two-set lead. He had outplayed Ivanisevic in the tight corners at the end, and his return on set point was a gem.

As Sampras recollected vividly in 2019, "I knew I had to make Goran play on those second serve points. That was the key for me against him. On that set point in the second set tie-break, his first serve up the middle was huge and it was going to be an ace, but I managed to stab at a forehand and I got him stuck. Then I hit a passing shot and he hit it off the frame. That return of serve was one of the best of my life. I still think about it every now and again. And that cracked his back and put me up two sets. That was one of those times I screamed out because I felt like I got him."

Understandably, Ivanisevic was deflated. Without losing his serve once, he was down two sets to love. He had done very little wrong and had made many correct decisions. But he was in a dire predicament against a more polished and complete player than he was. Sampras was not going to lose from this commanding position. Not now. Not on this court. Not with the most prestigious title in tennis on the line.

The American was out to take the third set as quickly as possible. He played every point with heightened interest. Ivanisevic was depressed by the score-line and Sampras would not let him forget about it. The American started the third set with his 17th ace and held at 15. In the next game, an astonishing backhand passing-shot winner off a deep volley from Ivanisevic put Sampras ahead 0-40 and he broke at love for 2-0. He held easily at 15 for 3-0 and then broke at 30 for 4-0 with a low backhand passing shot down the line leaving Ivanisevic helpless.

Having achieved that second break, Sampras shouted "Yeah!" knowing victory was certainly at hand. He took the next two games swiftly, closing out the match entirely on his own terms, winning 7-6 (2), 7-6 (5), 6-0. Serving into the sunshine was no facile task. Sampras put only 50% of his first serves in for the match, but won 90% of those points and was victorious on 60% of his second-serve points. Remarkably, Sampras got 56% of his returns back in play, 12% better than his opponent. And Sampras was giving much less away than Ivanisevic, making 39 unforced errors, 35 fewer than the decidedly less-disciplined Ivanisevic. Sampras had defended his title and had lost only one set in the fortnight. He had held serve in 103 of 106 service games across seven matches through the fortnight and had not been broken against Ivanisevic. He had held back a rival in the final who had beaten him in five of eight previous meetings, including once at Wimbledon. He had captured a fifth major singles title.

Sampras was proud of his effort against Ivanisevic on that occasion. Examining that triumph a quarter of a century later, Sampras said, "Beating Goran there in '94 was just the start of my dominance at Wimbledon. He had a bit of a letdown in the third set because he had played as well as he could and he was still down two sets to love. After I won that match, I think people feared me a little more. My game was getting better and grass was my surface. That was definitely one of my best finals."

In an interview for this book, Ivanisevic spoke about that 1994 loss to Sampras on the Centre Court. He remembered,

Goran Ivanisevic fell victim to Pete Sampras in the 1994 Wimbledon final

"The problem was I knew and he knew that for like 15 or 20 minutes at a time nobody was going to touch the ball, him or me, because of the way we serve. But he was the one who put one or two more returns in play for the tie-breaks and he put pressure on me to volley well. And then in the third set he really picked his game up and I didn't have any chance. No chance. Not that I played wrong or badly. He was just a better player than me."

And so Sampras had won four of the last five majors and his second of 1994. He was having the finest season of his professional career. He left Wimbledon feeling he was on top of the world, determined to stamp his authority on the game even more. He had captured the most prestigious title in tennis even more convincingly than the year before, defending his crown at the cost of only one set over the fortnight. There was one more major left in 1994 at the U.S. Open and that was his chief goal for the rest of the year. But not long after Wimbledon, he would get injured at the worst possible time.

Playing the tall Dutchman Richard Krajicek in a Davis Cup match at the Netherlands, Sampras was utterly at ease in moving ahead, winning the first set 6-2. But he lost that clash in four sets as his left ankle hindered him. It turned out to be tendinitis. That injury kept him away from all of the hard court tournaments leading up to the U.S. Open, leaving Sampras in no position to defend his title. In the round of 16 he lost in five sets to the Peruvian Jaime Yzaga, the same stylish player who had beaten him at his first U.S. Open in 1988.

Over the autumn, however, he found his groove again on the court and started replicating much of the sparkling form he had demonstrated in his almost unblemished first half of the season. He needed some time to bring out his best tennis again. But after a semifinal setback against Becker in Stockholm and a quarterfinal defeat indoors against Agassi at the Paris Bercy Masters 1000 tournament, Sampras won the title in Antwerp, Belgium over Sweden's free swinging and overpowering Magnus Larsson and then closed his regular season campaign by coming through at the ATP World Tour Championships in Germany. In the semifinals of that season-ending tournament, having already sealed the season-ending No. 1 world ranking for the third year in a row, he toppled Agassi in a stirring match against his foremost rival, who concluded that year deservedly at No. 2. Down a set, Sampras reached a second-set tie-break. Leading 5-3 in that sequence, he played one of the most spectacularly inventive points of his career.

Sampras served-and-volleyed, punching a backhand first volley down the line to the Agassi forehand. Agassi sent a dipping forehand pass crosscourt, forcing Sampras to play a difficult forehand finesse volley short down the line. Agassi anticipated that play with uncanny alertness and managed to dig out the low ball and angle a backhand acutely crosscourt. Agassi's well executed passing shot pulled Sampras off the court and seemingly had his fellow American beaten with the angle and placement. It should have been a winner. But Sampras, knowing the value of this point, understanding that he could not afford to lose it, realizing that this was a critical time to rely not only on his speed but also his intuition, chased that ball down unswervingly. With his back to the net, he chipped a backhand down the line past Agassi for a magnificent winner. Sampras leaped into the air, pumping his fist, recognizing the magnitude of the moment, delighted that he had executed a shot magnificently that even he could not have envisioned. Seldom was he as demonstrably emotive on a tennis court.

He subsequently won that tie-break 7-5 and took the match 4-6, 7-6 (5), 6-3. The following day, Sampras came from behind to defeat Becker in a four-set final, winning that prestigious title for the second time. The ATP Tour Championships was regarded by the authorities as the definitive season-ending tournament. Sampras had succeeded in claiming that crown. But, in the fragmented tennis world at that time, one more big money event remained on the calendar, the Grand Slam Cup in Munich.

In the semifinals, Sampras moved past Ivanisevic 10-8 in the fifth set. He took on the big-hitting and free-wheeling Magnus Larsson of Sweden in the final, falling in four sets, dropping a pair of tie-breaks in the process. Larsson was one of the taller men in the sport at the time, standing 6'4" and weighing 205 pounds. He was ranked No. 19 in the world. When he was at peak efficiency and Sampras was slightly off his game, the Swede could be burdensome for the American.

Larsson had not beaten Sampras in four previous meetings before this one, and his performance was first rate across the board. Yet Sampras was concerned not simply with the loss itself, but by the state of his health. As he recalled in 2019, "I had this ulcer for at least two years in that period where I would get sick before some matches. It happened before I played Andre in Miami that year [1994] and before I played Todd Martin in the semifinals of Wimbledon. I woke up that morning feeling sick and had a bunch of water and I threw that up. It all kind of came to a head the day I played Larsson in Munich. I drank liters of water and I threw it all up. I went out and played and lost and I felt tired. If you look at pictures of me from a few weeks earlier at the ATP Finals, I look really skinny. You can see it in my neck. An ulcer is not like indigestion or heartburn. It is a severe injury in your stomach. I was internalizing emotions and feelings and bottling them all up."

Sampras realized after getting sick prior to his appointment with Larsson that he needed to figure out what was triggering these stomach ailments. It was happening too often—not on a weekly basis but every couple of months, or thereabouts. He went back home to Tampa, Florida and did an Upper G.I. test with a doctor and it was diagnosed as an ulcer. At that time, Sampras was taking a strong anti-inflammatory called Indocin.

As he said, "At 23 or 24, around the same time as the ulcer, I had a dead arm that was very achy so I started taking Indocin, which is a strong anti-inflammatory. I was taking it too much, taking it before every match to the point where even if my arm wasn't hurting I would take it because I knew the arm probably was going to hurt. So my doctor told me this was very tough on my stomach and said I should take the Indocin when I was eating. I can't remember when, but I started feeling a little nauseous at times after a meal. I was dealing with this for a couple of years, feeling nauseous, having stomach issues and continuing to take the Indocin. I had to get off the Indocin. The doctor in Tampa put me on a six-week program of taking medication so I took a few pills a day and that cleared the ulcer up. But I always had a sensitive stomach so I had to be aware of spicy foods, big meals and just being more aware of what I was eating. I was stressed out a lot and you carry all of your stress in your stomach."

Through that period, Sampras tried to keep his mind off of his stomach issues and keep on performing majestically. He was winning. He was the sport's preeminent player. He was focused entirely on staying at the top. That is why he put himself through some debilitating times.

"I just ignored it," he said in 2019. "I just wanted to keep on winning, even though I was uncomfortable, even though I was getting sick. I woke up and my will to win just trumped everything. I would get sick and it was my will to stay No. 1 that mattered. It was not easy, but I just dealt with it. Maybe my energy wasn't as high as I needed it to be. I was dealing with a sensitive stomach. Throughout that 1994 year when I played Larsson at the end in Munich, I remember all of these episodes of getting sick. I was just uncomfortable. Why I just kept it to myself beats me. I didn't tell anyone and just kept it private. Looking back, I should have done something about it sooner."

Elaborating on that thought, Sampras said, "I do regret not communicating better with my team and whoever was close to me about my stomach and the ulcer and what was going on. Being a Dad now, I know how important it is to get things off your chest. You want to know what is going on with your kids. I would hate for my two sons to not share something important like that with me that they are going through. So I look back at my mid-twenties with some regrets. I never wanted to show any vulnerability or insecurity. I didn't want to make a big deal out of things. This was always my feeling about life and tennis. I found myself at that time in '94 and those years around then really internalizing a lot, which contributed to the ulcer. A lot of it was my personality, keeping things close to me and not sharing a lot of my feelings. That was just how I was."

He did eventually confront the stomach problems. But he had another significant challenge that stayed with him for the rest of his career. Not uncommonly for someone of Greek heritage, Sampras had a blood disorder called thalassemia that was known to cause fatigue and could cause anemia.

On the most scorching days, when temperatures soared and the sun was beating down oppressively, Sampras was susceptible to deep fatigue on the court in long and draining contests, particularly on the most stifling afternoons. So he was confronting thalassemia at the same time as his ulcer and well beyond.

He explained, "Thalassemia is a low red blood cell count and a lot of Greek people can get it. It was on my Mom's side of the family. As a kid I never thought twice about it and when I first turned pro it never was an issue, but as I got older my doctors told me to eat more protein and take supplements. You need to bring up your red blood cell count to get your energy. And for me it was always a struggle. I did get tired, especially in the heat. I felt I was working a lot harder just to keep up."

Sampras paused briefly before adding, "I trained hard and worked hard but always felt at times that my energy was a little low. I tried more supplements, more red meat and more protein but in the heat of battle at times I did get winded in Australia a few times and in other matches. As I got older I had to take more of a look at my protein intake. My doctor would say to eat steak, chicken, steak and more steak. I was always working on it. And it was tied in for a time with the ulcer."

Despite these internal battles and inclination to keep things to himself, Sampras won more prolifically than ever before in that 1994 season. His numbers were outstanding. He captured ten titles—a career record for a single season that he would never equal—and won 77 of 89 matches. For the first time in his career, he won tournaments in the same year on indoor carpet, grass, clay and hard courts. Had his season not been so sorely disrupted over the summer, undoubtedly Sampras would have taken a few more titles and probably another major—the U.S. Open.

But there was little for the best player in the world to complain about. He had celebrated a second two-major year in a row. He had lived on the edge of invincibility during the first half of the season when he avoided injuries and performed ceaselessly with spirit and panache.

At the end of 1994, Pete Sampras now understood himself more fully than he ever had before. His priorities were well established. His vision of who he was and where he was going was uncluttered. He could not wait to get on with the rest of his career. As fate would decree, 1995 would be one of the most emotional years of his illustrious career, on and off the court.

# CHAPTER 8

# A LIFE-ALTERING EXPERIENCE LEADS TO A SIXTH MAJOR

Knowing how much he had raised his personal stock and standing in his immensely productive 1993 and 1994 campaigns, Sampras dove into the following season determined to maintain and even increase his status as the central figure in the world of tennis. He had a clear sense of purpose and a substantial supply of self-conviction based on the growing foundation of his success. He had every reason to approach 1995 in a very optimistic frame of mind.

But, during the Australian Open in January, as he was in pursuit of another major title, Sampras's world was turned upside down. Tim Gullikson found himself battling a health crisis and it struck in the middle of the tournament. He was seriously ill.

As Tom Gullikson reflected, "Tim had his first episode in the fall of 1994 in Stockholm. He collapsed in his hotel room and had multiple stitches. They got him to the hospital but unfortunately never checked his brain. They only checked his heart. Like a lot of athletes, he had a bit of an enlarged heart. Five weeks later Tim and Pete were in Germany for the ATP Finals. His wife Rosemary was talking to him on the phone while Tim was at his hotel and he started garbling his words. Rosemary was an intensive care nurse before she became a lawyer, so she knew the symptoms right away."

Rosemary Gullikson telephoned the hotel and asked them to go to her husband's room because she knew he was having an episode. As Tom Gullikson said, "Tim was having another seizure but unfortunately they never checked his brain, which to me is unbelievable. They just looked into the whole heart issue. He recovered from that, but we all were concerned."

Before Sampras played an early round match at the Australian Open of 1995, Tim Gullikson had another seizure, this time in the locker room. Tom Gullikson recalled, "I remember being in there with Pete and Tim. Pete was getting ready to play and all of a sudden Tim has this seizure. The locker rooms guys did a great job and I went with Tim to the hospital. They got him there in about five minutes. I spent three or four nights in the hospital with Tim and then they finally took an MRI of his brain. I talked to the doctor and he told me 'This doesn't look good for your brother. These four spots on his brain look like brain tumors but you can't confirm that until you do a biopsy. We are not going to do that here. We will put him on medications so he doesn't have a seizure on the plane ride back to Chicago.'"

Sampras kept playing his matches at the Australian Open while trying to keep his mind on his mission, but visited his close friend and coach on a daily basis. A date was determined for Tim and Tom Gullikson to fly back to the U.S. but the doctors felt it would be good for Tim's morale for him to go out to dinner the night before with friends before he went home. Tom Gullikson said, "The night before Pete played Courier in the quarterfinals, I invited some special guests to dinner with Tim including Pete, Jim, Todd Martin and a few other friends. We just had a small party and a nice dinner and showed our support to Tim. The next day Tim and I were on that plane back to Chicago."

Speaking about that dinner in 2019, Courier was still deeply moved by the memory. He said, "It was a very somber affair. Ian Hamilton from Nike was there. We had been to the hospital to see Tim. It was a rough situation. A whole group of us were trying to put a smile on a serious situation when there were a lot of question marks and unknowns with Tim flying back the next morning on the eleven o'clock flight. My coach Craig Boynton was with me then and Paul Annacone was there for Pete and it was definitely nice to have all of us there together. It was a good show of solidarity for people we cared deeply about that were going through something really difficult. We [Sampras and Courier] still had work to do in Australia."

That next evening, Sampras and Courier engaged in a classic contest, with Sampras dropping a pair of tie-breaks before making a spirited comeback to win in five sets. In the first game of the final set, with Sampras serving at 30-0, a fan yelled out, "Do it for your coach!"

Sampras, however, clarified in 2019 that he did not really hear that spectator, but soon he started to cry. After a quick hold, he walked to the changeover and the tears continued. Courier held on in the second game as Sampras remained in his vulnerably emotional state, fighting in vain to stop the tears. Serving in the following game at 1-1, the tears were streaming down his face and he kept wiping them away. It was as poignant a moment as he would ever experience on a tennis court. As Gullikson said, "That was just raw emotion that Pete showed when he cried. In a weird way, it was like the first time people saw that side of Pete because everybody thought he was a tennis machine who didn't have emotions."

In that fifth set, Sampras was demonstrating to the fans something those in his inner circle had always known—that he had a large heart, exceedingly strong mind and deep sensitivity. Courier understood why Sampras was flooded with feelings of sadness for Tim Gullikson, but he felt he had to do something to ensure that the match could continue.

After Sampras served an ace for 30-0 with the score locked at 1-1 in the fifth, Courier looked across the net at his emotional opponent and said, "Are you all right, Pete? We can do this tomorrow."

STEVE FLINK

Undoubtedly, Courier was genuinely empathetic about his friend's plight and in his mind was looking for a way to help. But however Sampras interpreted that remark—as a jab or just pure sympathy—he was snapped sweepingly out of his state of mind.

Courier clarified in 2019, "We were in a situation where Pete needed to come out of the emotional situation he was in and get back to playing tennis. We had 15,000 people in the middle of it with us. I knew Pete well enough that I thought I could help him get back into the competition. That was my only thought. We had to get the show back on the road. He was really struggling, so how do we do it? So I did what I did, and said what I said, and Pete reacts brilliantly the way he did in times of crisis in his career and starts throwing down aces. He refocuses and finds his way to the finish line. And then we shake hands and we are both on the training table so fatigued, laying side by side, both of us cramping up and getting treatment. And we are just talking to each other. It was certainly one of the most memorable moments of my career and one of the more remarked upon moments of any match I was ever involved with. Pete certainly had a different vantage point coming out of it than I did, which I respect. He was living what he was living and I was living what I was living. It was definitely a moment in time. It was intense."

Courier explained how that moment played out from his point of view. He said, "The choices are that either Pete comes out of it on his own—which didn't seem like it was happening—or someone would try to help him out of it, whether it was me or the chair umpire. We are the only two people who have a way to do that because the people in the crowd are just making Pete more emotional. And if the chair umpire does it, then it is going to come at a cost. So my option was to not say anything or let the chair umpire assess Pete time violations. Or I could say something that I think will bring Pete back to where it comes back to the tennis. The emotion is still a factor, but it is no longer the overarching factor in the result. So as I look back at it today, that is the way it shapes out."

Sampras put on an astonishing display of professionalism and character, serving aces while the tears were still flowing. Soon after the Courier remark, Sampras recovered his composure and he played a first-rate fifth set, completing a 6-7 (4), 6-7 (3), 6-3, 6-4, 6-3 triumph.

Reflecting on that moment later that year, he told me in a piece I was writing for *World of Tennis*, "At that one moment I just couldn't control my emotions. I had this image of Tim lying in the hospital bed crying and I had been keeping everything inside me until then, so I just cracked."

As he examined that singular experience through the longer lens of history, Sampras better understood what it felt like to be in his shoes at that time. He said in 2019, "I look at it now that Jim was genuinely trying to help out the situation, trying to get me out of whatever I was going through. What irked me was that the crowd laughed when Jim spoke to me across the net. It wasn't necessarily what Jim said, but more that the crowd laughed. I just felt a little exposed at the time and I remember that the light switch went on. But the reaction of the crowd didn't sit well with me. Jim was just trying to change the mood and that definitely got me locked in. Even right after, it was like the pink elephant in the room. We were around each other for the next bunch of years, but Jim and I never addressed it. It was almost like we talked about it through the media. We never had a conversation about it. Maybe it was my poor communication skills and how I was back then. I didn't want to talk about it. I just put it somewhere else."

Courier said in 2019, "I don't think there was ever a thought to have a conversation about that moment. It never would have occurred to me unless I felt there was a problem, which I did not. In the end, I felt an immense sense of pride about what Pete accomplished and what he did with his ability and the same for myself. I look at the way Pete handled himself throughout his career, the dignity that he showed and continues to show whenever he pops up in the tennis world and I admire the hell out of it having known him since the beginning. And likewise for him. Both of us have a lot to be proud of and a lot to talk about whenever we get together because we have gone through the worst together and come out on the other side healthy. I am talking 10,000 feet now in the big picture. I feel really good about it."

Prior to his meeting with Courier, Sampras had already fought back ferociously from two-sets-to-love down against Magnus Larsson. After the Courier win, he ousted Chang to reach the final. Now the defending champion collided with none other than Agassi for the title and their four-set contest was played out at a lofty level. Sampras took the first set, dropped the second and on they went to a pivotal third-set tie-break. Sampras was serving at 6-4, double set point in that sequence. He swung his first serve out wide to the Agassi forehand in the deuce court, a tactic that worked frequently over the years in big matches. But Agassi anticipated this serve and blasted a return down the line past the charging Sampras for a winner.

Agassi saved the second set point, prevailed in the tie-break and moved purposefully to a 4-6, 6-1, 7-6 (6), 6-4 victory. The 24-year-old from Las Vegas had never played this major before, but he was magnificent from the backcourt against Sampras, operating with uncanny efficiency and sending his shots across the net with sustained power, depth and precision. Had Sampras secured the crucial third set, he would have been hard to stop. But, despite losing in the final of 1995's leadoff major, he came away from the experience both emboldened and astutely aware of life's sometimes cruel fragility.

As he told me later that year, "I did not like it when I lost to Andre, but when I hopped on the plane the next day I had learned a lot about myself and about how important Tim is. In the tournaments after that, I was playing very up and down for a while, and I could hear Tim's voice on the phone when we spoke. He was extremely worried. This put everything into perspective for me. Tennis is a great game and I want to win every match I play, but it is not the most important thing in your life. Your health is most important. This is so unfair because Tim doesn't have a bad bone in his body. It just shows me how vulnerable we all are."

Shielding Sampras against that vulnerability was Paul Annacone, who stepped in to coach Sampras during the Australian Open when Gullikson was hospitalized, and took over at the helm both before and after Gullikson passed away in May of 1996. In the interim, he travelled with Sampras and spoke regularly with Gullikson and the situation sorted itself out very well.

As Annacone said in an interview for this book, "It was very tricky in the beginning. The hardest part for me going into it was making sure I didn't mess anything up. I had been coaching a little bit and winding down my career as a player, but I had known Pete since he was 16 when we became friendly. I knew Gully very well so when he had to go home from Australia they said 'Would you mind just staying and helping until we figure out exactly what is going on?' So that was an easy one for me. The theme behind it all was, 'How do we make some good out of a horrible situation'?"

Annacone realized from the outset that luck was on his side in guiding Sampras. As he said in 2019, "First of all, Pete was a great player and he was only 23. He was really pretty darned clear about what he needed to do to be successful, so there weren't a million moving parts. And he wasn't overly emotional. Those two things in retrospect to me are the biggest challenges about coaching at the professional level. How much volatility is there emotionally and how many moving parts are there? The third part is: how well does the player know himself or herself? Pete ticked all of those boxes extremely well. That is what made it so easy for me. The icing on the cake was that Gully was my buddy. He was amazing. He helped navigate the situation with me about how much information to give Pete and when to give it, what to look for and the best way to communicate. Those were all the things that a new coaching relationship needs to have and Tim Gullikson was the maestro."

Sampras adjusted remarkably well to not having Gullikson on the road with him and being accompanied by Annacone. In some respects, the coaching transition was seamless because Annacone's personality and style suited

Sampras similarly. But, understandably, despite speaking regularly with Gullikson on the telephone, even though he got along very well with Annacone, Sampras was still worried. His results were not nearly as consistent as had been the case in 1994; during the early stages of 1995, he was sporadically brilliant but his week-in, week-out performances were less reliable.

After the Australian Open, he was beaten in the semifinals of Memphis, narrowly bowing out against Todd Martin 4-6, 7-6, (6), 6-4. It was the kind of hard-fought and tight match that Sampras was accustomed to winning, but he could not close the deal. He fell in the round of 16 of Philadelphia against the Dutchman Paul Haarhuis, a surprising loss at an indoor event. He came through at the Masters 1000 tournament in Indian Wells, toppling Agassi 7-5, 6-3, 7-5 in the final. But a few weeks later, Agassi turned the tables on his compatriot, succeeding in a final-set tie-break as the two icons collided in the Miami Masters 1000 final for the second year in a row.

In his four clay-court tournaments on the road to Roland Garros, Sampras made it to one semifinal in Hamburg but lost early in the rest. Having reached the quarterfinals three years in a row at the French Open, he seemed likely to get at least that far again, but he was upset in the first round by world No. 24 Gilbert Schaller of Austria, losing that encounter in five sets.

Now he gladly left the clay behind him and headed to Great Britain and the grass courts that brought out the best in his game and his outlook. The week after Roland Garros, he was victorious at the Queen's Club tournament, cutting down the left-handed Guy Forget, the same guileful Frenchman who led their head to head series 4-2 heading into this showdown. Sampras, who finished with a 5-4 career record versus Forget, took this final in two tie-breaks.

And so he went to Wimbledon in search of a third crown in a row. This was going to be his make or break tournament of the year. He had not won a major since Wimbledon the previous year. He needed this one badly.

Annacone recalled, "I was worried after the French Open about how he would react since he didn't play well there, but Gully was great when I talked to him about that. He said, 'Pete doesn't wallow around in the past. He will move on to the next thing extremely well. Once he gets on the grass courts he will be fine.' And Pete was very calm on the way to London from Paris. He said, 'It didn't go the way I wanted. We have to figure out a way to keep getting better on that surface but now we play on the grass and I have to get comfortable serving to targets and have a different return mentality.' There was no big drama. It was really like a math equation for him. He just didn't miss a beat. He was amazingly pragmatic. We got over to Wimbledon and he just goes out there at times like that and believes in big moments."

Sampras may have been more disconcerted than he had let on to Annacone. As he told me in an interview for *World of Tennis* in the autumn of 1995, "When I got back from the French Open, that was the lowest point I had felt in three or four years. I talked to Paul Annacone and my parents and they gave me all the support I needed. When I talked to Tim, he told me to go to London and try to win my third Wimbledon. Tim really encouraged me. He was going through the toughest fight of his life with [cancer] treatments and this and that and here he was telling me to have a positive attitude. There was a bit of irony in that."

The triumph at Queen's Club was a positive step, but Sampras recognized that Wimbledon was a fortnight unlike any other in his profession, a grass-court festival that thoroughly captured the imagination of the public and the tournament he wanted more than any other each and every year. He was wounded internally by the plight of Tim Gullikson and in constant touch with his friend. But he knew that Wimbledon required his full attention and a day-in and day-out devotion. He wanted a third crown in a row on the Centre Court wholeheartedly.

At the beginning of the tournament, however, he was not at the top of his game. Confronting Germany's funky left-hander Karsten Braasch in the first round, he did not win entirely on his own terms. Sampras was victorious 7-6 (4), 6-7 (2), 6-4, 6-1 over the No. 120-ranked player in the world. Toward the end of the third set and right on through the fourth, he elevated his game significantly. His second-round assignment was against Great Britain's Tim Henman, a confirmed serve-and-volleyer who would reach four semifinals at Wimbledon in the future.

Henman was only 20 and still evolving as a player. Sampras took him apart 6-2, 6-3, 7-6 (3). In a third-round meeting against compatriot Jared Palmer—an All-American at Stanford University who won the NCAA Championships in 1991—Sampras started apprehensively but turned the corner at the end of the second set and came through 4-6, 6-4, 6-1, 6-2, defeating his fellow American for the second year in a row at the All England Club.

He then took on Greg Rusedski, a left-hander who grew up in Canada but was permitted to play later under the British flag because his mother was from that country. Rusedski was a big server who reached the U.S. Open final a couple of years later. Sampras was a 6-4, 6-3, 7-5 round-of-16 victor and did not lose his serve across three sets. He was clearly the better player and a vastly superior returner, yet Rusedski sat at many of the changeovers inexplicably wearing a wide grin on his face, as if he was winning a match that he was clearly losing. Asked afterwards how he felt about that, Sampras playfully said, "I wanted to wipe that smile off of his face." That sardonic line was greeted with much laughter among the reporters in the room.

Having done battle with Rusedski on the Centre Court, Sampras played his quarterfinal on Court One against Japan's instinctively cagey Shuzo Matsuoka. Matsuoka was problematic for Sampras for a while, but the American figured out the right solutions and soldiered on to a 6-7 (5), 6-3, 6-4, 6-2 victory.

Now, in the penultimate round, Sampras found himself up against a familiar figure in the towering southpaw Goran Ivanisevic. They were colliding for the third time in four years, having split the previous two battles in the 1992 semifinals and 1994 final. This time, both players were primed for a crucial appointment. Ivanisevic had dropped only one set in five matches on his way to his duel with Sampras. He had toppled the formidable Todd Martin and the well-rounded Kafelnikov in the two previous rounds.

The first set of the Sampras-Ivanisevic semifinal was settled on a razor's edge. Sampras took it in a tie-break by nine points to seven. But, serving at 4-5 in the second set, hoping to at least reach another tie-break, Sampras was broken by the Croatian. At 30-40 in the tenth game, he fell behind in the point and never recovered. His forehand first volley down the middle had no bite on it. Ivanisevic had him on the defensive and eventually his heavy hitting succeeded. It was one set all.

And yet, immediately after that jarring moment, Sampras found an opening and took it. Consecutive double faults from Ivanisevic gave the American a 15-40 lead. Ivanisevic unloaded on a first serve to the backhand side of his opponent and Sampras went with the chip return, keeping it low. Ivanisevic was forced to play an awkward half volley, which he sent into the net. Sampras was on the ascendancy again, up a break at 1-0 in the third set. He made that count and moved ahead two sets to one with an insurance break at the end of the set.

Once more, Ivanisevic battled gamely from behind. Sampras served at 3-3, 30-15 in the fourth set but Ivanisevic released a forehand return winner off a second serve, followed with a forehand passing shot on the next point and then broke when his backhand return drew a forehand volley long on the stretch. Sampras had missed five out of six first serves in that game and it cost him the set. Ivanisevic took it 6-4.

Now it all came down to one set between two prodigious servers who were throwing everything they had in their arsenals at each other. Sampras was built for these circumstances because of his unflinching temperament and his coolness in the heat of battle. He commenced the final set with typical clarity of purpose, holding at 15 in the first game and then securing the critical break in the second game. At break point down, Ivanisevic muffed a forehand first volley wide down the line.

From a break up in the fifth set of a semifinal or final at a major, no one was better than Sampras. He would stubbornly protect his delivery, play every point on his serve with deep intensity and keep closing in on victory with an unwavering feeling that he was simply not going to be halted. He held at the cost of only one point for 3-0. In his next two service games, he did not concede a single point. Serving for the match at 5-3, he lost the first point, won the second with a service winner, and then unleashed a pair of aces for a 40-15 lead. Ivanisevic saved one match point with a freakish winner off the net cord, but Sampras closed it out on the second with a first serve to the forehand in the ad court that Ivanisevic could not return. Victory had gone deservedly to Sampras 7-6 (7), 4-6, 6-3, 4-6, 6-3. Ivanisevic had served 38 aces, 17 more than Sampras. He won ten more total points in the match than Sampras. But the American was the better big-point player, more reliable when it mattered, utterly calm under duress.

He had garnered a place in the final after a pendulum-swinging, nerve-wracking, gut-wrenching win over a rival who often stretched him to his limits. Speaking about his 1995 semifinal win over Ivanisevic in a 2019 interview for this book, Sampras said, "I wasn't quite as sharp against Goran as I was the year before in the final. I felt like he wanted it a little more. It was a semifinal so there was not quite the same pressure in that way, but because of his serve he always puts you under a lot of pressure. If you make a few mistakes, which I did in '95, it will cost you and I lost a couple of sets. But I was able to tough him out and get some relief out of that. John McEnroe had a comment after that match with Goran that it was like the Lakers were playing the Jazz. The Lakers always found a way to win in the end and maybe with me and Goran, I would find a way to get through it. Tennis is like boxing with two guys battling it out and one guy always seems to find a way to win at the end. Maybe Goran just felt a little nervous. There were a lot of different reasons why I always seemed to find a way."

Ivanisevic said in an interview for this book, "Pete gave me a couple of chances in the beginning. I maybe should have won it earlier, but I didn't. If you don't take those chances early in the match, then later on he will give you less and less chances, and he was just serving better and better toward the end. In the important points and important moments he was the better player. He kind of knew me. He just knew I was going to do something stupid, bad volleys or double faults, something like that. He didn't make those mistakes. I did."

For Sampras, playing Ivanisevic in the semifinals was ideal preparation for taking on Boris Becker in the July 9, 1995 final. Becker, of course, was another big server, but perhaps less intimidating as an adversary than the tall southpaw from Croatia. Sampras respected Becker and had some extraordinary skirmishes with the German, particularly indoors in the German's homeland. But, for the most part, Sampras was not unduly daunted by Becker.

"The way I looked at it," recalled Sampras, "if I could just get a few second serve looks, make him play and hold my serve, I felt it could go my way. If I just kept doing what I was doing, it was fine. Boris wasn't a natural volleyer so I felt if I could get the ball down on him with my returns and serve well myself I could wear him down."

Becker came into the final on the heels of one of the most uplifting triumphs of his career. In a semifinal confrontation with the top seeded Agassi, Becker was in an abysmal bind. Agassi was striking the ball supremely, returning Becker's serve with blinding returns at his feet and out of his reach, controlling his own service games meticulously with the purity of his ground strokes and the extraordinary accuracy of his passing shots.

Agassi not only won the first set commandingly 6-2, but moved out in front 4-1 in the second set with a two-service break lead. But Becker pulled off a startling comeback to prevail in four sets. It was a tremendously gratifying win for the German, who had not beaten Agassi in nearly seven years, not since he overcame the American in a July 1989 Davis Cup contest. Sitting courtside with the Becker contingent was his coach Nick Bollettieri, who had been Agassi's guiding force for so long until they parted ways acrimoniously a few years earlier.

In the final, Becker picked off where he left off against Agassi. Both men powered their way into a tie-break in the first set without a service break for either participant. Sampras had been victorious in six of seven tie-breaks across his career against the burly German, but he lost this one. Becker was ahead 4-2 before Sampras collected three points in a row. But Becker rallied from 4-5 with two top notch serve-and-volley points and a crackling low backhand return that forced an error on the volley from Sampras. Tie-break to Becker 7-5.

Sampras was down a set but was not out of sorts about it. "It was another hot day," he recalled, "but I always felt good against Boris. You can lose a set on grass and be playing fine. I remember getting on top of him in the second set and when I got my returns going in the third and fourth, he got tired."

At 1-1 in the second set, Sampras found his range on his returns and laced a forehand winner down the line followed by a forehand pass up the line. Then he sent a return at Becker's feet, setting up a winning backhand passing shot to reach 0-40. The crowd applauded politely but almost dispassionately and Sampras allowed himself the luxury of a light moment he seldom experienced on the Centre Court. He glanced in their direction, raising his palms, urging the fans to be more enthusiastic. The fans loved the gesture and acted accordingly, smiling and applauding unreservedly. He wanted more appreciation and found a gentle way to have that wish fulfilled.

Recollecting that moment with some amusement, Sampras said, "I was saying, 'Show me a little love.' There were times I was playing great tennis and the way I made it look people could maybe take it for granted. I remember hitting that backhand passing shot and it was almost like I had hit another ace, like no big deal. Any time I showed emotion with the crowd they were so shocked. It was like, 'Oh, he is human.' I learned that as I got older."

Relaxed after establishing that connection with the crowd, Sampras secured the first service break of the match at 15, building a 2-1 second-set lead. That game turned the match decidedly in his direction. He broke again for 4-1 with the persistence of his backhand returns compromising the German. He kept holding comfortably and served out the set in the eighth game, holding at 15 with three aces, coming through convincingly 6-2.

Sampras was feeling close to unstoppable now. His tennis was gelling in every way, from his steadily improving returns, to his play in the forecourt, to the cornerstone of his game—that incomparable serve. Becker had done very well to salvage a first set that could have gone either way, but the heaviness of his movement was increasingly apparent and his serve, however potent it remained, could not match his younger adversary's delivery.

The 23-year-old Sampras had considerably more spring in his step than the 27-year-old German. He was the decidedly superior athlete, the swifter man covering the court and his skills at the net surpassed Becker by a wide margin. At 1-1 in the third set, Becker labored through a six-deuce game on his serve, realizing that falling behind here could dampen his chances significantly. Both men had opportunities. Becker had three game points and saved three break points. But then he double faulted to give Sampras a fourth break point and the American made this one count, chipping a backhand return down the line and coaxing Becker into a forehand volley error.

Buoyed by that break, sensing that he had full control of the match, delighted that under the broiling sun his searing shots were succeeding, Sampras held at love for 3-1 and nearly broke Becker again before the German rallied from 15-40 in the fifth game. But Sampras was serving with astonishing power, accuracy and rhythm. On his way to 5-3, the American was giving nothing away on his serve. His love hold in the eighth game was his fourth in a row without the loss of a point.

Becker, however, remained resolute, closing out a tough deuce game on his serve with two aces, forcing Sampras to serve out the set. With the keen instincts of a champion, Becker pressed Sampras tenaciously on the American's serve in the tenth game. The German created some consternation among Sampras fans when he advanced to 0-30. But, as he so often did under duress, Sampras responded mightily. An excellent second serve to the Becker backhand provoked an error: 15-30.

Two aces—the first out wide, the second down the T—lifted Sampras to 40-30. Becker saved that set point with a scintillating down-the-line backhand return that was as good as a winner, but Sampras once again raised the stakes and demonstrably declared his greatness. A second serve ace out wide gave the American a second set point. Recognizing the importance of this game, he screamed "Come On!" urging himself on. Then he served another ace—his 16th of the contest—to seal the set 6-4, yelling "Yes!" pumping his fist, walking to the changeover commandingly, believing that he was going to win this tennis match.

Becker was understandably deflated. From 30-30 in the first game of the fourth set, he double faulted twice to lose his serve. That was an irrevocable blow to the three-time former champion's chances. Sampras served two more aces and stunningly produced a winning overhead from near the baseline on his way to 2-0 before Becker held in the third game. When Sampras served consecutive aces to establish a 30-15 lead in the fourth game, Becker playfully placed his hands over his eyes, pretending to be blindfolded and swinging at a serve he could not see. That was his way of conceding that he simply could not read his opponent's unimaginably deceptive delivery. That self-deprecating display from the German went over well with the Centre Court audience.

Sampras magnified that image with a game closing ace for 3-1. He nearly sealed the verdict in the next game when he had Becker trapped at 15-40, but the German guilefully directed a couple of serves into the Sampras body to get back to deuce and eventually held on. On his way to 4-2, Sampras emblematically left Becker befuddled. The American lunged for a backhand drop volley, forcing the German to scamper forward. Becker scraped that ball back but, as the German slipped to the turf, Sampras lofted a lob volley winner over his opponent's head into an empty space for a winner.

Becker was spent. At 2-4, 30-30, he double faulted and then a Sampras chipped backhand return found the edge of the sideline. He had gained the insurance break. Serving for the match in the following game, he produced his 23rd and final ace on the penultimate point of the confrontation and then took the last point on an errant forehand return from Becker. Sampras had sparkled across the last three sets of a 6-7 (5), 6-2, 6-4, 6-2 triumph. He had not lost his serve for the second straight year in a Wimbledon final. He had distanced himself from Becker across the board. He was the Wimbledon champion for the third consecutive year. No American man had ever swept three Wimbledon singles titles in a row.

Reflecting in 2019 on what the media called his "Three-Pete," Sampras said, "I think there was more of an appreciation of what I was doing. My first Wimbledon win they didn't know me that well and my second they still didn't know me and maybe thought I was a good guy, but the third one I felt they were thinking, 'Okay, he has won three in a row and we have got to appreciate what this guy has done.' So I did feel from a popularity standpoint winning against Boris in '95 kind of shifted how people saw me, with a different kind of appreciation. I definitely felt that more as I got older and the third Wimbledon against Boris was kind of the start of it."

He always celebrated competing at Wimbledon. It was his home abroad. Sampras appreciated the U.S. Open enormously as well, and took immense pride in his many triumphant journeys at the championships of his country. But the U.S. Open was a louder New York showcase, an American sporting festival that attracted fans from across the spectrum of entertainment and brought in observers who were not necessarily steeped in knowledge of tennis.

Wimbledon sharply contrasted from the Open as a dignified setting with more polite audiences and a deeper sense of decorum. The atmospherics at the All England Club seemed to suit Sampras to the hilt. After his 1995 triumph, the fans in Great Britain almost adopted Sampras as one of their own and embraced his unwavering sense of fair play. In turn, Sampras was unfailingly appreciative of Wimbledon as a showcase for his talent.

Pete Sampras won Wimbledon for a third year in a row in 1995

As he said in 2019, "Wimbledon had a big impact on me as a kid. We made it a family outing to go watch the Wimbledon final at the Jack Kramer Club when our television was broken. There was something about the echo of the ball in the Centre Court that I loved and the royalty in the box. It felt bigger than a tournament. This was the Granddaddy of them all, the Super Bowl of tennis. Wimbledon. Wimbledon. Wimbledon. And it was Borg, it was McEnroe, it was Becker winning at 17. Not that the Open wasn't great because it was, but the quietness of Wimbledon suited my personality."

Expanding thoughtfully, Sampras added, "I just liked things in a certain way and Wimbledon was more regimented. I felt comfortable there. The U.S. Open was bigger and louder and there was more of a buzz in the stadium. You felt the fans were more separate from you and they weren't even watching the match sometimes. That unsettled me at times. Getting in and out of New York was definitely more stressful for me than Wimbledon, where I rented a quiet house. I just had a routine at Wimbledon and a regimen. It all fit. In New York, you noticed the traffic and the noise. If I went back to the Open today, the anxiety would come back to me. Going back to Wimbledon would be more mellow. I got over the mental hurdle at some point of not liking playing on grass and started to improve. I got into my routine. There were no surprises and not much wind. The U.S. Open was always windy. That could make a lot of players uptight. As an American it was a great feeling and I loved playing at the Open, but I always felt more at ease when I played Wimbledon."

By 1995, Sampras had clearly found his groove on the lawns of Great Britain and it was no accident that it would be his most successful major. At that stage of his career, Sampras liked where he stood in the hierarchy of the sport and appreciated how much progress he had made in the space of a few short years as the game's leading player.

He said, "I was feeling good about where I was. My game was good. You get to a point where you just figure it out. That is where I was. I have seen it with players like Roger and Novak in the last ten to 15 years. At 22 or 23 they figure it out, and they know they belong. After that third Wimbledon, I was adding up my majors and I just wanted to keep it going. Physically I was good and mentally I felt strong. There were no concerns. I was in the prime of my career. When you are in your mid-twenties and recovering well and you are healthy, it feels good. It was fun and winning that Wimbledon in '95 for three in a row was calming."

And so Sampras left Wimbledon exhilarated and relieved, victorious at a major for the sixth time, glad to have turned his 1995 season around and eager to get on with the rest of the year. "Winning Wimbledon saved my year," he said a few months later. Sampras had taken the most prestigious title in tennis, but he was not willing to slip into complacency after a fulfilling victory. The next major in New York meant a lot to him as well. He would make that his chief priority soon enough.

# CHAPTER 9

# THE END OF A SPECTACULAR SUMMER

The summer of 1995 was strikingly similar to that same stretch of time in 1993. Wimbledon was colossally important to Sampras and always the one he wanted more than any other. Coming down from that emotional mountaintop was inevitable. He put so much into winning at the All England Club—and sacrificed to such a large extent in pursuit of this overriding goal—that it took a while to rekindle his inner drive and reignite his game.

In his first tournament after Wimbledon, he got to the final of the Masters 1000 final in Montreal. Sampras played well enough in the title round, taking the first set before bowing against Agassi. In Cincinnati, he was beaten by Stich in the quarterfinals and at Indianapolis he was ousted in the semifinals by Bernd Karbacher of Germany, the world No. 27.

Some of his boosters might have been worried that he did not win a hard court tournament leading up to the U.S. Open at Flushing Meadows and some may have been concerned that he lost a few winnable matches. But not Pete Sampras. He had played 12 matches in those three tournaments and that was more than enough to be prepared for the last major of the season. He was not losing conviction. The notion was to bring out his best in New York when it mattered the most.

He started his campaign for the U.S. Open title against a Brazilian left-hander named Fernando Meligini, who reached the top 25 in the world four years later when he made it to the semifinals at Roland Garros, as well as having a good win over Sampras on the clay in Rome. On the hard courts at Flushing Meadows, however, he was no match for the American. Sampras took apart the 54th-ranked Meligini 6-0, 6-3, 6-4. That victory put him into the second round against Jaime Yzaga, who had taken two five set matches from him at the Open—in the American's 1988 debut and again in 1994.

But this time around, Sampras was more than ready for the Peruvian, overpowering him 6-1, 6-4, 6-3, serving 16 aces in the process and never losing his serve. He had launched his bid for a third U.S. Open title with two confident performances. But his next assignment would be a tense meeting against an 18-year-old Australian who already had one of the game's biggest serves, not to mention a potent ground game and a readiness to approach the net.

Mark Philippoussis was a burly Australian who faced Sampras in an afternoon weekend clash on Louis Armstrong Stadium. Sampras had never played the 6-foot 4-inch, 200 pound Philippoussis before. It turned into an uncomfortable encounter because the Australian was going for broke, serving almost recklessly at times and playing fearlessly. He took the first set in a tie-break and then made a concerted effort to win the second, climbing from 1-4 to 4-4. When Philippoussis served to stay in the set at 5-6, he had a game point to reach a tie-break, missing a forehand inside-in attempt for a winner.

A dipping down-the-line backhand pass from Sampras caused Philippoussis to miss a difficult forehand volley on the stretch, giving the American a set point. He sealed it with a solid forehand return off a first serve, putting just enough pressure on the Australian. Philippoussis netted a forehand. The set belonged to a relieved Sampras 7-5.

Seemingly, the 24-year-old American had scampered out of danger to level ground at one set all. He proceeded to open up a 4-0, 40-0 lead in the third set. Sampras double faulted on the next point, double faulted again at 40-30 and served a third double to lose his serve. Rarely did he unravel like that with a big lead. Philippoussis held on in the sixth game and then, shockingly, Sampras served three more double faults in the seventh game to lose his serve again, this time at love. He now had served 13 double faults in the match.

Back into hazardous territory was Sampras. Philippoussis struggled but held on for 4-4. Both men held easily to make it 5-5. But by now the American had rediscovered his service rhythm. He served two aces in establishing a 6-5 lead. He was absolutely determined to gain a break and avoid the uncertainty of another tie-break. He followed a forehand return in and then put away a forehand volley: 0-15. An elegant, dipping backhand pass opened up the court for a forehand down-the-line passing shot winner: 0-30. Next, Sampras chip-charged off the backhand return, coming in down the middle, dispatching a forehand volley into an open space: 0-40.

Philippoussis was down triple set point. He saved one by provoking an errant backhand pass from Sampras but, on the second, Sampras rolled another backhand pass at his opponent's feet. Philippoussis was trapped, netting a half volley off the backhand. Sampras had managed to win that complicated set 7-5 with his mental toughness, moving out in front two sets to one despite squandering the 4-0, 40-0 lead.

The fourth set was straightforward. Sampras conceded only two points in his first three service games and then broke for a 4-2 lead. Down 0-40 in the seventh game, he collected five consecutive points, closing that game with his 26th ace. Two games later, serving for the match, Sampras held at love, completing the job with his 27th and 28th aces. Sampras had prevailed 6-7 (5), 7-5, 7-5, 6-3, but candidly told the media afterwards, "That was a dangerous match."

Recollecting that 1995 duel, Sampras said in 2018, "I was a little uncomfortable playing someone for the first time, a little on edge playing Mark. He can put you on your heels. That was a strange match and I was probably careless, but he was similar to me and I didn't like playing guys that play like me. It was a bizarre and ugly match. It wasn't pretty."

Toughened by the unexpectedly close encounter, Sampras found himself up against his old buddy Todd Martin in the round of 16. After capturing the first set in a tie-break over his 6-foot, 6-inch adversary on a windy evening, Sampras pulled away 7-6 (3), 6-3, 6-4 without losing his serve in the three sets, winning 56 of 61 first serve points. That solid win took him into the quarterfinals against Byron Black of Zimbabwe, an outstanding doubles player who came from an accomplished tennis family. His younger brother, Wayne, reached the world's top ten in doubles. His younger sister, Cara, won the French Open mixed doubles in 2002 and the Wimbledon mixed title with Wayne in 2004. Moreover, she won ten majors altogether in doubles, including five at Wimbledon.

Byron Black did not fare quite as well as his two siblings, but he did win the 1994 French Open with Jonathan Stark of the United States. He simply did not have enough firepower to seriously threaten Sampras in their 1995 U.S. Open quarterfinal. To be sure, Black had upended the powerful Swede Thomas Enqvist and No. 8 seed Michael Stich to reach the quarters, but against Sampras he was outclassed.

Sampras sprinted to 5-2 before Black took the first set into a tie-break. Once Sampras connected immaculately with a running forehand passing shot to seal the tie-break seven points to three, there was no stopping him. From 2-2 in the second set, he won 10 of the last 12 games. He served 22 aces and did not ask any more from himself inspirationally than was necessary, recognizing that he had a big weekend ahead against two of his premier rivals.

In the semifinals, Sampras opened the "Super Saturday" program against Courier, a revitalized figure during this Open. He was seeded No. 14, which seemed far too low for a player of his stature, yet his results that year had not been up to the level he wanted. Nevertheless, he crushed the No. 3 seed Muster and defeated No. 5 Chang in three tight sets to earn his appointment against Sampras. Courier was back in the groove from the baseline and was looking very much like his old self.

This was a high quality contest from beginning to end. As Sampras recalled, "I remember we both played quite well that day. We started at 11 am. I always liked playing Jim and practiced with him so many times. I was comfortable with his game and kind of loved the matchup. I could get in on him and attack his backhand. I always had good results against Jim and that match at the Open was hard fought. He was playing well at the time. But I was getting my game going. It was just a good, clean match from both of us. I remember when we started off there wasn't much energy in the place, but by the time we finished there was very good energy as the stadium filled up."

The Sampras assessment is accurate. Up until 4-4 in the opening set, with the crowd steadily filing into Louis Armstrong Stadium, both men were holding with ease. Sampras dropped only five points on serve in that span while Courier lost only two points out of 18 on his delivery. Sampras, of course, was serve-volleying forcefully on his first delivery and picking his spots on the second. He was smothering Courier with the attacking game. But Courier was retaliating with his own brand of persuasive hard-court tennis, serving as big as he could and backing it up with his signature shot—the inside-out forehand. He could hit so hard off that side that it was difficult for opponents to find his much more vulnerable two-handed backhand. Lendl had brought that shot into vogue across the eighties but Courier had taken the inside-out forehand to a new level in the nineties with his singular potency.

The Courier forehand was the primary reason this U.S. Open semifinal was so closely contested. But it was late in sets that Sampras so frequently raised his intensity, found his full focus and ensured that his game soared to another level. That mentality was the difference against an unwavering Courier.

Down 30-40 on his serve in the ninth game, Sampras sent a first serve to the Courier backhand and followed it in, punching a forehand first volley crosscourt. He anticipated the passing shot, closing off the net for a forehand volley winner. Courier garnered a second break point but Sampras delivered a kick serve high to the Courier backhand and the return was long. Sampras followed with an ace and then punched a firm first volley down the line to provoke a forehand pass into the net tape from his opponent.

Sampras had saved two break points and took a 5-4 lead, but Courier held at 15 for 5-5 with a searing forehand winner down the line. Sampras double faulted twice on his way to a 30-30 deadlock in the eleventh game, but served an ace out wide for 40-30 and then tested Courier with the second-serve kicker up high to the backhand. Courier netted the return. 6-5 for Sampras.

Courier was serving for the second time to stay in the set. He advanced to 30-15 but Sampras approached to the Courier backhand, drawing an errant passing shot for 30-30. Sampras then went backhand to backhand with his opponent and it was Courier who blinked, driving a two-hander wide. That gave Sampras a set point with Courier serving at 30-40. Sampras drove a flat forehand down the line that clipped the net cord and fell over. That fortunate winner could not have come at a better time. Set to Sampras 7-5.

Sampras found some excellent serving rhythm in the second set. In gaining a 4-3 lead, he released ten aces and won 16 of 20 points on his delivery. But Courier was not backing off. His forehand was flying off his racket with stunning speed and precision. He held on for 4-4 in a deuce game with an ace. Sampras served at 30-30 in the ninth game and got his first serve in. But, surprisingly, he stayed back. That move backfired. Courier took control, cracked an inside-out forehand fiercely and set up a winner. On break point, Courier looped a backhand return down the line into the Sampras strength, but it worked. Sampras drove a forehand down the line into the net.

Having achieved his first service break of the match, Courier exploited it to the hilt. He was pushed to deuce again on his serve but closed out the set when Sampras blocked a forehand return long. Courier prevailed 6-4. It was one set all.

Now, on this hot day in New York, Courier had to like the fact that he had made certain this would be at least a four-set contest. That was to his benefit. Courier was supremely fit, a warrior through and through and a player who prided himself on his penchant to wear down opponents with his physicality and his almost tangible will to win.

Yet Sampras was an indefatigable fighter who knew how to battle his way fearlessly out of the trenches. He would have much preferred to win that second set from Courier and march inexorably toward a straight-set triumph. But when asked to define who he was as a competitor at consequential moments, Sampras would almost always meet that challenge.

At 2-2 in the third set, Sampras found himself in one of those predicaments. Courier connected impeccably with a passing-shot winner, Sampras double faulted and then Courier drilled a crosscourt forehand return for another winner. Sampras was down 0-40, behind triple break point. He sorely wanted to avoid going down a break here after losing the second set. Courier would have been bursting with energy, confidence and inspiration.

Sampras maintained his serenity. He serve-volleyed behind a heavy kicker, closing in with conviction for a backhand first-volley winner. He then went wide in the deuce court with a slice serve and Courier could hardly touch it. After missing his first serve at 30-40, Sampras found the opening to attack off the forehand, punching a backhand volley down the line to the Courier forehand. Sampras was extraordinarily alert now, spinning to make an acrobatic high backhand volley winner for deuce. An ace out wide gave Sampras game point and a serve-volley into Courier's body forced his fellow American into a netted forehand return. Five straight points for Sampras from triple break point down had taken him to 3-2. It was the single most important game of the match. Sampras had played percentage tennis to hold on to his serve. It was soundness, intelligence, competitive stability and calculation that took him where he wanted to go.

Courier then had to demonstrate his composure in a tight corner, saving a break point in the sixth game when Sampras missed a running forehand. The four-time major champion held on steadfastly for 3-3. Both men held easily through the next three games, but Courier then had to serve to stay in the set at 4-5. He led 30-0 but missed one shot off each flank. At 30-30, Sampras went for his favorite running forehand, driving that shot from well behind the baseline with trademark velocity. His shot landed inside the Courier service line and not far inside the sideline for an eye-popping winner. The buzz among the audience was unmistakable. Their applause was unrestrained. They fully appreciated Sampras's speed, power, elegance and athleticism.

It was set point for Sampras. Having just made his signature shot as he so often did when the stakes were highest and the odds appeared to be slim, Sampras now opted to go with a heavily-looped topspin backhand crosscourt. He was daring Courier to make his favorite inside-out forehand off a high and awkward ball. Courier's shot landed wide. He stared at the linesman incredulously, not believing that he could have missed that shot. But the call was correct. The television replay on CBS confirmed that irrefutably.

Sampras had regained the upper hand, taking the third set 6-4 to lead two sets to one. With the advantage of serving first in the fourth set, Sampras was behind 15-30 but he emphatically put away one of his leaping overheads that always went over well with the crowds. He soon held on for 1-0. Sampras had a break point in the second game but Courier took it away with a backhand crosscourt winner, holding for 1-1. Courier was not going away. He fashioned a 15-40 lead on the Sampras serve in the third game but missed a backhand return and then was aced down the T on a second serve by a resolute adversary. Sampras had battled back to deuce but Courier garnered a third break point. Sampras stayed with the tried and true, kicking another second serve to the Courier backhand to elicit a return mistake.

Sampras held on for 2-1. With Courier serving at 2-3, Sampras had two more break points but he could not convert as the spirited Courier held on for 3-3. Both players were unstoppable on serve over the next five games. Sampras won 12 of 13 points on his serve while Courier took 8 of 11 on his. But when Sampras held at love for 6-5 with his 25th and 26th aces of the day, Courier headed to the changeover knowing full well he would be serving to stay in the match for the second time.

This was when Sampras fans sensed he was going to bear down inordinately hard and go after a break at full force. He had done just that in the first set and the philosophy now was no different. Sampras had an uncanny knack for breaking at this precise juncture in a set. He was one of the great tie-break players in the history of tennis and trusted himself invariably in those sequences. His career record in these sequences was 328-194 (62.8%) and only four players (Federer, Arthur Ashe, Djokovic and the left-handed Ecuadorian Andres Gomez) had posted higher winning percentages in the pressure cooker of tiebreakers as the 2019 season concluded. But when he had a chance to take care of business and succeed sooner, that is precisely what Sampras did.

With Courier serving at 5-6, 15-15, Sampras sent a heavy topspin backhand crosscourt to the Courier backhand, getting that shot up high to the two-hander of his opponent. Courier could not handle it: 15-30. Sampras sent another tantalizing backhand topspin return down the middle and Courier wanted to step in and blast it. But he pulled a forehand wide: 15-40. Sampras was right where he wanted to be, at double match point. Courier came forward but Sampras caught him in his tracks with a low backhand passing shot down the line. Courier uncomfortably half-volleyed crosscourt off the forehand, directly into the famed Sampras forehand. Sampras saw his opening, sending the passing shot down the line for a match-concluding winner.

Sampras had beaten Courier 7-5, 4-6, 6-4, 7-5 in one of the best played matches in their long rivalry. All four sets had been closely contested. But, as so often was the case over the course of his career, Sampras was the better player on the biggest points. He habitually lifted his game and found some magic when he needed it the most. This was not accidental; it was a striking and recurring chord in the music of his many sterling performances at the tail end of majors. Modest to his core, Sampras said in 2019, "I ended up squeaking that one out against Jim."

And so he had booked his appointment for the final. Later on that Saturday afternoon, Agassi and Becker would meet in a contentious semifinal, reprising their duel in the same round at Wimbledon. After that victory, Becker had made some disparaging comments about Agassi that had not gone over well with the American when he read the remarks later. Their meeting this time turned into a grudge match, with Agassi upending the German in four sets.

Interestingly, Sampras had been asked after his win over Courier on CBS television for his prediction on the Agassi-Becker match. Normally, someone in his shoes would simply praise both opponents for diplomatic reasons without projecting who would win, but Sampras was forthcoming. He freely projected an Agassi victory. Sampras recalled, "I just felt it was a tough matchup for Boris and Andre was the best player in the world at that time. I just figured he was going to roll into the final."

Sampras added, "By '95 I had been in quite a few of these finals [this was his ninth major final and he was chasing a seventh title]. With my experience I felt pretty good going into that final with Andre. I knew the routine with the 4 pm start and when to eat, when to practice. So it wasn't anything special I did that day. It was just straightforward preparation, just thinking about what I was trying to do in that match, trying to dictate play. I was talking to Paul Annacone before I went out there about a good game plan. I went into the match obviously nervous but prepared and calm. Andre is a tough matchup for me if I am not playing well."

Pete Sampras rips a backhand at the 1995 U.S. Open

Agassi had captured four tournaments in a row and 26 consecutive matches across the hard court summer. He had been unbeatable on that surface. Brad Gilbert—an estimable player in his own right who had peaked at No. 4 in the world in 1990 after finishing two seasons among the top ten—had started coaching Agassi in 1994. At the end of that summer, the unseeded Agassi had captured his first U.S. Open.

In a 2019 interview for this book, Gilbert recalled Agassi's golden summer of 1995 and the path to the U.S. Open final. He said, "Andre had an unbelievable summer but it was almost like, 'Did he play a little too much?' He was thinking about not playing New Haven—which was his last tournament before the Open—but he ended up playing it and winning it. Then he had a five-setter early at the Open with Alex Corretja and a tough four setter with Petr Korda and then he had a four-setter with Becker in the semis. So I remember the morning of the final against Pete, we went out to hit and Andre was a little bit tired. He did not quite have the spark he did earlier in the summer, but I still felt like he was on one of those rolls where he couldn't lose. But you knew at that point if Pete had one of those days, maybe he was the only guy who could beat Andre. And I could see early on that Pete was a different player than when he played Andre in the finals in Canada a month earlier."

Annacone recalled how Sampras felt as he headed into one of the most important matches of his career. He said, "I remember talking to Pete and saying, 'Okay, what is the best way to bring this to him?' And he said to me, 'This is going to be fun. Andre has played great all summer and I like how I am playing here. It is always a great matchup and I know what I have got to do to be successful.' I am paraphrasing here but he said something like 'Andre hasn't faced a ton of adversity this summer. I want to see if I can really push him and I know I can. With my serve and my athleticism I am the one guy he will struggle against in big moments. This is going to be great.' And Pete wasn't throwing cliché's around. He really believed what he was saying."

Sampras and Agassi had an idyllic day for their September 10, 1995 showdown, a duel contested on the five-year anniversary of their first final-round meeting at the Open. The skies were a bright azure blue, there was a healthy breeze and the temperature was comfortably in the seventies. They could not have asked for more. Sampras got his teeth into the contest swiftly. He did not miss a first serve in the opening game and volleyed crisply, holding at 15 to set a certain tone right off the bat. Agassi answered by playing his service game impressively, passing Sampras cleanly with a crosscourt backhand and rifling a forehand crosscourt winner. He held at love for 1-1.

The first opening for either player came at 2-2, when Sampras found himself down 30-40 after a double fault. He met that moment ably, serving down the T at 123 mph and forcing Agassi to net a stretch forehand return. He then pulled Agassi off the court with a wide serve in the deuce court to set up a backhand first-volley winner. Agassi netted a forehand passing shot on the next point. From break point down, Sampras was all power, precision and purpose, holding on for 3-2.

Remarkably, Agassi won 16 of 18 points on his serve up until 4-4, but now the set was getting more serious. Although Sampras missed four of six first serves in the ninth game, he held at 30, backing up his second serve skillfully from the backcourt as he stuck with his policy in those days of staying back on the second serve frequently while always going in behind the first delivery.

Agassi was in the unenviable position of serving at 4-5, realizing that Sampras was inevitably going to apply some scoreboard pressure, knowing that the outcome of this opening set would be critical—especially for him. Sampras advanced to 30-40 but Agassi saved a set point there when his adversary netted a forehand chipped return off a first serve. But Agassi administered a self-inflicted wound on the following point with a bungled forehand swing volley.

Sampras had arrived at set point for the second time. This one he wanted badly, but Agassi also fully understood the magnitude of the moment. The fans in Louis Armstrong Stadium were enthralled as the two combatants went full throttle in not only the best backcourt exchange of this match but also the finest rally of their careers in a match as consequential as this. It was a beauty and the one-upmanship was extraordinary. They went corner to corner, side to side, pace versus pace. On the 20th stroke, Sampras pounded a forehand crosscourt that took Agassi well off the court. Agassi went down the line to the Sampras backhand, realizing he could not recover. Sampras set up impeccably with his excellent racket preparation and drove his topspin backhand crosscourt at a safely high trajectory. His point-concluding shot landed in an open court for a dazzling winner. The set belonged to Sampras 6-4. As the crowd showered both players with a rousing round of applause and many stood on their feet, Sampras pumped his fist in recognition of a signature moment.

"I remember that point as if it was yesterday," he said in 2019. "We were feeling each other out and trying to get used to the conditions with the wind and the balls and the court. It just all came down to that big set point and there was a sense of urgency. I win this point and it changes the whole dynamic of the match. So we got into this grinding rally and all of a sudden I was moving him and he was moving me. We were going back and forth and I think me being a better mover than Andre helped me in that situation. I hit a couple of big running forehands and it ended when I hit the backhand winner. It was a magical moment for me. The crowd got very into it and it set the tone for the match."

Sampras paused for a moment to collect his thoughts and then added, "We both knew that point was huge because I got a set lead and when I get a lead I get better. It broke his back a little bit and I felt as the second set went on I wanted to keep it going. Andre was not going away, but I felt this was mine to win."

Annacone also carried that point around in the eye of his mind happily across the years. He said, "It is a huge generalization but that point was Andre's forte and not Pete's. This was about will and moving your opponent side to side and punishing them. But Pete with his sheer will was like, 'No, I am Pete Sampras and I am going to win this.' So he ends up hitting that backhand winner and it really looked like Andre's legs were done. You could see he couldn't even go after that ball. And to me that was Pete saying in essence, 'Let's see how Andre deals with adversity now that I have got my nose out in front.'"

Agassi wasn't surrendering by any means. He gave himself a break point opportunity in the first game of the second set. Agassi hit deep down the middle and Sampras was well behind the baseline. But that did not stop him from walloping an inside-in forehand cleanly for a crucial winner. He took the next point and then closed out that hold with an ace down the T. The next game went to deuce twice but Agassi was feeling the force of Sampras's game and the size of his opponent's big-match reputation. At break point down, he missed another swing volley. Sampras was up a set and a break, leading 2-0 in the second.

He was rolling now. Sampras advanced rapidly to 3-0, holding at 15 with an ace. He served three consecutive aces and held at love for 4-1 and released two more aces in holding at 15 for 5-2, finishing off that game with an excellent forehand approach down the line setting up a high backhand-volley winner down the line.

Two games later, Sampras had a set point at 5-3, 40-30. Agassi saved it adeptly with one of his trademark rolled forehand passing shots crosscourt. A diving Sampras could not make the volley. Sampras earned a second set point but Agassi retreated quickly for an overhead and put it away with gusto. When Sampras pulled a forehand wide, Agassi went to break point, an honorable effort on his part. But at this critical moment, Sampras was his typically unyielding self. He unleashed a 125-mph first serve into Agassi's body on the backhand side and the game's foremost returner sent his return wide down the line.

Sampras was in full pursuit of this critical hold. A slice serve wide in the deuce court lured Agassi into an errant return, giving Sampras a third set point. He missed his first serve but then aced Agassi down the T on a second serve. The set went to an inspired Sampras 6-3. He was ahead two sets to love.

Early in the third set, Sampras seemed likely to close out the account in straight sets. He broke for a 2-1 lead. But in the fourth game, the attacking American double faulted consecutively to trail 15-30. Agassi opportunistically took the next two points to break for the first time and rally for 2-2. He held at 15 for 3-2. Those two games significantly altered Agassi's state of mind. Both players held serve comfortably from there until Sampras served to stay in the set at 4-5.

He double faulted to fall behind 30-40, and then saved a set point. But an obstinate Agassi garnered a second set point and on this one he was magnificent. Sampras served-and-volleyed but the return was low. Sampras was unable to do much with the first volley and Agassi stepped in and blasted a forehand passing shot down-the-line winner. The top seed had taken the set 6-4, and he was back in the match.

Sampras was not worried. As he recollected, "Andre is a tough guy to hold serve against and I did a good job the first couple of sets, but it's hard to keep it up. If you lose your momentum on your serve and miss a few, you are hitting second serves and getting into these baseline points. It was hard for me to keep up that pace and he kept hanging around and returning well. He did not wear me down, but he broke me a few times. That was not devastating to me. I was concerned, but I still had a two-sets-to-one lead. I thought, 'Let's get back at it in the fourth.' It is just hard to maintain that level against him with the serve-and-volley tennis that I was playing. He is a difficult person to close out. He got into it and the crowd got behind him. They wanted to see more tennis. And here we were in a dogfight."

Indeed they were. In the opening game of the fourth set, though, Sampras had an opening at break point. Agassi's half volley sat up for Sampras, who lined up a forehand inside-in passing shot. Agassi was totally stranded but Sampras did not have quite the margin for error he needed. His shot went into the net tape. Agassi held on gamely, but Sampras's serving in this set was the best he would release all match long. He held twice at 30 on his way to 2-2. And then he had the audience gasping at a gem of his own making. He started with an ace down the T. Then another ace down the T. Next an ace out wide. And finally another ace down the T, his 20th of the match. With four swings of the racket and a stunning love hold, Sampras was locked at 3-3 in the fourth with his biggest rival.

"Serving is interesting," said Sampras in 2019. "Sometimes you are a little tired but it can help your serve a little bit in some ways. It relaxes your arm and it relaxes you. If you are too amped up, you can lose your rhythm. I remember in that fourth set, I found a rhythm. And the better I am serving, the more he feels under pressure. I think with those four aces in a row it was kind of like, 'I am not going anywhere.'"

Neither was Agassi. He kept holding to lead 5-4, making Sampras serve to stay in the fourth set. On the first point of that tenth game, Sampras stayed back on his second serve but came forward dynamically behind a forehand down-the-line approach, closed in tight on the net and put away a forehand volley crosscourt off Agassi's backhand pass. He held at 15 with his 22nd ace. It was 5-5.

Now Sampras displayed his late-set big-point propensity again when it would mean the most. If he did not break here, a tie-break would decide the fourth set. Sampras would have surely been the favorite in that sequence with his serve. But with a few timely and boldly-struck returns, Agassi might have forced a fifth set. A tie-break came down to a form of high stakes poker. Sampras figured it was time to go full force after a service break, as if to underline his superiority. He never shied away from these situations.

On the first point of the eleventh game, he invented a seemingly impossible acute angle crosscourt for his topspin backhand, with his shot landing near the sideline and just in front of the service line. Agassi was pulled way off the court, and his crosscourt response was just where Sampras wanted it. Sampras approached down the line with a backhand chip and Agassi's running forehand topspin lob missed by a wide margin. Sampras prevailed in a 15-stroke rally to reach 0-30 and then a flustered Agassi double faulted.

That mistake put Agassi behind 0-40 but he served an ace and hit another unanswerable first serve. Back to 30-40 was the top seed. Sampras looped his second-serve return safely, not that deep but at a high trajectory. Agassi thought he had an opening to step around for a forehand, but it was a tougher shot than he realized. Pressing, he drove it long. Sampras had the break for 6-5. No one was more reliable in that situation. He relished the chance to serve out a match. Not only was he the best server of his own era, but arguably the finest of all time. He opened the twelfth game with his 23rd ace of the day, going down the T with Agassi leaning the other way. On the next point, he looked in a vulnerable position up at the net as Agassi ripped a passing shot mightily. But Sampras made a startling forehand stab volley that left Agassi frozen. Agassi then missed a forehand down-the-line return off a second serve, sending that shot wide. Sampras fittingly ended the match with his 24th ace and his tenth of the set for a love hold, going down the T, completing a well-deserved 6-4, 6-3, 4-6, 7-5 victory.

Sampras responded to that major triumph the way he would other standout occasions throughout his career, raising his arms distinctly but not arrogantly, sincerely acknowledging the crowd, basking in the glow of victory with an air of originality. It was a ritual of sorts and his way of letting observers everywhere know how much he cared about his craft and what it took to succeed on the premier stages. But by no means was Sampras showing off after these landmark triumphs. He was simply reaching out quietly to the audience.

Mary Carillo was in the CBS booth for that Open final and she always looked forward to the way Sampras celebrated his victories. She recalled in 2019, "He would raise his arms in triumph with both coming up at the same time. That always seemed very Greek to me. He was like a Greek God and I am sure he didn't mean it to look like that, but I just saw it that way. It was an iconic gesture and unconscious, which makes it even better. It was a triumphal look, a statement to raise your arms like that and hold it there and smile. He didn't have to scream and blow kisses. He just had this beautiful coda to some remarkable performance that he had just thrown down. Oh my God, I just loved that."

Michael Chang felt similarly about Sampras's unabashed joy in winning a major. He said, "If you ever looked at the way in which he wins a Slam, at the end of championship point if you look at his face, you can see his appreciation in knowing what he has accomplished. People sometimes did not see that about Pete. They see maybe not as much flamboyance as Andre, but at the end of the day, Pete was all business. And from a player's perspective you had to admire what he was doing."

Told how much Carillo and Chang admired his post-match routine at the majors, Sampras said, "I always remember Borg going down to his knees at Wimbledon. For me, I just felt like putting my arms in the air. But I was always sensitive about knowing how to win and how it comes across. I never wanted it to look at it as being wonderful or 'look how great I am.' I see the same thing in my two kids now who are both understated, which they got from me. I look at the players today and see Rafa putting his arms in the air and going down to the ground. He is a grinder and that is who he is. He is great. I love that in him. But I was a little more dialed back. I realize in this day and age people want to see a Nadal expressing himself so openly, but I just didn't fit that bill. I just felt good about trying to achieve great things and expressing gratitude for people who helped me. I look back at it now and I certainly could have been more open, but it was who I was. I just downplayed everything and didn't want to make a fuss about what I was doing."

That was the essential Pete Sampras—unpretentious, not carried away with his fame or his stature, refusing to glorify himself, entirely grounded. Sampras was delighted to have won such a monumentally important match at the last Grand Slam championship of 1995, overcoming a uniquely revered rival in a battle of renowned Americans at the U.S. Open. He had made amends for his loss to Agassi in the Australian Open final at the start of the year and for falling short against his fellow American earlier in the summer in Canada. He had been beaten in three of his previous four meetings against Agassi. But this was the most significant match they would play in all of 1995 and probably their most crucial contest ever. It was an incomparably satisfying win for Sampras because it was fundamentally a battle to determine who would be the best player in the world for the year. The crucial win reinforced his inner belief that he could bring out his best when it mattered the most. It was not the best tennis match he ever played—although he gave an extraordinary performance—but it was surely right up there among his most important triumphs. Just as he had done at Wimbledon earlier in the summer, Sampras had raised his game decidedly at the end of another major, this time in New York. He had concluded summer with one of the best big-match performances of his career.

For Agassi, the setback had long lasting implications. After dominating the game during the summer—winning those 26 consecutive matches and not losing a match on hard courts over that span—he lost the biggest one he played on the premier stage in American tennis with the last major of the season on the line in New York as the sports world watched with heightened interest. Agassi was shattered about the outcome and devastated that he had lost the most momentous contest he would ever play against Pete Sampras.

He would finish that year at No. 2 in the world, but in 1996, despite winning a gold medal by taking the singles title at the Olympic Games in Atlanta and reaching two semifinals at the majors, he dropped to No. 8. By the fall of 1997, he slipped all the way down to No. 141 and played a couple of Challenger tournaments as a means to work his way back up to where he belonged.

That prolonged slump and identity crisis of sorts could largely be attributed to the bruising defeat he suffered against Sampras in New York at the 1995 Open. He would say that day he was exhausted by his long campaign across the summer and depleted by playing so many matches on the hard courts.

Agassi told the media afterwards, "I just think it has been a long summer. I had a couple of days off before I played Boris in the semis and that helped me a lot. I mean, in the first set, that long set point we had, it was like, I mean, I felt my legs... It was way too early in the match to be feeling the way I was feeling. When you play the summer tournaments, that is the price sometimes to pay when you win a lot of matches. I guess

I was lacking a little strength, a little pep in my step [today].... I didn't quite have that little extra that I know I needed."

Gilbert—who later worked with both Andy Roddick and Andy Murray and established himself as one of the premier coaches in professional tennis—remembered in 2019, "Andre got a second wind and a second life and won the third in that '95 final at the Open. I had the feeling in the fourth set that he was going to turn this thing around and go to five and make it a physical battle. I had a feeling he was going to come back and win that match. When you are on a big winning streak like Andre's, you always find a way to win. You might say that Pete had to play the absolute best tennis of his career in those situations and he did. He knew that if he didn't have a day like that when Andre was near his best [it would not be enough]. Pete had this ability to rise above everything with this sense of calmness about him. And Andre, for as many times as he played him, he just didn't have a good enough beat and read on Pete's serve. That serve was unbelievable. He didn't telegraph nothing."

Sampras was asked how he rates that appointment with Agassi among the most important matches he ever played. Is it right up there?

"Yes," he responded. "I think of my first time winning Wimbledon [1993] and that [1995] U.S. Open. Every major is special but because of the rivalry with Andre and because of what we were doing at the time, it just transcended the game. I remember Arnold Schwarzenegger was there and John F. Kennedy, Jr. When you are in it and playing, you don't think about that, but looking back on it now it was one of those moments when you had the perfect storm. It was fun to be a part of it."

Examining the way he regrouped in the fourth set and closed out that final, Sampras said, "With my style of play things can change pretty quickly. We went from 5-5 in the fourth set to, boom, ten minutes later I am holding the trophy. It was such a big, big match. The aftermath was really interesting in how it affected him. Little did I know that with the winning streak and him losing to me that it would affect him as much as it did. It really took him a few years to recover. Mentally it was devastating for Andre because he did beat me over the summer, but then for the biggest match in the world, the one that everyone remembers and what we play for, he didn't quite get there. I think that popped his balloon and shattered him for quite a while. With me, it just got me going even more as far as my confidence. I turned it on when I had to. Andre was the best player in the world at the time we met at the Open, so to beat him on that stage with both of us being Americans was definitely one of the best highlights of my career."

Looking at that match in the context of his illustrious rivalry with his fellow American, Sampras again said in 2019, "That 1995 Open final was a pivotal point for both of us. It really shook him for the next year or so. He felt he was playing really well but he was thinking, 'When Pete is playing well I can't beat him.' I think there was a little bit of that feeling, like 'Damn, he got me again in a big match. I might beat him in Montreal but in the U.S. Open he finds a way to win.' Deep down, I think that really bothered him."

That was surely the case. Agassi offered his share of alibis after losses to Sampras on auspicious occasions. He would lose four of his five major final-round meetings with Sampras over the course of their careers. The prevailing view among many authorities was that he never quite came to terms with the fundamental fact that Sampras was better than he was, especially when it counted the most.

Reflecting on his rivalry with Agassi, Sampras said, "I always respected him and he was the same way with me. Maybe we are not going to play golf together or have dinner, but there is nothing wrong with that. I could call him tomorrow on the phone and we would have a fine conversation, but we will always be different people. There is just a bit of oil and water with us."

Sampras expanded, "Jim Courier and I were at one time close and it was noticeable when we went our separate ways when we were competing in really big matches, but Andre and I were never that close. It took time for our relationship to evolve. I did get to know him better through playing Davis Cup together like we did in '95. We were good. We got along well throughout our careers but he was more expressive than I was and he would put me on my heels even when I was practicing with him, grunting loud with a different energy than I was used to."

The Sampras-Agassi rivalry peaked in 95 with their battle for supremacy as the two best players in the world. Annacone vividly recalled that period and his recollections of the buildup to the U.S. Open final were particularly sharp. He said, "Andre had just been smashing everybody all summer and Pete at the Open basically said, 'Not so fast. This is the finals of the U.S. Open. I am not everybody.' It was amazing. Andre is such a great champion. He is so emotional and I always felt he was more susceptible to these peaks and valleys because he was an emotionally driven player with great heart, great empathy and a great kind of broad perspective. That is harder to manage as a pro tennis player. You have this expansive perspective yet you can still have the laser-like tunnel vision focus at the big moments. That is what Pete had without all the complexities of being Andre Agassi, which is this brand, this icon-philanthropist. Pete just loved the challenge of playing Andre and he was one of the few guys that could handle Andre's weaponry."

After he had completed a triumph over Agassi that would have such lasting ramifications for both players, Sampras was sitting on his court side chair, getting ready for the presentation ceremony. He saw the microphone that CBS had placed nearby, looked into the camera and spoke from the heart to Tim Gullikson. Gullikson was home and Sampras knew he was watching and wanted to reach out to him over the airwaves. He said, "That was for you, Timmy. I'm coming to Chicago and I am going to beat you at some golf in a couple of days. Thanks for your help, bud."

Remembering that poignant moment in a 2019 interview for this book, Sampras said, "Tim obviously wanted to be there. He was going through his brain treatments. I was just thinking about him and wanted to shout out to him. We had talked a bit before the match and he was still very much a part of my tennis at the time, but obviously things were getting serious for him. So I wanted to let him know I was thinking about him. It just came to me quickly to say that to him. It was not premeditated. The camera was right in my face so it was in the moment. I knew he was watching so I wanted to include him in this big win. It was just a very tough situation for him."

Sampras had good reason to be content. He had captured two majors in a row, ruling at the most prestigious tournaments in the game of tennis. He now had seven major titles in his growing collection. And he had demonstrated that peaking at the landmark events was more than ever his highest priority.

In the weeks following the Open, Sampras performed at a reasonably high level as the season came to a conclusion. He reached the final indoors at Lyon, losing to Wayne Ferreira, a burdensome rival from South Africa. Ferreira would add triumphs in his next three contests against Sampras to this one, improbably ousting the American four consecutive times. In Essen, Germany, Sampras was beaten by Muster. His finest tennis of that stretch was indoors at the Paris Masters 1000 event, defeating Courier and Becker back to back at the end to claim that crown. At the ATP World Tour Championships in Germany, he was beaten in the semifinals by Chang.

But there was one more monumental task ahead for the American, who finished a third year in a row as the No. 1 ranked player in the world. He travelled to Russia with the American team to represent his country in the Davis Cup Final on indoor clay at Moscow. On the opening day of that historic occasion, he met the Russian Andrei Chesnokov. Chesnokov was an accomplished clay-court player, a former French Open semifinalist and a backboard from the baseline.

Sampras dropped the first set, took the next two and was ahead 5-4 and 6-5 on serve in the fourth. But they went to a tie-break, which was locked at 5-5. Sampras was two points away from a triumph, but Chesnokov outperformed Sampras in a 24-stroke rally from the backcourt and then the American double faulted. The match proceeded to a fifth set and Sampras was behind, serving at 3-4 and fully understanding the gravity of his plight.

He promptly held at love, broke at love and then served for the match at 5-4. On his second match point in that tenth game of the fifth set, the two warriors fought it out in a 25-stroke rally. Sampras ended it with a flat forehand approach that left Chesnokov unable to respond. But as soon as he saw that the point and the match were over, knowing he had toughed-out a five-set win, Sampras collapsed with cramps on the court. Captain Tom Gullikson and the trainers carried him off the court and into the locker room.

Since Courier lost that day to Kafelnikov, the two teams were tied at 1-1, but Sampras volunteered to play the doubles the next day, joining Todd Martin for a straightforward victory over Kafelnikov and Andrei Olhovskiy. On the third and last day of the competition, Sampras crushed Kafelnikov in straight sets and the U.S. had won the coveted Davis Cup for the first time in five years.

It was one of Sampras's finest hours. At the end of a memorable year, he almost single-handedly led his country to victory on his least favorite surface. As Todd Martin recalled, "Watching Pete struggle but win a critical point the first day against Chesnokov was inspiring, exciting and fun. You are watching him grind out a match more than you have ever seen. Pete was not a grinder. And when he seized into a full cramp, part of it was, 'What just happened?' Pete was in great shape and it wasn't like we were playing in a sauna. It was indoors in Moscow. But he got into this full body cramp. Pete and I had played some doubles together and we won Queen's that year. We were good friends. I think his confidence was high with me on the court. He knew exactly what he was going to get as far as a teammate was concerned. And then he beat Yevgeny, who was one of the smarter players around and difficult to crack as far as putting him out of sorts. Pete just got better with his game and better physically as the weekend went on. And I think he was extra motivated against Yevgeny personally because most of us looked at Kafelnikov as a likely competitor for being the best player in the world. Pete wanted to move the ball forward for the team. That is what he did, and more."

Carillo was there in Moscow, calling the matches for ESPN. She said 23 years later, "The muddy clay was tricked out by the Russian Federation. Agassi was over there as a spectator, but he didn't want to play and he had let the team down. It was the end of the year and everyone was whipped. Chessie [Chesnekov] made you hit a million balls on clay and the place was going crazy when Pete played him on the first day. It could not have been a more uncomfortable environment for Pete and he really came through and then he came through again the last day to win it for the U.S. by beating Kafelnikov. And that was after winning the doubles with Todd Martin in between. That was one of the most remarkable achievements in his career."

Wimbledon. The U.S. Open. Davis Cup. It was a singularly impressive year for Sampras in many ways because of that trio of triumphs. He won five tournaments and 72 of 88 matches despite the turmoil in his personal life surrounding Gullikson's health. Sampras looked forward to a similarly productive 1996 campaign after securing six of the last 10 majors. He was unmistakably in the middle of his prime and many of his largest dreams had not yet been realized.

# CHAPTER 10

# A REWARDING TRIUMPH
# IN NEW YORK

Having such a short off season after his Davis Cup
exploits at the end of 1995 was an impediment to Sampras as
he went "Down Under" for the Australian Open at the start of
1996. He faced Philippoussis in the third round and this time
the imposing Australian carved out a 6-4, 7-6 (9), 7-6 (3) victory,
exploding with 29 aces and not losing his serve. Sampras was
broken only once in this battle of big servers but "The Scud" was
in an almost unconscious state playing for his fervent brigade
of boosters."

Putting that defeat behind him in short order, Sampras
won a couple of tournaments consecutively back in the U.S.,
trouncing Agassi 6-2, 6-3 in the final of San Jose, California,
handling Chang and Todd Martin back to back for the crown
in Memphis, Tennessee. He lost in the quarters at Indian Wells
and the semifinals at Miami, falling against Ivanisevic in the
latter.

But he soon took two more titles at Hong Kong and
Tokyo. He had secured four titles in the still young 1996 season
and was riding high, but soon Tim Gullikson passed away in
early May. Sampras was one of the pallbearers for his close

friend and coach. It was a devastating juncture in his life. Gullikson was only 44. Sampras had respected his highly-valued friend for much more than his coaching acumen. They had formed a friendship based on mutual respect, the same values, similar senses of humor and much common ground. And all through Gullikson's battle with brain cancer, Sampras had been more than attentive, making certain to stay in regular contact and visit whenever possible.

As Tom Gullikson said, "Pete was great about coming to see Tim. They had such a good relationship. Pete would stop by and see him once in a while and show his support and his love of Tim. They talked on the phone a lot. And Tim had talked a lot with Paul Annacone about how to help Pete out. It was a tough time for everybody. Tim fought the battle the best he could fight it and then he passed away in May of 1996."

The loss of Tim Gullikson left a sizable void in Sampras's life and his spirits were severely dampened in the weeks that followed. Leading up to the French Open, Sampras was not in his prime playing condition. And yet, somehow, with only two matches in the World Team Cup as clay-court preparation, Sampras celebrated his finest French Open ever, toppling a pair of two-time champions in Courier and Sergi Bruguera, as well as Todd Martin, on his way to the semifinals. All three of those wins were recorded in five sets, Sampras rallied spectacularly from two sets down against Courier.

But, on an oppressive afternoon with the temperature soaring into the mid-90s, Sampras wilted in the heat and lost to Kafelnikov, bowing in straight sets against a player who only beat him twice in 13 career head-to-head meetings. Kafelnikov would win the title two days later over Michael Stich. If Sampras had found the energy and wherewithal to beat Kafelnikov, it might have been a golden opportunity to win at Roland Garros, but he was simply not in the best of shape after mourning over Gullikson. Facing Stich, it would have been an atypical clay-court match for both competitors, with predominantly short points. Sampras would have stood a very good chance of succeeding.

"I was with him in Tampa before the French Open," said Annacone, "and he hadn't even been practicing. How he got through all those five setters I don't even know. But he just ran out of gas in the semifinals."

At Wimbledon, Sampras seemed on course to win a fourth title in succession but lost to the big serving Richard Krajicek of the Netherlands, the eventual champion. Krajicek unloaded 28 aces and won 91% of his first-serve points in a 7-5, 7-6 (3), 6-4 upset of the top seed. The quarterfinal match began under dreary skies and Sampras was unable to convert several break points in the opening set. Krajicek erupted at the end of the set with some timely and explosive passing shots. There was a long rain delay the first day and the third set was completed the following afternoon. Sampras did not have his best stuff but Krajicek—who finished with a 6-4 career head to head edge over Sampras and won four straight matches in their series starting with this skirmish—sparkled. "He served Pete off the court. That would happen only once in a while," said Annacone.

He had played some good tennis in the last two majors, but still Sampras was searching for his first major of the year at the U.S. Open. Over the summer, he won Indianapolis over Ivanisevic and was eager to peak in New York. He was still clearly the best player in the world, but Sampras sorely wanted to validate that status by winning one of the four majors. This would be his last chance.

As he mentioned in an interview for this book, "I had been having a good year but not at the majors. Going into the Australian I was tired after Davis Cup at the end of '95 and I lost to Philippoussis. The French Open was a good run and then I lost to Krajicek at Wimbledon. The Open was my last opportunity to win a major that year. I would reflect at the end of each year on how I did at the majors so I went into that Open a little stressed and concerned about not being as dominant. I was feeling my own pressure that I was putting on myself."

Sampras waltzed through the first round, defeating world No. 164 Jimmy Szymanski 6-2, 6-2, 6-1. But in the second round he was pushed to the hilt by world No. 47 Jiri Novak of the Czech Republic. Four years later, the 6'3" Novak surprised Sampras in a Davis Cup match at Los Angeles, but on this occasion Sampras came through 6-3, 1-6, 6-3, 4-6, 6-4. He saved a break point at 2-2 in the fifth set and navigated a victory from there, but it was a hard-fought battle that he did not easily survive.

Sharper in his next outing, Sampras removed Alexander Volkov 6-3, 6-4, 6-2 in the third round. It was the third time he had beaten the left-hander at the Open, all in straight sets. Next on his agenda was the daunting Philippoussis, the same player who had given him a scare the year before at the Open prior to knocking the American out of the Australian Open earlier in 1996. But in this showdown under the lights, Sampras was on heightened alert. Although he connected with only 52% of his first serves, he never faced a break point and returned exceptionally well off his backhand to romp 6-3, 6-4, 6-4.

The victory over Philippoussis sent Sampras into the quarterfinals against Alex Corretja, the wily Spaniard better known for his clay-court skills. On paper, it looked to many who had underestimated Corretja like a routine victory for the defending champion, but it turned into one of the most memorable matches of Sampras's illustrious career. Corretja was seemingly overmatched on hard courts against the heavy favorite, but he was as guileful a player as there was in the game and he had taken Agassi to five sets at the U.S. Open of 1995. Although he was ranked only No. 31 in the world, Corretja was a whole lot better than that. A few years later, he would be the runner-up to countryman Carlos Moya at the 1998 French Open and he would rally from two sets down to stop Moya in the final of the ATP World Tour Championships at the end of that memorable season. Corretja ended 1998 at No. 3 in the world and climbed to a career high at No. 2 early in 1999.

Sampras and Corretja took the court in the latter part of the afternoon. Sampras had misgauged the starting time of the match and had not fueled himself with enough food or fluids. He was pushed hard in the opening set and had to lift his game significantly at the end to salvage it. This was a draining late summer, New York afternoon when they started and it took Sampras a while to get going. Corretja, meanwhile, was strategically sound, in control from the baseline and determined to gradually grind his renowned adversary down.

At 5-4, Corretja served for the first set. The Spaniard had his first set point at 40-30 but Sampras went on the attack, punching a forehand volley deep to set up a backhand volley on the stretch into the open court. Corretja served an ace for a second set point but, once again, Sampras came forward, approaching deep to the backhand and then putting away a forehand volley. Sampras eventually broke back for 5-5.

The rallies were long and beneficial to the Spaniard. Sampras was clearly not playing this match on his terms. He was being forced to engage too often in taxing exchanges. John McEnroe joked in the USA Network commentary box, "This is Flushing Meadows, not Roland Garros."

That opening set was settled in a tie-break. In that sequence, the American poured in five of six first serves and did not lose a point on his delivery. At 6-5, he surprised Corretja with a heavy first-serve kicker that bounced extra high and gave Corretja no real play on the backhand return. Sampras succeeded seven points to five and led one set to love.

But, as afternoon morphed toward evening, the war of attrition took its toll on Sampras. He was winning some quick points on his first serve, going in behind it and volleying skillfully. Yet he was picking and choosing on the second serve and was sometimes too respectful of his opponent, frequently getting bogged down in debilitating rallies. At 5-6 in the second set, Sampras fought hard in a three deuce game and saved a couple of set points. On the third one, he came in down the line off the backhand. Sampras seemed certain to win the point. But the Spaniard specialized in counter-attacking and found spaces that did not appear to exist. He connected improbably with a dazzling forehand crosscourt passing shot that landed on the sideline. 7-5 for Corretja. One set all.

Sampras had lost an emotionally and physically-depleting set. There was less spring in his step. Corretja was making him play interminably. At 4-5 in the third set, the American steadfastly saved two set points on his own serve. But, two games later, serving to stay in the set for the second time at 5-6, fighting hard to reach a tie-break, Sampras was broken. At 30-30, his first volley behind the serve had no stick on it and Corretja passed him off the backhand cleanly. That put the American down set point. He served-and-volleyed and then retreated for a Corretja lob. Under normal circumstances, the point would have been over. His overhead was the best in the game and arguably the greatest in history. But Sampras was fatigued. His smash landed long. Corretja had taken a second straight 7-5 set, moving out in front two sets to one.

Early in the fourth, however, Sampras found renewed vigor. On break point in the third game, he came in on a topspin backhand crosscourt to the Corretja backhand, read the response, and elegantly angled away a forehand drop-volley winner. The rest of that set, he served magnificently, winning 16 of 20 points, holding at love the last two times and closing out that chapter with an ace down the T, his 19th of the match. The set belonged to Sampras 6-4.

Sampras had rallied to make it two sets all. But he was clearly weary, trying to conserve energy and cognizant that Corretja was feeling a lot more energetic than he was. Meanwhile, the Spaniard was serving surprisingly well himself and not giving the American many openings. In the fifth set, both men were holding comfortably most of the way through. Corretja backed up his serve staunchly, dropping only seven points in six games. Sampras was largely untouchable but he did struggle once at 2-3, holding on after two deuces. Otherwise, he conceded only four points in his remaining five service games.

Serving to stay in the match at 4-5, Sampras was three points from defeat at 15-15 but an excellent first serve drew an errant return. He followed with an ace and a well-executed backhand drop volley into an open court. At 5-6, Sampras held at love to make it into a tie-break.

Now drama flooded across Louis Armstrong Stadium and the fans showered Sampras with as unbridled a brand of support as he would ever experience at the championships of his country. They would play a pivotal role in pulling him through when his resources had dwindled dangerously low. He was relying now on his spirit, self-belief and willpower more than anything else to bring a bright ending to a long journey from the middle of the afternoon into the evening. Not normally a proponent of fifth set tie-breaks, Sampras was relieved that this match would end in one of those sequences. A drawn out fifth set might have been beyond his limits.

Serving at 1-1 in the tie-break, Sampras walked back near the fence and vomited. He was given a time violation warning before spinning his serve in weakly. He somehow won that point with a stinging forehand inside-in that provoked an error. Sampras was throwing every fiber of his being into all of the points, but in between he was slumped over his racket, searching for energy and inspiration, summoning whatever he had left emotionally into battling on.

The only strategy was to go for winners as soon as openings were available. He missed with a bold forehand for 2-2 but went to 3-2 with a forehand inside-in winner and then missed another daring forehand. As the players changed ends of the court at 3-3, the crowd was chanting, "Pete, Pete, Pete" imploring him to find a way to win, letting him know they fully sympathized with his plight. Their unabashed outpouring of affection was an immeasurable boost to Sampras. He promptly pounded a huge first serve down the T to lead 4-3 before Corretja made it 4-4.

The pattern continued. Sampras struck another flat forehand crosscourt winner, leaving Corretja sprawled on the court. But he was very unlucky on the next point. Corretja totally shanked a forehand return that landed in the corner. Corretja took that point by advancing to the net for a forehand volley winner. Sampras should have been ahead 6-4 with two match points but was instead locked at 5-5. He pressed forward and leaped for an overhead that was more like a high forehand volley, drawing a backhand passing shot wide.

It was 6-5 for Sampras and match point for the American. Corretja was serving. Sampras went for another forehand winner on the run but netted it. Then Corretja employed one of his heavy looping shots to set up a winner and now the Spaniard had a match point with Sampras serving at 6-7. His first serve had little on it but he found an avenue to the net and punched a low forehand volley crosscourt. Corretja had a good play on it, but Sampras anticipated where the crosscourt passing shot was going. He lunged to his right and drop-volleyed into the open court. Winner. 7-7. Pandomonium erupted in the stands.

The crowd was cheering as ardently and unrestrainedly as they had all match long. Now, at 7-7, Sampras missed a weak first serve. Realizing that he had almost no alternative, he went for his second serve unhesitatingly, sending it out wide to the forehand, risking a double fault. Corretja was leaning the other way. The serve was magnificent. Ace. 8-7 for the American. A crescendo of cheering rose from the seats of the New York audience. Sampras had match point for the second time. Corretja missed the first serve, paused, and served again. The place was eerily silent until the beep of the Cyclops machine was heard. Double fault. It was only the third in five long sets for the Spaniard. Sampras had succeeded despite feeling as abysmally as he ever would on a tennis court, winning 7-6 (5), 5-7, 5-7, 6-4, 7-6 (7).

It had lasted four hours and eight minutes. Corretja had served two more aces than Sampras, 25 to 23. The Spaniard had won 218 points in the match, five more than the American. Corretja had traveled to the edge of a career-altering triumph, moving within one point of a monumental victory. Pete Sampras had somehow survived an ordeal, winning without anything like his best stuff, fighting gallantly, moving on to the semifinals. It was the single most courageous triumph of his tennis career. The two players embraced at the net, fully appreciating that they had just shared one of the great New York moments in sports across that decade.

Sampras vividly recalled in 2019 what he endured 23 years earlier and how he managed in the end to get across the finish line after he was so compromised physically and feeling ill. It was an ineffably gratifying experience to survive under those circumstances with the crowd unabashedly behind him and Lady Luck beside him. He did not particularly like the way he played, but was exceedingly proud of how he competed.

Looking back on that character defining match, Sampras said, "I didn't prepare well. I ate too early and the match before mine took a long time so I walked out there low on fuel to play Alex. Everyone thought it was going to be an easy straight-sets match but I knew it was going to be a fight. He could play on hard courts and he made me work, serving kickers to my backhand and hitting high balls to my backhand. That was always my struggle—the high backhand. Alex took advantage of that and wore me down."

Sampras elaborated on his plight, saying, "I was just feeling heavy and tired and was sort of grinding along. So we got into this long battle. In the fifth set, I wasn't feeling too good. I reached for a coke, had a few sips of that and ate a banana. I was working a lot harder than I wanted to and there were nerves and stress and we got into the tie-breaker. My stomach was crampy and a little queasy and my back was not feeling good. I was kind of dehydrated but I wasn't sweating. And then I got sick on the court and threw up the banana and the coke. What saved me was that it was almost over because we were in a breaker, so I did not have to play it out."

In addition to knowing there was a finish line not far ahead as he played that tie-break, the fervor of the crowd propelled the American past his deep fatigue.

"That crowd was going nuts and getting behind me," he said. "They could see I was suffering. They were aware of that. When I play, it almost always looked easy but they were seeing, 'Pete doesn't look good. He is not playing well. He is really grinding it out here.' So it opened their eyes that as talented as I am, and as much as they felt everything comes easily to me, there is grit there in me and a little grind. They could see I was fighting my ass off to try to win this match. I was dead. I was completely fatigued. I was exhausted."

Summing it up more than two decades later, Sampras said, "I felt that was one of my grittiest wins. It just shows you that if you are not playing well and not feeling well like I was, tennis is one of those sports where there is just one guy out there. And when you are not at your best, you still have to find a way to win. That showed me and maybe a lot of other people that you can still find a way by winning ugly, by just scrapping and clawing and digging it out of the dirt as they say. That match showed me and my opponents, and maybe the tennis world, that there is a lot of fight in me. I showed people that I am not a robot. Only when I am pushed do you see it. I was definitely pushed past my limit, but by that point in my career I had a very strong will. I had not won a major all year. I really wanted to win that U.S. Open."

Corretja was a wounded warrior when it was over, psychically more than physically. He had played the hard court match of his life, exceeding the expectations of nearly all observers, nearly bringing down a great champion very much against the odds. He was, of course, deflated in many ways after losing by the skin of his teeth, but ultimately not discouraged.

As he said in an interview with me for *Tennis Championships Magazine* in 2016, "That match was unbelievable. It was a turning point in my career. That day I was playing against the best player in the world on his court, so even if I lost that match it was a great experience for the future for me. It opened up my eyes to realize I could become a better player. Pete and I had a good relationship. If I had lost that match to another guy I would have been more upset, but Pete was always very respectful to me."

As Annacone said, "This match was analogous to when he played Courier the year before at the Australian Open and he broke down crying. Pete Sampras isn't used to letting anyone know how he feels, what he is thinking and how he is processing stuff. They didn't know Pete. And that was a huge advantage for him on the tour. He was this enigmatic guy. He was Pete Sampras and was kind of legendary. He didn't mean it in a way to be rude or insulated. This was just Pete, a middle-class Greek kid who didn't need seven million friends. He had his group around him and life was simple and that was it. He was not a gregarious person. So when he broke down against Courier and we saw him getting sick against Corretja, that was hard and even brutal for him because he didn't want people to see that."

Annacone talked with Sampras after the Corretja match, and tried to help him put it all in perspective. "I said to him, 'Pete, the biggest challenge you have is that you did what everyone on the planet does, except it is in front of millions of people. That's hard. But it does not short circuit your ability to find a way through.' And that is what is amazing about Pete. Whether he vomited in the match against Corretja or broke down in tears against Courier, even after matches like that, he is not dramatic about it at all. He is like, 'Yeah, I got through it, so how do I now move to the next step?' And that ability to synthesize what is happening in the moment, and get through no matter what the adversity, can't be taught. Only the greatest of the greats do that. His ability to deflate pressure and take the air out of the balloon of expectations enabled him to get through and move on. That is what he did after Corretja."

Another crucial figure in the Sampras professional universe at that time was his trainer Todd Snyder, a man he valued highly. Sampras spoke effusively about Snyder's role in his career in a 2019 interview for this book. He said, "I had been having some injuries week to week with different tape jobs from different trainers. I have very sensitive feet and I knew Todd a little bit when he was working for the ATP Tour. Todd knew his business and knew the body. He was really good at taping. At that point in my career I was making good money and I wanted peace of mind that my body was going to be taken care of. When you see someone like Todd who is good at what they do, you jump on it. So I asked him while he was working for the ATP Tour to come work for me. He is a great and supportive guy who helped me mainly with injuries, massage, stretching and taping. He is very smart. We had a good relationship. I hired him away from the Tour because I trusted his expertise."

Snyder was very helpful to Sampras after the taxing battle with Corretja, knowing how the world No. 1 could reach into his recuperative powers and flourish. Sampras put a lot of stock in the fact that he had two days off after his ordeal with Corretja. He felt that was just the reprieve he needed to get on with his unwavering pursuit of the crown over the weekend.

As he explained, "That was huge having the two days off. I would have been ready with one day off. You put your shoes on and go again. But I was sore as hell and tired. I got an IV after the Corretja match and that thing is a wonder drug. If I had needed to play on Friday instead of Saturday, that would have been fine, but the extra day really helped. I did not even go out to the site. I just stayed away and then played my semifinal against Ivanisevic."

The big Croatian left-hander was a menacing man to confront on any surface, but the fact remained that on hard courts it was not quite as daunting a task to play him. Ivanisevic could still exploit his incomparably crackling serve and back it up adequately on the volley as he frequently followed his first delivery in. But he was more vulnerable on the hard courts because it was easier for Sampras to expose Ivanisevic's groundstroke inconsistency and impatience. And Ivanisevic did not get away with as many mediocre volleys as he could on the lawns of Wimbledon.

After getting goaded into far too many long backcourt rallies in the Corretja encounter, Ivanisevic was the ideal opponent for Sampras. He knew he could find holes in the Ivanisevic backcourt game any time they got into a rally. Sampras settled into the match comfortably and confidently and was the decidedly better player over the first two sets.

Sampras started the way he would have scripted it, breaking Ivanisevic in the second game on a double fault, dropping only six points in his five disciplined service games. That set went to the American briskly. He took it 6-3. The second set was strikingly similar, although Sampras worked harder to hold serve. At 3-3, he broke a dispirited Ivanisevic on a cluster of unjustifiable errors from the southpaw. At 5-4, Sampras served out the set with the authority and self-belief he almost always did, holding at love, releasing a pair of aces. He was ahead two sets to love and resolute about closing out the contest in three straight sets. The final was the next day. Getting off the court as soon as possible was his clear priority.

Sampras served beautifully all through the third set, winning 24 of 29 points on his way to a tie-break, picking apart his adversary comprehensively, giving nothing away. But Ivanisevic was also unbreakable and his serving numbers were nearly identical to those of Sampras. They went to a tie-break and the defending champion raised both his game and his intensity. On his way to 5-2 in that sequence, he served two aces and did not concede a point on his delivery. When he sent a backhand pass low down the line to provoke Ivanisevic into an error, Sampras was precisely where he wanted to be, at triple match point, leading 6-3 and serving the next two points.

He serve-volleyed on the first one and the return was low. Sampras made a reasonably deep forehand first volley crosscourt, but Ivanisevic had time to set up and simply teed off. His backhand pass blazed crosscourt supersonically for a stunning winner. He walloped that shot with such stunning velocity that it was as if he thought the match was over and was simply going for broke. Sampras was trying to serve and volley behind another second serve on the next point at 6-4, but double faulted off the net cord. He still had a third match point in hand when Ivanisevic served at 5-6, but the left-hander refused to miss in this carefully orchestrated rally. The point lasted 27 strokes but Sampras ultimately drove a backhand pass long. Ivanisevic had saved three match points to make it back to 6-6. Sampras would garner a fourth match point opportunity when he led 8-7, but Ivanisevic was revitalized. He saved that one with an unstoppable serve-and-volley combination and eventually triumphed 11-9 in the tie-break.

The 1996 U.S. Open was one of the grittiest and most emotional Grand Slam tournament wins for Pete Sampras

Sampras said in 2019, "I had the match in my hands and I was perturbed at myself that I let that third set slip away. I wanted to save my energy for the next day. You are in a match like that and you expect it to go a certain way. You let it slip and then you have to play another set. I let him off the hook for a second."

Perturbed or not, Sampras had a penchant for moving past exasperating experiences like the one at the end of the third set and remaining fully focused on what was ahead. The third set was gone. He could not afford to dwell on that or beat himself up emotionally. And so he moved on calmly to the fourth set, looking to wrap it up there, but realizing that Ivanisevic had a different perspective.

At 2-2 in the fourth, Sampras saved a break point and held in a long game with his 21st ace of the afternoon. Ivanisevic was breezing through his service games rhythmically, but at 3-4 he fell into a 0-40 hole. Sampras was at triple break point for a chance to conclude the contest on his own serve. But Ivanisevic was undismayed. After Sampras missed a down-the-line passing shot off the backhand, Ivanisevic surged to deuce with consecutive aces, the first out wide and the second down the T. He had lifted his total of aces to 30.

Ivanisevic made another first serve at deuce, but Sampras chipped a backhand return deliberately short to coax his adversary into an error on the forehand approach. At break point for the fourth time, Sampras experimented with the same formula, chipping a forehand return off a 128 mph thunderbolt, keeping that shot low, drawing Ivanisevic forward again. Ivanisevic netted his approach. The crowd erupted. Sampras was exhilarated. He had the break for 5-3 and then held at 15 to close out the account, pouring in two more aces, winning 6-3, 6-4, 6-7 (9), 6-3. He had not lost his serve even once across four sets and, after some unexpected apprehension, succeeded in the end.

When it was over, Sampras spoke with Annacone and expressed his disappointment in himself for not getting the job done in straight sets, but his coach reassured him, "You are in the final of the U.S. Open. You are right where you want to be. That is what matters."

And so Sampras clashed with Chang in the title round on September 8, 1996. Chang had played spectacularly to crush Agassi 6-3, 6-2, 6-2 in the semifinals. He served 16 aces, did not face a break point all day and won 87% of his first serve points. Chang had altered his philosophy by this stage of his career, going for bigger first serves even if that meant lowering his percentage, feeling it was important to make sure he got his share of free points. In the Agassi match, that philosophy was very rewarding.

In those days, the women's final at the Open was played right before the men's title round duel on Sunday afternoon. But during the presentation ceremony following Steffi Graf's triumph over Monica Seles, the skies opened and a heavy rainstorm erupted. Sampras and Chang were delayed for about three hours. That was good news for Sampras. The cooler evening conditions seemed better suited to him, although not a disadvantage for Chang.

Speaking about the match 22 years after it was played, Chang said, "The first set I was almost too pumped to play. Probably what I should have done after the three-hour rain delay was to go out and hit a few balls like Pete did prior to walking out for our match. I just had so much adrenaline that I actually couldn't play in the first set."

Conversely, Sampras came out of the gates arrestingly, aware that a blazing start had served him well in other Grand Slam finals, determined to take on the front runner's role and impose himself as only he could. He was confident after winning eight of his last nine head-to-head meetings with Chang.

As Annacone said, "I talked to him before that final and said, 'Let's think about this matchup. Tell me what tennis shot you have to be afraid of with Michael Chang? Andre is a shot maker and if you miss your targets he is going to rip returns. Becker is powerful and Goran has a huge serve. We know Michael is not going to beat you with weapons. So how does he beat you?' Pete said that Michael would just make him hit one more shot on every point. So I said, 'Exactly, he is the best counter puncher in the world right now. He moves incredibly well, so I want you to go into every point thinking you are going to hit one or two more balls and not overplay. It is totally up to you if you hit your targets on your serve and put pressure on his second serve."

As the first set unfolded, Annacone sensed that Sampras was "the clearest I had ever seen him" in terms of a game plan. Annacone recalled, "It was a joke that first set. It looked like he was playing a guy ranked 60 in the world. Pete was totally comfortable and not overplaying. It was amazing because he just went through Chang like no one can."

In that opening set, Sampras showcased his excellence immediately, serving two aces in the first game, making five of six first serves, holding at 30. He broke Chang at the cost of only two points for 2-0, connecting for a forehand winner and then a forehand passing shot in that game. Down 0-40 in the third game, Sampras swept five points in a row, starting that comeback with an ace, finishing the hold with an unstoppable first serve down the T. On went an unswerving Sampras to 3-0.

The fourth game featured Sampras at the absolute peak of his powers. He produced a winning forehand return down the line, another forehand down the line into the clear and a backhand winner down the line on his way to 15-40. With Chang serving at 30-40, Sampras moved in swiftly behind an inside-out forehand return and caught Chang going the wrong way. Closing in, Sampras punched a forehand volley behind his adversary with regal authority. It was his fourth outright winner of the game. He led 4-0. In the following game he saved a break point and reached 5-0 with an ace down the T.

Sampras took that set 6-1, serving three aces in the seventh game as if to underline his supremacy. At the beginning of the second set, the world No. 1 was still striking the ball with sweeping self-assurance. Chang was shaken, losing the first two games, winning only one point in the process. In the first game he missed all five first serves and double faulted at 15-40. Sampras took the second game at love on his own serve.

After Chang got on the scoreboard in the third game, Sampras held at 15 for 3-1. When he served his second ace of that fourth game to move ahead 40-15, the crowd seemed almost numbed by his extraordinary performance. He lifted up the palms of his hands as if to say, "Hey, don't I deserve a little credit for playing this well?" The moment was reminiscent of his outreach to the Wimbledon audience during his final with Becker the year before. The U.S. Open crowd responded by lifting their level of appreciation. But they sensed the match might soon be over the way it was unfolding.

It was not. Chang was an unwavering warrior. He obstinately asserted himself, holding at 15 in the fifth game, breaking Sampras at 30 in the sixth on a double fault and then losing only one point on his serve in the seventh. Chang led 4-3. He had won 12 of 16 points and three successive games and gained some encouragement. But that fleeting hope evaporated rapidly.

Sampras was in no mood to relinquish his authority. Not now. Not with the U.S. Open title on the line. Not with Chang on the other side of the net. He served an ace out wide and then an ace down the T for 30-0 in the eighth game and held his serve at 15 for 4-4. Sampras wanted to negotiate a service break badly in the ninth game and bargained hard to get it. Serving at 30-40, Chang netted a backhand approach. Sampras had broken for 5-4 by unveiling everything that was admirable in his arsenal — stinging flat forehands, a biting sliced backhand down the line on the run, considerable depth and uncanny court sense.

Serving for the set in the tenth game, the first point set the tone Sampras wanted for that entire game. He served and volleyed and Chang tossed up a topspin lob. Sampras leapt off the ground for one of his trademark athletic overheads, putting it away forcefully. He held on at 15 to take that set 6-4. Now he was one set away from a fourth U.S. Open title. But the fact remained that Chang was on the other side of the net. He would not surrender. His spirit was undiminished.

Chang turned the third set into his best of the match. On his serve, he was getting on top of the rallies, reducing his mistakes significantly and finding his range. He won 24 of 29 points on serve and kept Sampras largely at bay. Sampras held all through the set as well, but he was precariously perched at the end. Serving at 5-6, down set point, he missed his first serve and stayed back on the second. Chang found an opportunity to get to the net, coming in off the forehand. But his approach clipped the net cord and gave Sampras time to line up a piercing forehand pass crosscourt. He drove it flat, hard and low and Chang netted a forehand volley from close range.

That was a tough break for Chang. Sampras needed three game points but he made it to 6-6 with a well-disguised topspin backhand winner down the line. He had missed nine of twelve first serves but, from set point down, held on more than anything else with tough mindedness.

The tie-break was one that Sampras did not want to elude his grasp. The longer Chang lasted in a match, the more dangerous this fellow became. No one understood that better than Sampras. He played every point in the tie-break as if his entire year depended on winning it. In many ways, that was the case.

Sampras gained the quick mini-break, rolling a topspin backhand with excellent depth, backing Chang up and then implementing an inside-out forehand that landed on the sideline. He took both points on his serve for 3-0 before Chang succeeded on both of his service points to close the gap. Serving at 3-2, Sampras won the pivotal point of that sequence. Staying back on his second serve, Sampras seemed compromised by Chang's blazing forehand return directed deep down the middle. It should have given Chang the point. But Sampras took it on the rise and sent a forehand back with good depth. The rally continued until Sampras decided it was time to end it, going inside-in off the forehand for an outright winner.

That clutch piece of business lifted Sampras to 4-2. As Chang remembered more than 22 years after the fact, "I ran around my backhand and cranked that forehand return as hard as I could and my shot was literally almost on the baseline. He just flexed it back deep and I was thinking, 'Oh my Gosh, are you kidding me?'"

Chang came in on the next point behind a backhand down the line, approaching off a low ball. He could not get enough on that shot. Sampras passed him cleanly down the line off the forehand to make it 5-2 and then arrived at 6-2 when a Chang forehand down the line landed long. Chang saved one match point, but Sampras went to his trusted first serve down the T in the ad court at 6-3. Uncharacteristically, he did not serve and volley, but that did not matter. The Chang forehand return was well long. Sampras was the victor 6-1, 6-4, 7-6 (3). He had captured his eighth major singles title and was climbing the historical ladder of the sport faster than he could have imagined. From match point down against Corretja in the quarterfinals, Sampras had gathered his strength, reached back with all of his resources and claimed a major at the last hurdle, defeating an unbending Chang.

As Chang said in 2018, "I kept fighting and fighting and I felt like I was starting to get a bit of an edge. I thought it was starting to turn a little bit in that third set. I had the set point. But Pete played a good tie-breaker to close it out. I hit some good shots but all credit to Pete. He just stayed tough and served well when it counted. I didn't make any errors or anything like that. He just played tough."

"It was huge to close out Michael in straight sets," said Sampras in 2019. "You don't want to let anyone back into a match like that. Closing out a third set against a really good player is not easy, so it was nice to do that. It was just a long second week and a bit tiring. I was still dealing some with the 'Chang Curse' and really started dominating him before that and from that point on. It was a tough but not a pretty victory in the end. It was good hard court tennis. I felt I wasn't at my best. But it was one of my more satisfying wins because of what I was going through that year with Tim Gullikson passing away, so getting through the Corretja match and then ending the tournament beating one of my oldest rivals since I was a kid was very satisfying."

Not even a bizarre stunt from a grandstanding fan could dampen Sampras's effusiveness. Right after the triumph, he went to a familiar routine that was his custom after some of his most important finals. Sampras gently tossed his racket into the crowd, hoping it would land in the hands of his friend Phil Knight of Nike. But in the commotion of spectators trying to grab the racket, a fan claimed he was hurt in the hubbub. Those who saw Sampras toss the racket were very dubious of the fan's contention.

As Sampras remembered it 23 years afterwards, "I was on such a high after winning the event. I remember my agent at the time told me that my racket hit a fan in the eye. Then this article came out and the fan had a couple of quotes about athletes that were just random and out of the blue. I wasn't sure what his message was, but this fan wanted an apology. I was still on Cloud Nine and it didn't make any sense to me. I spoke to Robin Finn of the *New York Times* and she did a story on it. I think that diffused everything and made this guy look a little ridiculous. It just went away. It was bizarre. It seemed like someone trying to make a name for himself. I tossed the racket and it was just a guy who wanted some attention but he went about it the wrong way."

That triumph meant that 1996 had been another great year. He defined himself and his seasons by what he did at the majors. This U.S. Open was one he sorely needed and the only time in his sterling career that Sampras would rescue himself from match point down during the course of a major to win it in the end. That remarkable feat was realized seven years earlier at the Open by Becker in 1989 and was later replicated by Andy Roddick in 2003 and Djokovic in 2010. These were four towering competitors who could all confront pressure and not buckle.

For Pete Sampras, that U.S. Open was just the tonic he needed to turn 1996 into his kind of a year. He would say that winning in New York made playing the tournaments for the rest of that season more enjoyable. He had his big prize and his validation for being at the top and now could try to pocket a few more important titles.

Sampras played four more tournaments after the U.S. Open, winning in Basel, losing a five-set final to Becker in Stuttgart, falling early in Paris and then coming to Hannover to complete his season. During the round-robin portion of that tournament reserved for only the top eight players in men's tennis, Sampras was beaten by Becker again. But he met the German once more in the final round.

Their indoor duel to decide who would win the ATP World Tour Finals was a dandy. Before the two combatants walked on court, they stood a level above the court for the introductions with the theme music from the movie "Rocky" reverberating throughout the arena. In other cases at different venues, this kind of a buildup would have been regarded as hyperbolic and theatrical and perhaps seen as a cheap imitation of authentic art.

Not in this case. Sampras and Becker never contested a better match against each other anywhere in the world. They played arguably one of the ten best matches of all time. With the German crowd cheering Becker on unabashedly in a Davis Cup atmosphere, and two prodigious servers at full force fighting furiously in fast indoor conditions, the tennis shined. These were indeed a pair of heavyweights presiding in the tennis arena, playing aggressive, fast-charging, uncompromising serve-and-volley tennis in an ideal setting for an audience thirsting for this kind of high octane confrontation. It was the last big match of the year in tournament tennis, with only the Davis Cup Final remaining on the agenda.

Becker took the first set, breaking Sampras for the only time in this mind boggling tennis match. Sampras struck back mightily to win the second in a tie-break and replicated that feat in the third. The serving from each of these eminent men was out of this world. The fourth set went to a third tie-break in a row and Sampras was poised to end it there. But Becker fought off two match points, winning the gripping sequence 11-9.

Sampras could easily have been dismayed by his misfortune. Becker had the capacity crowd feverishly pulling for him to succeed in his home country. He was their hero. He had been a prominent player since 1985, when he won his first Wimbledon at 17 and established himself as the youngest man ever to claim that crown. Now, 11 years later, playing prime time tennis in the twilight of his career, feeding off the highly-animated audience, Becker was on the verge of a splendid triumph in his homeland at the biggest indoor tournament of them all—and the most prestigious event outside of the four majors.

But Sampras did not want to lose to his respected rival for the third time in a row during the indoor swing. He had not come this far to fall short in a classic confrontation. At 4-4 in the fifth and final set, Sampras had a crucial break point. He laced a backhand passing shot down the line for a winner and then shouted out to himself as most of the audience sat in stunned silence. Relieved that for the first time all day he had broken Becker's serve, Sampras closed it out in a hard-fought final game, winning 3-6, 7-6 (5), 7-6 (4), 6-7 (11), 6-4.

Speaking about that match 22 years after it was played, Sampras confirmed that this was a singular experience for him beyond the realm of the Grand Slam tournaments. It was a victory he always savored.

"It was one of the best matches I was ever a part of," he said. "Playing Boris in Germany on a fast court which was a good court for me and a great court for him, we both played really well. I remember the crowd being very much for him but very fair to me. It was this back and forth match and I had those two match points in the fourth set but I finally got him at 4-4 in the fifth. I hit that backhand down-the-line pass and screamed out after I did it because he is so tough to break in those conditions. It was so tough to get a hold of him. At the end, I was exhausted and my legs were tight. I was physically and emotionally spent from the long year and the match. We had a nice embrace at the net when it ended, just two guys who respected one another that competed their asses off for four hours and I managed to squeak it out. It was two great players playing well at the same time in his homeland."

Atmospherically, Sampras rarely experienced anything like that extraordinary meeting with Becker in Germany. He said in 2019, "That was a very loud crowd in a small kind of hall. It was deafening, one of the loudest crowds I have ever heard. They went ballistic, but those things happen and it is the mental wherewithal that matters. You see it in the great players today like Roger, Novak and Rafa. They recover quickly and then you get back to work. That match I played with Boris was an epic, the most epic match I was a part of outside of the majors."

He came home and had a short time to digest his stirring victory and appreciate that remarkable year and how it had all ended in an indoor gem of a tennis match. Sampras could be proud of his eight titles over the course of that season and his 65-11 match record. He had worked hard, persistently and long. He had finished at No. 1 in the ATP Rankings for the fourth consecutive year. That was all well and good. But he would soon turn his full attention to the 1997 season and a quest to keep capturing the game's most prestigious prizes. At 25, Sampras knew full well that he was very much in the summertime of his talent, but realized he could not afford to slip into complacency as he pursued his overriding goals.

# CHAPTER 11

## ON TOP AGAIN DOWN UNDER

Less than two weeks into the 1997 season, Pete Sampras was back at work, playing his first tournament of the new year on the hard courts in Melbourne at the Australian Open. The brief off season since the middle of November had been beneficial, allowing him to recover from the rigors of a long and debilitating 1996 campaign. But he had now grown accustomed to being the best in the world. He was not overburdened as the favorite in the land "Down Under." He believed that no one was better than he was and wanted to give himself every chance to be holding the trophy at the end of the fortnight.

This was not to say that he took anything for granted or underestimated any opponent during a fortnight lasting until the end of January. In fact, the 25-year-old American left no stone unturned. He was a professional through and through, with no delusions. If he wanted to win a second Australian Open crown, Sampras understood that there would inevitably be some rugged skirmishes along the way. On the Rebound Ace hard courts that never were ideal for his game, he would be made to overcome some formidable adversaries. This was not going to be an easy tournament and Sampras realized he could be tested comprehensively at any time as temperatures

STEVE FLINK

sometimes soared to almost unbearable levels and opponents took him to his limits.

The fact remained that he was at the height of his powers and his indomitable will to win the first major of the new season was strikingly evident to both his peers and those who followed his career as fans or journalists. Sampras sorely wanted this Australian Open to set the right tone for the new year and remind everyone that he was still the man to beat on every big occasion save Roland Garros. And so he set out unambiguously to stamp his authority on the proceedings in Melbourne.

Sampras handled the Romanian Dinu Pescariu easily, taking their first-round encounter 6-2, 6-4, 6-2 without losing his serve. Facing another Romanian named Adrian Voinea in the second round, Sampras was down a set but he turned that battle around sweepingly, winning 3-6, 6-2, 6-3, 6-2. That triumph took Sampras into a third round collision against Mark Woodforde, a congenial left-hander ranked No. 28 in the world at the time.

Woodforde was a fine player in singles but he made his name and built his reputation as one of the great doubles players of all time. Alongside countryman Todd Woodbridge, Woodforde was victorious at no less than 11 major tournaments. Altogether, he won 17 Grand Slam titles in doubles, including the 1989 U.S. Open with fellow left-hander John McEnroe. His record was so far reaching that he captured major titles in men's and mixed doubles at all four of the Grand Slam championships. He would eventually be inducted at the International Tennis Hall of Fame.

But Woodforde was routed 6-1, 6-0, 6-1 by an unblinking Sampras, who moved on confidently to the round of 16 for an appointment against Dominik Hrbaty. The Slovakian was a big hitter from the baseline. He swung freely, went for his returns, and made more than his share of winners uncorked at blinding speeds from anywhere on the court. The 19-year-old knew he had nothing to lose against the best player in the world and the prohibitive tournament favorite.

Hrbaty was hitting out freely against Sampras on one of those impossibly scorching afternoons in Melbourne. The tell-tale sign of the heat extremity was the hat Sampras wore to protect himself from the sun's deep intensity. He only wore the hat on the most oppressive days and this was one of those. Down 5-2, Sampras took the first set into a tie-break. He led 4-2 in that sequence, but lost five consecutive points from there. Hrbaty won that tie-break 7-4.

But Sampras's discipline on serve and off the ground carried him through the next two sets. Hrbaty, however, was not surrendering. Blasting away off the forehand with impressive control, he broke for 3-1 in the fourth set and took that set 6-3. The teenager had pushed the top seed into a fifth set and Sampras was feeling not only the heat reflecting off the hard court but also the firepower of Hrbaty's unrelenting ground game.

The fifth set was treacherous all the way for the American, who was under siege on his serve and from the back of the court as Hrbaty fearlessly pursued a major upset. He broke Sampras in the third game and established a 3-1 lead. In the fifth game, Sampras was down 0-30 but at that critical moment he served an ace out wide in the deuce court. After taking the next two points with first serves that were too much for his adversary, Sampras served another ace, going down the T in the ad court to hold on boldly for 2-3.

Hrbaty held in a hard fought, two-deuce game for 4-2 and once more he put Sampras under considerable pressure on the American's serve. Sampras trailed 2-4, 15-40. If Hrbaty could take one of the next two points, he would be up two breaks in the final set and within striking distance of a stunning five-set upset. But Sampras sent a service winner down the T for 30-40 before connecting with another first serve that set up a penetrating forehand. Hrbaty netted a forehand. The error was clearly forced.

Back to deuce, Sampras served his 18th ace of the day, directing it down the T. Another unanswerable first serve on game point did the job. From 15-40 he had not missed a first serve, taking four clutch points in a row, holding on for 3-4. For the first time in a very long while, Hrbaty seemed to realize who he was playing and what was at stake. In the eighth game, Sampras reached 0-30 with a dipping forehand pass and a forehand inside-in return winner off a second serve. Shaken, Hrbaty double faulted. He won the next point but, at 15-40, served another double fault. He would finish with 15 doubles. Although the audacious teenager produced 21 aces, he faltered frequently on the second delivery. Sampras had no intention of letting Hrbaty get away with that.

Having broken back for 4-4, Sampras went to 30-15 in the ninth game, only to double fault two times in a row. On break point, he missed his first serve but was bold from the baseline, lacing a backhand down the line, rushing Hrbaty into a mistake. Sampras followed with two unstoppable serves, holding for 5-4. Hrbaty led 30-15 in the tenth game but double faulted for 30-30 and missed a two-hander long. At match point, Sampras recovered from a defensive position in the rally and then ran around his backhand, driving a forehand inside out. It landed safely near the sideline for a winner. He had survived a tormenting skirmish, coming through 6-7 (4), 6-3, 6-4, 3-6, 6-4.

That victory was a testament to Sampras's insatiable desire to succeed. He had been under siege all through the fifth set, but wanted victory so badly that he found a way to succeed with the depth of his determination when he was physically drained.

More than two decades later, Sampras recollected the surrounding factors with greater clarity than the match itself. He said, "I remember the night before they were talking about the record heat in Melbourne. They were talking about the conditions being the hottest in 50 years. I was concerned. The heat has always given me some issues and the match was early in the day session, so it was maybe not as hot as it would be at 3 pm, but I knew it was going to be a hot one. I also knew Hrbaty could play and he had big groundies. Anytime I put a hat on I am concerned. I don't like wearing hats, but it was more of a conditioning test than a tennis match that day. It was so hot that I remember going out there it felt like I was walking into a sauna. And that court didn't handle heat well. It just made it even hotter."

Assessing the match itself, Sampras said in 2019, "It could have gone either way. The heat got to me. Maybe experience got me through it. Maybe he got a little tight. But I was ecstatic to get off the court. Paul Annacone actually came out on the court and got my stuff. I just walked straight into the locker room. It was brutally hot. Today they would probably put the roof up on a day like that. It was very uncomfortable and that is when the level of tennis isn't great. I was certainly paying the price."

In addition to the extreme heat during the tournament, Sampras and the other players were adjusting to the balls. As Annacone recalled, "Early in the tournament, I was talking to Pete about the balls. Everyone was complaining about how heavy they were. It was hard to finish points. Every day in the newspaper, there was talk about the balls, but Pete hadn't said one word to me about it. So after one of his early round matches I said to him, 'Everyone is talking about the balls. What is your take?' And he said, "Yeah, they are heavy.' And it was like he was saying 'What is the big deal? The balls are heavy for everybody. What is the point of talking about it?' And that is one of the things that was so endearing about Pete. He was telling me that you can't complain about things you can't control. Just go out and play. It is what it is. I thought that was great."

After Sampras found his way past the dangerously free-wheeling Hrbaty, he met the stylish Spaniard Albert Costa in the quarterfinals. Costa was, predominantly, a clay-court player. In 2002, he would cap his career with a triumph at the French Open. By virtue of winning that major title, he climbed to a career high at No. 6 in the world.

When he went out into the Melbourne night to play Sampras at the Australian Open, Costa stood at No. 13 in the ATP rankings and he was seeded No. 10 in Melbourne. In the first round, he had upended Pat Rafter, the fast-charging Australian who would take the U.S. Open title less than eight months later. He was playing well and did not concede a set on his way to the last eight in the first major of 1997.

Having dealt with such stifling heat in his appointment with Hrbaty, Sampras welcomed fighting this battle out in the evening air. He was not at his very best, but his court coverage was substantially improved. He was much closer to a top of the line Sampras, serving magnificently throughout another five-set confrontation, bending for his low volleys with customary ease, making running forehands as only he could.

With some better fortune, his contest with Costa could have been more clear-cut. He took the first set comfortably, breaking right off the bat in the second game and making it count. 6-3 for Sampras. The second set went to a tie-break. If Sampras had succeeded there he would very likely have been a straight-sets victor. He lost only one point on his serve in the tie-break but never took a point on Costa's serve. The Spaniard was unerring, winning the tie-break 7-5. One set all.

Sampras was unflagging. He swept through the third set 6-1.The break he secured in the first game revealed the world No.1 at full force. The point that took him to 15-40 was a sparkler in every sense. He opened up the court with a sizzling crosscourt forehand, pulling Costa out of position. Then Sampras laced a backhand crosscourt approach shot. Costa went crosscourt with his passing shot, but Sampras's backhand volley down the line was too good. Costa could not do enough with his forehand pass and Sampras finished with an elegant forehand drop-volley winner. That eye-catching display encapsulated Sampras as easily the best athlete in the game of tennis. He was the most versatile and complete player in his profession by far. Two points later, he sealed that break with an inside-in forehand winner, another of his favorite shots. Gliding from there, he stormed to 5-1 and served four aces in a deuce game to close it out confidently 6-1. He seemed well on his way to a four-set win.

But, at 3-4 in the fourth set, Sampras lost his serve for the only time in the match, through little fault of his own. Costa had to work hard to hold in the following game, but he did. The set was owned by Costa. He won it 6-3. Surprisingly, the two players would settle the outcome in a fifth set.

At 1-1 in the fifth, Costa went all out for a break. Sampras led 40-0 in that game, but lost the next three points as the Spaniard battled back forcefully. Costa's one-handed backhand was a dynamic shot. He could explore any angle and thread the needle, finding the smallest openings and executing winners that sometimes seemed lifted out of dreams.

Sampras did not want to go down a break in the final set. At deuce, he followed a familiar pattern that carried him through so many matches, sending a first serve wide with slice, following it in swiftly and putting the backhand first volley away crosscourt. On his fourth game point, Sampras made a difficult low forehand first volley on the stretch, punching it crosscourt into an open space. Crucially, he had held for 2-1.

Bolstered by that important hold, Sampras broke in the following game, losing only one point, attacking a couple of times to win big points. Now ahead 3-1, Sampras led 40-30 when he sent a second serve down the T, just inside the center service line. Costa was leaning the other way. That gutsy delivery landed safely for an ace. Having moved to 4-1, Sampras trotted to the changeover, delighted to be closing in on his destination. Two games later, Sampras was taken to deuce by an obstinate Costa, but he served and volleyed behind a second delivery, going to the Costa forehand. Sampras directed a forehand volley down the line for a winner. A service winner down the T took Sampras to 5-2.

Costa was serving to stay in the match, but he could not pass that test. He won only one point as Sampras performed like the ultimate professional. The American was victorious 6-3, 6-7 (5), 6-1, 3-6, 6-2. He had played decidedly better tennis in the cooler evening conditions than he had against Hrbaty in the heat. It was a definite step in the right direction and a confirmation to Sampras that he was within striking distance of his loftiest tennis.

Speaking in 2019 of that 1997 duel with Costa, Sampras said, "He was always tough to play. He had a beautiful backhand and I remember how slow the conditions were. The balls were soft and they weren't going anywhere, so those were tough conditions for me, but the Costa match was a good one. I got into the net a bit and he stands pretty far back, but he was talented. All of those Spaniards played the same way against me. They tried to hit high to my backhand and I tried to get in and use my forehand. Albert always pushed me. That whole tournament was tough because I was not getting that many free points on my serve. I never liked the Rebound Ace surface, but at night it plays well and that was good quality tennis. I played better and felt better than I did against Hrbaty, which was a relief."

Now in the penultimate round, Sampras was pitted against the ever industrious and persistent Muster. The left-handed Austrian had ousted both Courier and Ivanisevic to reach this round and he was striking the ball well, running down balls inexhaustibly, retrieving with a regularity that left opponents dumbfounded. He was seeded fifth and playing top-five tennis beyond any doubt. But, playing Sampras on hard courts in the semifinals of a major on a hard court, looking for a game plan that would allow him to counter attack successfully against the premier attacking player in the sport, Muster knew full well that he would need to be at the very top of his game to have any chance at all to succeed.

Always admiring of Muster's work ethic and competitiveness, Sampras was aware that the Austrian could on occasion resort to possible gamesmanship. Later in this 1997 season, they would meet again in the final of the Masters 1000 tournament in Cincinnati, with Sampras a straight-sets victor on the hard courts of Ohio. As Sampras recollected in 2019, "Thomas was always fine and he would compete hard, but in this one case he got under my skin. In that Cincinnati final, right before I would serve, in the middle of my toss, he would exhale loud. I don't think you can do that so I said something to the umpire. He seemed to be trying to throw me off a little bit. I thought he was doing it on purpose but maybe he wasn't. With Thomas you never knew. He was a real grinder who got everything out of his game. I like him but what he did that day did not land well with me."

Sampras was primed for this 1997 meeting in Melbourne, feeling he held all of the winning cards, realizing he could control his own destiny. He broke Muster in the second game of the match, firing away freely off the forehand, rifling a winner crosscourt into a wide open space. Sampras surged to 5-0 before Muster finally won a game, but the American served it out with an ace out wide in the ad court to hold at 30. 6-1 to Sampras. Trouble for Muster.

Yet the Austrian left-hander played his finest return game of the match to move out in front 4-2 in the second set. A backhand return winner down the line got him to 0-40 and he broke at 30 with an inside-out forehand passing-shot winner. Muster held on for 5-2. He was in an enviable position, one game away from deadlocking the match at one set all.

Being down only one break against a player like Muster—who did not have an exceptional serve for a left-hander—was the reason the American believed he could pull out the set. He held at love with two aces in the eighth game. Muster rallied from 15-40 and had a set point in the ninth game. Sampras looped a backhand down the line and Muster sought to run around his backhand and blast an inside-out forehand. The tactic backfired. Not on balance, Muster netted that forehand. Sampras pounced, taking the next point before prevailing in a 14-stroke exchange. He did not put an overhead away, giving Muster a look at a forehand pass. But Sampras closed in swiftly for a backhand drop-volley winner down the line. He had broken back.

He quickly held for 5-5. Soon the set would be settled in a tie-break. The first point was deflating for Muster, who prided himself on his backcourt consistency. The two players had a 30-stroke rally but Sampras won it with a forehand crosscourt winner hit at a high trajectory, catching Muster off guard. Sampras bolted to 6-1 in that tie-break and came out on top 7-3.

Muster had boundless energy, an unmistakable sense of self and a strong fighting spirit, but he was down two sets to love against Pete Sampras. That was a quandary anyone would want to avoid.

Sampras was in his closing mode now. He broke for 2-0 in the third set, winning an 18-shot rally with a running forehand pass down the line off a high backhand volley from the Austrian. Muster was not that comfortable or competent at the net. Sampras exploited that vulnerability to the hilt, powering his way to 3-0 after a few deuces on his serve.

Now that the outcome was hardly in doubt, Sampras serendipitously hit one of the most remarkable shots of his career. Muster was serving at 0-3, 30-15. He pulled Sampras way off the court on the American's backhand side with a beautifully struck crosscourt forehand. A ballboy was crouched near the net. Sampras had to cover a lot of court to retrieve that shot and then go around the net post with his shot to avoid hitting the ballboy. He did just that. Somehow Sampras drove that backhand down the line and made this highly-improbable winner curl into the court. Muster bowed. Sampras grinned incredulously, enjoying the moment for all it was worth, realizing that he had magically invented a shot that he would probably not replicate for the rest of his career.

Asked in late 2018 if he recalled that golden moment, Sampras said, "Yes, I do remember that point. He hit a wide serve to my backhand and I just sliced it back. Then he hit this incredible forehand crosscourt and I just went for it on the run. It was all just reactionary. I felt it was an incredible shot. I knew what happened and he knew what happened, but no one else did. I put my hands in the air like to say, 'Did I just pull that off?' And he kind of bowed a little bit."

Muster did manage to hold on in that game despite that startling development, but Sampras was unstoppable. In his last three service games, he allowed Muster only one point. Sampras marched into the final 6-4, 7-6 (3), 6-3. He was clearly elevating his game down the homestretch.

"I always liked playing Thomas," said Sampras, "because I could always get my forehand to his backhand and get in on him. He stayed way back on the return and I felt I could hang with him from the baseline and wait for my opportunity. He was a fighter and a grinder who could annoy you a little bit, but I did not let that affect me out there. It was a good clean match. I was getting a little better as the tournament wore on."

Joining Sampras in the title round on January 26, 1997 was none other than Carlos Moya, a beguiling Spanish performer who had enjoyed the fortnight of his life in front of appreciative Australian fans. The 20-year-old crafty baseliner owned an excellent forehand and a first-rate two-handed backhand. He was quick with uncanny instincts and an appealing flair for the game. He started his remarkable Australian Open run by upending the defending champion Becker in a five set, first-round encounter. Moving on to the semifinals, he cut down 1996 finalist Michael Chang in straight sets. Becker was seeded sixth. Chang was the No. 2 seed. Those were big wins.

But the Spaniard must have felt as if he was stepping into another league when he confronted Sampras on a stifling afternoon in the title round meeting. The 25-year-old American had gone from the Hrbaty five set scare to the hard-fought five-set win over Costa to the straight-set removal of Muster. With each and every match, Sampras was improving markedly, raising his self-conviction steadily and believing increasingly that no one in the world was going to stop him.

An apprehensive Moya did not have the game on hard courts to seriously trouble Sampras. Perhaps a more daunting opponent on the day was the weather. Once more, the sky was clear, the sun was burning down on the Rebound Ace courts and Sampras opted to wear a hat again. That was a clear sign that he was concerned about the conditions. He wanted no part of an extended skirmish on this occasion. This was another crucial final at a Grand Slam tournament and he wanted to impose himself early, create immediate doubts in his opponent's mind, and claim a victory as rapidly as it could be found.

The way Sampras started gave him just the reassurance he needed. As so often was the case in major finals, he played a whale of a first set, looking to set the tone, hoping to make Moya feel his presence on the court. He embraced these occasions and trusted himself implicitly. And so the American went right to work with full clarity of mind and a sureness of purpose. He did not miss a first serve in the first game and he held easily at 15. Moya acquitted himself well in the second game with a love hold, concluding that game with an ace.

But from 1-1 in that opening set, Sampras controlled the proceedings. He held at 15 again. In the fourth game, Sampras made his move. The Spaniard was down 30-40. This was the first break point of the match. Sampras was not going to give it away. After an 18-stroke rally, Moya blinked. Sampras drove a forehand inside-in with admirable depth and Moya pressed, netting a forehand. It was 3-1 for Sampras. He would never look back.

Sampras held at 30 for 4-1, lost the next game, then held again for 5-2. Now Moya was serving to stay in the set and that proved problematic. He won only one point in the eighth game. On set point, Sampras executed a cagey backhand slice crosscourt, coaxing an errant backhand from the Spaniard. Set to Sampras 6-2. He was off and running.

The American was determined to take his game up another notch now. In the opening game of the second set, Sampras held at love, finishing off that game with a pair of aces down the T. With Moya serving at 15-30 in the second game, Sampras's court sense and spontaneous brilliance came into full view. He made a delayed approach behind a forehand inside-out, moved in alertly and punched a backhand volley winner crisply down the line off a sliced backhand from Moya. On the next point, Sampras chip-charged off the backhand and forced a netted backhand pass from Moya. It was 2-0 for Sampras in the second set. He had won eight of nine points.

And yet, Moya settled down impressively in the third game. Sampras reached 30-30 but missed two first serves in a row. Moya took advantage of that. A looped return deep drew a forehand error from Sampras and then a dipping forehand pass crosscourt was unmanageable for Sampras. Moya had broken Sampras for the first time. He would not do so again. Moya then held easily for 2-2.

Sampras was unruffled. Despite breaking a string in one of his rackets for the third time, he held for 3-2 at the cost of only one point. Moya retaliated with a love hold for 3-3. The next game was significant. Sampras was down break point at 30-40, but here his native intelligence as a tennis player was strikingly evident once more. He decided on a first-serve kicker to the Moya backhand, eliciting a backhand return wide.

Surprisingly, Sampras stayed back on his first serve for the next two points, something he rarely did. But he drew a missed forehand return from Moya and then worked his way in on a penetrating forehand approach to provoke a passing shot error. To 4-3 went Sampras. From there he was masterful. With Moya serving in the following game, Sampras once again outmaneuvered his adversary from the backcourt, winning a 16-stroke baseline rally at 15-15 with demonstrable patience. He then moved Moya side to side, came in on a crosscourt backhand and put away an overhead emphatically. Now, at double break point, he employed two down-the-line passing shots to keep Moya off balance. Then he chased down a forehand volley from Moya and passed him cleanly off the forehand, going down the line again. That point lasted 24 strokes. This was a confident brand of counter-attacking from a man more accustomed to the opposite role. Sampras, of course, could do it all.

Now leading 5-3, he trailed 0-15 but swept four points in a row by eliciting a stream of errant returns from the Spaniard. Sampras held easily to close out the set 6-3. Things had become slightly complicated after he had gone up a break early, but in the end Sampras channeled his energy and inspiration to achieve his objectives.

Moya fought hard but unsuccessfully to keep himself in the match during the third set, but, after four deuces, he was broken at 1-1 by an unwavering Sampras. The Spaniard conceded that game with an inside-out forehand mistake that came about because Sampras was keeping his shots so deep. Sampras was rolling now. He held at 15 for 3-1 and served a love game—which included two aces from 30-0—to reach 4-2.

Moya kept competing diligently, but could not halt a better player. Sampras was now serving up a storm, releasing three aces on his way to 5-3. In four service games during the third set, Sampras had given up a total of three points. Moya served at 3-5, opening with a double fault. When Sampras took the next point to reach 0-30 and place himself two points away from the title, he saw the television cameramen moving to the side of the court in anticipation of his triumph. They wanted to be ready to get the close-up of him claiming the crown. He looked over at them disapprovingly, as if to say, "Hold on, here, this isn't over yet."

Understandably, Sampras was, in his own quiet way, aggravated. He had more work to do. All athletes are superstitious, at least to a degree. He wanted to finish the job and was taking nothing for granted. No lead is entirely safe in tennis. In the semifinals of the Masters tournament at Madison Square Garden in January of 1985, Jimmy Connors established a 5-2 final set lead over Ivan Lendl and the television cameramen were highly visible at court side as the two combatants walked to the changeover. Lendl saw them setting up, knowing they were preparing to potentially capture Connors' expression in victory as soon as it occurred. Lendl proceeded to sweep 20 of the next 24 points and five games in succession to take the match away from Connors. The premature appearance of the television crew had clearly spurred Lendl on. He did not like being counted out and was decidedly sharper as he turned the match around.

Sampras was well aware of how matches could change course radically. He was determined to close out this contest with Moya and did not want to be the least bit distracted as victory seemed within his grasp. That moment remained vivid in Sampras's mind as he moved deep into his forties.

Pete Sampras grasped the Norman Brookes Challenge Cup for a second time as the 1997 Australian Open champion

"I remember it 100 percent," he said in 2019. "I looked to the right and they were getting ready for their shot, but I was so into what I was doing. I did not want anything to distract me. I am thinking, 'Let's not count our chickens here.' I just remember I was on edge a bit. You don't want to have anything get in your way."

Nothing did. He captured the next two points in a hurry. On his first match point, Sampras got to the net as fast as possible, played a backhand finesse volley short, forcing

Moya to lob long off the forehand. Sampras triumphed over the Spaniard 6-2, 6-3, 6-3. He connected in that contest with 75% of his first serves, a personal record for him in a major final. He still served 12 aces in a relatively short match. But his chief objective was taking advantage of Moya's defensive court positioning. The Spaniard was standing far behind the baseline on the return and Sampras's goal was to move in swiftly and take control at the net. Mission accomplished. Delighted to have it done, Sampras took his cap off and poured water freely over his head to cool off in the bright sunshine on a scorcher of a day.

Reflecting on the decisive win over Moya, Sampras said in 2019, "What I remember a lot about that match is that it was my introduction to playing someone with the Babolat racket. Moya's ball sounded a little funny coming off his racket. He was the first one to use that racket and was just coming up, kind of like a Costa or Corretja. But he was a little bit better with a slightly better backhand. He tried to attack my backhand. But I served well that day, got in on him and played some good, tough points against Carlos. I always felt when I played the top Spaniards that if I could beat them in some of those tough rallies I could break their will. That's what they do well. Obviously I did not want to do that too often, but I remember grinding through Carlos a bit. I felt I was timing it well. His level maybe dropped off a little and the next thing I knew it was a pretty comfortable straight-set win."

It was a satisfying way to start the year. Sampras had secured major title No. 9. He had won a second and last Australian Open on a surface that he found difficult to navigate. There was a growing feeling in the tennis community that he was destined to break Roy Emerson's men's record of 12 major singles crowns. The year 1997 was still young, but the feeling of lifting the trophy at the sport's places of prestige was far from old for Pete Sampras.

# CHAPTER 12

# TRIUMPHANT AGAIN AT WIMBLEDON

Having opened his 1997 season as stylishly and productively as he hoped he could, Sampras came back to the United States in the right frame of mind, determined to sustain the pace he had set "Down Under." He was victorious indoors in San Jose, California, taking the final after losing the first set and leading 5-0 in the second against Greg Rusedski. The left-hander, playing under the banner of Great Britain, had to retire with an injury at that stage. Across the country went Sampras to Philadelphia and in the final of the U.S. Pro Indoor he found himself facing the 24-year-old Australian Pat Rafter.

Rafter was then ranked No. 60 in the world. About six months later, this affable fellow would win the U.S. Open and, in his clash with Sampras, he performed commendably, pushing the American close to his limits before bowing out 5-7, 7-6 (4), 6-3. Rafter was coming forward with the ultra-aggression that was his trademark. He chip-charged frequently on Sampras's second serve and had success with that tactic because he was such a formidable figure at the net. Rafter volleyed aggressively, with impressive pace and unmistakable panache. And Sampras was in a transitional phase of sorts with his philosophy on coming in behind his second serve. By later in the year, he would do that more and more and from 1998 on, it became a staple in his game. His second serve was much too good to hang back behind it and having someone as capable as Rafter pressure him that way was an important factor in altering a tactical foundation in his game.

Nevertheless, Sampras had made the finest start of his career, winning his first three tournaments of the year, capturing 17 consecutive matches in that span. At Indian Wells, he suffered an understandable letdown, losing his opening round assignment with Bohdan Ulihrach as the balls often flew off his racket in the desert air with the high altitude. He then was beaten in a tight semifinal match at the Miami Masters 1000 event against the industrious Bruguera.

Sampras never quite found his competitive footing during the clay-court campaign. He did not win a match on the dirt en route to Roland Garros and then was ousted in the third round of Paris by Magnus Norman. The Swede was a first-rate clay-court competitor who reached the French Open final three years later. But having reached three quarterfinals and one semifinal in the previous five years, losing so early in Paris was disappointing for Sampras.

And yet, he now put the red clay campaign behind him and moved onto the grass in Great Britain. This was one of his favorite times of the year. Despite losing to Sweden's Jonas Bjorkman in the quarters at Queen's Club, Sampras was ready to reclaim his crown at the shrine of the sport. This was the major he had come to cherish more than any of the others, including even the U.S. Open that he valued so highly. Wimbledon had become his home away from home. He loved the feel of the place, the familiar sound of the ball coming off the strings of the racket and the incomparable atmospherics of the fabled Centre Court. Returning to the lawns of the All England Club for the most important fortnight of the entire year in tennis was a particularly joyous if sometimes stressful experience for the American.

In this 1997 edition of The Championships, Sampras was serving arrestingly from the outset, advancing through the early rounds with some timely returning and the distinctive competitive serenity that he displayed so regularly across the years. Taking on Sweden's Mikael Tillstrom—the world No. 54 who was a perennial top 100 player—in the first round, Sampras romped 6-4, 6-4, 6-2. He lost his serve only once and put in 67% of his first serves for the match. In a tighter second-round duel, he stopped Hendrik Dreekmann of Germany, coming through 7-6 (2), 7-5, 7-5 without facing a break point. In this collision, Sampras poured in 79% of his first serves, hit 22 aces and carved out breaks at the end of the second and third sets to get the victory.

Waiting for him in the third round was the diminutive Byron Black. This was their second meeting at Wimbledon, their third showdown at a major and their fourth duel overall. Sampras would eventually win all six of their battles at the cost of only one set. He made 75% of his first serves, released 13 aces and never was down break point in his 6-1, 6-2, 6-2 win.

Not until the round of 16 was Sampras seriously challenged. He was given a thorough examination by the mercurially explosive shot-maker Petr Korda, who was playing some of the finest tennis of his career. The left-hander was ranked No. 24 in the world when he walked on court for this crucial confrontation with Sampras. The following year, he would win his lone major at the Australian Open. Later, at the end of 1998, to the chagrin of Sampras and others who knew he was a very slender individual and could even seem scrawny at times, Korda was suspended for taking a performance enhancing drug.

In this appointment on Court 1, Sampras was coasting along with a 6-4, 4-2 lead but rain and darkness forced a postponement until the following afternoon. When play resumed, Sampras closed that second set quickly. From a two-sets-to-love position he was nearly impossible to beat. Not for five years—at the 1992 Olympic Games in Barcelona on clay against the Russian Andrei Chersakov—had Sampras lost after being two sets up and it would not happen again until an improbable Davis Cup match on grass in the spring of 2002 against Alex Corretja.

But Korda somehow escaped in the third set when he seemed certain to lose. Both players held serve all the way through to set up a tie-break. Sampras was utterly in command, ahead 4-0, when he netted a backhand return off a second serve. Surprisingly, that mistake seemed to irk him. He still was serving the next two points. He took the first one for a 5-1 lead and then serve-volleyed on a second delivery. Korda went down the line with absolutely no margin for error off his backhand side. The shot looked like it would be out all the way through the air until it curled at the last instant and landed just inside the sideline for an astonishing winner.

Sampras was inches away from a 6-1 lead with five match points surrounding him. Instead, Korda kept himself barely alive at 5-2 down. He made it all the way back to 5-5 but Sampras served his way to 6-5 and match point. Korda missed his first serve and then Sampras looked as though he had the upper hand in the ensuing rally. But, as Sampras slipped on the grass, Korda laced a forehand winner.

Sampras saved a set point at 7-6 and moved out in front again at 8-7 after serving an ace down the T. Korda was serving at match point down for the second time, but once more profited from his opponent losing his footing on the grass. Korda connected immaculately with a forehand passing shot. He took that tie-break 10-8, tightening the Sampras lead. The American was ahead two sets to one.

The fourth set was resolved in another tie-break, but Korda ran away with this one 7-1. When he finished that sequence off so convincingly, Korda jumped joyously in the air for one of his inimitable and bizarre scissors kicks. Sampras had not lost his serve, nor had he faced a break point. Yet he had been taken into a fifth set despite twice being a point away from a straight-sets triumph.

In the first game of the fifth set, Sampras reached break point at 30-40 by sending a forehand down-the-line approach deep to set up a forehand volley winner. Korda saved that break point with a blazing backhand crosscourt that rushed Sampras into a forehand mistake, but the American immediately garnered another. Not wanting to miss, knowing Korda might falter, realizing how sorely he needed to convert, Sampras blocked a first serve return off the forehand safely in play and Korda took the bait. He ripped a topspin backhand down the line somewhat recklessly. His shot landed wide.

Sampras's match-playing acumen had carried him to the critical break. The rest of the way, his serve was unanswerable. In five service games during that fifth set, he dropped only two points. He closed out the contest with his 27th ace, going down the T in the deuce court immaculately. Sampras put himself in the quarterfinals with a hard earned 6-4, 6-3, 6-7 (8), 6-7 (1), 6-4 triumph.

As he said in 2018, "Petr was always dangerous. I always felt like Court 1 played differently from Centre Court. It was a little faster. I wasn't that comfortable on it and Petr was a streaky guy. One break was always my philosophy on the grass. It was a relief to win that one. It was a little testy there. When Petr got hot, he could string together a lot of winners, but other times he did not. So you had to just ride the wave. But on grass if you make a few mistakes things can go pretty quickly. That is why I was glad to get that break early in the fifth."

Sampras was pitted against Becker in the quarterfinals. This was their third meeting at Wimbledon and the 18th head-to-head skirmish of their careers. Sampras led 10-7 in the series but had won both of their Wimbledon battles, prevailing in the 1993 semifinals and in the final of 1995. It was odd to see them playing as early as the quarterfinals. Becker was such a storied player and an affirmed grass court giant. But he had won only nine of the 16 matches he had played in 1997 and had not looked anything like the Becker of 1995 or 1996.

Still, this was Wimbledon, the place where he had established himself as an emerging superstar in 1985 when, at 17, he became the youngest man ever to rule as champion on the Centre Court. Becker was still capable of reproducing his old heroics under the right set of circumstances in a house he once owned.

Sampras took this match very seriously. He did not want to allow Becker any space to take over. The German's emotional intensity could be difficult to combat. The American came out of the blocks blazing, striking his returns cleanly, serving with pinpoint accuracy, moving with alacrity. Sampras was letting his adversary know that he was in a no-nonsense state of mind. This was his court now. Not even the redoubtable Becker was going to deny the American what he wanted.

Sampras made that abundantly clear when he broke for 2-0 in the first set with a crackling backhand return winner and then an unstoppable backhand pass. He was holding routinely and then broke again for 5-1 with another first-rate backhand return at the German's feet. Sampras had to fight hard to hold in the following game which lasted four deuces, but he did. After 23 minutes, he sealed the set 6-1.

Becker picked up his serving in the second set. There were no breaks. A tie-break would decide the outcome. Sampras was ahead 5-3, two points away from a two-sets-to-love lead. But Becker collected four points in a row to salvage it 7-5. It was one set all.

Sampras might have been disappointed to not seal that set, but he was typically composed and confident. At 2-1 in the third, he released consecutive backhand passing-shot winners to break. Sampras broke again in the sixth game and served it out in the seventh at 30. He won 16 of 18 points on serve in that set. It was a replica of the first set in many ways.

One break early in the fourth for 2-1 was all Sampras needed. He finished off a 6-1, 6-7 (5), 6-1, 6-4 victory with a flourish. Sharp and solid on his backhand returns and passing shots, serving rhythmically and deceptively, driving the forehand effortlessly, Sampras crushed Becker across the board. That result was not shocking, but what followed stunned the American.

When they shook hands at the net, Becker told Sampras it had been a pleasure playing him but he was not going to compete at Wimbledon again. He would later break that vow and play again in 1999, but that was not his intention at this time.

More than 20 years later, Sampras was still astonished as he reflected on that moment when Becker leaned over the net. As he said, "I was shocked. Just shocked. It floored me when he told me that up at the net. I had just won this great match and I am in my own little world. When you end a match, you normally shake hands and say 'Nice Match' and move on. But he stopped and said a few things and I did not know what to say. I think I might have said, 'It has been a pleasure playing you.' It was an eerie moment but he did come back a few years later. It was interesting that he shared that with me."

That victory over Becker lifted Sampras into a semifinal contest against the Australian Todd Woodbridge, much better known as one of the great doubles players of all time. With partner Mark Woodforde, Woodbridge won 11 "Big Four" prizes. He later took four more alongside Jonas Bjorkman. And he secured six additional Grand Slam titles in mixed doubles. Altogether, he amassed 22 major titles.

But Woodbridge had never gone this far at a major in singles before and he would not do so again. He had toppled No. 5 seed Michael Chang in the first round and No.12 Rafter in the round of 16. That was more than he could have imagined. Back in 1989, when Sampras was playing his first Wimbledon, Woodbridge had defeated the American in a four-set, first-round match.

But history was not going to repeat itself. Sampras was now clearly the best player in the world and Woodbridge realized that he had already exceeded his expectations by reaching the penultimate round. Sampras made this look like an early-round match. He released passing-shot winners at will, drilled returns at Woodbridge's feet, hit every spot he wanted on his serve and cruised to a 6-2, 6-1, 7-6 (3) triumph. The most suspenseful moment of the day occurred when Sampras was broken once at 2-1 in the third set. He had held 97 consecutive

After losing to Pete Sampras in the 1997 Wimbledon quarterfinals, Boris Becker told him that it would be his last match at Wimbledon

times since getting broken in his first-round match. But that only prolonged the match slightly, with Sampras closing it out predictably in a tie-break.

On the opposite half, unseeded Cedric Pioline had a good draw, taking out No. 15 seed Wayne Ferreira in the third round, Rusedski in the quarterfinals and then 1991 champion Michael Stich in an absorbing five-set semifinal. For the second time, the entertaining Frenchman had made it to a major final and once again his opponent was Sampras. That was not good news for Pioline.

He was 0-7 in his career against the American, including a straight-set loss at Wimbledon the year before. That was already problematic, but trying to beat Pete Sampras for the first time ever in the final of Wimbledon was an awfully tall task. Sampras was a fixture at the majors. He was 9-2 in major finals and had won his last four. He was a player made for auspicious occasions. His psyche was altered in the latter stages at the majors because he recognized that there were lasting repercussions. Victory and defeat were magnified. The wounds were much deeper for the loser, the rewards substantially larger for the winner. The big finals brought out the best in some players and the worst in others.

Sampras knew that Pioline would likely be apprehensive in his first Centre Court final on July 6, 1997. The world No. 44 double faulted on the first point of the match into the net, a clear sign of anxiety. But he followed immediately with an ace and managed to hold his serve at 30. Sampras took that in stride, holding at love. Now the burden was back on the Frenchman to avoid falling behind early.

He fought hard in the third game to hold on to his serve, saving a couple of break points. But, after three deuces, he was indeed broken. On his third break point, Sampras shortened his backswing on a backhand return and sent it down the line for a winner. Delighted with the quick start, happy with his execution on that accurate return, Sampras jogged self-assuredly to his chair at the changeover.

Pioline was aware that the set might be over. Although he was only down 2-1, getting that break back was very much against the odds. No one in the sport protected a service break lead more unbendingly than Sampras. He opened the next game with an ace and held at love to make it 3-1. After Pioline held his serve, Sampras unleashed two more aces in a hold at 30 for 4-2. The American did not need another break the way he was controlling the climate of the contest on serve.

Pioline held easily in the seventh game but Sampras began the eighth game with an ace and then won three second serve points in a row to hold at love for 5-3. Two games later, Sampras served for the set. At 30-30, he served an ace down the T. He then produced a deep second serve to the backhand, kicking it high to the Pioline backhand. The return went long. Sampras took the set 6-4. He was setting the tempo and playing this match almost entirely on his terms.

The Frenchman stayed with Sampras until the fifth game of the second set. Sampras had been coming over many of his backhand returns, but now he switched to the chip, winning a couple of big points by keeping those shots low. He broke at 15 for 3-2, and, buoyed by that development, unloaded three consecutive aces on his way to a love hold for 4-2. Returning superbly off the backhand again, Sampras broke in the seventh game. He then served out the set confidently, holding at 30 with a backhand first-volley winner down the line. The set belonged to Sampras 6-2. He was up two sets to love, one set away from a tenth Grand Slam singles title.

The Sampras backhand return was giving Pioline fits. The American broke at love in the third game of the third set. The standout point was his backhand return winner for 0-40 off an awkward body serve. Sampras promptly held at love for 3-1. He served another love game for 4-2, coming up with his 16th ace for 40-0. Two holds away from a fourth Wimbledon title in five years, Sampras advanced to 5-3 in a tough, two-deuce game. And then, serving for the match at 5-4, down 0-15 after Pioline connected for a return winner off his elegant backhand side, Sampras swept four points in a row. At 40-15, up double match point, he angled a slice serve out wide to the weaker forehand wing of Pioline and the Frenchman had no play on the return. Sampras succeeded 6-4, 6-2, 6-4, taking his second major of the season.

Sampras said in an interview for this book, "It felt good to win that Wimbledon. I remember Cedric beating Stich in the semis. That would have been maybe more of a challenge playing Stich. But Pioline was talented and he deserved to be in that final. Like for every final I play, you get more comfortable. You don't sleep well the night before, but you get into your routine. Cedric wasn't going to serve me off the court. I was going to have a chance to play and to use my serve-and-volley game. I think the moment got to him. He didn't play very well. He missed a few shots, threw in a few double faults and made it a little easier for me. Once I get on top of someone and he is not playing well, I can let my shoulders down and really play. I felt that was a good, clean grass-court match."

Sampras had finished off the best serving tournament of his career at any major. In seven matches, he had held serve in an astounding 116 of 118 service games. Five of his seven opponents, including Pioline, did not break him. He served 115 aces across the fortnight in only 24 sets. To be sure, his opposition was tougher in many of his other majors. In this case, Sampras did not meet a top ten player and the highest-ranked player he confronted was No. 18 Becker. But the fact remains that he was in a remarkable rhythm all fortnight long and it is doubtful that anyone could have beaten Sampras at Wimbledon in 1997. Very doubtful.

Over the summer, Sampras returned home to Tampa, Florida, where he lived and trained for a large chunk of the nineties. He would have much preferred to be in California where he had grown up. He loved that part of the country. But, as Mary Carillo pointed out, he was sacrificing the California life for a climate and location that was going to keep him at the top of the sport.

Carillo said in 2019, "The game just meant so damned much to Pete. He had to fight his own body. He had ulcers. And he continued to live in Florida all those years even though he wanted to be in California so badly, but he stayed in Florida to train because he wanted to end the year No. 1 year after year. These were the sacrifices he made and the stuff he did and he felt it was all worth it."

Sampras clarified how it felt to be in his shoes at that time. He said, "I felt like I needed to be in an area where it was easy to focus and find a climate that could get you in the best shape, especially over the summer. I had my trainer there in Florida [Pat Etcheberry] and plenty of practice partners and it was a good setup for me, a good place to chill and relax after being on the road. But also, it was right for me there. Being in L.A., it is so spread out and you are spending half the day in the car. It all worked out for me being in Florida. It was a little closer to Europe for flights and there were a lot of benefits. It was definitely a sacrifice, but I knew I was not going to be there forever. I was not able to see the family as much. I was in Tampa for quite a while. I was doing well and didn't want to change a good thing."

As for Etcheberry, a highly-regarded task master, Sampras said, "He was an old school sort of trainer who pushed me very hard. He was kind of a no pain, no gain trainer and we worked on specific foot drills on the clay courts. We did a lot of lifting in the gym, did some long runs and some sprint work. He was easy to be around, but he was a no BS sort of trainer who just wanted you to get your work done. He didn't want to hear how you were feeling or what was going on in your life. It was a good relationship and he got me in great shape."

Sampras had done it again at Wimbledon. But he was not content with winning his second major of the year. He sorely wanted another.

Sampras worked hard in Florida and had about a one month training period after Wimbledon and then he was almost letter perfect all week long at the Masters 1000 event in Cincinnati. He did not lose a set all week, knocking out Rafter, Kakelnikov, Costa and Muster in his last four matches. Although he was beaten the next week in Indianapolis by Magnus Larsson in a final-set tie-break, Sampras was well prepared and heavily favored to win the U.S. Open.

On Labor Day, he found himself facing the wildly unpredictable Korda, the same man who had given him his toughest match at Wimbledon by far. They waged a hard court war in New York. Sampras was up a break in the fifth set, leading 3-0. He later came within two points of winning this rugged round of 16 clash. But Korda edged him out in a tie-break at the end. Sampras's bid to win three majors in a single season for the first time in his career came to an end. He also lost his chance to win the Open three consecutive years. Had Sampras held back Korda, he would have met Bjorkman in the quarters, Rusedski in the semis and Rafter in the final. That title would almost certainly have gone to him. Korda may well have been the only man in the Open field who could have beaten Sampras.

But, as was his pattern in life, as he demonstrated so many times over the course of a sterling career, Sampras did not lose sleep over a lost opportunity. Agassi and other rivals could sometimes drown in a sea of self-pity, wrestling with the elusive past, usually to their own detriment. Sampras had a different mentality, moving on purposefully toward new targets, not worrying about what might have been.

He did some very productive work over the autumn. First, not long after the Open, the U.S. Davis Cup team assembled in Washington for the semifinal round in the World Group. Sampras crushed Philippoussis in straight sets on Friday afternoon. Chang upended Rafter the same day so the U.S. led 2-0 and then captain Tom Gullikson went for the kill, hoping Sampras and Todd Martin could topple the esteemed Woodies. But Woodforde and Woodbridge stopped the American tandem in four sets.

Sampras then had the chance on his own to clinch victory for the United States when he faced the newly-minted U.S. Open champion Rafter. The Australian scraped out a tight opening set tie-break 8-6, but then Sampras erupted. For two sets, he played unconsciously sublime tennis, serving stupendously, returning with impeccable timing, passing his aggressive adversary at will. He lost only five total points on his serve in the second and third sets and took the match 6-7 (6), 6-1, 6-1, 6-4. He would never play better tennis against Rafter and seldom would he surpass that form against anyone else.

Perhaps Sampras had a point to prove. He had wanted that Open crown now being worn by Rafter. Facing the man who had replaced him as the U.S. Open champion gave the 26-year-old American that extra layer of motivation. It was nothing personal, but simply a time to bring out the best he had to offer against a player who had established himself so recently in the elite circle of players who had claimed a title at a Grand Slam event.

As Rafter recalled in an interview for this book, "Pete came out and just kicked my ass. Too good. I won that first set, but he got angry and beat me. He was just a better player than I was. He went out and did the job and did it well. He had a bit of a purpose. He was fired up."

Sampras maintained a high level through the rest of 1997. He was playing some of the best tennis of his career during this span. After that Davis Cup semifinal when fans came up to Sampras and Chang to congratulate them on winning the Cup (not realizing there was another round to go in Sweden), Sampras was magnificent in closing out a stellar season. He was victorious at the Grand Slam Cup indoors in Munich, coming from behind to win a clutch four-set semifinal against Rusedski before eclipsing Rafter systematically 6-2, 6-4, 7-5. Beaten by Richard Krajicek in the round of 16 in Stuttgart, Sampras took the ATP Masters 1000 Paris indoor title, overcoming the impressive quintet of Becker, Korda, Muster, Kafelnikov and Bjorkman.

Bolstered by that remarkable run, he took the ATP World Tour Championships in Hannover, Germany. It was the fourth time he won the highly-coveted season ending tournament for the top eight players in the world. Beaten by Moya in his opening round-robin clash, Sampras performed prodigiously the rest of the way, defeating Rusedski, Rafter, Bjorkman and Kafelnikov without the loss of a set. He won three of his last four tournaments in 1997 with a flourish. Although he had to retire on opening day of the Davis Cup Final in Sweden at one set all and 1-2 in the third against the sometimes daunting Magnus Larsson with a leg injury, Sampras had to be content with the way he had concluded the year. He finished far ahead of his rivals to garner the year-end No. 1 ranking for the fifth year in a row, giving him a tie for the ATP record with fellow American Jimmy Connors (1974-78). For the second year in a row, Sampras garnered eight titles and in addition he won 55 of 67 matches.

Perhaps physically and certainly mentally weary after another long and demanding year, Sampras would struggle to find a winning formula in the early stages of 1998. His five consecutive years at the top had taken a toll. He had won no fewer than nine majors over that remarkable span and ten altogether in his career. And yet, his pursuit of the highest goals was undiminished.

# CHAPTER 13

# QUEST FOR AN 11th MAJOR

The first half of the 1998 Sampras campaign did not measure up to the second half of his 1997 season. He played ten tournaments on the road to Wimbledon, winning Philadelphia over Sweden's big-hitting Thomas Enqvist, taking the clay-court title in Atlanta over seasoned professional Jason Stoltenberg. But there were many setbacks. He did not lose a set on his way to the Australian Open quarterfinals, but the defending champion was ushered out of that tournament by a 23-year-old from the Czech Republic named Karol Kucera. Kucera was a stylist to his core, feeding off the pace of the sport's bigger hitters, counter-attacking with extraordinary quickness and a stunningly agile mind, displaying astounding feel and remarkable ball control.

Sampras would be on the right end of a 7-1 career series with Kucera. This was only their second meeting. And it all came together for Kucera in Melbourne. He had a high service toss that could give him issues on windy occasions, but in this instance he was untroubled in that department. He served 19 aces, 12 more than Sampras. He returned spectacularly, breaking the best server in the sport no less than seven times. He ran down Sampras' biggest shots and retaliated with uncanny strategic acumen. Sampras, meanwhile, had a bad night. Kucera won 6-4, 6-2, 6-7 (3), 6-3.

Sampras was the runner-up to Agassi in San Jose before winning in Philadelphia. Moving outdoors, he was ousted by Muster at Indian Wells and Wayne Ferreira in Miami. On clay at the Masters 1000 tournament in Monte Carlo, he came under the spell of "The Magician" Fabrice Santoro, a player with one of the widest assortment of shots in the game and unimaginable touch. Santoro stung Sampras 6-1, 6-1. Then Sampras won Atlanta on clay but lost to Chang in the round of 16 in Rome. Returning to Roland Garros for his ninth attempt at the French Open title, Sampras did not fare well, bowing out in the second round 7-6 (6), 6-3, 6-4 against Ramon Delgado, a 21-year-old clay-courter from Paraguay ranked No. 97 in the world.

In three consecutive major tournaments, Sampras had not gone past the quarterfinals. Not since 1991 had that happened to him. But he was back where he wanted to be, on the grass of Great Britain, looking to make amends at the All England Club. Although he was beaten soundly and surprisingly at the Queen's Club 6-3, 6-2 by the left-handed Woodforde, that loss to the world No. 66 would not linger long in his mind.

His overriding goal was to win a fifth Wimbledon and an 11th major title. Although the path leading to this point in the 1998 season had not been entirely what Sampras would have wanted, the fact remained that he approached every edition of Wimbledon believing that this was both his time and his turf. The preceding months were incidental to Sampras now; Wimbledon was his chief and only concern.

He drew Hrbaty in the first round, the same young fellow who had been so bothersome under a scorching sun at the Australian Open the year before. On the lawns of the All England Club, it was a vastly different story. Hrbaty did not have time to take his big cuts on service returns. The low bouncing grass courts in England were not to his liking. Sampras was serve-volleying as well as it could be done and taking complete command up at the net. He smothered his opponent with a barrage of big serving and forehand firepower from the backcourt. Sampras soared to a 6-3, 6-3, 6-2 triumph, serving 19 aces, losing his serve only once, winning 56 of 61 first-serve points.

In the second round, Sampras met Sweden's Mikael Tillstrom, a player to whom he never lost a match in six meetings. The year before at the All England Club, Sampras removed Tillstrom in straight sets and this duel was very similar. Sampras did not face a break point in a 6-4, 6-4, 7-6 (4) victory, making 69% of his first serves. He had moved into the third round comfortably, but now would confront a much more accomplished adversary.

Thomas Enqvist was the No. 17 ranked player in the world but he would peak at No. 4 in the ATP Rankings late the following year. At 6' 3" and 195 pounds, he was imposing. His power on serve and off the ground was not insubstantial. Sampras started this skirmish late on Saturday afternoon after rain fell Friday and caused the one-day delay. On Saturday, his serve was stunningly potent and accurate from the opening bell. The first seven points he served were all aces. He took the opening set 6-3. There were two more rain delays before a third, at 5-5, brought the curtain down on play for the day. With the middle Sunday of the tournament an off day for the players, Sampras and Enqvist did not return until Monday. The American took the second set in a tie-break and the match went to 4-4 in the third. Once more, rain intruded. At long last, Sampras advanced 6-3, 7-6 (4), 7-6 (3) after serving a total of 28 aces and not facing any break points.

In his round of 16 contest with the fleet-footed Frenchman Sebastien Grosjean, Sampras came forward relentlessly on his own serve, rushed his opponent into errors and probed from the backcourt until he could get the right ball to approach the net. Grosjean tested Sampras to a degree with his outstanding speed and a first-rate forehand, but the American always had the upper hand in a 6-3, 6-4, 6-4 triumph, serving 16 aces and getting broken only once.

Everything was shaping up well for Sampras as he shifted gears for a big server's contest against Philippoussis on

Court 1. The first set was the key to the outcome. Sampras came through in a tie-break 7-5. From there, he gathered strength and played from ahead with his usual self-assurance. One break in both the second and third sets was enough, carrying Sampras to a 7-6 (5), 6-4, 6-4 victory. Although he connected with only 46% of his first serves, Sampras never faced a break point in the entire match, proof that his second serve was so deep and biting that it was very much like another first serve.

Now the top seed was into the semifinals. Nearly every time Sampras stepped out onto the Centre Court, he was comfortable and inspired to perform in that regal setting. He was regularly and deeply appreciated by the British audiences over the years, celebrated for his enduring excellence, beloved as a sportsman of the highest order. Sampras was, in essence, one of their own. No British man had won Wimbledon in singles since Fred Perry took his third consecutive title in 1936. Because Sampras was so reserved, dignified and such a model of decorum, the British fans embraced him to a large degree as their favorite player; in their eyes, he was borderline British.

But, in the 1998 semifinals, Sampras was pitted against his friend and frequent practice partner Tim Henman, a quarterfinalist the previous two years and now among the final four for the first time. He was quick coming forward, a confirmed serve-and-volleyer and a player with a game tailor made for the grass. Moreover, he hailed from Great Britain and a large portion of the affectionate fans were thirsting for him to succeed against the four-time Wimbledon victor.

The Centre Court atmosphere was therefore more highly charged than usual. It was as if this was a Davis Cup confrontation and the 23-year-old Englishman was not only representing himself but also carrying the hopes of a nation on his shoulders. They fully recognized that Henman would be hard pressed to stop the world's greatest tennis player, but could still allow their imaginations to soar.

Amidst this uncommonly high tension surrounding the occasion, Sampras came out acutely aware of what he needed to do. He had not played Henman since their Wimbledon early-round meeting three years back. The British competitor had grown by leaps and bounds since then. Now he was ranked No. 18 in the world, headed for residence in the top five and prepared to do battle against a colleague he knew well.

As Sampras recollected in 2018, "I felt a little uncomfortable in that match. Tim and I were friends and he was getting closer and maybe was worthy of winning a Wimbledon. And there were expectations on Tim that year."

The American was sharply focused at the outset and did not lose a point in his first two service games. But Henman was punching his volleys crisply and holding his own. At 2-3 in the first set, Sampras was break point down. It was a pivotal moment. He aced Henman out wide in the ad court for deuce and took the next two points to make it to 3-3.

Relieved and more at ease, Sampras turned up the volume of his intensity and went to work even harder. With Henman serving at 30-15 in the seventh game, Sampras displayed his tactical acumen and keen instincts, employing a topspin lob to back Henman up and taking the net away from the Englishman. Sampras now came in behind a flat forehand, eliciting a passing shot error from Henman. At 30-30, Sampras rolled a backhand return at the feet of the incoming Henman, who could not get anything on his half volley. Alert and opportunistic, Sampras swooped in and put away a forehand volley. Shaken, Henman double faulted long.

Sampras had the break for 4-3 and consolidated it easily, holding at love in the eighth game. He was in full flight now, breaking Henman at 15 in the ninth game with a backhand inside-in return winner. The American had found his range on the backhand return, breaking a second time, taking the opening set 6-3.

When Sampras held at love to commence the second set, he had now won five games in a row and 19 of the last 22 points. His heavyweight game was making Henman look like a lightweight. Sampras was outperforming Henman in every facet of the game.

But Henman held on for 1-1 in the second set and then shifted to another gear while Sampras's form dropped slightly. On the first point of the third game, Henman's lob was good enough to prevent Sampras from putting his smash away. Henman got it back and then Sampras missed a forehand down the line volley. Henman followed with a forehand topspin lob winner down the line and a sparkling backhand pass down the line. Sampras served an ace at 0-40 but Henman broke at 15 with an excellent forehand down the line return coaxing a half volley error from the American.

The Centre Court crowd was pleasantly surprised. Henman had sunk his teeth into the contest. The British player held on for 3-1 and then broke Sampras again in the fifth game after two deuces. Henman improbably was ahead by two breaks in the second set. Sampras got one of them back in the sixth game when Henman double faulted at 15-40 and then the No. 1 seed held at 15 with an ace.

The Henman lead had been cut to 4-3, but he held for 5-3. Two games later, serving for the set and enlivened by the effusiveness of the fans, Henman held at love with a fine first serve into the body. It was one set all. In essence, the match was starting all over again.

Both players held without much stress until Henman served at 2-3 in the third set. Sampras advanced to break point and sent a backhand return down the line, keeping it low, hitting it hard. Henman seemed compromised. For an instant, Sampras seemed certain to secure a break and be back in command. But Henman's low forehand first volley was a beauty. He punched it crosscourt for a clean winner and then took the next two points. 3-3.

Sampras did not allow that tough stand from the British competitor to alter his mindset. The American held at love with an ace, his ninth of the match. Henman answered with an easy hold for 4-4. This hard-fought set was building to a crescendo. Both players were going full force after it. Sampras held at 30 with another ace out wide to make it 5-4, but Henman was not blinking, holding at the cost of only one point for 5-5.

The fans understood the significance of this set. So, too, did the players. Sampras served-and-volleyed remarkably well to establish a 6-5 lead, holding at 15. He would either win the set in the following game or have another opportunity to seal it in a tie-break. With Henman serving to stay in the set, and the score locked at 30-30, Sampras chipped a backhand approach effectively. Henman's lob was short. Sampras demolished it with an overhead winner. Set point for the American.

Henman wiped it away with a service winner down the T. But Sampras made a superb low forehand return crosscourt to force Henman into an errant forehand volley. The American had garnered a second set point, yet once more Henman was not found wanting. He rolled the dice in a way by driving a forehand inside-in, giving Sampras a chance to make his signature running forehand. But the American missed. Deuce again.

Now Henman gained the advantage, moving to game point, standing on the edge of a tie-break. He sent a beautifully-placed first serve down the T that might have been an ace against many other players. Sampras was at full stretch, but somehow he muscled a forehand return winner past a startled Henman, leaving the crowd gasping at that stellar display of grace and power under pressure.

Sampras was utterly determined to negotiate a service break here and avoid the potential lottery of a tie-break. He chipped a backhand return and followed it in. Having served-and-volleyed, Henman was confounded and helpless. Sampras closed in determinedly and directed a terrific backhand crosscourt volley behind Henman for a winner. For the third time, Sampras had advanced to set point. This one he converted, keeping his backhand return low at Henman's feet. Henman's half volley response sat up. Sampras lined up his backhand crosscourt passing shot and hit through it with force, generating as much pace as he could with enough topspin to make it dip. Henman was camped on top of the net but the speed of Sampras's shot was too much for the British player. He missed the volley. Sampras had taken the set 7-5.

He emoted freely, jumping for joy, clenching his fist, conveying that he was both exhilarated and relieved to be ahead two sets to one. His early evening expressiveness was welcomed by his wide legion of worldwide admirers who appreciated that Sampras was not a man who manufactured his emotions. Only selectively would he share how he felt with those who were watching and when he did the impact on audiences was therefore larger.

Down break point in the first game of the fourth set, Sampras characteristically released an unstoppable first serve to Henman's backhand side. Recognizing the significance of this juncture of the contest, Sampras comfortably conveyed his feelings. He passionately said to himself, "Come On!" Back to back aces carried Sampras to 1-0. With Henman serving at 1-2, 30-30, Sampras chip-charged off the backhand, punched a forehand volley crosscourt and then anticipated Henman's down the line passing shot. Sampras knifed his backhand volley crosscourt into an empty space. Chip-charging again on break point, Sampras was ready for Henman's forehand inside-in pass. He put away a forehand volley unhesitatingly and gave himself a fist pump. The American was up 3-1. He soon held at 15 with an ace for 4-1.

After both men held across the next three games, Sampras served for the match at 5-3. He produced two service winners and an ace for 40-0. Henman saved one match point, but Sampras came through on the second with an ace down the T. It was his 16th of the match and a symbolic moment. Sampras moved on to the final with a fulfilling 6-3, 4-6, 7-5, 6-3 win under difficult circumstances.

As he recalled in an interview for this book, "Because we knew each other so well and practiced so much, Tim was comfortable with my game. The more he saw my serve, he was getting on to me a bit. The third set was big. Those moments really changed the course of the match. In the fourth, I got a little better and he dropped off a bit, but the third was such a big part of that match. Getting to a tie-break, anything can happen, but breaking there in that last game to win the third made me feel so much better in the fourth. I remember how that game to close the third set relaxed me. There are moments in a match that are backbreakers. I knew that with 12,000 to 15,000 English people rooting for him, you are carrying that weight with you the whole time. I was aware of that so I showed some emotion when I won the third set."

And so Sampras had arrived in another Wimbledon final, the fifth of his career. For the second time in a title-round contest and the fourth time overall since 1992 at the All England Club, Sampras would have to deal with the ever-daunting Goran Ivanisevic in this July 5, 1998 appointment. The Croatian had survived a harrowing five-set encounter with 1996 Wimbledon champion Richard Krajicek in the semifinals. He was up two sets to one, 5-4, 40-15, double match point over the Dutchman. An apparent ace was called a let. Ivanisevic lost the set but eventually prevailed 6-3, 6-4, 5-7, 6-7 (5), 15-13.

This was the towering left-hander's third Wimbledon final. He thought this might be his breakthrough year on the lawns. His serve was overwhelming but perhaps not as astonishingly accurate as Sampras's and he was prone to double faults that could be costly, but the fact remained that Ivanisevic had the single biggest weapon in tennis with that deadly delivery. Whenever he stepped out onto the grass courts in Great Britain, Ivanisevic struck thunderbolts like no one else.

In seven matches at the 1992 Wimbledon—including his five set, final-round loss to Agassi—Ivanisevic served a total of 206 aces. On the way to this appointment with Sampras six years later, he had served 152 aces in six matches. Over the course of his career, he would release no less than 10,131 aces. Sampras knew full well as he headed into this Centre Court final that he would need to be nimble of mind and stout of heart to conquer the mighty southpaw Ivanisevic on the sport's most fabled court.

He did have a 10-6 career head to head edge over the Croatian at that point and had been victorious in two of their three Wimbledon meetings. But every time he took on this adversary, Sampras was understandably circumspect. It was

Pete Sampras had much to celebrate at Wimbledon in 1998

not entirely in his own hands. The points, as usual, would be swift, hard hitting and violent. It was a no rhythm, quick paced, high stakes matchup, as exacting as any he would ever experience.

Sampras had the first glimpse of a break at 1-1 in the first set on an afternoon that started with brilliant sunshine but later clouded over to some degree. As was the case four years earlier in the final, Sampras had the sun in his eyes on the Centre Court over the first hour or so. The left-handed Ivanisevic did not have the same issues. But Sampras did reach 15-40 on Ivanisevic's serve. He had four break points altogether in that four deuce game. But the southpaw held on for 2-1. Sampras had to save a break point in the following game, but he wiped it away. At 2-3, the American drifted into danger again at 15-40 but a backhand volley winner into the open court and a service winner put him at deuce. He held on for 3-3.

In the ninth game, Sampras had a break point, but Ivanisevic served into the body with slice to draw an errant forehand return from Sampras. On to 5-4 went the No. 14 seed. At 5-5, Sampras gave himself another look at a break, but Ivanisevic aced him out wide at 30-40 and held on for 6-5. After Sampras held his serve for 6-6, the set went to a tie-break. Ivanisevic was decidedly better in that sequence. He won all five of his service points, did not miss a first serve and closed out the tie-break 7-2 with an ace and a service winner.

Sampras got the early break for 2-0 in the second set but a plucky Ivanisevic broke back in the following game. Both men served magnificently the rest of the set. In his last five service games, Ivanisevic allowed Sampras only three points. The pressure was largely on the American. He could not afford to fall behind two sets to love against a server like Ivanisevic; he had to establish his authority now and treat every point like a match point.

Sampras moved ahead 3-1 in the tie-break, but then he did not make his first serve break wide enough in the deuce court. Ivanisevic drove a backhand return winner down the line and then blasted a pair of aces to lead 4-3. Sampras served his way into a 5-4 lead before Ivanisevic unleashed two devastatingly potent and unanswerable first serves in a row to the backhand, regaining the lead at 6-5.

This meant that Sampras was set point down. He missed his first serve but spun his second delivery to the backhand of Ivanisevic, who missed the return. Sampras advanced to 7-6 with a set point on the Ivanisevic serve. Ivanisevic slipped and fell coming in behind his first serve, but Sampras's chipped return off the backhand was wide. Ivanisevic garnered a second set point when he went ahead 8-7, but his backhand return off a better second serve found the net.

Now Sampras had a second set point of his own, but the velocity of Ivanisevic's first serve was too much. Sampras netted a backhand return. It was 9-9. As the players changed ends of the court, the Centre Court tension was almost tangible. Ivanisevic then served an apparent double fault. The beep of the Cyclops machine was unmistakable. But the umpire overruled immediately. An astounded Sampras bellowed, "Oh my God!" The reaction was understandable because now the point would be played over and Ivanisevic would have a first serve. Yet Sampras collected his composure at once. Ivanisevic missed his first serve and then sent a second delivery to the backhand. Sampras hit his return reasonably hard, but higher than he wanted. Ivanisevic, however, faltered at a crucial moment. His forehand volley was poorly executed and travelled well long.

Sampras was at set point for the third time, but this was the first one on his serve. The American steadied himself and released a first serve in the ad court to the Ivanisevic forehand. The big left-hander could not handle the difficult return. The set was in the Sampras victory column, 11-9 in the tie-break. After all of the anxiety and two set points against him, a deeply relieved Sampras was back to one set all.

Until then, Sampras was having serious doubts about the outcome of this final. He recalled, "I wasn't playing that well and felt maybe this was Goran's time. He won that first set and then we went to that second-set breaker and you feel like you are not getting the breaks. I was thinking maybe it wasn't my day. I actually kind of felt that during the match, like maybe I got through a couple of tight ones with Goran in the past, but thinking maybe I wore out my nine lives. So when that moment happened at 9-9 in the tie-break, you feel it is maybe not your day. But one thing led to another and I ended up winning that second set. I felt I had kind of escaped, so I was thinking, 'Let's get back into it.'"

In the fifth game of the third set, Sampras found an opening. On break point, Ivanisevic went wide with a first serve to the Sampras backhand, but the American read it well, chipping his return sharply crosscourt for a clean winner. Delighted with that excellent return and by going up a break in the set, Sampras cried out joyously, "Yeah!"

He was at one set all but up a break at 3-2 in the third. From that juncture, Sampras was unstoppable. In his last three service games from there, Sampras took 12 of 14 points. Serving for the set at 5-4, he was the ultimate professional and a closer nonpareil. He opened that tenth game with an ace and finished it off with another untouchable delivery. Two aces. A love hold. Two sets to one for Sampras.

At 2-2 in the fourth set, Sampras had a break point, but a body serve to the forehand from Ivanisevic was too good. The southpaw secured a clutch hold for 3-2. Sampras could have been well on his way to victory, but Ivanisevic was refusing to accept defeat. He proceeded to play one of the greatest return games of his career on an auspicious occasion to break for a 4-2 lead. It was breathtaking. On the first point of that stunning sixth game, he directed a low backhand return down the line off a first serve. Sampras made a decent backhand half volley crosscourt, but Ivanisevic drove a forehand passing shot winner on the run for 0-15. Another low return set up a gorgeous backhand passing shot crosscourt: 0-30. Sampras served wide to the backhand again, sent a first volley crosscourt, but Ivanisevic was in the midst of a magical spell, directing a down-the-line forehand pass for a winner: 0-40.

Sampras saved one break point but, at 15-40, Ivanisevic struck gold on another forehand crosscourt passing shot winner. Sampras had gone four-for-five on first serves but lost his serve at 15 as Ivanisevic pulled off four magnificent outright winners. Ivanisevic then held at 30 for 5-2. Serving for the set at 5-3, Ivanisevic held at 15 with his 30th ace of the day. Set to Ivanisevic 6-3. Two sets all. An astounding turnaround had taken place.

And so, for the first time in his career, Sampras was engaged in a five-set final at a Grand Slam event. Ivanisevic had played spectacularly to capture the fourth set. No one knew what to expect. Sampras was the best big-match player of the Open Era. Ivanisevic was one set away from a title he had wanted more than any other throughout his career. Neither the stakes nor the suspense could have been more substantial.

Despite two double faults, Sampras held at 30 for 1-0 in the fifth set. Ivanisevic made it to 1-1. Sampras stepped up his serving decidedly in the third game, making all five first serves, holding at 15, closing with an ace down the T. Ivanisevic stood his ground forcefully, holding at 30 for 2-2. With these two prodigious servers battling it out, a long fifth set seemed entirely possible. There were still no final-set tie-breaks at Wimbledon. Not until 21 years later, when Novak Djokovic toppled Roger Federer in a gripping final after saving two match points, would a final set at the sport's shrine be settled in a tie-break—and that was not until 12-12 in a phenomenal fifth set.

But in his 1998 duel grass-court duel with Ivanisevic, Sampras was finding a groove on his serve. He held at love for 3-2, finishing with his second ace of the game, sending this one out wide in the ad court. Ivanisevic may have been slightly fatigued after his debilitating semifinal with Krajicek, but Sampras, despite the almost unbearable tension of the afternoon, was feeling fine. He played an excellent return game. A low return set up a crosscourt forehand passing-shot winner. An impeccably executed low backhand chip return drew an errant volley from Ivanisevic: 0-30. The lefty won the next point, but Sampras went to 15-40 with a dipping backhand return forcing the southpaw to half volley weakly. Sampras then drove a backhand passing shot winner up the line. Now the big Croatian served wide and Sampras responded with a scorching forehand return at the feet of the incoming server. Ivanisevic netted his half volley.

Sampras had played his best return game of the afternoon to break at 15 for 4-2. He then held at 30 for 5-2. Serving to stay in the match, Ivanisevic was confronting a surging Sampras. The American started with a backhand inside-in return winner. Ivanisevic double faulted for the 20th time in the match to trail 0-30. A low chipped return from Sampras elicited a forehand first volley long: 0-40. Another finely-chipped return from Sampras made Ivanisevic half volley with no relish. Sampras moved forward for the forehand pass and a dispirited Ivanisevic sent a backhand volley long.

Sampras had broken at love to complete a pendulum swinging 6-7 (2), 7-6 (9), 6-4, 3-6, 6-2 victory, winning 16 of the last 19 points, taking four games in a row at the end. Not only did he have his fifth Wimbledon singles title, but the triumph was his 11th at a major, placing the American only one behind the widely-revered Roy Emerson of Australia for the men's record.

As Sampras said of that 1998 final 20 years later, "Goran steamrolled me there in the fourth set. I just tried to stay patient with him and hopefully get some second-serve opportunities and make him play. The match was just kind of touch and go. I really did feel it wasn't going to be my day, but the next thing I knew I had won the match. To be honest, I felt a little sheepish in the trophy presentation ceremony afterwards. I was holding that trophy up and Goran was just devastated. He felt like he let one get away and thought he should have won. I felt for him. He played better than I did, but I just managed to scratch and claw to get an opportunity and one thing led to another."

Sampras paused, and then continued, "I felt like I wasn't the better player that day. So how did I win? Maybe there was just something in the air. I can't explain it."

Ivanisevic recalled in his 2019 interview for this book, "From the beginning I thought I can't lose this match. I was a better player all through the match but I didn't win. I could break him whenever I want and I was playing better. I won that first set and then had those two set points in the second-set tie-break. And it is funny what happened. Pete had one of the best second serves in the history of tennis. It was always very deep and hard to return. So I was expecting a big second serve on those set points. So I went a little further back on the return. And I don't think he did it on purpose, but he got tight and on one of those second serves it landed short. I missed the returns. If I go two sets to love up there is no chance that he comes back."

How did Ivanisevic feel about coming back into the match later and forcing a fifth set? Was he somewhat fatigued after his long semifinal against Krajicek?

He responded, "Okay, that hurt me. That was the strangest semifinal ever because I had already won the match with Krajicek in the fourth set and we were shaking hands and then the guy called a let on match point for me and we played for two more hours before I finally won. That was crazy. But when I lost the third set with Pete, I still believed I cannot lose. That is why I won the fourth set, but then I played a very bad game early in the fifth when I was serving with new balls. I was finished after that. I lose my serve and it was bye, bye for me. You cannot do that against Pete after you have a chance."

Ivanisevic elaborated on his regret about not making certain when he had a chance to defeat a great champion he knew would never give up. He said, "Pete is a guy that, like in the movies, you shoot him but one bullet is not enough. He gets up. You have to make sure he is dead. I did not make sure he was dead. I had to shoot him a couple more times and I did not do it. That was a big mistake. You can't do that. Pete doesn't forgive you. Unfortunately, that was the biggest tournament in the world. Losing that game on my serve with the new balls when he was kind of down made him lift his game and that was it. I didn't have any chance on his serve after that. Zero. I was gone."

And yet, Ivanisevic lauded Sampras considerably for the way he competed that day and all through their respective careers. He said in 2019, "Pete could play some bad matches early in those big tournaments but he somehow would win and later in the tournament he was just better, better, better. And then you were gone. You thought you had him but you did not. He showed you how strong he was mentally. Sometimes he might not look like he was, but he was there. He was really there. Somehow he would beat you. Ninety percent of the matches we played would be 7-5 or 7-6 in the final set, or five sets. It was always tight but it was pretty much the same scenario every time, like copy-paste. Grand Slam Cup. ATP Finals. So many times it would happen to me."

Ivanisevic came out on the wrong end of a 12-6 career series with Sampras and the American captured ten of their last 11 meetings. At Wimbledon, Ivanisevic was beaten by Sampras in two finals and one semifinal. He only triumphed once over the American at that storied location. But some of the sting from those penetrating defeats was diminished when the towering Croatian won Wimbledon in 2001 as a wildcard ranked No. 125 in the world and he was deeply touched when Sampras conveyed his sincere and heartfelt congratulations later that summer.

As Sampras remembered, "I congratulated Goran when I saw him in Cincinnati for the first time after he had won Wimbledon. We had a nice moment there. I was happy for him."

Ivanisevic was deeply touched by that gesture from his old rival. He said, "Here is Pete Sampras who has won Wimbledon so many times and he comes up to me. He was not saying these things to me just to be nice. He really felt happy for me. I saw that he appreciated me and really respected me as a tennis player and a person. That was the first time he came like that to me and it is why he was No. 1 and the best. He was showing another aspect of his personality that people did not see often. He was genuinely happy that I had won Wimbledon. We were not best friends, but we had huge respect for each other. Pete was for me one of the best players in the history of tennis and I was lucky I could play at the same time and in the same era as him. I am honored I was part of the story, playing Pete Sampras in so many big matches. Nobody can take that away from me. When they talk about the Sampras Era, they are always going to mention me. I feel privileged to have played when he did."

Inarguably, the 1998 title-round duel between Sampras and Ivanisevic could have gone either way, but Sampras is perhaps downgrading what he did to win and Ivanisevic is being too hard on himself in evaluating his defeat. Sampras had to fight with quiet fury to avoid trailing by two sets to love, but he was the decidedly better player in the third set and the clearly worthy victor in the fifth. Moreover, he was the more well-rounded of the two competitors, volleying with significantly more flair and feel than Ivanisevic, demonstrably playing with more self-assurance and stability when the chips were down.

Annacone admired how Sampras managed his emotions during that tumultuous contest against an adversary who was such an overwhelming physical force. He said, "It was another great effort for Pete to deal with a guy like Goran who can take the racket out of your hand. Goran can really do that. After Goran played a really good fourth set, Pete just flushed that out of his system and then, bang, he wins the fifth."

To be sure, Sampras needed some good fortune to get through that gut-wrenching afternoon against a player who worried him more than any other on a grass court. But the old adage that "fortune favors the brave" applied to Pete Sampras on a day when he was not at his zenith. He won that one with his heart and his undervalued will. He took it with steadfastness and resolution. He succeeded because he was a champion of rare stature.

But the rest of the year was a complicated and often unhappy stretch for Sampras. Heading into each and every season, his goal was always to win at least one major and perhaps more. His highest priorities unswervingly were the Grand Slam tournaments and that is what drove him to dizzying heights. For the most part, he was not preoccupied with his ranking. He wanted to be the best in the world and finishing the year at No. 1 was a priority. He realized that winning one or two of the "Big Four" prizes—coupled with success in ATP Tour Masters 1000 tournaments and as solid a record as possible across the board—would ensure his status at the top of the rankings.

The 1998 season, however, was different in that regard for Sampras. He was aware that Connors had spent five years in a row (1974-78) at No. 1 in the official ATP Rankings. Now he had a chance to break that record and conclude six consecutive years as the preeminent player on the planet. As the second half of the season progressed, and certainly in every tournament he played after the U.S. Open, he was always thinking about realizing that goal. Always.

Over the summer on the hard courts en route to the U.S. Open, he was beaten by Pat Rafter in the final of Cincinnati. It was one of those matches he could have won easily, but it slipped exasperatingly from his grasp. Sampras took the first set with vintage play and nearly wrapped it up in straight sets. Rafter clipped the edge of the line on a second serve when he was break point down at 4-4 in the second set. Sampras had looked for a call, thinking it might have been a double fault that would allow him to serve for the match. But Rafter escaped with tenacity and persistence, took the second set in a tie-break and eventually prevailed 1-6, 7-6 (2),6-4. Serving for the match in the tenth game of a tense third set, Rafter was at match point, leading 5-4, 40-30, when his serve was called wide by the linesmen but overruled by the umpire. That controversial ace for Rafter brought victory to the Australian, while leaving the American dumbfounded. Sampras had lost a match that should have gone his way and he was very disconcerted about it.

The American stood there for a long moment, astonished to have lost in that manner, wondering how it got away. A few weeks later, a leg injury that he suffered in the second set of his semifinal with Rafter at the U.S. Open was clearly a factor in a five-set loss. Those were two big wins for Rafter over Sampras, but Sampras understandably felt they were matches he could and should have won. Sampras was a champion widely appreciated for his grace and dignity, but Rafter believed he had not been properly lauded by his opponent after claiming those victories.

He said in 2019, "I thought when I beat Pete he did not give me enough credit. I just thought, 'Mate, every once in a while just say, yeah, it was too good on the day.' That was all he had to say. I was just someone putting himself out there trying to do my best."

Rafter only toppled Sampras four times in 16 career clashes. Uppermost on his mind were surely those aforementioned back-to-back wins he had over the American in the summer of 1998 at Cincinnati and the U.S. Open. Sampras certainly would have responded differently to those defeats had it not been for the unusual circumstances.

In 2019, Sampras recalled the Cincinnati setback and said, "I lost a match I felt I should have won and went into the press right after the match on fumes. Someone asked what the difference was between Pat Rafter and me and I said, 'Ten Grand Slam titles.' That was a smart ass comment. I was just pissed that I lost and I meant nothing personal against Pat. He is a great player and a great gentleman. He interpreted it like I took a shot at him, but that wasn't my intention at all to do that. I probably should have waited 20 minutes before walking into that press conference, but in the heat of the moment you say something you maybe regret. That was the situation because I always complimented Pat."

The record is clear on that. Sampras lauded his adversaries for their finest performances consistently. He added, "Maybe Pat wanted me to be more complimentary and that comment didn't land well in Cincinnati. And at the Open I hurt my leg a little. I don't remember that one as well. But we cleared the air. He said a few things in '99 during the L.A. tournament that got back to me and caught me off guard. It was something like, 'I am glad I got No. 1 over Pete. Pete has never given me credit.' And I was thinking, 'Where did this come from?' He called me the next day and we cleared the air. I apologized for my comment in Cincinnati and explained that it was in the heat of the moment and I didn't mean to offend him by any means and that was really it."

Sampras drew a distinction between himself and Rafter as players with differing viewpoints and personalities residing in the same profession. He said, "The Australian mentality is that you compete, but then have a beer afterwards. Pat is more of a social guy than me. I was a little more to myself and a little more aloof in the locker room. That was just the way I was. I think Pat wanted me to be more one of the guys. Pat was one of the guys and I was not. I think he wanted me to be a little more relaxed, but I did not like to let my guard down. Guys today are much closer than they were back in the nineties. Pat is a nice guy and a great guy but I was just quieter."

Rafter agreed. He said in 2019, "Pete is shy but he is a really nice guy. I remember once an article about me was coming out and there were things in there that I hadn't said. I rang Pete up to tell him I had not said certain things [about him] that were in the newspaper. I didn't want to see him in the locker room the next week without talking about this first. And Pete told me he didn't care about that at all. He said, 'That stuff doesn't bother me.' And I was like, 'Okay, pretty cool.' After I got off the phone, I realized Pete doesn't take things to heart that much. He wasn't an overly sensitive sort of guy. I came away with a lot of respect for him."

These were two honorable human beings and shining athletes navigating the field of competition and ultimately doing their best to understand each other and respect their different mentalities. In any case, after that defeat against Rafter at the U.S. Open, Sampras was absolutely determined to secure that year end No. 1 ranking. Pursuing a more crowded schedule than he would have liked across the autumn, Sampras played seven tournaments after the U.S. Open. Chile's left-handed wizard Marcelo Rios and the remarkable Rafter were still in contention for the top spot. Sampras needed to keep accumulating ATP ranking points to maintain his position at No. 1.

Starting his quest in Basel, he lost a hard-fought, first-round match with old rival Wayne Ferreira. Sampras would eventually prevail in their career series seven matches to six, but he lost this one narrowly 4-6, 7-6 (4), 6-3. He then took the title in Vienna with fine wins over Henman, Todd Martin and Kucera, but had to withdraw from the quarterfinals in Lyon prior to his scheduled match against Tommy Haas with an injury.

Moving on to Stuttgart, he fell in a final-set tie-break against Krajicek in the semifinals. At the Masters 1000 event indoors at Paris, he was clearly favored in the final to beat Greg Rusedski, but the left-hander pulled off the upset. Still needing ATP Ranking points, he elected to play in Stockholm and now the American was at his wits end. Playing journeyman Jason Stoltenberg in the first round, he lost the first set in a tie-break. Playing tournament after tournament in Europe, sick of the travel and strung out by his obsession with the year-end No. 1 ranking, Sampras was understandably agitated.

The Swedish fans were astounded when they watched Sampras smash his racket on the court in utter frustration. He went on to lose that match in three sets, but venting in that fashion was therapeutic. As he told me in a piece I wrote for *The Independent* in London later that year, "I just threw my racket down after that first set and broke it in a million pieces. I was so stressed out from the whole race for No. 1. I wasn't eating or sleeping well. I have never done that in my career and I was on the edge. I just snapped for a moment but it felt pretty good to do it."

Reliving that experience in 2019, Sampras said, "I just wanted that record of being No. 1 six years in a row so badly, so I stayed over in Europe another three or four weeks. The way I looked at it, I had just this one chance to do it and I was obsessed. It can be a little dreary being in Stockholm and Basel and all of those places at that time of the year. So that put me on the edge when I played Stoltenberg. The fans could not believe it when I smashed the racket. I ended up losing that match. I look back on what happened there and wish I could have had more balance but, at the same time, who knows if I would have broken the record without being obsessed with it? It is one of my proudest achievements."

It had been one of the most trying periods of his career, but ultimately it was all worth it. Sampras sealed the No. 1 ranking during the round-robin portion of the season ending ATP Finals for the top eight players in the world. He cast aside Kafelnikov, Moya and Kucera without losing a set. In the semifinals, he had three match points against Corretja, but this time the Spaniard was the one who rallied from the brink to win. After that ironic twist, Sampras put the curtain down on his season. Of all the years he had been stationed at the very top of his profession, this was his least productive yet most commendable season. He won only four tournaments. He endured some heartbreaking defeats. He finished the year in an enervated state.

But the result of all that anguish was ineffably rewarding. As Annacone said in an interview for this book, "I remember we talked about it and he said to me 'No one has ever been ranked No. 1 six years in a row. You get only one chance. So I have got to try and figure out how to do that.' It was a big deal for Pete and a great accomplishment. I remember talking with Pete again later on toward the end of his career and he said being No. 1 six years in a row was his biggest accomplishment. I asked him to compare it to winning 13 and then 14 majors and he said this was harder because you get four chances every year to win majors, but only one chance to be No. 1 six straight years."

Speaking about the campaign he waged for world supremacy 20 years after the fact, Sampras said, "It was stressful—and maybe too stressful—hanging out for so long over there in Europe and trying to get that No. 1 ranking for six years in a row. But it was my one opportunity to break one of the all-time toughest records. Quite honestly, sitting here at age 47, looking back on that year, it feels like a great achievement. I know how hard it is to stay at No. 1 and to do it for six straight years is a beast. Who knows if that will ever be broken?"

The all-consuming nature of that campaign for No. 1 left Sampras thoroughly devoid of inspiration. He had run out of emotional energy. Numerically, it was his least successful of the years he celebrated at No. 1. He did win the biggest tournament of them all in Great Britain, but claimed only three other titles while winning 61 of 78 matches. It would be a while before Pete Sampras would recover his full field of vision as a tennis champion of the highest order. At the end of 1998, having realized such a lofty goal, after working overtime to achieve it, knowing this opportunity would never come his way again, he needed to step aside for a while and recover his zest for the sport. For the time being, Sampras was almost entirely spent, but his demanding quest for a record that meant so much to him had been realized. And yet, it left him empty of immediate ambition and ready to retreat for a while. He needed to rediscover the joy of playing high-stakes tennis on his own terms with his mind uncluttered, his body rested and his heart fully engaged in what he was doing.

# CHAPTER 14

# ON LEVEL TERRAIN WITH
# ROY EMERSON

It had been a very long time since Sampras had missed
a major tennis tournament. He had played 27 Grand Slam
tournaments in a row since he had last been a non-participant
in one of the premier events at the 1992 Australian Open. But as
the 1999 season was launched, he was still recovering from the
rigors of the grueling season he had just left behind. Needing
more time to rest both his mind and his body, he was in no
condition to make the trip "Down Under." He elected to skip
the season's first major.

He opened his campaign shortly afterwards in San
Jose, California and reached the semis. But an injury forced the
American to default against Philippoussis. Beaten by compatriot
Jan Michael Gambill in the round of 16 at Scottsdale and a
second-round victim of Spain's Felix Mantilla at Indian Wells,
Sampras was struggling to find his form. He lost to Krajicek in
the quarters of Miami and then shifted onto the clay.

Along the road to Roland Garros, he lost early in Rome,
took two of three matches in World Team Cup, but headed into
the French Open without much confidence. He lost in the second
round at Roland Garros to Andrei Medvedev, a formidable clay

court player who would reach the final. Medvedev was up two sets to love against Agassi before the American struck back boldly to win in five sets.

Sampras left Roland Garros in need of a boost and that is precisely what he got at the Queen's Club tournament on the London lawns. He had played six tournaments leading up to Queen's and had reached only one semifinal and one quarterfinal. But now he found the inner spark, upending Ivanisevic in the quarterfinals, ousting Hewitt in a final-set tie-break and then clipping Henman in a final that went down to the wire. Sampras was building belief again on the eve of the biggest tournament in the world.

As he said in an interview for this book, "It gave me some confidence to win that tournament and it let other players know that I was playing well and my game was coming around. Beating Tim in England again was nice and I went into Wimbledon with some confidence and momentum."

Always delighted to be back at the All England Club, determined to achieve a streak of three titles in a row for the second time at his favorite tournament—and the one that mattered the most to him—Sampras opened his bid for the title against a left-handed Australian named Scott Draper, ranked No. 75 in the world. He had won the Wimbledon junior doubles title seven years earlier. He was also a first-rate golfer who nearly made the cut at the PGA Queensland Championships in 2003 after shooting impressive rounds of 72 and 73.

But Draper was no match for Sampras at the tennis grass court capital of the world. He did not have the arsenal to threaten the tournament favorite. Sampras carved out a 6-3, 6-4, 6-4 victory without facing a break point. His next opponent was the Canadian Sebastien Lareau, the world No. 100. Lareau was a good doubles player who had won the 1990 Roland Garros junior title in that forum. More importantly, he would garner a gold medal in doubles alongside Daniel Nestor at the 2000 Olympic Games. But Lareau was out of his league playing Sampras in singles, falling 6-4, 6-2, 6-3.

Facing Sampras in the third round was a British wildcard named Danny Sapsford. He was ranked No. 595 in the world. This was the last match of his career. Sapsford acquitted himself well but did not have enough game to seriously bother the top seed. Sampras served 23 aces and was unbreakable, but Sapsford made the third set interesting before Sampras succeeded 6-3, 6-4, 7-5.

Now it was time for Sampras to meet the aforementioned Daniel Nestor, a left-handed Canadian who established himself as one of the finest doubles players of the modern era and one of the best of all time. Nestor would win 91 doubles titles with 11 partners during his stellar career on the ATP World Tour. He secured eight men's Grand Slam titles with three different partners, and four majors in mixed as well. He reached No. 1 in the ATP doubles rankings.

Yet, on his own, Nestor could not contain Sampras. The American's serving and his power off the ground were too much for the Canadian. He won 6-3, 6-4, 6-2. It had been a straightforward march for Sampras into the quarterfinals. He had not lost a set. He was playing very good tennis. He had preserved strength and vitality for the latter rounds.

Sampras then collided with a top of the line Philippoussis in the quarters. They had met eight times up until this juncture and Sampras had won six of those big-serving contests, including two wins over the Australian at Wimbledon. But the burly Australian was blasting away freely in the early stages of this skirmish and Sampras dropped the first set. A rusty Sampras had not played much since his fourth-round match for the better part of five days because there was so much rain. He opened the match with three double faults in the first game and was broken. That uncharacteristic start cost him the set. But, at 1-1 in the second set, Philippoussis hurt his knee. Sampras held for 2-1 but the Australian could not continue. Sampras prevailed: 4-6, 2-1, ret.

"That was a scare," Sampras said in 2019. "I didn't feel like I was going to lose the match, but I remember his monster game and huge first serve on grass were tough. With that kind of serve it could have been another Krajicek situation. It could have been that he would be too good on the day. Early in the second set he goes down with an injury and he is out of the match. I walked off the court feeling like I was being outplayed. I am not saying I was going to lose, but I knew this was a tough guy to beat that day. I walked out of there sort of relieved I was still in the event. If I had been down two sets and a break that would have been lucky. I was only down a set and we were on serve in the second. But it was definitely a scary match playing someone with that type of game. He had the tools."

Having won that contest under unusual circumstances, Sampras took on Henman in the semifinal round for the second year in a row on the Centre Court. He opened this encounter with a lack of rhythm and confidence on serve, double faulting in his first service game three times again. He lost his serve a second time to go down two breaks and Henman had enough of a cushion to close out the set 6-3.

Late in the second set, however, Sampras turned the corner propitiously, breaking Henman in the tenth game on a double fault from the British competitor. When he won that point and knew he was back to one set all, Sampras leapt into the air with joy, exuberance and relief, feeling he could now take control. He won the third set 6-3, but had to battle fiercely in the fourth. Henman saved a break point in the first game. After three deuces, Henman held on for 1-0. Not until Sampras served at 2-3 did either player have any other openings. The American led 40-0 in the sixth game but missed a backhand volley long, double faulted and was forced into a backhand half volley error by a terrific backhand return from Henman.

Sampras earned a fourth game point but double faulted again. Now Henman moved to break point but Sampras applied some extra kick on his second serve and his adversary totally miss-hit the return off the backhand. Sampras then pulled off a forehand half-volley winner and served an ace down the T for 3-3. At 3-4, Sampras drifted into danger again, serving his tenth double fault of the contest to fall behind 30-40. If the American had lost this point, Henman would have been serving to bring the battle into a fifth set. But Sampras was acutely aware of what he needed to do when he was down break point. His first serve hit the service line in the ad court and Henman missed the return. Sampras eventually got the hold for 4-4.

He had survived two arduous service games in a row, but his holds had not happened by accident. He had this striking propensity to respond to precarious moments with not only urgency but temerity. He simply would not buckle and the high tension surrounding him at those moments almost always brought out the best in Sampras. At times like that, he frequently took his tennis to another level and served with the power and precision that might have been missing when the stakes were not as consequential. Henman served at 4-4, cognizant that Sampras had kept him at bay when it counted. The Englishman's insecurity was evident. He missed an easy forehand first volley for 0-15 and double faulted on the next point. Sampras sensed his chance, sending a backhand return winner screaming past the incoming Henman. At 0-40, Sampras stepped up the pace of his passing shot and the speed of that backhand caught Henman off guard. He missed a backhand volley long.

Sampras had broken at love for 5-4. With his outstanding play on the big points and a stellar return game, Sampras was serving for the match. He lost the first point when Henman connected with a forehand return winner down the line, but Sampras collected four points in a row from there to close out the account stylishly, taking the last two points with service winners. His class frequently surfaced at pivotal moments. The way he had swept the last three games was ample evidence of that. He looked at Annacone and his supporters across the way, raising a fist quietly, gratified that he had made his way into another Wimbledon final. This would be his sixth. Sampras had never lost one.

In the title-round contest, he renewed his series with fellow American Agassi, the most important rival he would ever have. They had not met at a major since Sampras had taken their career-defining showdown at the 1995 U.S. Open.

Agassi had been almost permanently wounded by that defeat. His game deteriorated decidedly in 1996, but Agassi reached the semifinals of the Australian and U.S. Opens and took the Olympic gold medal in Atlanta without Sampras in that field. Agassi ended that season still among the elite top ten in the world at No. 8. But his 1997 season was abysmal. He did not even play any of the majors until the U.S. Open, losing in the fourth round there to Rafter. In the fall, he drifted down to No. 141 in the world and chose to play a couple of Challenger tournaments. He concluded the season at No. 122.

By 1998, Agassi was back at a much loftier standard. He did not make it past the fourth round at all four majors, but won five tournaments and ended the year at No. 6 in the world. In 1999, he had kept working diligently but his form fluctuated in the early months of the season. He did win Hong Kong over Becker, but that was his only bright spot prior to Roland Garros. Yet a big comeback win over the defending champion Moya at Roland Garros in the round of 16 propelled Agassi in Paris and eventually he made his stirring comeback to beat Medvedev in the final.

That was a landmark victory for Agassi. It gave him a career collection of the four majors. He established himself as the fifth man in tennis history to realize that extraordinary feat, joining Fred Perry, Don Budge, Roy Emerson and Rod Laver in that elite territory. He thus came into Wimbledon riding high. Nursing a shoulder injury before Roland Garros, he had essentially made up his mind to skip the tournament, but was talked out of that notion by his coach Brad Gilbert.

Now, back at the All England Club where he had been the champion seven years earlier, buoyant after his startling Roland Garros triumph, Agassi was revitalized and highly charged. When he took apart the polished serve-and-volley practitioner Rafter in the semifinals, there were many in the cognoscenti—players and press alike—who were picking him to beat Sampras.

John McEnroe was not one of them. The New Yorker and three-time Wimbledon champion was looking at this all-

American duel dispassionately, soberly and intelligently. He knew that Sampras was the far superior grass court player and understood that you underestimated Sampras on a big occasion—especially a Wimbledon final—at your own peril.

Speaking with fellow commentator Dick Enberg on NBC only minutes before the start of the Sampras-Agassi final, McEnroe was the voice of reason. Enberg mentioned that he had done an informal "little straw poll" to get prognostications on the match and that "more and more feel that this could be Agassi's championship."

McEnroe replied, "To be honest, Dick, I am a little surprised about that. Yes, Agassi had that incredible run in Paris. It was a miracle, but Pete Sampras is to me the greatest grass court player of all time and this is where he is determined to put his status with the Laver's, with the Bjorn Borg's, with the true greats. Now, Agassi suddenly with that win in Paris jumped, leapfrogged right to the area where Pete was, because Pete has not won the fourth one, being the French Open. So what we have suddenly is—let's face it—the dream, perfect matchup. I mean, what more could we ask for on July 4th than having these two guys—arguably the two best guys in the 90's, two of the greatest ever—fight it out right here at Wimbledon."

Having said that, McEnroe got to the heart of the matter at the end of his pre-match assessment when he proclaimed, "I have to give the edge to Pistol Pete Sampras on this surface."

The fans anticipated another spirited clash between the two iconic Americans on Sunday July 4, 1999. They had last gone up against each other at the shrine six years earlier, when Sampras had come through in that memorable five-set quarterfinal on his way to his first Wimbledon title. That was when Sampras was just establishing himself on grass. Now he was the unassailable 'King of the Lawns.' Agassi was exceedingly aware of the task at hand, but excited about being in his first final at Wimbledon since he took his lone title seven years earlier.

Annacone recalled the Sampras mentality heading into this historic encounter. He said, "I remember vividly that five minutes before Pete walked on the court for that match with Andre, we were standing in the locker room. The last day is always really cool because usually it is just the two players who have made it to the final, the two coaches and maybe a few former champions milling around. There are usually four to six people in the locker room, max. It is a little eerie. So five minutes before he walks on court and both players are kind of dressing and putting their shoes on. Pete is standing by the front door kind of jumping around and doing his warm-up stuff. He stops and looks at me with a big smile and goes, 'This is going to be a lot of fun.'"

That was a prescient remark from Sampras. He would indeed enjoy this match immensely. As he said in 2018, "It was fun. Andre was coming in after winning the French and I was doing my thing during Wimbledon '99. Playing Andre is always a challenge but going into the Wimbledon final, I had always played big servers. Now I was playing somebody that was going to stay back, so I knew I could play a little bit. In the beginning we were feeling each other out."

Indeed they were. In fact, both men were playing well from the opening bell. Agassi's ball striking from the backcourt was outstanding. Sampras was serving and volleying with power, purposefulness and polish. There were no tactical secrets from either man. They knew precisely what to expect. It was all about which man could take control with his distinctive style of play, who could play better tennis on the biggest points and how well each player could control their nerves on the occasion of all occasions in tennis.

Across the first half of the opening set, not much separated the two combatants. Sampras held at 15 in the first game, punching a forehand volley crosscourt into the clear off an Agassi backhand pass up the line. Agassi reached 1-1 at the cost of only two points. In the third game, Sampras was down break point. Agassi had just pieced together one his most favorite patterns, returning low down the middle, making Sampras half volley and stepping in to drill a backhand pass that was too tough to handle.

Sampras took his time at 30-40, wanting to avoid going down an early break. He served at 124 mph out wide in the ad court. Agassi had no chance. It was an ace for Sampras. He took the next point and then served another ace, this one at 123 mph down the T. He moved to 2-1, but Agassi swiftly reached 2-2 with an ace out wide in the deuce court. He lost only one point in that service game. Sampras followed with a love hold on his serve, releasing two aces and making one service winner. He put himself out in front 3-2.

For the first time, Agassi was hard pressed to hold his serve in the sixth game. In a three-deuce game, he led 40-15 but later had to fend off a break point, sending a 105 mph biting second serve down the T to draw a forehand return long from Sampras. On his fourth game point, Agassi held for 3-3, taking a short return from Sampras and rifling a forehand winner well out of reach.

The seventh game would be the defining moment of the match. A wide-eyed Agassi was explosive on his returns and was counter attacking at full force. A low forehand down-the-line return coaxed an error on the volley from Sampras. Then Agassi produced a pair of passing shot winners. It was 0-40 on the Sampras serve and the burden was on him to come up with something substantial. If he was broken here, it could lead to the loss of the set. That could have wounded his psyche while fueling Agassi with a large supply of encouragement. Sampras had to meet this moment forthrightly.

That is precisely what he did. He sent a first serve out wide to the Agassi backhand at 118 mph with superb placement, leaving Agassi helpless on the return: 15-40. His next first serve whistled down the T. Agassi's return barely made it over the net. Sampras calmly unleashed a forehand winner: 30-40. A service winner to the backhand took Sampras to deuce. An ace out wide gave him game point. And then he serve-volleyed behind a typically fearless second delivery, making a fine forehand half volley pickup and coaxing a forehand passing shot long from Agassi.

From 0-40, Sampras had swept five points in a row for a 4-3 lead. He had missed only one first serve in that span. His extraordinary discipline and poise under pressure were fully evident. That clutch comeback hold from Sampras had clearly rattled a now fragile Agassi. At 15-30 in the eighth game, he double faulted. Sampras was suddenly at 15-40 with two break point chances awaiting him. Only one was required. He took his forehand return off a second serve early, hitting it hard, rushing Agassi into a netted forehand down the line.

Sampras had the break at 15 for 5-3. In a four-minute span, he had sweepingly and permanently altered the course of the match. He realized how critical holding serve in the seventh game had been and now he was building considerable momentum. Agassi understood the depth of his difficulties. In situations like this one, when Sampras was serving for a set or a match, his habit was to raise the stakes exponentially.

On the first point of the ninth game, Sampras came forward behind the first serve as was his custom, but Agassi then backed him up with a good lob. Sampras hit a solid overhead, but could not put it away. Seemingly, Agassi was back in the point. He sent a backhand down the line off the smash with reasonably good depth, but Sampras was unimpressed. He answered with an immaculate flat forehand down the line. It was a timely and outright winner: 15-0 Sampras. Serving down the T on the next point, he elicited a high return from Agassi. Sampras closed in tight to put away a high forehand volley: 30-0. Agassi's backhand pass on the following point landed in the corner for a winner, but Sampras immediately released his seventh ace of the set, going down the T. Now at double set point, leading 40-15, Sampras went with a body serve to the backhand and Agassi did not come close on the return. The set was Sampras's 6-3.

Having won three games in a row, Sampras refused to take his foot off the accelerator. He broke at love to open the second set, boosted by a scintillating backhand down-the-line winner and a thundering forehand crosscourt return in that game. Sampras was up a set and a break. He bolted to

2-0 by holding at 15, commencing and closing that game with aces down the T. Sampras was playing irresistibly well. He had won five consecutive games and 21 of the last 24 points, predominantly because of his outstanding movement, inventive shot-making and serving of the highest order.

Agassi was down 0-30 in the third game after Sampras's excellent return set up a backhand crosscourt winner, but the bald-headed American held on with four points in a row. Implacably, Sampras held for 3-1. At 15-15 in that fourth game, Agassi angled a low backhand passing shot on the run, foregoing his two-hander and driving this shot with one hand. Sampras seemed to have little chance to make a play at the net. But he dove and made a spectacular backhand volley winner. Agassi was disgruntled. He stood there for a long moment, staring at his opponent incredulously. Sampras got up with blood on his arm, just above the elbow. He proceeded to ace Agassi consecutively, sending both first serves down the T at 124 mph and 127 mph respectively, closing out that game with gusto.

Sampras was thoroughly in the zone. He soared to 15-40 in the fifth game, but Agassi admirably fought his way out of that corner. After three deuces, he held on. In the following game, at 3-2, 30-30, Sampras sent a service winner down the T that Agassi could barely touch. He held at 30 with a forehand stretch volley setting up a backhand finesse volley winner crosscourt.

Agassi was perched precariously at 2-4 but he held at love in the seventh game and then advanced to 15-30 on the Sampras serve in the eighth game. Sampras aced his adversary down the T and took the next two points to build a 5-3 lead. Two games later, he served for a two-set lead. Sampras double faulted for 15-15, but swept the next three points with an ace sandwiched between two unstoppable first deliveries. Sampras had taken the set 6-4. From the middle of the first set to the end of the second, his tennis was nothing short of sublime.

Agassi made Sampras work harder to hold serve early in the third set, but to no avail. In the second game, he took Sampras to deuce but lost the next two points on return errors off both sides. In the fourth game, Sampras was at 30-30 on his serve but played an outstanding pattern point, directing a forehand first volley down the line, anticipating Agassi's backhand pass and punching a forehand volley winner crosscourt. He moved to 2-2. For the third service game in a row, Sampras was tested, trailing 0-30 in the sixth game. But a winning volley followed by two service winners in a row and then an unanswerable second serve propelled Sampras to 3-3.

Now he had his chance, surging to 15-40 on Agassi's serve in the seventh game, only to be denied. A well-placed first serve wide to the Sampras forehand drew an error and then Agassi raced swiftly across the court to chase down a forehand volley from Sampras, making his finest forehand passing shot of the match, sending that shot acutely crosscourt and out of reach. Agassi would hold on with gumption for 4-3 and then reached 30-30 on Sampras's serve in the eighth game.

Once more, Sampras played an important point with aplomb. He served and volleyed on his second serve, going deep and heavy to the Agassi forehand. Sampras got to the net quickly and put away a backhand volley. A remarkable body serve to the backhand took Sampras to 4-4. Agassi held comfortably for 5-4 but Sampras did not lose a point to make it 5-5.

How many times had we seen it? Sampras would be locked at 5-5 in a set. A tie-break seemed entirely possible and perhaps inevitable. But he would find a way to secure a break when it was most beneficial. With Agassi serving at 30-40 in the 11th game, Sampras wisely went with the safe chipped backhand crosscourt, making Agassi create his own pace. Agassi pressed, missing a backhand down the line.

Sampras was serving for the match. He directed a first serve to the Agassi forehand, and the return found the net tape: 15-0. An impeccably executed second serve at 113 mph down the T stifled Agassi: 30-0. Thinking an Agassi return might be going out, Sampras let it go. But the shot landed well in for a winner: 30-15. Agassi then rolled a forehand pass low crosscourt. Sampras dove but could not make the volley. He was bleeding lightly again above the elbow after that fall.

Andre Agassi lost his third major final to Pete Sampras 6-3, 6-4, 7-5 at Wimbledon in 1999

It was 30-30. Sampras was two points from an uplifting triumph. Agassi was two points away from his first service break of the match and an opportunity to play a tie-break. Sampras was ready to meet this propitious moment with no reservations. He served an ace down the T for 40-30. At match point, he missed his first serve but aimed boldly down the T on the second serve. It was a tournament closing ace, another signature moment in his career and a fitting way to conclude what was arguably the best tennis match he had ever played.

This was a virtuoso display on a stage he cherished. Sampras garnered Grand Slam title No. 12 and Wimbledon victory No. 6 in one fell swoop. For the second time in a seven-year span, he had captured the world's premier title three years in a row.

Sampras recollected that match with not only immense pride but also much clarity 20 years later. He said, "I got out of that game from 3-3, 0-40 and then new balls came out when he served the next game. Andre missed a couple. I raised it up a little bit. You just know there are certain moments in a match. He feels it and I feel it. There is a sense of urgency. So I got the break and served out the set and, boom, all of a sudden three minutes later I am up a set. Then I relaxed a bit and from the second set on, pretty much to the end of the match, I got in the zone where I was hitting my ground strokes very well and I felt like I had all the time in the world. My backhand was on. I was moving well and doing everything I wanted to do and serving very well. I was able to show my whole game."

Sampras added, "Andre wasn't able to break me and he was playing well. On the grass, I had time to play against him and that is what I always wanted on that surface. I got into those rallies and enjoyed it. I play my best tennis when I don't think. I remember that match I wasn't thinking much at all. It was all reactionary, just playing the next point and trying to dictate play. In the Wimbledon final, with Andre coming off the French win and me having a subpar year, it was a big win. My level from the second set on through the rest of the match made me feel I had hit the point of just being unbeatable."

Brad Gilbert was there in the friend's box for this historic final coaching Agassi, encouraged about his prospects. The loquacious Gilbert had been a fine player in his time. Between 1986 and 1990, he finished two years just outside the top ten in the world and two more in that elite category. He peaked at No. 4 in 1990. In 1994, he started coaching Agassi. They forged a strong player-coach bond. Gilbert was a master strategist who made Agassi think differently and more cerebrally about how he wanted to play the game.

Two decades after the Wimbledon final of 1999, Gilbert spoke in an interview for this book about his remembrances. He said, "I can tell you that as I was sitting in my chair when Pete was serving at 3-3, 0-40, Andre was playing incredible tennis. I didn't think anybody could beat him the way he was playing, not even Pete. Pete snatched that match in nine minutes like nothing I have ever seen. He held from 3-3, 0-40 with five absolute bombs and two of them were like second serve aces in the 120s. From there it was break, hold, break early in the second set and the next thing you know Andre was two sets to love down. It was one of those flashes of genius from Pete, kind of like what Fed does these days. It happens really fast. That nine-minute span was probably the greatest I have ever seen from Pete, that level where he took it from 3-3, 0-40, to 6-3, 1-0, up a break in the second. That was probably Pete's highest level ever."

"It was a joke how well Pete played the first set-and-a half," said Annacone. "Andre did nothing wrong. I remember watching that match and thinking 'This guy is unbelievable. In this environment, against this player, in this moment, he can just let his talent shine. He can quiet his mind and quiet his heart, know the strategy, hit the button and go. It is so hard for anyone to comprehend how difficult that is to do in that arena. He was the epitome of the maestro at that."

After playing the match of his life against his most revered rival to tie Roy Emerson for the largest number of major men's titles at 12, Sampras was splendid across the summer. At home in Los Angeles, he confronted Agassi in the final under the bright California sunshine on an idyllic Sunday afternoon. Sampras shined again in a crackling match, overcoming his fellow American in a pair of tiebreakers for the title. He moved on to Cincinnati and cut down Krajicek, Agassi and Rafter for the Masters 1000 title in Ohio.

Sampras was so filled with conviction that losing hardly entered his mind. He had won four tournaments in a row. He was eagerly anticipating the U.S. Open. This was one of the best stretches he had celebrated in a very long time. He had recaptured the brand of tennis that he loved to play above all else, crushing running forehands crosscourt with abandon, driving through his backhand, serving magnificently and volleying as skillfully as he had at any time in his career. His instinctive genius had come to the forefront once again.

Having played a lot of tennis in his two tournament triumphs on the hard courts, Sampras hit a physical wall when he went to Indianapolis. After splitting sets with countryman Vince Spadea in the quarterfinals, Sampras retired with an injury and his remarkable 24-match winning streak came to an end. But the injury was not serious. He came to the U.S. Open convinced that he could win the tournament, as self-assured as he had ever been for the championships of his country. He was the clear favorite for the last Grand Slam title of the season.

But, practicing with the Brazilian Guga Kuerten on the weekend leading up to the start of play in New York, Sampras hurt his back. It was diagnosed as a herniated disc. Heartbroken, he had to pull out of the tournament. The memory of that withdrawal lingered for a long while and struck a deeply emotional cord. Even in 2019, talking about that unfortunate development was painful for Sampras.

"I was pretty devastated, "he said. "I had so much momentum going into the summer after winning Wimbledon and playing so well in the final. You just carry that momentum with you and everything is fun and you are playing loose. I just felt really good going into the Open. I was prepared and playing well, practicing well and practicing quite hard. I was practicing with Kuerten on the Grandstand court and I got this uncomfortable feeling in my back. It just didn't feel right so I stopped playing. I went to get it tested and they said it was a herniated disc. I was really bummed out. I really felt that I was going to win another Open. There was no guarantee, but everything was on the line and I was looking forward to it."

He went home to California and initially was discouraged by his plight. As he told me in an interview for *Tennis Week* later that year, "I went through a huge wave of emotions. I couldn't wait for the Open to finish so I could put that to rest and move on. I couldn't leave my house for six or seven days because I couldn't drive. I was stuck there. Everything stops and you are doing rehab twice a day and you can get really frustrated. I was at the point where I was thinking 'I am done for the year. I don't want to play anymore. I have lost my ranking. I have lost the whole thing.' But you can't make decisions on emotion, especially when they are not good emotions. As I got more treatments, I had a better outlook. Time heals a lot of different wounds. I became hungry to play again."

He resumed tournament competition at the Masters 1000 event indoors at Paris in the first week of November and edged the left-handed Spaniard Francisco Clavet in a final set tie-break, but the back was not ready for that kind of punishment. He defaulted to Tommy Haas and flew home. The ATP World Tour Championships in Hannover was less than three weeks away.

Sampras told me in the *Tennis Week* interview that he was not discouraged by having to pull out of the Paris tournament. He said, "The Paraflex surface they put down in Paris has historically given me problems because it is soft and very gritty, so I felt my back get tighter as the Clavet match went on. It was just muscle spasms and muscles around my spine protecting themselves. The doctor in Paris told me I should not play in Hannover. But as I was laying on my back on that plane ride home, I remember telling my trainer that I was going to Hannover and I would win it."

True to his word despite the size of the challenge after playing so little tennis in that span, he did just that. In the round robin, he was still searching for self-belief and Agassi took him apart 6-2, 6-2. But he won his two other round-robin duels, cruised through his semifinal against Germany's Nicolas Kiefer and then turned the tables comprehensively on Agassi in the final. His 6-1, 7-5, 6-4 triumph over his most revered rival on a relatively slow indoor court in the title-round meeting at the ATP Finals was reminiscent of their Wimbledon duel. In this case, Sampras lost his serve only once but recovered from 0-3, 15-40 in the second set. He concluded the year on a high note.

Agassi had already secured the No. 1 year end ranking for the first time in his career after claiming two major titles. Taking the second of those majors at the U.S. Open was made a lot less complicated without Sampras in the field.

Sampras finished that year at No. 3, largely because he played only two of the four majors and just 13 tournaments altogether, completing only 10. That he won half of those events he completed was evidence of his enduring greatness. Sampras was victorious in 40 of 48 matches during that disrupted campaign. Had he been able to play a fuller schedule, he might well have stood at the top of the tennis mountain for a seventh consecutive season, particularly if he had been able to underline his summertime supremacy with a triumph at the U.S. Open. Nevertheless, he had played some of the finest sustained tennis of his career when he was at his best and that gave him ample incentive to push on purposefully into the year ahead.

# CHAPTER 15

# BREAKING THE RECORD AT HIS HOME ABROAD

At the first major of the new 2000 season in Melbourne, the two top Americans found themselves on the same half of the draw at the Australian Open. Russia's Yevgeny Kafelnikov—the defending champion and a perennial workhorse—was ranked ahead of Sampras at No. 2 in the world. A dream final between the reigning Wimbledon and U.S. Open champions was not possible.

Sampras never fretted about things like that. He took it in stride, kept his mind on his business and his form over the fortnight was impressive. On his way to the semifinal round, Sampras had only one dangerous moment. Playing Wayne Black—the younger brother of Byron Black, someone he had beaten three times at the majors over the years—in the third round, Sampras was down two sets to love but rallied to win in five. He lost only one other set prior to the semifinals.

And then he took on Agassi under the lights. They contested one of their most memorable battles across five exhilarating sets. Sampras tore his right hip flexor in the fourth game of the match, but he was able to play on productively nonetheless. He lost the first set, won the next two in tie-breaks and was within two points of victory at 5-4 in the fourth-set tie-break. Agassi was serving in tenuous territory, but he went for two relatively flat first serves and made them both. Sampras could not get the returns back in play. Agassi closed out that tie-break 7-5 and was too strong physically in the fifth set, winning the match 6-4, 3-6, 6-7 (0), 7-6 (5), 6-1.

Had Sampras pulled out that hard-fought fourth-set tie-break, he would have met Kafelnikov in the final. Perhaps he would have been hindered by the injury, but he still might have toppled the Russian, against whom he finished with an 11-2 career record. But the bottom line is that Agassi beat him for the second time at that major. Sampras served 37 aces and performed spectacularly in the second, third and fourth sets. But it was not quite enough for a victory.

As usual, he quickly left that disappointment behind him. After some uneven showings over the winter and into the spring, he won the Masters 1000 title in Miami over Gustavo Kuerten in an absorbing final. Leading two sets to one and 6-2 in the fourth-set tie-break, Sampras needed seven match points to finish the job, but he came through in a gripping clash 6-1, 6-7 (2), 7-6 (5), 7-6 (8).

The clay court season was not kind to him, culminating with a five-set, first-round loss to Philippoussis at Roland Garros. He left for Great Britain and reached the final at Queen's Club, losing on the lawns there 6-4, 6-4 to Lleyton Hewitt. But the five matches he played there gave him excellent preparation for Wimbledon. In search of a seventh title, he was ready and eager to move on to the All England Club.

His quest for the crown began with a routine 6-4, 6-4, 6-2 first-round victory over Jiri Vanek of the Czech Republic. In 14 service games, he conceded only 15 points. That sent the American into a second-round duel against the ever dangerous Karol Kucera, the same fellow who had upended him at the 1998 Australian Open. Kucera was a cagey and inventive player across the board with outstanding ball control and stellar counter-attacking instincts. His anticipation was uncanny and the more pace you gave him, the better he was likely to respond.

Kucera was ranked No. 44 in the world at the time, but he was a decidedly better player than that. He had climbed to a career high at No. 6 in the world in 1998 and had concluded that season at No. 8. He remained a top 20 player in 1999. No matter where he stood on the charts, Kucera was not in awe of Sampras or his Centre Court surroundings. Four years earlier on the same court, he lost 7-6 in the fourth set to the American in a tense third-round contest.

Against Kucera in 2000, Sampras was hobbled. He would win the first set nonetheless, but dropped the second and needed to have his ankle wrapped near the end of the third. Sampras eventually halted an inspired Kucera 7-6 (9), 3-6, 6-3, 6-4 on the edge of darkness, but he was limping constantly and clearly in pain. He left the grounds not long after that physically painful encounter and had an M.R.I. It was determined that he had tendinitis in his left shin and foot, but he was given the green light to proceed with the rest of the tournament.

Nevertheless, the deep discomfort did not disappear. He was not practicing between matches the rest of the way until a brief hit the day before the final. Fortunately for the gimpy Sampras, his draw had opened up and, even on one leg, his grass-court game surpassed the others in the field at the All England Club.

Reflecting on that arduous fortnight in 2019, Sampras said, "To put it lightly, I wasn't fun to be around. I was stressed. I wasn't sleeping well and wasn't sure what I should do, wasn't sure I should continue to play. It was just very difficult and I was very on edge and in a lot of discomfort, just trying to figure out what to do. I was getting injections before each match and getting injections is something I am not crazy about. Doing that made me feel it was borderline that maybe I shouldn't play."

But he wanted this title very badly, and, in the end, felt it was worth it to endure the injections and keep fighting through and past the pain. As he recalled, "I tried the injection before my third-round match and the pain went away for about an hour, but it would creep back in at the end of the match, so I couldn't practice and I was hobbled up. I iced it and stayed off it and decided this was what I was going to have to do—just keep getting the injections before each match. It doesn't last forever. It just masks the pain for a little while, so I was uncomfortable playing on the grass and not even hitting between matches. You are going out there cold without even moving your body. It is hard enough playing, but add that to it and it is very stressful."

Yet Sampras somehow survived. In the third round, after a couple of days off, he played fellow American Justin Gimelstob, the No. 99-ranked player in the world. Gimelstob had won a couple of major mixed doubles titles alongside Venus Williams and he was a respectable grass court player in singles. Gimelstob was a confirmed serve-and-volleyer and the 6'5" competitor was volleying remarkably well in the process of taking the first set from an off-key Sampras.

But Sampras turned the corner in the second set and never looked back. Gradually he found the range on his returns and discovered his rhythm on serve to win 2-6, 6-4, 6-2, 6-2. In the round of 16, he confronted the 28-year-old Swede Jonas Bjorkman, an outstanding doubles player who had resided among the top five in singles three years earlier.

But the aggressive-minded Swede—now No. 78 in the world—could not contain a determined and sharply-focused Sampras. The American did not need to stay on court any longer than was necessary. In 95 minutes, he cast aside Bjorkman 6-3, 6-2, 7-5, facing only one break point, volleying with both depth and feel, making his returns consistently off the backhand side. Encouraged by Annacone to display his intensity when the spirit moved him, Sampras fist pumped periodically and let both his opponent and his many fans know how much he cared about his craft.

That triumph over Bjorkman took Sampras into a quarterfinal contest against compatriot Jan Michael Gambill, a 23-year-old who stood 6'3", weighed 195 pounds, served big and hit his groundstrokes off both sides with two hands. When Sampras dropped the second set of their showdown in a tie-break and realized he would need to play at least two more sets, he could have been concerned. But that was not the case.

He broke once in the third set and once more in the fourth and came through 6-4, 6-7 (4), 6-4, 6-4 in two hours and 46 minutes. Sampras poured in 70% of his first serves and was not broken in the match.

Up next on the agenda was the world No. 237 from Belarus, Vladimir Voltchkov. He established himself as the first qualifier since John McEnroe in 1977 to reach the semifinal round of the world's most important tennis tournament. Among his victims were the No. 6 seed and 1997 finalist Cedric Pioline, and the wily veteran Wayne Ferreira. But Voltchkov was out of his league against a vastly superior opponent. Sampras was victorious 7-6 (4), 6-2, 6-4, losing only 12 points in 15 service games, facing no break points and returning with increasing efficiency across the last couple of sets.

Sampras was right where he wanted to be, back in the final of Wimbledon, one match away from breaking the record he shared with Roy Emerson for the most Grand Slam singles titles taken by a man. And yet, his opponent was by far the best player he would face over the fortnight. Patrick Rafter had won the U.S. Open twice, in 1997 and 1998. He was appearing in his first final on the lawns of the All England Club. He had beaten Agassi in a classic five-set semifinal. Rafter was going to be a "tough out" for Sampras, especially under these circumstances. Very few players backed up their serves as skillfully as Rafter, who could close in as fast as anyone for the first volley and take control unhesitatingly at the net. This formidable serve-and-volleyer was extraordinary in the forecourt; he volleyed out of the traditional Australian playbook, with aggression and polish.

But, despite the substantial pressure and realizing that physically he was going to be hard pressed to survive a long skirmish as he strove for a record-breaking achievement, Sampras was bolstered in the back of his mind by the fact that his parents had flown over from California to see him play the final. His fiancé, Bridgette Wilson, had made the request on his behalf, knowing how much it would mean to Sampras.

As he said in an interview for this book, "Bridgette called my sisters. We had talked about dreams, about things you would love to see happen. I had said my parents had never seen me win Wimbledon in person, or even seen me play at Wimbledon at all. Bridgette spoke with my sisters and it got back to my parents that I wanted them there. So they flew over and all they asked was not to be seated in the player's box and not be seen on television. But I knew they were there and that meant a lot to me."

Sam and Georgia Sampras were seated behind the court, but relatively high in the stands that Sunday July 9, 2000. And yet, inevitably, they were spotted by NBC, who captured their priceless expressions numerous times during the match. But the dignified couple were not aware of the cameras and were able to watch their son compete on this historic occasion without being self-conscious. They still must have felt as if they were sitting on pins and needles as they viewed a highly-charged collision. They witnessed their son enduring some bad luck in the first set and a measure of good fortune in the second. Sam Sampras was so nervous that he left the match for a while and tried to walk away his tension.

Rafter, meanwhile, had his own perspective as he appeared in his first Wimbledon final. In an interview for this book, he said, "Honestly, over time we lose a little bit of our memory, so I will tell you what I remember now, almost 20 years later. I understood that Pete was having a little problem with his ankle leading into our match. That was in the back of my mind going into the Wimbledon final and playing Pete, but I knew he was going to be tough to beat. I had come back after shoulder surgery and I was really happy to be in the final after a great match with Andre in the semifinals. I would say I did not have a lot of expectations when I went out there to play Pete."

The way Rafter looked at it, "Pete and I didn't match up very well, so I always found when Pete and I played it was pretty ugly tennis, while with Andre there was a good contrast in styles when I played him. When I played Pete, in the back of my mind, I always felt he did everything better than me and bigger than me. Our styles conflicted but there was no contrast. It certainly didn't make for pretty tennis. I just found it hard to get through Pete because he did everything better than what I did."

Making matters even more demanding for the players was the inclement weather. The final was delayed initially for about an hour. They walked on court at 2:51 and play actually started at 3:01 pm. The sky above remained ominously dark, but Sampras and Rafter ignored the atmosphere and settled into the first set purposefully. Each man was a virtual advertisement for the serve-and-volley game on grass, coming forward relentlessly, taking command at the net, leaving nothing to chance. They were playing grass-court tennis the way it was meant to be played, in an ultra-aggressive fashion, much like the protagonists in the 1971 Wimbledon had when the Australian John Newcombe defeated Stan Smith of the United States in a five-set final round duel played about five weeks before Sampras was born.

In the first four games, the returner was making no impression at all. Both Rafter and Sampras lost only one point in their first two service games. But Sampras found the first opening in the fifth game. Rafter had issued his familiarly sincere "Sorry, mate" apology after an errant toss on the first point and Sampras proceeded to play a couple of high quality returns that drew errors from the Aussie on the volley.

The American had 0-30 in the fifth game, but Rafter picked on Sampras's backhand the rest of that game to hold on a run of four points in a row, moving on to 3-2. Yet two games later, the Australian was back under duress. Serving at 3-3, he went to 40-15 but Sampras kept pressing him. That hard-fought game lasted six deuces. Sampras never had a break point but Rafter needed eight game points before holding after making 12 of 18 first serves. Some fine body serving to the backhand helped him gain that hold, but Sampras had kept a lot of returns in play and made it abundantly clear that he was better in that capacity.

The final had been underway for only 26 minutes when rain halted play for the better part of half an hour. When play resumed, Sampras promptly held at 15 for 4-4. In four service games, he had won 16 of 19 points. Rafter was not reading his serve even remotely well. The American plainly had the upper hand. Now he advanced to 15-40 in the ninth game as Rafter double faulted, but the Australian made a backhand volley winner down the line and followed with another backhand volley into the clear. Rafter saved a third break point with an excellent kicker to the Sampras backhand. After four deuces, play was suspended again.

By the time the players returned, it was 6:35 in the evening. That delay had lasted two-and-a-half hours. Rafter double faulted to give Sampras a fourth break point for a chance to serve for the set, but a deep first volley from the Australian was more than Sampras could handle. Rafter came through to hold for 5-4 after five deuces. Both players held easily from there to set up a tie-break. Sampras, however, had been more persuasive, winning 24 of 28 points on serve, putting 20 of 28 first serves in play (71%).

In the tie-break, both players were tight. But Rafter was in precarious territory again. Trailing 5-3, he put away a backhand volley cleanly and crisply. Sampras was serving at 5-4, but lost the following point, netting a half volley off one of Rafter's better returns. But Sampras took the next point for 6-5, reaching set point for the first time.

Rafter stayed with his tactic of the body serve to the backhand and the Sampras return was too high. Rafter punched a forehand volley into the clear. An ace gave Rafter 7-6 and a set point of his own. But Sampras swiftly retaliated, serving a pair of aces, the first out wide at 128 mph, the second at 130 mph down the T. He was at set point for the second time, ahead 8-7.

Rafter intelligently served down the T to the Sampras forehand in the ad court, eliciting a netted return: 8-8. A netted backhand return from the American gave Rafter a second set point. Sampras saved that one with a terrific body serve but then double faulted into the net. It was 10-9 for Rafter, who had arrived at set point for the third time. He got the first serve in, but the Sampras return was rolled perfectly off the backhand. Rafter missed his half volley: 10-10. He served wide to the Sampras forehand in the deuce court, eliciting a missed stretch return: 11-10 Rafter.

On his fourth set point, Rafter came through as Sampras went aggressively for his second serve, but sent it long for a double fault. Rafter prevailed 12-10 in that critical sequence. Not only had Sampras outplayed him for most of the set, but he had been up set point twice in the tie-break. Rafter had competed tenaciously to salvage that set and had served deceptively on the biggest points. A set that could have gone either way—and probably should have ended up in favor of Sampras—belonged to the opportunistic Rafter.

The pattern continued. After an easy hold at 15 in the first game of the second set, Sampras had a break point, but Rafter stifled him with another body serve kicker to the backhand. The Sampras return was long. Another opportunity had come and gone for the American. Rafter held after two deuces to make it 1-1. Sampras faced a break point for the first time in the match when he served in the third game, but a delicate and elegant drop volley that he kept low with sidespin got the American out of jeopardy. He held for 2-1.

Both men held with ease and professionalism for the rest of the set. Rafter was now adding velocity periodically to his first serve, holding with a 126 mph ace for 2-1 as an example. Sampras dropped only two points in his last four service games of the set after his early difficulty. Rafter lost only three points in his last five service games. And so they would fittingly settle the outcome of this set in another tie-break.

Sampras opened that sequence with a double fault and soon trailed 3-0. He missed an easy forehand down the line long to trail 4-1 and Rafter was now serving. The pressure was squarely on the shoulders of Sampras, who could not afford a two-sets-to-love deficit. As Sampras said in 2018, "I felt like I had outplayed him in the first set, but that is how grass-court tennis can be. I had a few chances but did not win the important points. And it was the same thing in the second set. I felt like I was on him a bit and that the floodgates could open if I took advantage. When he was serving at 4-1 in the tie-breaker, I just felt like maybe it was not my day. You have certain feelings in a match and I was starting to question it. Even though you feel like you are playing just as well as your opponent, in grass-court tennis you can get unlucky at times. It really comes down to having that calm steady nerve at times like that on the big points."

Rafter's recollected, "When I won the first set, I thought 'This is pretty cool.' You have got to get off to a good start against Pete because if you don't you are going to be in trouble. And then the match took its path and I got up 4-1 in that second set tie-breaker and all of a sudden the match was mine because Pete was struggling a little bit maybe with his ankle and maybe mentally he wasn't playing that well. I thought, 'If I get this set he is going to be totally deflated and it is going to be hard for him to come back from two sets to love down.' I was playing pretty decent tennis and I felt in a strong position."

But what followed in the rest of that tie-break permanently altered the complexion of the match and changed the face of history as well. Rafter connected with a first serve at 4-1, but Sampras made a solid return. Rafter could not do enough with the first volley and Sampras played his forehand pass with the percentages in mind. He hit it hard but cleared the net by a safe margin. Rafter netted an arduous forehand volley on the stretch.

As the players changed ends of the court, Rafter's lead was now more tenuous at 4-2. He then sent a second serve down the T to the Sampras backhand, but it clipped the net cord and landed long. Double fault. Serving at 3-4, Sampras kicked a first serve to the backhand and Rafter was on it, keeping his backhand return low. Sampras's backhand half volley down the line was not played aggressively. But it did go to the more vulnerable and less natural wing of Rafter. He missed the routine forehand passing shot flagrantly: 4-4. Sampras produced a first-rate wide serve to the forehand on the ninth point, drawing an errant return.

From 1-4, Sampras had surged to 5-4. Having come over his backhand return with topspin predominantly during the match as was his custom, he now chipped crosscourt off that side and it was a beauty, staying exceedingly low. Rafter half-volleyed weakly. Sampras ran around his backhand and went inside-out with a forehand passing shot for a dazzling winner. Delighted to be up double set point, buoyant as could be, Sampras gleefully pumped his fist, signaling to his supporters and the crowd at large that he was now fueled with self-conviction.

Rafter served at 4-6 and Sampras ripped a backhand return freely, hitting that shot as hard as he could. But the Australian directed an extraordinarily deep forehand volley down the line that was simply too good. It set up a winning volley. Sampras would have to serve it out at 6-5. On another kind of day in this identical situation, Sampras might well have gone for an ace, or at least a trademark big first serve that could get the job done with one swing. Not now. Not after all he had been through. Not in this critical situation. He went with a safe first-serve kicker to the backhand that was more like a second serve and closed in tight on the net. Rafter was unable to keep his return low. Sampras deliberately dispatched a forehand volley winner behind Rafter. He clenched his fist again. The set belonged to the American, seven points to five in a tense tie-break. It was one set all.

By capturing six of the last seven points to salvage that tie-break, Sampras was a man with another mindset. He was well aware that Rafter had to be distraught. The emotional turnaround at the end of the second set was monumental for both players. Sampras had moved past his earlier missed opportunities, allowing him to swing much more freely. As he said, "I just felt that winning that second set, I could breathe. I was so on edge for the first two sets, but I finally got him so I felt I could relax a little bit after I tied it up. I had dug a hole and now I was out of it."

He kept creating chances and realized sooner or later he would convert. Rafter was down 15-30 in the first game of the third but held on. At 1-1, Sampras had a break point but missed a forehand return long.

But in the fifth game, Sampras at last broke Rafter. Rafter rallied from 0-40 to game point, but Sampras's one-two punch of a dipping backhand return followed by an inside-in forehand passing-shot winner locked the score at deuce again. Rafter would have three game points altogether, but Sampras was unswerving. After four deuces, Rafter double faulted. Sampras was at break point for the tenth time in the contest, having been unrewarded on the previous nine. This time he converted. Much was made later about how Rafter netted a forehand volley, but too little was said about the accelerated speed of the Sampras backhand return that coaxed the error.

Exhilarated by that breakthrough, Sampras went four for four on first serves in the sixth game and moved swiftly to 4-2. Serving two games later, he held at 15 for 5-3. And then he served out the set with a majesty that was his trademark. Ace down the T: 15-0. Second serve ace down the T: 30-0. A 131 mph unstoppable first serve to the backhand: 40-0. And an ace out wide—his 24th of the match—for the hold at love. Set to Sampras, 6-4. He led two sets to one.

Both men held up until 2-2 in the fourth set, but thereafter Sampras took over the proceedings. The Centre Court was growing darker, leaving open the distinct possibility that the final could be postponed until Monday if Sampras did not run out the match quickly. He reached 0-40 on Rafter's serve in the fifth game, but the Australian made it back to 30-40. Sampras then miss-hit a backhand pass at a high trajectory, but somehow his shot landed in the corner.

Perhaps fate had played a hand on that point. Sampras thus was up a break, leading 3-2 in the fourth and closing in on a lofty historical landmark. But the next game was a fine skirmish within a larger war. Sampras double faulted to fall behind 30-40, but saved it nobly with a 119 mph second serve into the body on the Rafter forehand that the Australian could not manage on the return. After four deuces, Sampras served an ace followed by a service winner. He had held for 4-2. The rest was elementary. Sampras broke at 15 for 5-2 with a series of well-struck returns off the backhand. The last one—directed inside in by the American—was barely touched by Rafter as he lunged in vain for a backhand volley.

Sampras was two breaks up now, serving for the match at 5-2, looking to finish it off in the fast fading light. Television did not begin to capture just how deeply the darkness was enveloping the Centre Court. Sampras played this game masterfully, taking something off his first serve on every point, putting in four in a row, leaving Rafter helpless. Rafter got only one return back into play. Sampras had collected ten of the last 11 points in the match, winning 6-7 (10), 7-6 (5) 6-4, 6-2 at 8:57 pm. For the fifth time in his seven victorious Wimbledon finals—he never lost one at the shrine—Sampras had secured victory without losing his serve. Meanwhile, he raised his record in Wimbledon finals to 7-0. Heading into the 2020 season, Sampras's impeccable record in Wimbledon title round duels was equaled by Novak Djokovic at the Australian Open and surpassed at the majors only by Rafael Nadal (12-0) at Roland Garros during the Open Era among the men.

As he approached the net to shake hands with Rafter, Sampras was overcome by emotions. He crouched over and the tears would not be denied. He had his record breaking 13th major. He had the gratification of knowing that he had won this tournament despite having to move past his pain at the end of every match from the third round on. He had the pleasure of knowing that for the first time in his career his parents had been there in the stands to witness one of his major triumphs.

Before the presentation ceremony began, he looked up at his fiancé and his coach Paul Annacone, asking them where his parents were sitting. They pointed to where Sam and Georgia Sampras were located and his Dad soon waved at him through the darkness. Sampras made his way up there and hugged both parents. The picture of him embracing his proud father that was showcased in the newspapers the next morning was one Pete Sampras would cherish forever.

As he said in 2019, "They would probably have had to call the match in the next ten minutes so when we finished up, the weight of everything I had been through for those two weeks was just lifted off. My parents being there made me very emotional. It was a tough couple of weeks and even talking about it now, almost 20 years later, definitely triggers some emotions in me. It was an emotional time in so many ways, from my parents being there, to breaking the record, to the fact that I was engaged and everything was coming to a head. And I had this pure joy of that storybook ending with my parents being there to see it. Life is never perfect, but in that moment it was damned close."

Rafter, of course, was shattered. He said in 2019, "I remember choking really, really badly against Pete that day. It was my biggest choke ever. It was the finals of Wimbledon and I had my opportunity, but I gagged. My adrenaline really spiked after I got to 4-1 in the breaker. I had worked so hard and my heart rate was about 200. I could not control my heartbeat. So my serve and my forehand broke down then. When you have that massive adrenaline spike like I did, I guess it is like having a hit of a massive drug. It was really hard for me. I had no presence and no energy. Mentally I was so deflated and my body felt like I had been through a marathon. I had no energy in my legs."

Rafter realized his state of mind deteriorated after Sampras won that second set tie-break. "I really had a defeatist attitude and I didn't know how to break it," he said. "In my mind, I had lost the match and I couldn't find a way back. And it gave Pete so much good feeling winning that second set. All of a sudden his body lifted, his game lifted. I allowed him back in the match so he had this great, feel good attitude. I just wasn't good enough to keep him down."

Addressing the brief but enticing rivalry he had with Sampras from 1993-2001 that ended with the American winning 12 of 16 matches they contested, Rafter said, "I think it is a bit too much of a compliment to me to say we had a rivalry. We played each other a lot of times and I beat him the first time we met in '93 and a few times in '98, but I never touched him after that [with the exception of a World Team Cup duel in 1999]. Pete beat me five times in '97. Pete is one of the all-time greats and I was just trying to get the best out of my career. When Pete wanted to beat me, Pete beat me. In '98 he was struggling and wasn't having a great year and I beat him a couple of times, but the other times we played he beat me. The first time we played in '93, he just took me too lightly. So it is very nice to have those things said about me and Pete, but the real rivalry was Andre and Pete. I was just having to fill in a few gaps when Andre wasn't there along with guys like Kafelnikov, Moya, Corretja or those type of blokes. We all just stuck around to play when we could."

Redirecting his thoughts to the Wimbledon final of 2000, Rafter remembered, "By early in the fourth set it was getting really dark. But I didn't want to have the crowd coming back the next day. These were the thoughts going through my mind. In my mind, I had lost the match by then and I couldn't find a way back. I had the opportunity with Pete. All of a sudden it presented itself quickly to me and I wasn't ready for it."

Sampras's tennis down the stretch was magnificent. The match might have taken an entirely different course if Sampras had exploited his openings in the first set, or if Rafter had closed out the second. Once Sampras made it to one set all, however, he was unshakable.

"I had that new lease on life sort of feeling," said Sampras. "He felt the pressure and weight of that. He was feeling he was going to lose it, like I had in the second set. I started feeling good and I finally broke him in the third and kept the momentum and carried that into the fourth. The pressure I was putting on his service games maybe got to him and I was just in the zone and trying to keep it going the way I can on grass."

Looking at the larger picture, Sampras said in 2018, "Definitely as I see my parents getting older and my Dad is slowing down a little bit, you get more sentimental and you look back at moments like Wimbledon 2000 with a completely

Pete Sampras and Patrick Rafter after Sampras won his record-breaking 13<sup>th</sup> major singles title at Wimbledon

different set of eyes. I really felt for my parents and how they raised me and seeing me play and win Wimbledon, just being in that moment. That is just an incredible feeling looking back at it almost 20 years later."

It surely was a fortnight unlike any other in the life of the greatest men's tennis champion in the history of the United States. It was incomparably fulfilling to win a seventh Wimbledon and secure a 13th major simultaneously, to stand on top of the ladder as the man with the most Grand Slam singles titles of all time. He had realized an overarching goal. He was about to turn 29. His wedding would be less than three months later, on the 30th of September in Los Angeles.

Life could not have been much more fulfilling for Pete Sampras. But breaking a record he had sought for so long and making the ultimate commitment to marry Bridgette Wilson meant that his career would be altered. His motivation to be the best player in the world and remain the sport's central figure would almost inevitably be diminished.

"Definitely the week in and week out dominance and wanting to be No. 1 went away after Wimbledon in 2000," Sampras said. "It went away after being No. 1 for six years in a row. Something left me a bit. I still felt I could do some damage in the majors, though, and I was still playing at a high level."

But he realized that his life was changing at the end of his twenties. He had been involved in a few serious relationships when he was younger, but he saw something different and more substantial in his fiancé. Bridgette Wilson was a young woman made for him in many ways.

They had met in 1999, but it did not take Sampras long to reach the conclusion that he wanted to spend his life with Wilson. As he reflected, "It was huge being with Bridgette. She has such a good head on her shoulders and the last few years of my career she was a great sounding board, almost my therapist. It was a quick engagement. We got engaged within nine months. I proposed to her before that summer of 2000 and we got married on September 30. I knew she was the one for me and knew everything she is about and the good family she came from. She is a very good person. I was ready to settle down and have some stability. Now I sit here about 20 years later and we have done so well. I was 29 when we got married. I wanted to have kids over the next couple of years and see where my career was going and that was how it happened."

It was a complicated time. He had just broken a record that had had coveted for a very long while. There was nothing left on his competitive horizon to play for; he had done it all, with the exception of winning the French Open. He reflected, "There was a lot going on at that time, but I had met someone who made me happy and we were going to get married soon. But professionally, after Wimbledon, I was struggling. It was the timing of everything and the circumstances of breaking the record with my 13th major. I had all those years at No. 1 and I was catching my breath. It was interesting. You get to a point where you don't feel like digging as deep at some of the events week in and week out. I didn't have that in me. But I still felt I could win more majors. I lost that will and I was okay with not being No. 1 anymore. I burned that candle much faster than, say, Roger Federer."

And yet, he deeply appreciated the relationship that changed his life irrevocably. Sampras said, "Bridgette was there for me. She was all in. She put her career aside after we were married. She had done *The Wedding Planner* which is a big movie, but Bridgette always wanted to be a mother. That is why I knew she was the one for me. She loved her work and was very good at it and did 30 movies, but ultimately she wanted to be a wife and mom and not be pulled in other directions. Since we have been married she has done maybe a little work, but taking care of our kids has been her main job. She couldn't imagine sitting in a makeup trailer for herself, doing movies and missing something with the kids. It is rare to find that in this town. A lot of ladies have a hard time giving up the attention or the notoriety, but I knew Bridgette wanted to be a mom more than anything else. I believed her and believed in her. She had that thing that I didn't see in anyone else I dated, so that was the clincher for me."

At the end of that summer in 2000, he made a spirited run to the final of the U.S. Open. Confronting Krajicek in the quarterfinals, he dropped the first set and trailed 6-2 in the second set tie-break. Down quadruple set point, he swept six points in a row to make it one set all. That comeback was strikingly reminiscent to his Wimbledon final with Rafter. Sampras upended Krajicek in four sets, halted Lleyton Hewitt in the semifinal round, and faced the mercurial and often enigmatic Marat Safin in the final.

Although Safin had saved two match points and toppled Sampras a few weeks earlier in the Toronto Masters 1000 quarterfinals, the American was the heavy favorite to win their final at the Open. But Safin played the match of his life and was oblivious to his surroundings and the situation. He was victorious 6-4, 6-3, 6-3. It was an astonishing display of tennis, both on serve and off the ground, even on the return of serve. Safin was devastatingly potent. He was knocking the cover off the ball, but hardly missing. Quite simply, he played out of his mind. Safin never again performed with the same unconscious brilliance through the rest of his career.

For the second year in a row, Sampras ended the season stationed at No. 3 in the world, finishing behind Kuerten and Safin. Sampras lost to Kuerten 6-7 (5), 6-3, 6-4 in the semifinals of the ATP World Tour Championships that had shifted locations from Germany to Lisbon, Portugal and the Brazilian then startled Agassi in the final of that prestigious event. Had Sampras beaten Kuerten in their penultimate round duel (or if Agassi had upended the Brazilian), Safin would have ended that campaign as the top-ranked player in men's tennis. Taking only two titles all year long, Sampras was not in the running for No. 1 as the year concluded, but he won 42 of 55 matches.

The 2001 season commenced for Sampras with a four-set, round of 16 setback against Todd Martin at the Australian Open. Sampras owned a 17-2 career winning record over his countryman going into that contest and he had defeated Martin no fewer than 13 times in a row. He reached the final of Indian Wells before losing to Agassi 7-6 (5), 7-5, 6-1. In his first career confrontation against Andy Roddick, Sampras lost in Miami to the 18-year-old in a big-serving battle.

He never got going during the clay-court season and was knocked out in the second round at Roland Garros by Galo Blanco of Spain. And so he set his sights on Wimbledon, but lost there in his only official career meeting against a player who was destined to break his record for Grand Slam titles eight years later. Switzerland's immensely gifted Roger Federer defeated Sampras in a Centre Court, round of 16 chestnut 7-6 (7), 5-7, 6-4, 6-7 (2), 7-5. The poise of the 19-year-old was extraordinary.

In the days when the grass was playing faster, the young Federer served and volleyed regularly and his play at the net was remarkably good. The Swiss attacked persistently, serving and volleying no fewer than 109 times, winning 75 of those points. He was a different player in those days, more a product of that particular time. The quicker courts were abundant worldwide. And Federer was very comfortable coming in and taking command at the net.

Sampras, however, had his chances. At set point in the first set tie-break, he got a questionable call on a Federer first serve that was called in. Sampras passionately believed it was out. Anguished by that misfortune, Sampras let the umpire know of his disagreement, but there was no Hawkeye back then. A challenge was out of the question.

After winning the second set, Sampras bungled one of his normally trustworthy leaping overheads at 4-4, 40-30 in the third set and soon thereafter lost his serve and the set. And in the fifth and final set, he had 15-40 on the Federer serve at 4-4 but could not convert.

Across the summer, he lost his second match of the season against Agassi in the final of Los Angeles and was runner-up to Tommy Haas at the Long Island Open. Those showings were nothing to scoff at. But then Sampras came alive vibrantly at the U.S. Open and had his finest run ever at a major he did not win. In the round of 16, he brought down Rafter in four terrific sets. Having reached the quarters, he eclipsed Agassi 6-7 (7), 7-6 (2), 7-6 (2) 7-6 (5). Not a service break was to be found by either player in this four-set, masterfully played skirmish. It was the most absorbing and best played match of a 34 contest career series between the two dynamic Americans.

Before the start of the fourth set tie-break, Sampras and Agassi were showered with a standing ovation by the appreciative fans on a New York night stretching into early morning. That prolonged ovation was not simply a salute to the two icons for their stupendous play that evening, but also a stirring tribute to the breadth and scope of their entire careers. Agassi had played better in some of his triumphs over Sampras, and vice versa. But, on both sides of the net, in terms of high quality tennis from beginning to end, this was in a class by itself as their best match ever against each other.

As Sampras said in 2019, "It was just one of those nights in New York that everything turned into a home run with two guys playing great at the same time. It could not have been scripted any better. When everyone just stood up and applauded before that last tiebreaker, for the first time in my life I think I got out of my mindset of playing the match. It was like, 'Oh my God.' I appreciated it for about ten seconds. At the end the nerves got to both of us, but this was just high quality tennis the whole match, two guys with respect for each other going toe to toe and playing at the highest level. People don't realize how hard it is to not lose your serve for three-and-a-half hours against one of the best returners of all time."

Playing Safin in the semifinals, Sampras turned the tables on the Russian, reversing the result of the 2000 final with a 6-4, 7-6 (0), 6-3 triumph. Sampras had last ruled at the Open in 1996, but now he had removed the three men who had taken over the tournament since his previous victory, defeating the 1997-98 victor Rafter, 1999 champion Agassi and the defending champion Safin. Only Hewitt stood between Sampras and the title. The American had eclipsed the Australian the previous year on the same court in the semifinals, but this time he had run out of emotional intensity and physical firepower. The 20-year-old ousted a player ten years his senior 7-6 (4), 6-1, 6-1.

And so, for the second year in a row, Sampras had been beaten in the final of the championships of his country. In 2000, he had defeated Hewitt before losing the final to Safin; in 2001, he defeated Safin but bowed out against Hewitt. Clearly, Safin played an inspirational match in 2000 and Hewitt was virtually letter perfect off the ground in 2001. But Sampras at the tail end of his twenties and start of his thirties was clearly compromised by playing the semifinals and finals on back to back days.

"As you get older," he said in 2019, "that Saturday-Sunday schedule they had at the Open for the semifinals and finals was tough. I felt a little flat and those two guys were hot. Safin just overpowered me and I came in half a step slow. And with Hewitt, that was a tough second week with Rafter, the four-set epic with Andre and Safin. Having a day off would have been nice, but it is what it is. I was still playing fine, but it just looked in those finals that I was a little long in the tooth and feeling it. I didn't have the pop. And I also remember in one of those years [2000] I won my semi and should have gone back to the hotel room and rested, but I went up and spent an hour with

Bill Clinton in one of the suites. It was a great honor to meet him. I don't know if I was feeling a little too confident about the next day, but it doesn't matter: if the President asks you to come up and meet him, you do it."

Sampras had some shoulder issues after the 2001 U.S. Open and entered only one more tournament that year. He finished with a mediocre 35-16 match record for the season. He did not win a tournament all year long after taking at least one title every year from 1990-2000, falling to No. 10 in the ATP rankings.

Meanwhile, his partnership with Annacone came to an end, although they would later reunite. Sampras felt he needed to get the council of other voices of wisdom and Annacone understood. As Annacone said, "When we split up at the end of 2001, I realized we should have done that a little bit earlier. The message was just flat and I was going through my divorce, so I was not the cheeriest guy to be around. That was hard for Pete and I apologized to him for that because it was tough for him, tough for me and tough for my ex-wife, too. But the tough part for him was because he was on the road with me. It was the right thing for him at the time to get a new voice and he kind of struggled for a while. We stayed in touch and I would send him faxes to tournaments and wish him good luck. I was running Player Development for the USTA at that point."

But, even when he was sorting through his coaching complexities and surmising what to do, Sampras was convinced that he could still capture another major title. He was not preoccupied with the growing chorus of skeptics. It did not matter that much to him that some people who should have known better were counting him out. Deep in his psyche, Sampras remained certain he could still succeed on the premier stages. The critics be damned; no one was a better judge of what Pete Sampras could do than the man himself.

# CHAPTER 16

# FINAL CHAPTER OF A STERLING CAREER

Embarking on a campaign that he did not know would be his last as a professional tennis player on the ATP Tour, Sampras struggled to get his season on track. He had Tom Gullikson by his side as his coach, which was poignant in many ways. Not only was there the obvious connection that Sampras had with Tom's late twin brother Tim in the coaching box, but Tom had been his Davis Cup captain in the 1990's.

As Gullikson recalled, "I just went down to Australia with Pete and it was more of a temporary thing, kind of a stop-gap measure. He knew me well. Pete was not in the best place in his career and quite honestly I went down there feeling I didn't want to coach him long term because I much prefer for everyone to remember what a great partnership he had with Tim. He lost in the fourth round to Safin at the Australian Open and certainly didn't play his best tennis. After that we just parted ways which was fine with me and fine with him as well, because at that time I did not have the time to commit to all the traveling. I was quite happy to have been his Davis Cup captain and leave it at that. We parted ways as friends and we have always been friends."

Gullikson remembered Sampras turning to the highly regarded Jose Higueras—former coach of Courier among many others—as his new coach. As Gullikson pointed out, "Jose is very big on practicing hard and hitting a lot of balls and that is not in Pete's m.o. Pete is more of an artist and a feel player and an athlete. He is not the kind of guy who is going to do two-on-one drills for two hours a day like Courier would for example."

Beaten by Todd Martin in his 2002 debut at Adelaide, knocked out in a four-set, round-of-16 skirmish by Safin at the Australian Open, his results improved somewhat over the spring under Higueras, but this was not a top of the line Sampras by any means. He reached the semifinals at Indian Wells before losing to Hewitt in blustery conditions and was runner-up to Roddick on the clay in Houston after toppling Agassi in the semifinal round.

And yet, he lost an agonizing, five-set Davis Cup clash on grass against Corretja after taking the first two sets. Not since the Olympic Games in 1992 had he bowed out in a match after establishing a two-set lead. On the European clay, he did not fare well. He did not win a match at either Hamburg or Rome and was beaten in two out of three contests at the World Team Cup.

In his 14th and final appearance at Roland Garros, he was ushered out of the French Open in the first round by Italy's Andrea Gaudenzi, a player ranked No. 69 in the world. Shifting from clay to grass, Sampras fell early on the lawns of Halle against Germany's Nicholas Kiefer. Amidst this disconcerting slump, he headed into Wimbledon hoping to rekindle some magic and find a path toward an eighth title at the All England Club.

That scenario did not pan out. In the second round, Sampras faced "lucky loser" George Bastl of Switzerland out on the old Court 2, better known as the "Graveyard" of champions. In that setting, many renowned champions had suffered stunning losses, including John McEnroe at the hands of Tim Gullikson in 1979 and Jimmy Connors versus Kevin Curren in

1983. It was a distracting and noisy setting for Wimbledon and it seemed like another world compared to the fabled Centre Court or even Court 1.

Sampras would surely have handled Bastl on the Centre Court comfortably enough, but he was out of sorts in an unfamiliar location. Bastl captured the first two sets before Sampras battled his way back into a fifth. But the career journeyman Bastl pulled off a startling 6-3, 6-2, 4-6, 3-6, 6-4 victory over the seven-time Wimbledon champion.

To just about anyone else of stature who had tasted a defeat of that nature, the word humiliation would spring to mind. But Sampras was made of a different stock. He recognized that he was not himself at this juncture of his career. This loss was surely a low point for him. He had been beaten, but the unshakable American was not defeated. That was what made him who he is—the ever present sense of self. He was not giving up. To the contrary, he was moving on and driven by powerful private engines to ignore those who thought that he was through, and, even more so, to prove a point to himself.

Was the Bastl defeat a blessing in disguise? He answered in 2019, "The blessing in disguise was getting back together with Paul Annacone. We had this great run, but you get to the point where you want to hear a different voice. But after we split up my whole coaching situation was a mess. I was with Tom Gullikson a little bit and with Jose Higueras. Jose was not in a place to be totally invested in me at the time and it just accumulated over the months. I was working hard but, as you get older, you almost need more of a friend/therapist more than you need help with your forehand."

Continuing with his musings on his feelings after the shocker at Wimbledon, Sampras asserted, "After that Bastl match I just felt completely empty and dejected. I just felt lost and I didn't know where to turn. I just played horribly against Bastl on Court 2. When you are not confident out there, anything can happen. Five years before that on Court 2, I would have been fine. But I just felt uncomfortable with my game. I think the last eight months accumulated led to that one match. I just remember sitting on the side of the court, playing with my strings and thinking, 'What the hell just happened?' I was still putting in the time and effort but maybe my swagger went away. It really hit me hard and coming home was not easy. I had to do some soul searching. I was talking to my wife, Bridgette, quite a bit. I always felt in a safe place talking to her and she was almost my therapist. Jose and I had a talk and decided it was best to end it."

That brought Annacone back into the fold. Working for the USTA, he had been at Wimbledon. Sampras may have been muddled in his mind about why he was so far off key on the court, but the clarity of his deep-picture thinking was as sharp as ever. He knew it was time to reunite with Annacone and wasted no time making that decision.

As Annacone said, "I was running Player Development for the USTA when he lost to Bastl. I remember going back to my apartment afterwards and getting a call from Pete. He said, 'Did you see the match?' I said that I had. He asked me what I thought about it in general. I said, 'Do you really want to know what I think?'"

Annacone told Sampras, "Okay, here is the thing: you have achieved everything you want to achieve in the game and you have broken all of these records but you are at the stage of your life where you are tired of practice, tired of the travel and tired of being a star and signing autographs. You have got a great wife and she is totally supportive of you, but when you are tired from all these other things, even as great as you are, you can't walk on the court and give yourself the best chance to win matches. It is not possible. Pete, you are great. Great doesn't all of a sudden go away.'"

Having said all that, Annacone added, "Pete, there are three of four things you need to do as far as tennis is concerned. You do that and you are going to win another major. It might not be next week but you are going to win another major."

An hour later, Sampras called Annacone back and said, "I am ready. I want you back sitting in my box when I win another major. I want you sitting with Bridgette."

Annacone still had his USTA obligations but he got clearance from them to work with Sampras again. Sampras dove wholeheartedly into the summer hard-court season, but the losses did not cease. He was beaten in a third set tie-break by Tommy Haas in Toronto and he fell in another final-set tie-break contest to the left-handed, big serving Australian Wayne Arthurs in Cincinnati. Taking a wildcard into the Long Island ATP event, he was beaten in three sets by the Frenchman Paul-Henri Mathieu, then ranked No. 85 in the world.

He had split six matches across three tournaments leading up to the U.S. Open, but was undismayed. As Annacone recalled, "He was playing fine and the thing I loved about it was he was having no reaction. It was the old Pete again and there was no, 'Oh, no, what is wrong?'"

Sampras recollected, "I had a mediocre summer but everything was okay. Paul and I were talking about it and trying to figure this out. But I just always had this belief that I could get my game going and turn it around. I could play a bad match one day and come back the next day and play great. Why I was able to do that I don't know. So I just went into the Open and Paul said, 'You have won this four times. It is not an accident. It is because of who you are and the type of game you have. You just have to make sure you play the right way.' He just instilled that confidence in me and encouraged me to have some energy out there and not feel sorry for myself."

The first few rounds in New York went smoothly for the No. 17 seed. He moved past Spain's Albert Portas—the world No. 76—6-1, 6-4, 6-4, playing that afternoon contest in a half-full Arthur Ashe Stadium with fans scattered all over the grounds watching other matches. In the second round, he took on Kristian Pless and dismissed the Danish competitor 6-3, 7-5, 6-4 under the lights.

And so Sampras had advanced to a third-round appointment with Great Britain's Greg Rusedski, the 1997 U.S.

Open finalist. The match was not scheduled on Arthur Ashe Stadium but on Louis Armstrong Stadium.

When play commenced on Sunday evening, Sampras was behind 5-3 in the first set but he broke back in the ninth game after saving two set points before rain postponed play until Monday evening. Sampras had to erase another set point at 5-6 on his serve. In the ensuing tie-break, he missed only one first serve. Ahead 5-4, he unleashed a pair of aces, taking the tie-break 7-4 and gaining a one-set lead.

Rusedski rallied to win the second set and then the third was settled in another tie-break. Sampras seemed safely ahead at 4-0 but over-anxiously netted a smash from almost on top of the net. Rusedski followed with two aces to narrow the Sampras lead to 4-3. But Sampras connected with a big second serve to elicit an errant return from Rusedski and then a 129 mph first serve down the T was unanswerable. Sampras had moved to 6-3. He took the next point dynamically, using a low return to set up a forehand inside-in passing shot. He was backing up as he made that dazzling winner, but his timing was immaculate and the power was astounding. Tie-break to Sampras 7-3. He led two sets to one.

Once more, Rusedski roared back, breaking early in the fourth set, winning it 6-3. On to a fifth set the match would go. But Sampras had the advantage of serving first in the final set. In his first four service games, Sampras allowed Rusedski only four points. At 4-4, however, he was pushed to 30-30 and thus, deep in the fifth set, stood potentially only six points from defeat.

Wisely, Sampras sliced his first serve wide to the highly vulnerable Rusedski backhand in the deuce court. That biting delivery provoked a netted chip return. Sampras took the next point on another missed backhand return, holding on for 5-4. On his way to 30-40 in the tenth game, Sampras produced three vintage forehand passing-shot winners, giving himself a match point on Rusedski's serve. Rusedski served a thunderbolt at 130 mph down the T, but inexplicably stayed back behind it. Sampras made a solid return down the middle and then approached down the line off the forehand on his next shot. Rusedski barely missed a forehand pass up the line. Sampras raised his arms in both relief and exhilaration. He had won 7-6 (4), 4-6, 7-6 (3), 3-6, 6-4. This would be the last five-set match of Sampras's career and he finished with an impressive 33-15 record.

Rusedski did not endear himself to fans of Sampras with his ungracious post-match comments. He said, "I lost the match. He did not win it... He's not playing that great. I'd be surprised if he wins the next match against Haas....He's a step-and-a-half slower coming to the net. You can get the ball down. He's just not the same player. I mean, he's a great player from the past. You're used to seeing Pete Sampras, 13-time Grand Slam champion. It's not the same player."

Sampras insisted genuinely and convincingly in a 2019 interview for this book that Rusedski's remarks meant nothing to him. He felt that Rusedski simply posed problems at that time with his game. Sampras said, "Playing someone like Greg is uncomfortable. He doesn't give me a lot of rhythm with his big, tough lefty serve. I just hung in there and was relieved to get through that match."

Addressing Rusedki's post match comments, Sampras said, "Honestly, no disrespect to Greg, but it was him. It wasn't Courier or Agassi. It was just Greg being Greg. I was told about what he said, but it didn't affect me. If McEnroe had said something, I would have felt that a little more. Greg was bitter and pissed that he lost and we all say certain things at those times. I wasn't paying much attention to it. I would go into my own little world when I would play these majors and I just don't let anything get in the way of winning."

Sampras made those remarks with unmistakable sincerity. He was not concerned with Rusedski's lack of tact. But John McEnroe and Jim Courier believed that the provocative words of Rusedski served Pete Sampras quite well.

As McEnroe said in 2018, "Rusedski had one of the bigger mouths in tennis. When he made that comment about Pete not being the same guy, to me that is sometimes chalkboard material. Why did the guy have to open his mouth? Guess what that is going to do? It was going to unleash something. It was just unnecessary to throw that in there. It turned out to help Pete a little bit, just a tiny bit when you need to get over the hump and people are writing you off. Then, all of a sudden, it all came together and as it was playing out I was thinking Pete was going to win the whole thing."

Courier was essentially in accord with McEnroe. He said, "Rusedski did Pete a favor by smack talking before their match and in my recollection that lit Pete's fire. Pete was very prideful and Rusedski wasn't particularly well liked on the tour at the time. He had a knack for saying the wrong thing at times. I wasn't in the middle of it but it certainly looked like Pete had something to prove."

For his part, Rusedski sounded sincere as he reflected on the episode 17 years after the fact in an interview for this book. In his estimation, he meant no harm and was simply trying to be candid when he made his post-match comments. He did not believe he was being disrespectful but clearly misinterprets why his comments were viewed by nearly all of the tennis community as sour grapes.

Rusedski said in 2019, "I don't think it really came off as disrespectful what I said. It was kind of truthful because Pete's form coming into the Open was not great. He was struggling for match play. He had lost to George Bastl on Court 2 at Wimbledon. Everybody was saying what I was saying—that Pete had slowed down and was a step slower than before, so that was basically the chat in the locker room. So it was actually just an honest opinion I was expressing. I just said what I felt. At the time that was my truth in my situation, but I don't think I said anything rude or impolite."

Admitting that he was disgruntled by losing such a close contest against Sampras, Rusedski recalled, "On match point I hit a shot really close to the line that was called out, but we had no Hawkeye back then. It would have been nice to get a replay on that. Obviously I was frustrated and maybe I could have delivered my comments in a more relaxed manner as I am doing today, but my feeling at the time was that everybody in the locker room was thinking and feeling what I was saying. Maybe my tone could have been different and I could have put it in a nicer way. I just felt at the time that I probably should have won that match."

Told that Sampras maintained that his remarks neither motivated nor bothered him, Rusedski said, "Pete is a pretty horizontal sort of guy and pretty chilled out. He is a relaxed guy. McEnroe and Courier might have said it motivated Pete and maybe it did, but then the other aspect to look at is that Pete and I had a lot of big points in our match and he managed to win those big points. Sometimes it is one match like the one we had that can turn things around and then everything just flows for a great player like Pete. Maybe with our match that is just where he flicked the switch and got his mojo. Pete would tell you if what I said afterwards motivated him or not, but I don't believe it made a difference with him winning or losing the tournament that year. I would just take Pete's word for how he feels about it because he is an honest guy. You spend enough time with Pete, and Pete calls a spade a spade at the end of the day. So I would take the point of view that our match just played Pete into form and then he found his game."

That may well have been the case. Sampras was relieved and exhilarated to have come through in the clutch against Rusedski. Be that as it may, he had to keep going strong. He was pitted against the No. 3 seed Haas in the fourth round, looking to make amends for the hard-fought loss he experienced over the summer against the German, hoping to take his game up a notch from the way he had performed against Rusedski. That is exactly what he did.

The turning point of the memorable evening was when Sampras served at 4-5 in the first set. He released an ace for 40-0 and an easy hold looked likely. But Haas rallied to deuce. The No. 3 seed lofted a lob deep enough to prevent Sampras from putting away an overhead. But, on his next shot, Sampras approached on a forehand down the line, anticipated Haas's passing shot and put away a backhand volley winner authoritatively at an acute angle. Sampras held on after another deuce for 5-5, broke in the 11th game and served out the set at love, firing two aces in the process. He had won ten of the last 11 points to move out in front.

Sampras got an early break in the second set. At 5-4, he closed it out on his serve. Down break point, he sent a first serve to the Haas backhand and closed in quickly behind it, knocking off a forehand volley behind Haas for a winner. Soon he led two sets to love. They went to a third set tie-break. Sampras was ahead 4-3, three points away from a straight-set triumph. But he lost that tie-break 7-5, necessitating another set of tennis and a longer night for the American.

The fourth set stayed on serve until Haas sought to reach another tie-break. The German was serving at 5-6, 30-30 when Sampras attacked, coming forward for a textbook backhand volley winner. He had gone to match point. Haas's second serve bounded off the net cord and landed long. Double fault. Match over. Sampras moved on to the quarters with his 7-5, 6-4, 6-7 (5), 7-5 victory.

As Sampras said in 2019, "It had rained a lot and it was humid. These matches were taking a toll on me with the physical part of playing a lot of service games and all the serving-and-volleying. I felt that the fourth set win against Tommy saved me some energy going into my next match with Roddick. Tommy was a real solid player and he made me work, but I played good serve-and-volley tennis against him."

His opponent in the last eight would be none other than Andy Roddick, the young man with the high aspirations and a blindingly explosive serve that was not as elegant as Sampras's nor quite as precise. The fact remained that his serve was magnificent and a weapon feared by anyone who stood across the net from him. Roddick was a very tough man to break and a ferocious competitor. He would win the U.S. Open the following year and finish that campaign at No. 1 in the world. And in 2017 he would receive the sport's ultimate honor when he was inducted at the International Tennis Hall of Fame.

Courier felt that Sampras had the versatility in his game to make it a tall task for Roddick to stop him in this generational battle of Americans on a festive New York evening in front of an audience comprised almost entirely of effusive fans. He said, "That certainly felt like a match where Pete had the tools to beat Andy and just disrupt his game. Pete had a huge amount of pride playing against the young American lion trying to take his seat at the table."

Sampras and Roddick walked out into the windy evening on Arthur Ashe Stadium after the national anthem was sung beautifully by Melissa Errico, the wife of U.S. Davis Cup captain Patrick McEnroe. The atmosphere in that arena was highly charged. The audience was celebrating one ascendant American who was appearing in only his third U.S. Open at the age of 20 and another enduring icon they had known for ages. Roddick was a champion in the making and a young competitor who seemed certain to succeed at the highest levels of the game.

Across the net stood Sampras, a champion deeply appreciated for his tenure as a top flight player. Twelve years earlier he had won his first Open. Now he was playing the championships of his country for the 14th time and seeking a fifth crown in New York. The fans were decidedly on Sampras's side for sentimental reasons, knowing this might be his last chance to come through on the hard courts in Ashe Stadium, realizing that his days of dominating the game were over. They were aware that Sampras had withstood some difficult times over the last couple of years and that made many of them more sympathetic to and appreciative of a man they had too often taken for granted.

Roddick vividly remembers that night. He had won both of his previous meetings against Sampras, one on hard courts in Miami the previous year, the other on clay in Houston earlier in 2002. Both of those skirmishes had turned on first set tie-breaks taken by Roddick. This one would be very different.

Speaking about it retrospectively in a podcast I did with him for the USTA during the summer of 2018, Roddick said, "Pete went right through me that night. I had beaten him in Miami and Houston, but I think I had naively made the mistake of thinking that those were the same as a U.S. Open version of Pete Sampras. He came out there and was inspired. He had a huge chip on his shoulder and rightly so. I would say the coverage from the media coming out of the summer bordered on disrespectful. He caught some bad press and some personal press. It was almost like for a moment in time people had kind of forgotten how good he was capable of playing."

From the opening bell against Roddick, Sampras was finely tuned. Although he missed all four first serves in the first game, he made one ace on his second delivery and held at love. That was just the start he needed. He proceeded to play an excellent return game, approaching on the Roddick forehand to force a netted pass, walloping a forehand inside-in winner, and punching a backhand volley winner after chip-charging to the Roddick backhand. With that flourish, he was at 0-40. Roddick rallied to 30-40 but missed his first serve. Once again, Sampras chip-charged off the backhand and then punched a forehand volley down the line with good depth. Roddick was trapped. His backhand pass was easily anticipated by Sampras, who sent a backhand volley down the line with sidespin. Roddick had no chance to make a passing shot. Sampras had the quick 2-0 lead and he pumped his fist to celebrate the moment. He then held at 15 for 3-0. He had collected 12 of 15 points in building that lead.

Sampras was assiduously protecting that service break lead. After Roddick got on the scoreboard, Sampras held at love for 4-1. Roddick held easily in the sixth game but Sampras served two aces en route to a hold at 15 for 5-2. Serving for the set two games later, Sampras released a couple of aggressive double faults. It was 30-30. But Sampras swung his slice serve out wide, followed it in, and sent a backhand first-volley winner crosscourt. At 40-30, his second serve whistled down the T and caught the center service line. Ace. Roddick was akin to a spectator. Set to Sampras 6-3. In five service games, he won 20 of 24 points.

Early in the second set, Sampras was behind break point at 0-1. He had missed three first volleys on his way to a 30-40 deficit, but he punched a forehand volley crosscourt into the corner for a winner. On the next point, a fine pickup backhand half volley led to another forehand volley winner. Now at game point, Sampras served into the body on Roddick's backhand side and drew the error. 1-1.

Roddick might have been quietly rattled about not converting his first break point. Sampras broke him at love in the next game as the younger man double faulted twice from 0-30. Sampras held at 30 for 3-1. After Roddick took the next game, Sampras went 0-for-6 on first serves, but it didn't matter because his second serve was so prodigious. He volleyed brilliantly in establishing a 4-2 lead. Searching for an insurance break, Sampras found it. With Roddick serving at 30-40 in the seventh game, Sampras struck one of his signature running forehands crosscourt. Roddick netted a forehand under duress. It was 5-2 for Sampras. He trotted to his chair at the changeover, delighted with where he stood in the score-line.

At 40-15 in the next game, Sampras serve-volleyed, sending his backhand first volley deep crosscourt. Roddick made an impressive pass down the line, but an inspired Sampras moved with remarkable alacrity to his right and reached back almost behind him from a deep position to direct a forehand volley crosscourt into an open space. That point was emblematic of Sampras performing with the verve and intensity that made him such an unshakable champion. The set went decidedly his way, 6-2. He led two sets to love. The New York fans were thoroughly enjoying Sampras's clinically unassailable play. Sampras was so sprightly that he looked younger and sharper than he had in a long while.

Roddick was not one to surrender in the least, but he seemed dispirited. Sampras was unleashing his full groundstroke arsenal, covering the court magnificently and leaving his opponent with very few options. Sampras broke in the first game of the third set and promptly held at love. Although his first serve percentage was much lower than usual, Sampras had won 23 of 25 points when he managed the wind well enough to get the first ball in. He was up 2-0 in the third swiftly. Roddick's professionalism was apparent as he held serve four times in a row from there, but he was not threatening Sampras much at all in his return games. On his way to serving for the match at 5-4. Sampras lost only four points on serve in that third set. He trailed 15-30 in the tenth game, but a service winner to the backhand made it 30-30. A service winner to the forehand lifted Sampras to 40-30. On match point, he served-and-volleyed skillfully, making a stellar half volley off a fine return from Roddick. Roddick's passing shot was low, but Sampras was there for the forehand drop volley down the line. Roddick scampered forward but hardly touched the ball: 6-3, 6-2, 6-4 Sampras. He finished at 47% on first serves, but faced only one break point and went unbroken. That said everything about the extraordinary quality of his second serve and the soundness of his first volley.

"That was a nighttime match and I always felt good going on that court in the evening," said Sampras in 2018. "I chipped-and-charged and kind of took it to him. It wasn't a great serving night but I felt good with my game. I had gotten through a couple of tough matches and Andy had that big serve, but I felt I could get into some of these rallies with him and see what I could do. I felt I was playing better and had found my game there against Andy. It just did wonders for me for the rest of the event over the weekend because I was getting a little tired."

Elaborating, Sampras said, "The Andy match was physically not easy but it helped me to recover a little. Purely from a physical standpoint, it gave me a couple of days off and some time for the weekend push. It was a good match for me with my level getting better. The crowd was rooting for me as the older guy. People are quick to think after a match like mine against Bastl at Wimbledon that you should probably move on, but they felt for me and were cheering me on. I was showing some emotion and it felt good. Everything was going well."

The draw had opened up nicely for the semifinal. Kuerten had toppled the No. 2 seed Safin in the second round but he was beaten by the Dutchman Sjeng Schalken in the round of 16. Schalken then upended the dangerous No. 28 seed Fernando Gonzalez in a fifth-set tie-break. The Dutchman was a workhorse who would peak at No. 11 in the world the following year. Standing 6'4", weighing about 180 pounds, very fit and a player who was not afraid to confront bigger names—he had nearly toppled eventual champion Lleyton Hewitt that year at Wimbledon in the quarterfinals—Schalken had to be taken seriously.

Nonetheless, Sampras had never lost to him in four previous meetings. He did not necessarily need to be at peak efficiency to overcome the 25-year-old with one of the best one-handed backhands in the sport, but he also did not want to get bogged down in a long and strenuous contest the day before the final. Sampras had the advantage of playing in the opening semifinal late on Saturday morning and he wanted to get the job done in straight sets.

Sampras had a significant opening in the second game of the match as Schalken was down 0-40, but did not convert. Schalken held on. That changed the shape of the entire set. Sampras lost only four points in six opening set service games, but never came close to breaking Schalken after his early opportunity. Yet he was awfully sharp on his way to a commanding 4-0 tie-break lead before double faulting. Schalken took two points in a row on serve, then two in a row on the Sampras serve.

Improbably, Schalken had swept five points in a row and led 5-4, with two service points to come. Sampras knew he could not afford to make a mistake in the next rally, which lasted 16 strokes. He was going backhand to backhand when Schalken blinked, missing a crosscourt shot wide. But Schalken took the next point and so Sampras was serving at 5-6 and set point down. His big-point prowess was fully

Pete Sampras was seeded No. 17 at the 2002 U.S. Open

on display here. He sent an impeccably-placed first serve
down the T, closed in tight and put away a backhand first
volley down the line. 6-6. Another serve-volley combination
was letter perfect, setting up a backhand volley winner down
the line: 7-6 Sampras. Now Schalken was serving to stay in
the tie-break, down set point. Sampras suddenly accelerated
the pace off his forehand crosscourt and caught Schalken
off guard. The Dutchman missed. Set to Sampras 7-6, eight
points to six in the tie-break.

As Sampras walked to the changeover with an unmistakable spring in his step, he was captured by the CBS camera looking up at the loud and animated crowd and saying, "That's what I'm talking about!" It was one of those highly unusual overtures toward the audience made by a man known for his stoicism and introverted manner.

Recalling that moment 17 years later, Sampras said, "It was out of the ordinary for me, but I remember talking to Paul Annacone earlier in the tournament and he told me to let the crowd know I heard them. I had a few moments those two weeks at the Open like that, subtle moments even in the Roddick match. As you get a little older you honestly need a little help and encouragement. Paul told me to appreciate the fans. He dropped that one little hint and it just stuck in my mind. You are slowing down. I was 31 and knew this could be it. But for me to look into a crowd is shocking. You watch Nadal now with his emotion and the crowds know it and expect it. I was never going to go crazy, but it felt good to show a little emotion without being insincere. I was just getting out of my own way and letting loose a little. Throughout my career I would just do my thing and the court was almost separate from the crowd, but by now the blinders were not on so much and you can use the energy from the crowd."

At 3-4 in a second set that had been entirely on serve, Sampras was down 0-30, but he attacked to draw a passing-shot error, served two aces in a row and connected with another unstoppable first serve, holding on tenaciously for 4-4. At 4-5, Sampras was tested again, trailing 15-30. An ace out wide at 116 mph brought him back to 30-30. He held on at 30 for 5-5. Serving at 5-6, he was down 15-30, but took three points in a row, entering the tie-break after another timely ace.

Schalken was a tough competitor. He led 3-1 in the second-set tie-break, but Sampras secured four points in a row for a 5-3 lead. Schalken took the next point, but now Sampras had the set on his racket as he served at 5-4. He went to 6-4, releasing a deep second serve, drawing a return error. Now ahead double set point, Sampras went wide in the deuce court with an excellent first serve, pulling Schalken off the court. The return went predictably down the line. Sampras picked it off handsomely, sending a backhand first volley crosscourt for a winner. Tie-break to Sampras 7-4. He was now ahead two sets to love.

The comeback in the second set tie-break by Sampras had essentially dampened Schalken's spirit while raising the American's morale. An excellent chip and charge from Sampras that led to a forehand volley winner angled crosscourt gave the American a 3-1 lead in the third set. He kept holding and expanded his lead to 5-2. With Schalken serving to stay in the match, Sampras chip-charged to pressure Schalken into an error at 30-30. At match point, he went to the chip-charge again, read Schalken's backhand pass and punched a backhand volley winner impeccably down the line. Sampras had been opportunistic in winning 7-6 (6), 7-6 (4), 6-2.

"I did not play my best," Sampras said in 2019. "We played the early semifinal and there was not much energy in the crowd. I just felt it was a grind, but I was reasonably solid. It wasn't a beautiful match, but I did what I had to do. I just knew I would have to step it up against either Andre or Hewitt in the final. I really didn't care who won that match. I was thinking it would be pretty cool to play Andre once again at the Open but, on the other hand, I was thinking maybe a little revenge against Hewitt for the year before. I did not see their match. I had a massage and did press and by the time I got back to the hotel their match was kind of over and I knew I was playing Andre."

What a stunning development this was for American tennis fans assembled in New York at the last major of the 2002 season. The No. 17 seed Sampras was in his third Open final in a row, very much against the odds after his difficulties over the course of the season. His 2002 match record coming into the Open was just above .500 at 20 wins against 17 losses. He had last won a tournament of any kind at Wimbledon in 2000. Since then, he had played 33 tournaments but had not taken a title in that span. But he was not a man who dwelled on negative historical data, not when he had an opportunity like this, not at a time when he had rediscovered his zest for the game and the majesty of the way he could play on big occasions.

Agassi was seeded sixth. He had captured four singles titles across the 2002 season, including two Masters 1000 events at Miami and Rome. Sampras had prevailed in their lone meeting that season at Houston on clay in the semifinal round. But overall Agassi's form had been decidedly more reliable than Sampras's in this 2002 campaign, leading too many observers who should have known better to regard him as the favorite. Not only had he played the second semifinal the day before—going four hard and taxing sets against Hewitt—but, in addition, he had never beaten Sampras in three previous showdowns at the U.S. Open. Twice, Sampras had ousted Agassi in the final, first in 1990, again in 1995. Moreover, Sampras had surprised many learned observers when he toppled Agassi in their splendid 2001 Open quarterfinal.

Nonetheless, Agassi was not approaching this encounter in a melancholy frame of mind. He was buoyant in some ways after beating Hewitt. The affable Australian Darren Cahill had previously coached Hewitt, but he had taken over from Brad Gilbert as Agassi's coach at the start of that 2002 season. Cahill was unimpeachably astute in the coaching role. As a player, he peaked at No. 22 in the world in the late eighties and advanced to the semifinals of the 1988 U.S. Open. But Cahill was establishing himself as one of the great coaches of the modern era as he worked so successfully alongside Agassi in 2002 and on through the rest of the American's illustrious career, which concluded four years later at the Open.

As Cahill recalled in a 2019 interview for this book, "Andre's semifinal match at that 2002 U.S. Open with Hewitt was pretty emotional for both of us. Lleyton was the defending champion. I knew it was going to be an incredibly tough match and Pete had played first that day and had a pretty easy match with Schalken. Andre's match with Lleyton was incredibly physical and he did amazingly well to win that match. I remember he could have won it in straight sets. He was ahead two sets to love and had a bit of a chance to wrap it up but I remember saying to myself when he lost that third set, "God. Even if he wins this match, losing that set is going to hurt Andre for tomorrow in the final, knowing that he had to go to a fourth set. But he won that fourth to take the match and I have got to say that he was feeling good physically."

Recollecting that evening before the final, Cahill said, "Andre knew the battle he was going to be in for against Pete the next day, but that night before the final was spent celebrating the effort of beating Lleyton. We had a pretty relaxed night. We were renting a house in the Hamptons about an hour away from the city, so we took a nice drive out there and our wives had dinner for us with the kids and the family. Honestly, Andre wasn't struggling physically. He just went into the match the next day against Pete feeling confident. He was never overconfident against Pete but he was feeling if he played his best tennis he could win that one."

During the early stages of this historic final-round contest on September 8, 2002—precisely six years to the day Sampras had last ruled at the Open—the tennis was first rate on both sides of the net. Sampras had been showered with affection from the fans all through the tournament. They had cheered him on unabashedly in match after match. But the audience on this Sunday afternoon was conflicted. Many of them were sentimentally on Sampras's side, but Agassi always had a large legion of boosters whenever he performed in New York.

The atmospherics only heightened a large occasion. In his pre-match interview just before walking out on the court, Agassi had told 1978 U.S. Open singles finalist Pam Shriver on CBS, "Hopefully, I'll make him [Pete] serve lights out today in order to get it done."

The remark was prescient. That is exactly what Sampras intended to do. Every battle he fought against Agassi was essentially about the ferocity of his serving and the way he backed it up at the net versus the blockbuster returning and backcourt brilliance of Agassi. The outcome of their showdowns came down to which man could more consistently obtrude with their playing style.

Sampras had indeed been serving "lights out" across the fortnight, holding serve in 104 of 108 games, bombarding his opponents with 111 aces in his six previous matches and unleashing the most convincingly big and devastatingly potent second serves of his career. He was supremely confident about how he was playing and the way he was serving.

As he recalled, "I felt good going into the match. I had talked to Paul about coming out there with energy, dictating play off his second serve, going for the backhand, keeping the ball away from the center of the court and not getting into those long rallies. It is a different mindset when you are older like I was then. I had won a lot of majors, so there was not the same sense of urgency. But this was it: who knows how many more chances I would have to get back in this position?"

The evidence of his self-conviction was revealed in the first game of the match. He held at love, served a pair of aces and missed only one first serve. Agassi answered with a love hold. Each man held at love from there to make it 2-2. In the fifth game, Sampras was tested on his delivery for the first time as Agassi kept his returns low and passed well off the forehand. Agassi took Sampras to deuce, but Sampras's second serve came in at 116 mph to the Agassi backhand. Agassi netted the return. Sampras followed with an ace out wide in the ad court, his fifth of the set. 3-2 for Sampras.

Agassi maintained his high standards in the sixth game, going five for six on first serves and releasing two aces, including a game closer for 3-3. But the color of the contest then changed significantly. Sampras started the seventh game with an ace down the T at 132 mph. He served another untouchable delivery down the T for a 40-15 lead and held at 30 with his third ace of the game, this one out wide to the backhand. In four service games, he had sent out eight aces.

Serving at 3-4, Agassi could feel the heat, weight and diversity of his opponent's game. Sampras reached 15-15 with a scorching forehand down-the-line winner. On the next point, Sampras's signature running forehand elicited a short ball from Agassi, but it was up high. Sampras's topspin backhand approach went down the middle and Agassi had an opening to pass him crosscourt. He missed it wide. Now Sampras sent another heavy and penetrating forehand return with good depth, drawing an error from Agassi: 15-40. Down double break point, Agassi missed his first serve. Sampras chip-charged off the second serve and Agassi pulled his passing shot off the backhand wide.

Sampras had gained a very timely break for 5-3 and that gave him the chance to serve for the set in the ninth game. On his way to 40-15, Sampras served three more aces, the last one down the T. But his attempt at a second serve ace down the T just missed as he double faulted to make it 40-30 and then Sampras punched a forehand first volley narrowly wide. Deuce.

Agassi had ignited the crowd. A set that seemed over was very much alive. Agassi advanced to break point, but Sampras was imperturbable. He placed a big second serve down the T with slice. It clipped the center service line and skidded out of Agassi's reach. That clutch ace, his twelfth of the set, took him back to deuce. Agassi then missed a passing shot, giving Sampras a third set-point opportunity. This time he converted. Serving-and-volleying behind a kicker on the second delivery, he closed in purposefully for the first volley off the backhand side. With polish, he directed it down the line for a winner. The set was in the Sampras victory column. Despite missing seven of ten first serves, he held on to close that chapter with temerity, prevailing 6-3. After sealing the set on his own terms, Sampras urged himself on with a "Yeah," thoroughly gratified to be up a set in this riveting final-round skirmish.

The momentum was entirely with Sampras and Agassi was hard pressed to reverse it. At 15-15 in the opening game of the second set, Sampras came over a backhand second-serve return, following that shot in to provoke an errant backhand pass. An overwhelmingly powerful forehand crosscourt from Sampras on the run rushed Agassi into an error: 15-40. Now Sampras chip-charged off another second serve return and Agassi missed the backhand pass.

Sampras had the immediate break at the start of the second set and promptly held at love. By taking eight of nine points, he had bolted to 2-0, securing five games in a row to lead by a set and a break. Agassi obstinately fended off a break point in the third game but Sampras was serving stupendously. He opened the fourth game with his 13th ace, going down the T at 130 mph. He would hold at love for 3-1 before Agassi swept four points in a row for an easy hold. Yet Sampras answered with a love hold of his own for 4-2 as Agassi was unable to get a single return back into play.

Sampras was relishing playing with the lead. He broke again for 5-2. Serving for the set in the eighth game, he rallied from 15-40 to deuce but was then stifled by a slightly miss-hit Agassi forehand crosscourt return winner. A topspin lob from Agassi on the next point was too good. He had broken Sampras for the first time and then he held in the ninth game.

Now Sampras made certain he would serve out the set convincingly. A second-serve ace down the T took him to 15-0. He then served and volleyed masterfully. His deep forehand first volley was so good that Agassi's backhand down-the-line pass was unthreatening. Sampras covered the net swiftly, putting away a forehand volley into the open court. A superb second serve out wide was unanswerable. And then, as if to underline his supremacy, Sampras served his 16th ace of the day to hold at love. He had played an arresting and authoritative brand of tennis, taking the set 6-4, moving ahead two sets to love.

As he reflected more than 16 years later, "It was kind of similar to Wimbledon '99 the way I played those first two sets. It was the best I could put together, serving and volleying great, making him move and winning these groundstroke rallies. I felt he played fine but those first couple of sets I just played a very, very high quality of tennis."

Cahill was deeply impressed by the way Sampras sparkled in the early stages. He said, "Pete just came out and was on fire those first couple of sets. Andre barely touched the ball."

Sampras had put forth a golden display of shotmaking to build that lead. As he always did, Sampras made it all look remarkably easy, but, in fact, the process of performing so mightily was much more difficult than it appeared. Sustaining that level of excellence was going to be an arduous task for the 31-year-old. At 2-3 in the third set, he had to work hard to hold serve. Agassi had three break points in that game, but Sampras erased them all with a superb backhand volley winner and two aces. After four deuces, he held for 3-3 with his 23rd ace of the encounter.

Serving at 4-5, Sampras was extended to deuce by a markedly improving Agassi, but two outstanding second serves enabled him to hold on. With Agassi serving in the 11th game, Sampras went to 0-30 but Agassi met that moment boldly, holding on for 6-5. Sampras was serving into the wind during the 12th game. He fought wholeheartedly to lift himself into a tie-break. He had five game points but, after five deuces, Agassi benefitted from an uncharacteristic error from Sampras at the net. Sampras came in behind a second-serve kicker, but with the court wide open he netted an easy first volley. Set to Agassi 7-5.

The crowd was eupeptic. Agassi had prolonged the battle through force of will, significantly improved returning and sheer persistence at the end of the third set. Sampras was understandably disappointed, but not unduly dismayed. As he said in an interview for this book, "I remember when I missed that easy forehand volley the crowd got very loud. It was like, 'All right, we are in a dogfight here.' Losing that third set was a little deflating. Physically I was feeling it in my legs and feeling the weight of all the matches I had played. This was my fifth match in seven days, which is not easy."

One of Sampras's most undervalued qualities was his temperament. He was so strong mentally and so clear in his convictions that he would simply go back to the basics of his work, focus on what was ahead and not worry about what might have been. That discipline was put to the test early in the fourth set. Serving into the wind at 1-2 in a critical seven deuce game, Sampras had five game points that eluded him and then Agassi garnered a break point.

Agassi's return was excellent, down at the feet of the incoming Sampras. Sampras improvised creatively, digging out a delicate finesse backhand half volley that died short in the court. Agassi chased it but had no play. That magical piece of ingenuity took Sampras back to deuce. Cahill remembered it vividly as he spoke in 2019. He said, "Andre was starting to get on top and Pete was looking like he was getting tired. It was a pretty strong breeze Pete was serving into. Andre's return was great but Pete's half volley from behind him was unbelievable. It became a drop-volley winner. My heart sank because every tennis player who has been in that position knows that was it. It was a massive turning point in the match."

Yet Agassi still moved to break point for the second time. Sampras surprisingly stayed back on a second serve, something he rarely did in those days. But once more his uncanny feel and extraordinary court sense came fully and richly into view. He angled a soft slice backhand short crosscourt to draw Agassi in. Agassi had almost no alternative but to go down the line over the highest part of the net with his two-hander. His shot hit the net tape.

That clutch play from Sampras locked the score at deuce for the seventh time. He took the next two points with first volley winners and held on his sixth game point. To 2-2 went Sampras after that steadfast stand. In the fifth game, Sampras reached 0-30 but Agassi served his way out of that deficit methodically. Sampras was unshakable, serving three consecutive aces in a love hold for 3-3. He had elevated his total of aces to 30.

And yet, if he had been competing in the days of the Hawkeye replays that did not start at the Open until four years later, Sampras might have served another five to ten aces that afternoon than his eventual total of 33. Periodically during this match and many others, he would quietly let a linesman or the umpire know that he believed a serve that had been called out was actually on the line. Sampras had a particularly good eye for where his serves landed.

Speaking about Hawkeye in 2019, Sampras said, "When I first heard the challenge system was coming, I wasn't a big fan of it, but looking at it today I would have loved to have had it when I played. Just knowing how hard it was for linesman to see my serve, I would have felt a lot better sleeping at night that the satellite got the call right and there was not an error by a human. So I would have loved the challenge system. I could tell if I had served an ace or not. I could just tell. I know it when I miss it. It is like a pitcher throwing a pitch. You know if you have hit that corner and I knew from all the years of hitting a lot of serves and being good at it. I had the feel for whether it was in or out."

Sampras concluded his career after this U.S. Open final round contest with 8,713 aces across 984 matches. But no one kept track of his countless service winners. And he was a peerless big-match player who saved his best quality serving for the biggest occasions.

Both players were looking for that one crucial opening for a service break in this fourth set. Sampras was nearly there in the seventh game, reaching break point. But he missed a crosscourt backhand chip return wide off a first serve. Having dodged out of danger, Agassi held on to shift the burden of pressure back onto the shoulders of Sampras.

Sampras served at 3-4, 30-0. He had commenced that game with his 31st ace of the day and then punched a classic backhand volley into the clear. But he double faulted aggressively twice to allow Agassi back to 30-30. Sampras had a couple of game points that were denied by an unwavering adversary. Sampras then went for another big second serve but double faulted, allowing Agassi a break point opportunity. Sampras did not back off, serving and volleying on a second delivery. The kick bounded high. Agassi netted a backhand return. Sampras took the next point with another unstoppable serve-and-volley package. His forehand first volley was a winner. That was the 100th time he had approached the net and Sampras had won 65 of those points. Numbers like that are hard to beat. That percentage demonstrated that Sampras's unrelenting attacking game was proving superior to the superb counter-attacking of Agassi.

Sampras closed out the crucial eighth game with an ace out wide, his 32nd of the match. It was 4-4. For Sampras, this meant it was time for an all-out bid to close out the account on his terms, to avoid any possibility of a fifth set.

On the first point of the ninth game, his forehand return blazed crosscourt, putting Agassi on the defensive. Sampras then stepped in and drove a backhand crosscourt with interest. Agassi had no way to answer that one-two punch: 0-15. Another scorching return from Sampras put him in full command and left Agassi compromised. Sampras followed with an inside-out forehand winner: 0-30.

Agassi took the next two points, only to double fault. He saved himself at 30-40 with a backhand winner up the line. A dazzling backhand down-the-line passing shot winner gave Sampras a second break point, but he missed a running forehand topspin lob long. Deuce. Sampras, however, was utterly determined to secure this break. A penetrating forehand down the line provoked a backhand slice error from Agassi. It was break point for the third time. Agassi's first serve went to the Sampras forehand. Sampras's flat and deceptively heavy return had good depth. Agassi could not respond off the forehand.

Sampras had sealed the break for 5-4 in the fourth. And so he went to his chair at the changeover for the last time ever in an official tennis tournament, knowing he was within striking distance of a record-tying fifth Open and 14th Grand Slam title, realizing he was one hold away from moving past two years of vexation, comforted by being in control of his own destiny. He then walked out to serve for the match. Intuitively, he knew precisely what he had to do. On the first point, he sliced his first serve to the Agassi forehand, deliberately not trying to hit it too hard or make it that exceptional. He was serving and volleying in percentage fashion, demanding that his fellow American come up with something spectacular. The serve stayed low. Agassi netted the return: 15-0. Sampras sent a first serve down the T to the Agassi forehand and the return was long: 30-0. Now he missed the first serve, but gunned the second delivery down the T at 119 mph.

Agassi did not see it coming. He was coldly beaten by Sampras's audacious second serve ace, his 33rd of the match: 40-0. Agassi saved one match point with a forehand passing shot winner, but, at 40-15, Sampras served and volleyed elegantly to the Agassi backhand, punched a backhand volley down the line and a heavy-footed Agassi could not get much on his forehand pass. Sampras was stationed near the net and easily dispatched a backhand volley short crosscourt into the clear. He had bested Agassi 6-3, 6-4, 5-7, 6-4 for his 64th career title.

He broke into a broad grin, made his way over to the side of the court and climbed into the stands to share the triumph with his wife Bridgette. They embraced. He had played 33 tournaments since winning his last one at Wimbledon more than two years earlier. Now he had stepped back into the winner's circle at the last major of the 2002 season, on the same grounds in New York that he had claimed his first major crown 12 years earlier over the same estimable opponent in the final. Moreover, he established himself as the only man ever to capture U.S. Open titles in both the 20th and 21st centuries.

Recalling the fourth set and the finish line, Sampras said, "I felt my energy drop and he got a hold of my serve a little bit. I was getting a little tired. I just sort of hung in there and played a good game at 4-4. I just felt the fifth would have been a major struggle. I was not feeling great so, getting that break at 4-4, my emotions shifted 180 degrees. Serving for the match downwind made things a little easier. I was very happy. Two years of struggling and trying to find your confidence and get rid of all your insecurities about where you are with your game made me feel a bit of vindication. I knew that people were laughing at me and rolling their eyes that I felt I could still win the Open."

Following up on that theme, he said, "I am human. As you get older you are sensitive to what people are saying and writing. You get wind of things and try to rise above it, but you hear things from different commentators and writers and you walk into press conferences and it is like people have the nail in the coffin. I felt that. But I always had the confidence in my own game that I could turn it on at certain moments and try as hard as I can and not let anything get in my way. It just felt great to win that Open."

Agassi was philosophical about the defeat and fully cognizant of why Sampras had garnered the victory. He said in his post-match interview, "I've said this for years now that Pete's game is able to raise itself at the right time. While his discipline and the daily grind of what it takes to be at his best at the top has gotten tougher for him, there's still a danger in the way he plays the game and how good he is. Anybody that says anything different is really ignorant. They don't know the game of tennis because Pete has a lot of weapons out there. I'm well aware of that."

In 2019, Cahill looked retrospectively at the Sampras-Agassi clash and said, "It is difficult when Pete serves that way because he always ups his level when he plays Andre. He knew that Andre didn't have a great reach on the return of serve and there wasn't much difference between Pete's first and second serves. Basically he was playing with two first serves. If Andre got his racket on the ball, he would make great things happen. So Pete knew he had to play a little more redline than he did going up against other players. Andre had to start guessing on which way Pete's serve was going and that is why Andre got aced a lot. His reach wasn't like a Djokovic or a Murray these days."

Having said that, Cahill added one essential point about the greatness of Sampras: "The brilliance of Pete was how he was able to sustain his level over five sets. Pete was just incredibly good at playing the score and playing to his strengths. He had the ability to take time away from the opponent out of nowhere. He knew exactly where to position himself on the court. His tennis IQ was incredible and we saw it that day against Andre in the U.S. Open final."

Rusedski was back home in Great Britain and he watched Sampras overcome Agassi on television. He said, "I thought Pete played great in that match. He had gone on a magical run in beating Haas and Roddick and Andre. That is what great champions do. They find a way to lift their game. It was an amazing result for Pete to come through and win that U.S. Open in his last-ever tournament. What a way to finish and what a fitting way to do it, beating his big rival Agassi. It was a fairytale and an ideal way for Pete to finish his career, winning in America in his last tournament at the U.S. Open. He beat all of those guys convincingly. In life, some things are meant to be, and for Pete that was meant to be for him to win that U.S. Open title in the best way possible."

Rusedski's view was shared by many in the tennis community who appreciated what it took for Sampras to climb back up the mountain again and play top-flight tennis when it really counted. As Tom Gullikson reflected, "That was one of the great comeback stories in tennis what Pete did at the Open. The fact that he could make one more great run and find within himself the ability to raise his interest level again and overcome his doubts and fears to reach that Grand Slam championship level one last time from a very low place at Wimbledon was amazing."

"I was extremely impressed," said Martina Navratilova in 2019. "The older you get, the more difficult it is to win. When you don't win for a long time, confidence is a big thing. The seed of doubt has grown into a tree. The way he overcame that shows how strong Pete was mentally. He was able to zero in and play by memory. You talk yourself into the confidence, into believing you can still win. Knowing what can go wrong and how muddled the mind can get, it was very impressive that he could quiet down all that negative noise and still believe he could win a major. I was winning everything for a long time until 1987, but that year I didn't win a tournament until Wimbledon. I found so many ways to lose matches. Your game is still there but so much of it is mental where it is easy to doubt yourself. But if you are great, you talk yourself back into believing. That is what Pete did."

Tracy Austin marveled at how Sampras pulled off such a phenomenal feat. She says, "It was just amazing. He didn't have great results in that period leading up to the U.S. Open. Most players need those match wins to back up their confidence going into a major and win. There are only a few people like Serena Williams, Roger Federer and Pete who have such a strong inner belief that they might not need the match reps and wins. Pete was able to elevate from ordinary play by his standards in the summer to winning the Open. I don't remember thinking he was going to win it. You see the trajectory and the journey he made and that was special."

Billie Jean King examined the Sampras win at the Open to some degree in terms of how he felt about playing Agassi overall. In her view, it was preordained in some ways. She said in 2019, "I think Sampras felt if he played his best and Agassi played his best, he would beat Agassi nine times out of ten. And I think Agassi felt the same way."

The way Ivan Lendl looked at it, Sampras fit into a familiar pattern among champions who look for that last window of opportunity, and find it. He said, "If you look at the history of our game, most No. 1's get one opportunity somewhere down the road when they are not expecting to do that much anymore and they grab it. They know how to win. It is like riding a bike. That was Pete's opportunity and he took it."

Chang virtually echoed Lendl in his assessment. He said, "The motivation for Pete at that last U.S. Open was very evident. He went through the draw and had his opening and opportunities and he knew. It was like, 'This is my chance.' And he took advantage of it. If the opportunity presented itself he would be there and take advantage of it as only Pete can."

In an interview for this book, Rod Laver said, "Pete always had that championship nature. Winning that U.S. Open at the end was a great tribute to him. Most top players don't stop that way, leaving the game on top. He did it. Pete was just a great champion who knew how to win under pressure."

Annacone treasured the memory of Sampras's triumph over Agassi as he spoke about it in 2018. He said, "I will never forget sitting courtside and watching the big screen with Andre and Pete standing in the hallway before their final. To this day I have never had a feeling like that in tennis. The hair on my arms and legs was totally standing and it was just total goosebumps. I thought the building was going to collapse when they flashed to those two guys in the hallway. This is where it had all started 12 years earlier with the same two guys in the final. I remember Pete saying the night before their '02 final, 'This is awesome. This is exactly where I need to be. I get to play Andre.' He totally embraced the rivalry."

Making it all the more remarkable in retrospect is the fact that Sampras was indeed wrapping up his career right then and there. Beating Andre Agassi in the final of the U.S. Open was his last official tennis match. How could anyone leave the sport under more extraordinary circumstances? How many athletes could turn that kind of dream into reality?

Annacone said, "I couldn't believe that he was able to win this match and then never play again. This is the most amazing thing to me of all, the most incredible thing in sports that I have ever seen."

One of the unsung heroes in the Sampras camp was his trainer for the final years of his career. Brett "Moose" Stephens, an Australian who played an important role in helping Sampras deal with a rigorous schedule that tested him to the hilt during the second week.

As Sampras said, "I had moved from Florida to L.A. a few years earlier and felt I needed more balance in my life. I knew Moose a little bit on the tour and he was always laughing and outgoing, always the jokester of the locker room and a fun guy to be around. When I knew I was moving to L.A. I asked him if he would consider training me. So I hired him to come to L.A. and we would train on the UCLA track. He got me in the best possible shape. He is one of the fittest guys you could ever be around. He made fitness his life and worked out three hours a day. I was looking for someone like that. Pat Etcheberry had been a no pain, no gain guy and that was great for a certain time in my career. But you have to be aware of your body and Moose was a little more delicate. We played beach volleyball and would interact with some other activities to keep it fun and loose. In that last Open he was a big help to me. I had some tough battles. The work that Moose and I did off the court really paid off. He was such a good guy to have on my team because of his energy and how positive he was."

Sampras wholeheartedly believed that the way he played at that 2002 U.S. Open, he would have easily handled the Sampras of 1995 or any of his other prime time seasons.

He explained in late 2018, "Maybe I was more complete. I hit the ball cleaner and was able to swing harder with control as I got older. You just get better even though you slow down a little bit. I can't really explain it, but I remember on Tennis Channel recently they put on a Novak-Roger match from 2009 or around that time. The tennis was really good but it is better now. The more you do it, the better you get at it, and your competition gets better. Maybe in my time Safin and Hewitt pushed me to get better. It is interesting to me that as you get older you do get better. I can't give you a perfect answer for it. Maybe it is just the evolution of tennis. The 2002 Pete would have beaten the 1995 Pete or the 1990 Pete. It just tells me I was playing at the highest level possible at 31 years old at the U.S. Open."

Todd Martin was thoroughly in accord with his old friend, rival and Davis Cup teammate as he talked about Sampras in 2019. And he made the case even more powerfully.

Martin said, "Pete at the Open in '02 would have killed every other version of Pete. Pete at that Open was the best Pete he had ever been. You can't reproduce success without getting better. Pete was bigger, stronger, faster and more skilled at the '02 Open. He played with a more dominating presence."

Pausing briefly to collect his thoughts, Martin continued, "The only thing that was different was if you look at any of the ten or 12 tournaments he played before the 2002 Open, he was not the psychological competitor that he had been previously. But as soon as he got a little momentum at the Open, he was suffering from flashbacks because this was the 2002 physical Sampras. Whatever the best version of Pete Sampras was previously, psychologically that is who he was. And so it was basically the old and improved Sampras. He took his dominance from earlier in his career and imparted it on his improved physical game that he had been having trouble sorting out. So every crack in his armor that existed from 2001 until the Open of '02 got filled or welded shut for that tournament. And for those two weeks he was nearly flawless."

McEnroe respectfully disagreed that the 2002 U.S. Open Sampras was better than the Pete of his prime years. Asked if the Sampras of 2002 at the Open beats the 1995 Sampras, McEnroe said, "I don't think so. I think he was peaking in the mid-nineties. He found a comfort level mentally. I would say when he beat Agassi in the '95 Open final pretty handily, around that time that was the best I ever saw him play at a time when he felt he could do anything. In '02, I believe he felt he just had to be aggressive, take it to guys and not think about anything else. He certainly was playing at a very high level at the '02 Open, but I just don't think overall, if you looked at the whole package, that he was quite as good as he was or as confident as what he was before."

Navratilova was conflicted as she analyzed the Sampras who won the 2002 Open and compared him to the player he had been before. She said, "It's a hard comparison. As you get older like Pete was in 2002, you get better in some ways, but then you lose a little bit of speed and endurance, and maybe the nerves get in the way a little bit. You know more about the game and your technique has probably improved. It would be a tossup. It is impossible to know how much worse some things get and how much better other things do. You are more fearless when you are younger and confidence wins matches. You forget how to lose. Maybe you are a better player when you are older, but not as consistent. It is impossible to answer."

The view here is that a strong case could be made that the Sampras at Wimbledon in 1999 and on through the hard court swing that sizzling summer in the U.S. was the best he would ever be. There were also large portions of 1997 — particularly at Wimbledon and across the last couple of months in that memorable season—when his tennis soared to unsurpassable levels. In the final analysis, it is impossible to determine. What was more consequential is how he concluded his career so spectacularly and played sublimely across that New York fortnight. The triumph was immensely gratifying, as psychically rewarding a tournament as he could ever savor. Was he a better player than ever before at that last U.S. Open or not? The case has been made both ways, but this much is certain: he played magnificently all through that fortnight and pulled off a staggering feat after a long and often disconcerting dry spell that probably no other player could have endured. And then he went through the process of determining whether or not there was a reason to keep going.

Sampras remembered the feeling afterward his singularly satisfying 2002 U.S. Open triumph. He said in 2019, "I had to figure out what was next with my tennis. I didn't know what to feel. I flew home the night I won the Open and just enjoyed that. Two or three months later I was talking to Paul about what was next and getting ready for Australia, but I was not emotionally ready. So I felt I would see how I felt about playing Indian Wells or Miami in 2003. I was still hitting balls but just didn't want to do the work it took for the reward at the end. It just seemed unbalanced to me. I didn't feel like doing the practice or the gym work. Something just came out of me that I can't really explain. The moment when I knew I was going to retire was when I was in Palm Desert watching Lleyton Hewitt play a first-round match at Wimbledon in 2003, thinking that was the last place I wanted to be. That was when I knew I was done."

Annacone recalled it slightly differently. He said, "We literally went six months of hitting a couple of days and then not hitting, getting ready for a tournament he did not end up playing. We had so many great talks about life. And then in April, when we were getting ready for Wimbledon, I walked in the front door when I came by and he said, 'I am done.' I said, 'Done with what?' And he said, 'I am not playing anymore. I am done.' He explained that he had done everything he wanted to do. He said he realized why he played and that was to prove to himself what he could do. He said he didn't need to prove anything anymore."

At the U.S. Open of 2003, an official retirement ceremony took place. Sampras had a lot of family there, including his parents. His wife and infant son, Christian, were out in the evening air on Arthur Ashe Stadium, sharing the celebration with him.

No farewell could have been more fitting. Sampras had essentially announced himself to the tennis world at 19 when he became the youngest man ever to win the U.S. Open in the springtime of his career. Twelve years later, in the autumn of his career, with so many skeptics writing his professional obituary, when most of the tennis community at large was highly skeptical, he had closed the curtain with another triumph at the Open.

Reflecting on his sterling career now almost two decades after it ended, Sampras mused, "I could sit here now and look back on it and say, 'Should I have tried a different and larger racket for the French Open? Sure. Do I wish I had communicated better about my health and that I didn't have an ulcer for two years? Yes. I really do regret not communicating better with Paul Annacone and my team and whoever was close to me about what was going on."

Having said that, Sampras believed, "There are always some regrets. Internalizing a lot of stuff contributed to my ulcer. I do remember one conversation with Paul Annacone in 1998 when I was trying to break the No. 1 record and I told him I was stressed out and struggling. My hair was falling out. I let my guard down, which was unusual. But I have very few regrets. I look more at the positives. I achieved some amazing things. I didn't want to show any vulnerability. I didn't worry about what people were thinking. Being self-willed and self-focused with the blinders on made me a great player. I kept things close to my vest."

Following up on that theme, Sampras said, "You look at Roger and Rafa and Novak today and they are much more social and more outgoing than I was and maybe it is through social media and where we are in society. Maybe if I had been playing now I would have been more like these guys. It is just a different mentality. In my generation everyone was a little more separate and we all got along fine, but now Roger has Rafa's text number and they all text each other and have Instagram. Knowing Roger a little bit, I guess he can be the life of the party in the locker room. I was more in the corner away from everyone and I loved it on the last weekend of Wimbledon when nobody was in the locker room. I am a lone wolf. I get energy being by myself. I like being alone. That is how I am wired and how I have always been and it was the way I liked it throughout my career."

Speaking of how he viewed his illustrious career, what meant the most to Sampras was his longevity. "Being the best in the game for almost half of my career meant a lot to me," he said. "I did it in a certain way that was humble and it was my style. I feel I was a talented player with a big game that made guys uncomfortable. I just tried to conduct myself the way I am, in a very understated way, keeping my emotions in check and being a good role model for kids on behavior. That was important to me and at the same time that is who I am. I let my racket do the talking and played big matches well and I felt that the bigger the match was, the better I am."

He had established himself as arguably the best player in the history of the game with his unimaginable six years in a row at No. 1 and extraordinary 14-4 record in Grand Slam finals. He had gone out on a high note. As Monica Seles said in summation, "It was a storybook ending to a great career.

Walking away is very hard for an athlete. You always ask yourself that question—when is it time to go? And for him that was as perfect an ending as you could write, winning the Open in his home country and [eventually] saying I am closing this chapter of my life."

# CHAPTER 17

# THE SAMPRAS LEGACY

When Sampras bid farewell to the game in 2003 after completing his sterling career with that stirring fortnight at the U.S. Open the previous year, he left behind a shining legacy. Many believed then that with his 14 majors, six years in a row at No. 1 in the world and an unparalleled capacity to rise to big occasions and bring out his best when it mattered the most, he had the credentials to be viewed as the greatest player in the history of the game. Although the prevailing view soon changed among many in the cognoscenti to regard Roger Federer, Rafael Nadal or Novak Djokovic as the best ever based on their numerical supremacy, the fact remains that Sampras was indomitable. He belongs prominently at the table of elite figures who must be considered in any discussion of the best players ever.

No one could have foreseen in August of 2003 that by the end of 2019 those three estimable performers would all have surpassed Sampras's men's record at the majors. At that point, Federer had collected 20 "Big Four" prizes, Nadal had taken 19 Grand Slam tournament titles and Djokovic had secured 16 majors. That trio of icons all stepped into the circle of rare champions worthy of consideration for the distinction of G.O.A.T (Greatest of All Time).

Sampras himself was highly impressed and even astonished at how swiftly these players managed to all move past him on the historical ladder at the major championships. He never assumed his record would remain safe forever, but was amazed at what the towering trio accomplished in such a short span.

At the end of 2018, Sampras said, "I was just flabbergasted that these three guys would win so many majors combined in the past 15 years. I did think Roger had a realistic chance when he got to seven or eight majors and was so dominant, but for Rafa to come up and dominate Roger for a while—and then Novak to dominate both of them—these three athletes are three of the greatest of all time. What they have done is a testament to their hard work and dedication to the game. They keep pushing each other. I can't say enough good things about them."

That gracious comment gets to the essence of who Sampras is. But Ivan Lendl, for one, believes Sampras was unlucky not to have a longer reign as the all-time title holder for singles at the majors with his 14 championships. As Lendl said in 2018, "Pete got a little bit cheated by history with these three guys coming along when they did. Because of Rafa, Roger and Novak, nobody is talking about Pete. They could have come along not when they did, but in 30 years or 70 years or whatever. Then Pete would have been 'The Man' for a lot longer. Pete didn't get the opportunity to have everyone talking about him because these guys are phenomenal and they are just cleaning up and not letting anybody else take anything."

Interestingly, Sampras is responsible in some ways for the way today's players think in terms of their chief goals and priorities. Before he came along, top competitors were not as preoccupied with the majors. Previous generations of great performers wanted to win Wimbledon and the U.S. Open more than anything else, but the shape of the sport was different. From the advent of Open Tennis in 1968 until Sampras climbed through history so steadily across the nineties, there was less clarity about what really mattered.

The Australian Open had some very lean years with weaker fields for the most part until they moved from grass courts to hard in 1988. The French Open went through a similar slide in prestige during the seventies before recovering stature over the eighties. As Sampras grew into his talent and built his reputation so regally in the nineties, as he started closing in on a record number of major singles titles, he put an emphasis on the Grand Slam tournaments that had a lasting impact on the importance of the majors in the minds of future champions like Federer, Nadal and Djokovic. Sampras believed the majors were what really mattered historically. He always spoke his mind with clarity and conviction on that topic.

Asked in 2019 if he may have changed the philosophy of how great players define themselves, Sampras said, "Maybe there is some truth to that. As I got closer to breaking the record and had nine or ten majors, it became a conversation piece in the press. I wanted to break the record for the most majors and I talked about it. The game is not all about numbers, but having a chance to end my career with the most majors was important to me. And I raised the point that the majors were superior to all of the other events. That made me push harder for those tournaments. That was how I was raised."

Did Sampras find it satisfying that he used his influence as an all-time great to color the conversation differently and make others look at tennis history through another lens? Did he alter the outlook of those that have followed him and surpassed his total of majors like Federer, Nadal and Djokovic?

He responded to those questions this way in 2019: "I think I am part of that. I never wanted to bag on other tournaments, but I looked at certain things as black and white and this was a black and white thing. You based your year on what you did at the majors. If I won eight tournaments and none of them were majors, that would be a good year but not a great year. I was very open and honest about that. My year was measured on the Slams. I feel good about being honest about how I felt about tennis and all of sports. Now players are all talking about their majors and records and this generation is handling it all very well. As I sit here now, Roger has 20 majors and Rafa 19 with Novak a few behind. That is sort of the storyline for this generation and these three guys."

So how should authorities assess Sampras in light of the prodigious achievements of the superstars who have followed in his footsteps? There are different schools of thought on this question.

Perhaps Todd Martin offered the best analysis. He said in 2018, "Any discussion on who is the greatest of all time is a flawed discussion from the get go. You have different equipment, rackets, shoes, grips, strings—and all of that has impact. You can't compare any one set of statistics. As soon as you choose who is there for the most years in a row at No.1, then you have to look at the most weeks at No. 1, or who had the most Slams, or who had the most other tournaments. At some point you run out of data to compare and, at the end of the day, you just have to say Laver was the best of his time, Borg was the best of his time, Sampras was the best of his era, and Federer, Nadal and Djokovic have all taken runs at being the best of their time, with Federer the most so."

Annacone pointed out in 2018, "The game is so different now. It is not even the same sport. Pete's style of play is totally different from what we see today and there is a reason for that. So when people say, 'Who is better, Borg or Pete?' or "Who is better, Pete or Rafa?'—the greats of any era will adapt. That is the answer. Pete would have been a different player today, but he would have adapted. It is the mindset that leads you to be viable in your era. Pete would have been right in the mix today. Right in there."

Djokovic alluded to the changing face of the game and technology's role in altering the shape of it when he was interviewed for this book in 2019. He asserted, "It was a different kind of era for Pete. The technology has improved so much with the rackets, which nowadays are much better than they used to be in terms of the fabrics, the acceleration, the speed, the control and everything it gives you. You don't have as many serve-and-volleyers as you used to have back in those days when Pete

Pete Sampras won Wimbledon seven times, a major part of his career legacy

played. When he played, you had to rely more on talent and think through the game more. It is not like we are not thinking through the game now, but I think the game is probably more physical now. The rackets help you execute certain shots more than used to be the case."

Tracy Austin is certain that Sampras would have adjusted. She said in 2019, "I always believe a champion of Pete's quality would have been a champion in any era. Pete was a strong, strapping 6'1" and he would have been absolutely fine no matter when he played. If you have got the physicality and the athleticism and the movement like Pete, you are going to come through in any era."

John McEnroe said in 2019 for this book, "I have seen pretty much everybody and I would be pretty hard pressed to not say that Federer, Nadal, Pete, Djokovic and Laver are the top five guys ever, and not necessarily in that order. To me, Pete is the best fast-court player that has ever played."

Michael Chang made a cogent point when he spoke about Sampras and his status among the best ever to play the game of tennis. He proclaimed in 2019, "Pete is absolutely one of the best ever. Absolutely. There is no question. When Pete was dominant there were probably not just two, three or four guys capable of winning a Slam title, but 12 guys with a legitimate chance to take a run at a Slam title. There was Pete obviously, Agassi, myself, Courier, Ivanisevic, Bruguera, Krajicek, Becker, Edberg and others. It is not like the generation we have now with Rafa, Roger, Novak, Murray, Wawrinka—four or five guys who have really dominated, and a couple of guys like Delpo [Juan Martin Del Potro] sneaking in there. It wasn't like that in Pete's time."

Chang added, "In some ways it was a little harder to play in our generation because there was a little bit more of a mix of styles. Pete was beating the serve-and-volleyers, beating the baseliners, beating the guys who were cranking on the serves and playing with the spin, beating every type of player. The only type of player he really had trouble with was somebody who really knew how to play on the dirt. There is just no question if you take Pete's results and look at the situations he was put in under pressure in the big match environment, he came to play and his record shows it."

Courier followed up on one of Chang's themes concerning how Sampras defined his greatness. He said in 2019, "Pete was just an incredible champion. He should go down as one of the game's all-time great closers. His record in Grand Slam finals is better than anyone else's [except Roy Emerson at 12-3] as far as I can tell as far as winning percentage at 14-4 (.778). And his last couple of losses against Safin and Hewitt at the U.S. Open was when they still had the back-to-back Saturday semifinals and Sunday final. That hurt him at the end. With a day off, he probably would have won at least one of those matches. He is as great as everyone says he is."

There is a strong consensus on that point. But too many people lost their clarity of vision on Sampras after he had been gone from the game for nearly 20 years and was fading from their memories. Even the sport's most ardent fans too easily forget just how towering a champion Sampras was and how far ranging his skills stretched on a tennis court.

Mary Carillo is not among those who allowed Sampras to be diminished in the sharp eye of her mind. Carillo's appreciation of Sampras always knew no bounds. She said in 2019, "I totally believe that in the mists of time people have forgotten how great Pete was. Okay, he never won the French, but 14-4 in Grand Slam finals is a hell of a record. And had Pete played at a time when three of the four majors were on grass, he would have had over 20 majors. No doubt. What was so impressive about his run at Wimbledon was he was playing great grass-court tennis against great grass-court opponents when the grass really played like grass. It isn't like Federer winning Wimbledon these days, and I am not denigrating Roger's opponents. But Pete was going up against Ivanisevic and Krajicek and Rafter and all of these serve-and-volleyers. I just don't think people remember how much tennis meant to this guy. It drives me nuts. And I believe the quality of the opponents Pete faced in his career was more impressive than any other No. 1 player faced."

Asked to comment on Carillo's cogent point of view that he confronted the toughest cast of rivals in his generation of any dominant champion, Sampras said in 2019, "Watching a lot of matches at Indian Wells this year and seeing it up close and in person, I tend to agree with that. There is a lot of sameness out there with the players. The playing styles are similar for the most part. There are three or four great guys who have been better at the same game for the last 15 years. In my time there were more types of dangerous opponents. You had Goran Ivanisevic, Richard Krajicek, Boris Becker and guys who could serve you off the court. You were up against different styles of play. You have got Andre Agassi one day, Stefan Edberg the next day and then someone else after that. Now it seems like everyone plays almost the same. It is just that Novak, Rafa and Roger are so much better at it. If I had played only serve-and-volleyers for 15 years, it would have made my career less stressful. Roger feels if he plays well he is going to win and the same for Rafa and Novak. They don't feel threatened. It is a movement game today and a lot more physical and those three guys move better than anyone else. But no doubt Roger and Rafa and Novak are just great, great players."

The way Mats Wilander looked at it, Sampras set himself apart with his clear superiority over all of his chief rivals who represented varying styles of play. He was 20-14 against Agassi, 16-4 vs. Courier, 12-8 vs. Chang, 12-7 vs. Becker, 12-6 vs. Ivanisevic, 12-4 vs. Rafter, and 8-6 vs. Edberg. Moreover, he finished 5-3 against Lendl, 3-0 over McEnroe and 2-0 over Connors, although all three members of that powerful trio were past their primes. He relished competing in the sport's most storied arenas against the best players when the stakes were highest.

As Wilander said in 2019, "Pete always struggled on clay but on the other surfaces he was always the heavy, heavy favorite. The head-to-head records he had separate him from Federer and Nadal, who always struggled against one opponent or one surface. Roger always had the Rafa problem and Rafa always had the Novak problem. But Pete in his era being the heavy favorite everywhere else but clay puts him at the same level as Novak, Rafa and Roger because of the dominance on faster surfaces. When it counted and he was up against the best players in the world, you would back Pete, period. With Novak now and Pete in his time, when they are playing well, they are really untouchable."

When asked for his assessment of the Sampras legacy in an enduring sense, Edberg characteristically got right to the point. "Pete is one of the greatest all-around players we have ever had. Winning Wimbledon seven times tells you a lot, doesn't it? Being No. 1 six years in a row tells you he was one of the dominating players of all time. When I was playing, Pete was the best player I faced because he could always raise himself on the important occasions and he had that great serve-and-volley game with the huge forehand, plus he was such a good mover."

At the heart of his greatness was Sampras's supreme athleticism. When Billie Jean King was asked to comment for this book on the Sampras legacy, she said unhesitatingly, "He is just an all-time great athlete. He could have been a baseball pitcher with his elasticity. He was quick, smart, intuitive and instinctual, just an incredible athlete. He would have been amazing in any sport—football, basketball, baseball. Look at that running forehand he had and his overhead with the vertical jump. We are lucky to have him in our sport."

Carillo's work as a broadcaster has extended well beyond the boundaries of tennis to the full spectrum of sports. She said, "Pete was such a terrific athlete, better than anybody else out there. He was one of the best athletes I have ever seen and I have covered 14 Olympics. He had great body awareness and self-awareness, beautiful balance, terrific first step. Technically and tactically, everything seemed organic to his game. Everything made sense. And he had this air of ownership about it all."

That was evident to all who watched him across his 15-year pro career. And those who played him at the highest levels of the game were keenly aware of his capabilities. As Pat Rafter said in 2019, "Pete is someone who will go down as one of the greatest players of all time. He may not get mentioned as much as he should be because he is so quiet and reserved and shy. But I think he will become more appreciated over time and remembered more maybe in the next generation, a little like Rod Laver is now. We did not see Rod for a long time but then he started coming out more to the Australian Open and other places and everyone loved that. Maybe Pete will have some of that in the next generation and then he will be better understood for how great he was. I hope so for Pete. He just doesn't blow his own horn."

Martina Navratilova felt something of a kinship with Sampras as an outstanding attacking player who was at her best on fast courts. She examined Sampras's legacy in that light and asserted, "He was the last of the great serve-and-volleyers and even as the courts got slower he was still able to impose his style on the other players. If he ever could have played with the rackets we have today, he could have won the French Open. He just played the game the way I believe it should be played, which is to force the action. He wasn't waiting for the other guy to make a mistake. Pete just did his thing and there was no controversy. He did not call attention to himself. He did all of his talking with his racket. I liked that."

What Darren Cahill liked was Sampras's way of carrying himself. He saw Sampras as the consummate champion. Cahill said, "I have Pete Sampras right up there with the best of them. The greatest ever discussion is a tough one because we have got so many different generations of players and so many great players who have given back to the game and Pete is right up there as well for what he accomplished and how he did it. No question about it. And Pete is a good guy off the court. That goes a long way. He has got a lot of friends in tennis."

Upstanding, self-sufficient, driven inexhaustibly to succeed when it mattered the most, Sampras was a professional through and through and a craftsman of the highest order. Perhaps Monica Seles summed up his legacy as well as anyone.

She said, "His enduring legacy is as a tennis player. He was a player's player. I always looked at him that way, kind of how I looked at myself. He always gave 100% every match and he kept his tennis and his personal life separate. He just played tennis at an amazing level for a long time."

## AN OUTSTANDING SPORTSMAN

All through his career, Pete Sampras built an excellent reputation for himself not only as a champion, but also as a man who cared deeply about how he conducted himself in the public arena. He was a quietly ferocious competitor, immensely ambitious, giving everything he had year in and year out to realize his largest dreams and most concrete goals. But Sampras did not sacrifice his soul in pursuit of his aspirations. He refused to surrender his integrity for a shortcut to success.

As he said in 2019, "I was raised as a kid to act a certain way. I am a bit introverted and I don't like to show much emotion. If I did I would feel a bit embarrassed out there. I think it all came from my parents. As I became a young adult playing in front of people on television and in person, I just felt this is who I am. You might have a few moments here and there, but generally speaking I would have felt embarrassed for myself and for my family if I acted out. It just wasn't my personality to be emotionally upset out there. I didn't let things affect me. My goal was to win. Getting upset would have taken a lot out of me. I never wanted to show up my opponent or rub it in."

Sampras never took it for granted when fans approached him to compliment him on his conduct. As he said in 2019, "People come up to me who say I was a good role model for their kids because of the way I handled myself on the court and that means more to me than anything, knowing I had that effect on some people who have watched me play and might think,' I want to be like Rod Laver or I want to be like Pete.' I was just raised to be a good sport win or lose, to shake hands and get off the court. There are no disputed line calls or getting into it with opponents. That is not my personality, not my deal. Everyone has a different personality and I am more like Borg or Edberg, the sort of role model where we keep our head down and just play. Maybe during my career I was seen as a bit aloof and hard to figure out. But people get more sentimental for older athletes. I never changed for more publicity when people wanted me to act up, or to say or do more when people felt I wasn't exciting enough. From the time I was 19 until I retired at 31, I felt like I didn't change at all for anybody. I am proud of that. I didn't fall into the trappings of being somebody I am not. I was raised to be a tennis player—not a celebrity. That was who I was."

Todd Martin said, "If there was one thing Pete emulated from Rod Laver growing up, it was sportsmanship at all times. The number of times when Pete let anything bother him on the court in his whole career I think you could count on a couple of hands. If you look at it in terms of when it was really evident that something was bothering him, it might be on one hand. He didn't get the accolades for that because it was in vogue to say that tennis had lost its personality. Pete at the end of the day was a tennis player, as he said in his acceptance speech when he was inducted at the International Tennis Hall of Fame in 2007. He was maniacally focused on being the best he could be, so he knew if he let something bother him that would work against his overall objective of being the best tennis player in the world."

Martin contended in 2019, "Looking at where our culture was then and where it is now, if you throw athletes into a larger bucket they would be referred to as celebrities and they were expected to embody charisma. Pete was an athlete. For some to call him boring, I think he was just above that frankly. Pete was saying he was an athlete, not a celebrity. He was all right with that. It was a sign of the times we were in and it continues to be a sign of the times. It is a little more aglow than it has ever been."

As he reflected on Sampras and his sportsmanship, Martin said, "Pete is from a family of tight-knit Greek Americans. Family was hugely important to him and they still are in Southern California. These are things that come from the utmost of grounding in childhood so when Pete says he did not want to embarrass himself he also means he did not want to embarrass his family. Pete kept his life simple in the best sense. He woke up, read the newspaper, did his work, went back, had room service, watched a movie and went to bed—did the same thing the next day. That was fulfilling for him. He knew what he wanted. And it was fulfilling to him to be regarded as a great sportsman."

Martin's sentiments were echoed in many ways by a wide range of others who shared their views for this book. Lendl asserted, "Pete was a true gentleman, on and off the court. I have never seen Pete throw a racket or curse the umpire. He was a fantastic role model for kids on how to conduct themselves. If anybody with good values as a parent wants their kid to play tennis and their kid is going to play and act like Pete Sampras, they have got a winner."

Navratilova viewed Sampras through the same prism. She said in 2019, "Pete was a gentleman. He just played ball. You never saw him take a bathroom break to disrupt the rhythm of an opponent. As amazing as Roger is, he has done that, maybe just a few times, but he has done it. They are all playing some kind of game, looking across the net to see how their opponent is reacting or whatever. It is subtle. Pete never played that game at all. He was like an old time gentleman, a Roy Emerson type, or a Rod Laver. Just get on with it. He was just a very professional, matter of fact gentleman."

Courier stood across the net from Sampras 20 times across their careers, was his Davis Cup teammate and was even a doubles partner early in their careers. He said, "We all know how incredibly well he comported himself through a lot of ups and downs. He respected the game. He respected his peers. He was one of the game's great gentlemen."

Chang concurred. He said, "Pete actually knew the history of tennis quite well. He had a passion for the game but also an appreciation for the sport. That was always evident, even early on in the juniors. You could tell he loved the game very much. He never lost that focus of what tennis is about—the appreciation for the talent he had been given to play the sport. As a fellow player, you did not want to be on the other side of the net from him, but at the same time you had to admire what he was doing to focus on the goals he set for himself. Pete was totally a straight shooter."

The way Carillo looked at it in 2019, Sampras's legacy was not hard to define. She said, "Class. If I had to attach one word to him, that would be it. And after that I would say dignity. After that, athleticism. What makes me smile when I think of Pete Sampras is how he comported himself, what he wanted to be and the pains he took to live up to his own gold standard. That is what I am going to remember most about him."

Wilander admired the way Sampras carried himself and his total lack of gamesmanship. He said in 2019, "He had absolutely the highest grade of sportsmanship you can ever have. And that is without trying to be popular in any way, shape or form. I never felt he was out there for a popularity contest. It is a winner-take-all contest and he did it with grace and sportsmanship and respect for the game which was always there."

## THE EVOLUTION OF THE SAMPRAS GAME AND HIS TACTICAL ACUMEN

The cornerstone of Sampras's game through the heart of his prime was always that incomparable serve. In the eyes of many seasoned observers and fellow players, it was almost like poetry in motion. The sleekness of the delivery, the mastery of the mechanics, the reliability of his ball toss, the elegance of the motion—all of these elements made the Sampras serve arguably the greatest the game has yet seen. His priorities were consistently unimpeachable. Sampras was disinterested in breaking speed gun records on the serve. His velocity was extraordinary, but more significantly he could place it impeccably, disguise it with uncanny regularity, move it around both the deuce and ad court boxes more precisely than anyone else and count on it endlessly at consequential times.

Sampras was not only the best server in the game but he also had one of the biggest deliveries. Nevertheless, he was not consumed with "bringing the heat." He paid little attention to the mph numbers during matches and was more than happy to let players like Ivanisevic, Philippoussis and Rusedski serve at slightly higher speeds than he did, breaking into the 140s with their biggest serves. The highest recorded Sampras serve at Wimbledon was 136 mph and there were six years at the All England Club when his fastest serve was 130 mph or above. The fact remained that he had very little ego about those figures. Location and deception were his twin highest aims.

Asked in 2019 how much attention he paid to the serving velocity numbers or tried to see how his speeds compared to other big servers at the majors, he said, "It didn't affect me one bit. It was a curiosity to look up and see 127 mph or whatever, but it didn't affect anything regarding the match itself. It was like a side note if someone served 140 mph with the crowd oohing. Yeah, it gets your attention but it wasn't anything I worried about or focused on. You peeked over for a second and then it was off to the next point."

In an 11-year span at Wimbledon from 1992-2002, Sampras only once finished at the top of the serving speed charts and that was in 1998. But he finished among the top five in seven of those years and failed to finish among the top ten only once. His serve was always up there among the biggest but he was willing to leave it at that—and not get carried away with a velocity contest.

As Billie Jean King attested in 2019, "Sampras had the best serve ever not just because of the speed but because of his placement, spin and control. When I talk to young people I tell them to get a loop of Pancho Gonzales, Serena Williams and Pete, in particular Sampras. Serena's is beautiful, too, because her's is so simple with the timing and the rhythm. I have always said you are only as good as your second serve because you can't just rely on having a great day on your first serve. Sampras had two first serves. He could do whatever he wanted and was so flexible. You can pull his arms back and his elbows would touch easily. The elasticity of the arm is what makes greatness in serving, just as it does for a baseball pitcher."

King was in her element, speaking eloquently about the Sampras serve, clarifying what made it outstanding. She continued, "Martina Navratilova had a great serve, but she couldn't whip it like Sampras. He really has that whip. Name me one person who has a better serve than Sampras? He kept it so simple. It was just beautiful."

Navratilova said, "Pete had amazingly loose shoulders and he was very flexible. So he is able to get more turn and bend through his shoulders and accelerate more because he has got a longer path to travel. That is where he was getting all of that snap at the top of his serve. It was effortless. He was able to spring load his serve better than anyone else because of his flexibility. Combine that with the power he had with that little extra pop on it and the extra kick. And what he would be doing with the serve today using these rackets—wow!"

Looking at him historically as a server, Navratilova asserted in 2019, "His serve to me is top three of all time, period. I mean, John Isner may have a bigger serve, but then how does he back it up compared to Pete? Pete had that amazing serve and backing it up combination like Roger Federer. Pete was doing the one-two punch at the net whereas Roger does it from the baseline. So Pete's serve has to be right up there."

As Sampras said in 2019, "The serve evolved into my biggest weapon after coming together in that 1990 season. Obviously, being a serve-and-volley player helps your serve. I think everything just led to this weapon that I had that won me a lot of majors and got me out of a lot of trouble. I felt it was hard to read with my power and pace. I could find my spots. At 4-4, 30-30, fifth set of Wimbledon, I am your guy to hit that big second serve. Later in my career, my second serve became more and more of a weapon. That second serve turned out to be probably my biggest weapon, probably more than my forehand in a lot of ways. I felt it deflated a lot of players when they could not get my second serve back."

Darren Cahill paid Sampras the ultimate compliment with his assessment of the American's incomparable serve. He said in 2019, "Right now, if I had my career to do over again and was asked whose serve I would take, I would pick Pete's. Simple as that. Even with all of the great servers in today's game, I would still take Pete's because the guy had the ability to hit his spots, and to up the tempo of mph when he needed to. It was just incredible."

From the second half of 1997 onward, Sampras started coming in on almost every second serve as it became a larger part of his arsenal. That made him even tougher to break. As he explained in 2019, "What happened is I would serve and volley on both serves on grass, but then I would get to the hard court season and stay back on some second serves. But as my second serve got better on the grass, I started to serve and volley more on the hard courts and then I became more confident and used it as a bigger weapon. Early on in my career, I used the second serve as a weapon, but I wasn't as confident in my serve-and-volley game from maybe the time I was 20 to 25. It took me a few years. Guys like Rafter were starting to attack my second serve so I said, 'Okay, I have to serve and volley and see how that goes.' Then the confidence came for me and my second serve just got better as I got older."

Martin could not have agreed more with that Sampras assessment. He said, "As soon as Pete started serving and volleying on first and second serves, he came to the net more often in his return games as well and imposed himself as an athlete more. That is where the real benefit of beefing up his second serve came in because then it really was relentless."

Annacone recalled, "It took me a while to get Pete to serve and volley more on the second serve. And the great example was that '99 Wimbledon final against Agassi. His second serve speed average was up nine mph from where it was the rest of the tournament. I told him afterwards and he said, 'I figured it was harder.' I asked him about the mentality of that and he said, 'Two reasons. One, I have to against Andre. And two, because I can.'"

Undoubtedly, his commitment to getting in behind that second delivery constantly was one of the central changes in the evolution of his game. It made him an even more intimidating aggressor. In the first half of the 1990's—largely from 1990 to 1993—Edberg benefitted from Sampras staying back so often on his second serve. The Swede was among the best at chipping and charging on second-serve returns. In some cases, he provoked double faults from Sampras by employing that tactic—or just from the mere threat of that option being employed. Like Rafter later on, Edberg could apply pressure with that net rushing play.

In August of 1993, Edberg stopped Sampras 6-7 (3), 7-5, 7-6 (5) in the semifinals of Cincinnati. Sampras served 16 double faults and surely Edberg's chip-and-charge pressure was one of the chief reasons that happened. Edberg remembers how Sampras altered his ways later on strategically and got to the net regularly behind his second serve.

"If you want to stay at the top of the game," Edberg said in 2019, "you can't just sit back and do the same things you did repetitively. So with time, Pete got more experience and fine-tuned his game. He maybe got a little more offensive towards the end of his career and that is quite natural that he should do this. He just attacked more and was the one making the play going forward instead of being the one chasing the ball at the baseline. He had a huge second serve, so he had all the weapons to get in. It made life more difficult because you can't just push the return back."

Meanwhile, Sampras's play in the forecourt improved significantly as he gained the conviction to come forward relentlessly behind the second serve. Over the second half of his career, he was even more fearless on his second delivery, willing to risk more double faults by going for more speed, reaping the rewards of his dauntlessness. His volleying became more natural and he was increasingly adept up there, digging out the low volleys, making impossibly difficult half volleys look routine, putting away the high volleys emphatically and anticipating beautifully. As he said, "Serving and volleying is about rhythm and it is a fine art. It takes a certain movement and athlete to do it. Definitely my volleying improved the more I served and volleyed on my second serve."

John McEnroe pointed out, "I don't think people realize what a good volleyer Pete was. He was a damned good volleyer, right up there with some of the best. I don't know if he was the best volleyer who ever lived, but he was very underrated."

Tom Gullikson observed from close quarters including his Davis Cup captain's chair on countless occasions how well Sampras came to understand the territory of the net and how beautifully he anticipated up there.

As Gullikson said, "Pete's serve was so great that he didn't always have to make many tough volleys when he hit his spot on the serve, so others like Rafter and Edberg got more credit for being great volleyers. But Pete was a great volleyer. He had incredible hands and great instincts. He was so athletic and he covered the net really well. It is one thing to have decent technique on the volley and another thing to understand how to cover the net and take away what look like obvious passing lanes. Pete did that very well."

Sampras's athleticism came into play just as prominently when he was going for his renowned running forehand, sending fear into the hearts of his rivals as they stood there helplessly when he connected with that potent shot and blasted it crosscourt so potently and effortlessly.

As Billie Jean King said, "On a big point, that is the one shot you had to avoid because he was going to burn you—even if you thought you had him. You had to get him way over to the backhand and then hit a perfect volley or groundstroke to the other side. Pete was so quick. I don't think we have ever had a better athlete in the game."

Picturing the shot in the eye of his mind, Mats Wilander marveled at that Sampras running forehand. "I still do a lot of clinics," he said late in 2018, "and I have a drill where you have to go out wide to your forehand and keep it in play. I always say, 'The greatest running forehand was Pete Sampras's.' When he ran wide for his forehand, the cool thing about it was the point was over. There was no defense. It was like Edberg coming to the net or Nadal getting hold of a forehand in a rally. After three or four shots, the point was over. Sampras's running forehand was like, 'Here he comes! Here he comes!' Your level of enthusiasm went through the roof when Pete started running for the forehand. He was 100 % committed to hitting it as hard as he could and the ball was not coming back."

But Wilander believed that perhaps the single most underrated attribute of Pete Sampras was his big-point situational acuity and his propensity for playing on his own terms and making his opponent miserable in the process. He said, "Pete did not get the credit he deserved for the skill it took to play so well at the end of sets, at 5-5, deuce, or in tiebreakers. He had a lot of guts in big time moments. The credit we don't give him is his knowledge of how to put together service games and return games when it really mattered to him and how he made you feel as his opponent. I played him a few times. He is not trying the first few points of my service games and it is 15-15, because he hits one winner and one in the fence. Then suddenly he hits another winner. I haven't hit a proper shot in those first three points and it is 15-30. Then suddenly he decides to rally with you and I have no feel or timing because I didn't touch the ball in the previous game when he served. But now at 15-30 he is making me play. Pete doesn't get the credit he should have for how awful he made his opponents feel and the lack of rhythm he gave us. You felt, 'Come on Pete, you can't do that to me!' He could just tap into that awfulness you felt playing against him."

Asked if Sampras knew precisely what he was doing with his disruptive pattern of play, Wilander said, "Exactly. Tactically he knew exactly what he wanted to do. He would start to chip and give you dead balls and you can't do anything with a dead ball. Then he relies on his movement and some defense, but then he refuses to play defense. And then when you would come in, he would rip a passing shot and if it goes in, great, but if it doesn't you don't get to hit a good volley. No one has ever played like Pete Sampras did tactically."

Sampras responded to Wilander's assessment in a typically analytical way. He said, "The way I played, I didn't give anyone any rhythm. They didn't know what was coming. I wanted the match to be dictated from my end. I was the one making the errors and hitting the winners. It was based on what I was doing, the serve and volley, going for my second serves, never giving guys an opportunity to get control of points. It was just how I played and I guess players weren't comfortable with that. It wasn't my intention. My serve-and-volley game was just very straightforward and it would put people on edge. That was plenty fine with me."

Courier experienced the instinctive genius of Sampras many times himself. "I tell this to anyone who asks what it is like to play Pete Sampras," he said in 2019. "A lot of times we would both hold the first four games of a set. And then at 4-4 you are serving and all of a sudden he strings together a couple of points, he chips and charges on your second serve, you miss another shot and the set is over. You wonder what the heck just happened because you thought you had been outplaying him. That is what playing Pete felt like because he could summon his greatness late in a set. He just had that knack. And he wouldn't be bothered by not playing well in your service games because he would just keep holding serve. He just had that knack."

Priming for crucial points, sensing the moments that irrevocably counted and almost automatically elevating his game at those times—that was Pete Sampras. And he did it with a completeness and repertoire that set him far apart from any of his contemporaries. While he was lauded by so many authorities for having almost inarguably the finest first and second-serve package ever—and that signature running forehand—Sampras was under appreciated for the virtuosity of his entire game. His overhead may well be the best of all time as well and not simply because he would play the leaping "Air Sampras" smash that captivated galleries everywhere he went. The excitement he created with the suspended-jumping overhead only obscured the excellence of his conventional overhead.

He had very few weaknesses. To be sure, his adversaries tried to pick on his backhand, peppering away to that side. The high backhand could give him problems and on his off-days, when his timing was not in sync, he could miss-hit topspin backhands. And yet, off waist-high balls, he could do spectacular things from that wing. Meanwhile, he had an uncanny capacity to bide his time off the backhand, keep the ball in play without being too adventuresome and then find an opening to move around to unleash his lethal forehand. He would often loop the backhand down the middle or crosscourt and coax forehand errors from the likes of Agassi, Courier and Chang as they looked to end points with winners off tantalizing balls above their shoulders.

But above all else, Sampras was made for the monumental occasions. First and foremost, he was an elegant stylist who happened to be the tennis player's tennis player. As Tom Gullikson said, "Pete really was an artist. He wasn't like a Courier or a Lendl who would want to go out and do drills for four to five hours a day. Pete was about feeling the ball and much more into the artistry of the game than about the grind. He was a shotmaker. He was 'The Great White Shark of tennis' for a long time, no doubt. He was the main predator."

He was also an unwaveringly dedicated individual who was a total professional entirely focused on winning the premier prizes by sacrificing just about everything in pursuit of the highest honors. McEnroe said that what set Sampras apart above all else was "his single-mindedness." He said, "To me, he pretty much gave up everything. He was an introverted guy to begin with, so maybe that suited him, but the ability to more or less live and breathe tennis 24/7 and not have anything get in your way and be at Wimbledon four weeks and not leave your house—I am exaggerating slightly, but he would go practice, come back, eat at his house, and maybe once in a blue moon go out. It was this willingness to sacrifice everything—which is so difficult to keep going—that set him apart."

Todd Martin chimed in, "In some ways I envied Pete. He could simplify his life so well. I was fairly simple in my own way, but never able to simplify my existence enough to where I could cope with that amount of isolation day in and day out. I embraced that isolation when I was in my training mode, but I would have struggled remaining sane if at Wimbledon I had locked myself into the flat for 21 straight days the way Pete could do. That wouldn't have worked for me. I envied it because when somebody like Pete can be fulfilled and comfortable with that amount of focus, and not fatigue themselves, they are better for it in a competitive sense."

Sampras appreciated the comfort he found in settling into that routine at Wimbledon during the heart of his prime. That was how he wanted to conduct his business during the single most significant fortnight of his year and he reflected on it fondly in 2019.

"I preferred to be a little isolated," he said. "I had the flat at Wimbledon and I had a chef there. It was convenient to just stay in. Sometimes going out is nice just to change it up, but the majority of the time I just stayed in and kept to myself. I had that routine of eating dinner, getting a massage at eight or nine o'clock, watching a movie and calling it a night. It was easier that way. Earlier in my career, I stayed at the St. James Hotel during Wimbledon and went out to dinners, but sometimes that wears on you. I liked the routine when I stayed in the flat. It worked. I had the same chef for all of those years. I was happy to stay in and keep things low key."

The way Sampras displayed such supreme discipline across the years, it was no accident that he only lost four times in eighteen finals at the Grand Slam events. He prepared himself fully for those occasions and put himself in the right psychological space to perform at an optimum level when it mattered the most. He was not afraid to lose and believed unhesitatingly in his capacity to prevail when the stakes were highest.

As he said, "I felt very calm going into those finals. And as humble as I feel I am, these major finals was kind of where you could show off. I just felt fully confident in my ability being out there at those times. The circumstances didn't overwhelm me. As I won a few Wimbledon finals, I started feeling very relaxed. It was almost like going from the practice court to the Centre Court. Nothing really changed. No matter how big the match was, I had this inner belief, this quiet belief, that I was better than everyone else. I felt I had the game and I had the nerve. I don't mean this arrogantly at all. There were just times I felt unbeatable and I wanted to shine."

He did just that, winning ceaselessly with self-restraint, speaking volumes with his racket, representing himself virtuously. Through it all, from his teens into his thirties, he sparkled on the stages of prominence over and over again. Among the men, only Ken Rosewall captured majors in his teens, twenties and thirties before Sampras realized that considerable achievement. Since he left the game, the only man who had realized that extraordinary feat as of 2020 was Rafael Nadal.

Above all else, his legacy was largely about the clarity of his mind and his imperturbability. As Djokovic said, "Pete had the champion's spirit. That is his legacy. In the moments when most players would break down, he was the guy that showed the resilience and mental strength and the laser-like focus that separated him from everyone else and made him an all-time great. That is why I think his legacy and his mark on the game is so huge, especially for someone like me that looked up to him so much. You can only hear me speaking in superlatives about Pete Sampras."

# CHAPTER 18

## IMAGINING SAMPRAS AGAINST DJOKOVIC, FEDERER AND NADAL

Stepping into a time warp, how would Pete Sampras have fared against the mightily accomplished trio who followed in his footsteps and amassed so many majors after he left the game? By the end of 2019, they had collected 55 majors among them, and counting. All three—Roger Federer, Rafael Nadal and Novak Djokovic—had moved past Sampras on the Grand Slam tournament historical ladder.

But the imagination soars when thinking about how Sampras would have acquitted himself if he had competed in his prime during the era of Federer, Nadal and Djokovic. A wide range of authorities weighed in on this compelling topic for the purposes of this book and their responses were fascinating. The strong consensus is that the American would have done quite well against the renowned trio.

As Billie Jean King said, "He would have been 1, 2 or 3. Pete could have stayed with them because he is close enough generationally and because he is such a great athlete. If you take clay out of it, he would have been ahead of Nadal and probably neck and neck with Federer, even though Federer would have been in his face all the time. Pete might have had to use a two-handed backhand now and flatten it out. It would have been a great matchup between Pete and Roger, who beat Pete that one time [2001] at Wimbledon. Novak would have been a tough one, and their matches would have been great. But I think Pete would be winning a lot against him, too. Pete as an athlete definitely would have held his own with all of these guys. You adapt your game to the era you are playing in."

Navratilova said in 2019, "Clearly, Pete was at his best when it mattered the most. He was able to keep his nerves in check better than anybody else. He would have been able to compete with these guys for sure today. People talk about his backhand, but I can do things now I never could have done 20 or 30 years ago. Even though I am not even close to being as strong as I was back then, I can come over and hit a topspin backhand when the ball is over my shoulder. It was not possible then. You couldn't do that with the other rackets. Pete would have gotten creative, like McEnroe would have."

Turning her attention to the specific matchups, Navratilova said, "I think the one Pete would struggle with most of the three would be Rafa. He would struggle with the leftiness of Rafa and the big topspin to his one-handed backhand. That is rough. Even Roger can't handle it. I think Pete could handle the amazing craftiness of Roger because he was also very good at the cat and mouse stuff, taking pace off, hitting a little floater on the backhand and then ripping the forehand. Those would be beautiful matches between Pete and Roger, amazing to watch from a spectator perspective. They would be pretty evenly matched. Roger would be better on clay but it would be even Steven on the other surfaces and Pete would have the edge on grass because of him coming to the net and forcing the action. And against Novak, it would depend on the speed of the court. Pete would obviously try to find his way to the net and pick his spots on the serve and volley. Maybe he would serve and volley 80% of the time instead of almost 100% and try to mess up Novak. Novak's return is so unbelievably good. It would be 50-50 with Novak maybe having a slight edge because he doesn't ever miss a ball."

Interestingly, Djokovic shared Navratilova's view that Nadal's whirlwind topspin might have made him the most difficult member of the renowned trio for Sampras to confront. As Djokovic said, "If Pete would play against Rafa, he wouldn't like the Rafa spin. Rafa's heavy topspin in general is very difficult to handle and, especially with the eastern grip that Pete used to have, I think he would probably prefer playing against Roger and me than against Rafa. But obviously on the grass with the ball staying low and Pete slicing the approach shot and coming in, that surface would probably work the best for him against Rafa."

Speaking of how he would envision himself facing Sampras, Djokovic said in 2019, "It would be great to witness these kinds of matchups. When it comes to my matchup with Pete, it would be very interesting to see how I deal with his serve, which was his biggest asset and biggest weapon, both the first and second serves. He had probably the best second serve of all time. And Pete moved so well at the net and was smart in opening the court and finding holes in his opponents' games and exposing them, especially on quicker surfaces. It would be very interesting how I as a baseliner would deal with his aggressive style of tennis. It would be a tough matchup for sure. Regardless of how good my return might be, it would be very close with Pete in his prime and me in mine. It would be a thrill to experience it but we can only visualize and imagine it."

Edberg said in 2019, "Pete probably would do extremely well I would imagine against Rafa, Roger and Novak. He has got so many weapons he would be making a lot of trouble for these top guys today. I still believe this is a golden generation and I don't think we will ever see something like this again with three incredible guys dominating the game to an incredible extent. But Pete qualifies very close to this group. He would have done very well against them. That is for sure. They would have had less titles with him around."

The Swede added, "A player that could really serve and volley so well like Pete would make it a lot tougher for these guys. The difference is that the balls are heavier today and the courts are a little bit slower. The rackets make it easier to return. I like the contrast of Pete and Rafa. Roger and Pete are more alike. So having Pete play Djokovic or Rafa would be more interesting in a way because the contrasts are bigger, but Pete would keep the points as short as he could and the other guys would try to keep the points alive. Pete would definitely be very hard for them to beat on the grass. Watching Pete and Rafa would be a good setup and I would pick Pete most of the time on grass. Obviously on clay it would be the opposite all of the time."

Ivanisevic examined these dream matchups similarly to Edberg. The accomplished left-hander remained around the sport's central circles long after he retired, coaching a number of leading players including Marin Cilic when Cilic was victorious at the 2014 U.S. Open and joining Djokovic's coaching team in 2019. Ivanisevic said in June of 2019, "I think Pete would do well against Djokovic and Nadal. I don't know about Federer because their games are more similar. But Pete's game is completely different from Nadal and Djokovic. They don't like playing against someone like Pete with the attacking game. They would not have much rhythm against Pete and he would have his big serve and big forehand going for him. Pete was the guy who could very quickly adjust and he would if playing Nadal or Djokovic."

Robert Lansdorp witnessed all of the great players over the course of the Open Era and coached one champion after another over those decades. Asked about the imaginary rivalries pitting Sampras against Federer, Nadal and Djokovic, Lansdorp responded, "I think he would beat Federer most of the time. Federer is such a great player but with Pete's serve and volley he would be brutally tough to beat for these guys. The returns nowadays are pretty big, but Pete would have served and volleyed definitely on his first serve and on the second serve sometimes and his volley was unbelievably good. Federer is a nice guy and a great guy, but I don't care what they say about him: he could not volley the way Sampras volleyed. No way. Sampras had unbelievable volleys and great first volleys. There was no body jerking with Sampras. His volleys were effortless."

When he examined in his imagination Sampras versus Nadal and Federer, Lansdorp asserted, "I definitely think he would have beaten Nadal on hard courts and on grass. The way Djokovic plays is incredible, but Pete would have the edge just because of his serve and volley and getting in a lot. Djokovic is no pushover and the guy is always in position, every time he hits the ball. You rarely get him out of position. So Novak is really tough, but I just think Pete was such a natural serve and volleyer that he would have done really well against Djokovic."

Rafter said, "On grass Pete would have been the one guy who would have worried these guys. If they had all been around at the same time, Pete would have competed really well with these top guys today because he had such an amazing serve and the ability to come up with the right shot at the right time."

Tracy Austin asserted in 2019 that she dislikes generational comparisons. She said, "I hate to compare eras but I think a champion's mentality is always a champion mentality. He probably would have made some adjustments in his game and might not have been a pure serve-and-volleyer because you can't in this era. But Pete is such a great athlete. Who knows if his game would have developed differently? I always believe a champion of Pete's quality would have been absolutely fine in any era. If you have got the physicality and the athleticism and the movement, you are going to come through in any era. The champion's mentality sets him apart."

When Lendl took on this topic, he sounded much like Austin. "I am going to say this," said the eight-time major champion who finished four years at No.1 in the world. "Every player, whether it is Pete, Andre, McEnroe or myself included, if we were put into today's game with everything these players have at their disposal—and I am talking about equipment, training, and so on—we would find a way to compete. Every

Pete Sampras with Hall of Fame journalist Bud Collins and Rod Laver at his 2007 International Tennis Hall of Fame induction in Newport, R.I.

No. 1 could do that. Just like Jack Nicklaus would find a way to compete with Tiger Woods, Ben Hogan would find a way to compete with Nicklaus, and so on. Guys don't become No. 1 in the world for no reason. They work hard and figure out a way to become the best in the world. And so Pete would clearly hold his own with these guys today at the top, but I am not going to compare how he would match up with Rafa or Novak because times are different, balls are different and equipment is different."

Many in the know share that view, but John McEnroe was willing to engage in some interesting conjecture during his 2019 interview. He said, "If you are going to put Djokovic against Pete on a grass court, it would be hard for me to say, 'Oh, Djokovic is going to win that.' I could see Novak winning some of those matches but I also see Pete maybe winning the majority of the time. On a slower court I would see Novak winning but, because you are talking about some of the all-time greats of tennis, you have to say that they could turn the tide. So Pete could have beaten Novak sometimes on a slower court. We are talking about things we will never know. With Rafa, to me the mentality edge would pretty clearly go to Pete if they were both at the peak of their games on grass. So then you say what grass are they playing on —the old grass I played on or Pete played on that was not as good or the grass now?"

Courier addressed this topic thoughtfully. He said, "Look, Pete would certainly be playing with the same technology as these guys, the bigger racket and the Poly strings. He would have a lot more spin on his shots and a lot more control out of the corners. Pete was an amazing mover, a fantastic athlete, very nimble. And with his serve I think he could stay with anyone. Rafa certainly is going to be a big challenge for anyone on clay and Novak's such a good wing man at getting his racket on returns, but still, something inside me tells me Pete at his very best would still find a way to win his share of matches against these guys, as great as they are. Would he have a winning record in their head to heads? We will never know."

Continuing down this analytical path, Courier added, "A lot of it would come down to the speed of the courts. If he was playing on the speed of courts we played on in the 90's, his record would be quite good because these guys don't play on fast courts that often. They would have to use their defensive skills. Pete would have taken their time away at a place like the ATP Tour Finals indoors in the 90's when the courts were so fast. It is a great parlor game."

Wilander made the case that Sampras's game "would hold up on any fast surface. I think he would beat Nadal on grass actually, but the game and the surfaces are so different today from what they were and the balls are so much heavier today....But we have to remember that Pete was not only a great player but he played so many great matches. You could rely on him playing great in big matches. These days the surfaces are more similar than when Pete played. The top players are allowed to play their game on any court at any time against any opponent. They are allowed to do what they do best, whereas in Pete's day you just couldn't do that. On the slower [clay] court you had to change your game and he wasn't quite able to do that. You don't get to see Nadal playing his worst game at Wimbledon, which would be serving and volleying. We saw Pete having to play from the baseline on clay and it didn't work. We don't see Novak change anything on any surface. He thinks he does, but to the naked eye it is all just a different color on the same surface and the game is exactly the same."

Carillo observed all of the great players who have emerged in the Open Era that commenced in 1968. She won the French Open mixed doubles alongside McEnroe in 1977 and established herself as a inimitably astute commentator starting the early 1980's.

She said in 2019, "I genuinely believe Pete is there with a fistful of guys who could live on the same court at the same time, taking Rafa's domination on clay away from the conversation. The matchup I would have enjoyed the most would be Pete against Novak. Novak is so aggressive now from the serve and the return. It would be amazing watching those two. They would split matches only because it doesn't matter how well you serve, it doesn't matter how well you return: Pete had that great gunslinger attitude about him and would know he would need to go big early. He would know what to do against Novak. That matchup would be a joy to watch."

Shifting to Sampras taking on Federer and Nadal, Carillo said, "That one match Pete and Roger played at Wimbledon in 2001 was glorious. I still think Pete would serve and volley if he played Roger now and that would be fun. Pete would not go away from his own great gifts. Rafa has so much work on the ball that it would not be easy for Pete handling shot after shot and trying to volley because Rafa would certainly demand that Pete hit incredibly tough volleys off very tough topspin. I would love to see that one as well."

Sampras had his own thoughts on this imaginary series as he spoke about it in 2019. He said, "They are all different. I think Novak in a lot of ways would probably give me the most problems because he has by far the best return of all time. I always said Andre's return was the best and his return was great. But you could get it by him. With Novak, I would have a hard time getting my serve by him because he is just a better athlete than Andre. Novak would give me a hard time because he hits such a good, deep ball and returns so well. I would have to work hard to hold serve against Novak. It would be interesting to see the length of his return. I have never seen anything like that. It is aggressive and he has that stretch on the forehand and his athletic ability. I would try to get in on his second serve and try to do something with that, but his flexibility, stretch and reach are unlike anything I have ever seen."

Shifting to the charismatic Spanish southpaw and the Swiss Maestro, Sampras said, "I feel I could potentially get in on Nadal because he stands so far back to return. I feel it would be a little bit like playing Corretja because he would have one pattern of playing to my backhand and Rafa does that better than anyone. So that would be a struggle, but I feel I would be able to get in on him and impose my game. With Roger, I feel I could also get in on him some and attack the backhand return and try to hold serve that way. He possesses a bigger serve than Rafa or Novak and he has that great weapon on the forehand. Roger misses a little more, but of the three he may be the most dangerous guy. I would have my hands full with all three guys."

Nevertheless, Sampras had an ingrained belief in himself that he could deal with the severity of every challenge that would come his way.

Recalling his four exhibition matches against Federer in Asia and at Madison Square Garden in 2007 and 2008–he won one of three contests in Asia, took the Swiss to 7-6, 7-6 in another, served for the match at Madison Square Garden and even led 5-3 in the final-set tie-break of that contest before losing—Sampras said, "When I was 36, I stayed with Roger in those exhibitions and made it competitive. I just feel with my serve-and-volley game I would be in all of those matches. Obviously Roger is a great player, but I felt I could play with him even well past my prime. I just feel with my serve-and-volley game I would be in all of these matches. There is nobody in the past or the present I feel I couldn't play with."

He did not say it with even a trace of arrogance; he simply amplified what we all saw and heard from him during his heyday. He was confident with good reason. Sampras had the upper hand against every one of his chief rivals. It did not matter whether they were attacking players or confirmed baseliners, big servers or staunch defenders, outstanding counter attackers or chip and chargers. His game was fully equipped to handle all kinds of opponents, especially in high stakes conditions. He called the shots.

Sampras played the game on his own terms at all times in medium to fast court conditions. His self-conviction was demonstrably displayed in the matches that mattered most. Watching him compete in front of impassioned audiences against this celebrated trio of Federer, Nadal and Djokovic on the premier stages with the most prestigious prizes up for grabs would have been compelling. The feeling grows that Sampras would have presented these three luminaries—and anyone else in the upper regions of the sport who has emerged since he retired—with tactical and technical issues they have not experienced against anyone else. We can only imagine how captivating it would have been to see a prime time Pete Sampras confronting the men who have followed him at the summit in the world of tennis.

# CHAPTER 19

# THE GREATEST AMERICAN OF ALL TIME

Across the realm of history, American men have often been in the forefront of the game. Some of the sport's most iconic figures have hailed from the United States and many of them have transcended tennis. In the 1920's—the decade when the game started fully capturing the public imagination—Americans made their presence known surpassingly. They have ruled at the majors, dominated over long stretches, altered the face of tennis on many levels, and raised the bar of competition over and over again. These players have been indispensable, far reaching and unassailable. Their contributions have been immeasurable.

"Big Bill" Tilden was arguably the first authentic superstar of tennis. Between 1921 and 1930, he was victorious seven times at the U.S. Championships and thrice at Wimbledon. He was a master strategist and a superb technician and tactician. He wrote some excellent and enduring instructional books on the game that reflected his incomparable knowledge of tactics and court craft.

Tilden was indisputably the finest tennis player of the 1920's. He played on much longer after turning professional in the 1930's. Other great American competitors emerged in that era, most prominently the Californian Ellsworth Vines, a spectacularly explosive player who took three major singles titles in the early 1930's and later turned pro. Vines served prodigiously and was a powerhouse off the forehand.

But that decade's best American player was the red-headed and immensely ambitious Don Budge, another gifted Californian who developed one of the standout backhands of all time. Budge was the first player ever to secure a Grand Slam, sweeping all four majors in 1938.

Over the course of the 1940's, Jack Kramer took his potent attacking game to a level of importance never exhibited before. He played "The Big Game," serving and volleying with singular distinction. Kramer left amateur tennis after taking Wimbledon in 1947 and the U.S. Championships twice—in 1946-47. He was the dominant professional player thereafter well into the 1950's. In the first half of the 20th Century, no one did more to advance the game and how it was played than Kramer. But his multi-faceted contributions off the court later in his life may have obscured his extraordinary gifts as a player of rare stature.

From the late forties as an amateur into the early 1970's as a professional, Richard "Pancho "Gonzales was a major force, establishing himself as one of the leading Americans and best players of all time with his incomparably beautiful serve, terrific technique at the net, the force of his powerful personality and the range of his ambitions. Gonzales was perhaps the single most intimidating of all the great players from his or any country.

In 1955, Tony Trabert celebrated a magnificent season to conclude his amateur career, winning three of the four majors and 18 of 23 tournaments. He won five majors in singles altogether, had a distinguished pro career and demonstrated a propensity to play almost equally well on every surface with his all-court mastery. He belongs on any list of the top ten Americans.

Moving on into the Open Era which commenced in 1968, Arthur Ashe distinguished himself as the first African-American man to win a major when he was victorious at the initial U.S. Open that year. He went on to rule at the Australian Open two years later and prevailed at Wimbledon in 1975. Ashe's potency on serve and his glorious backhand were the leading features of his exhilarating brand of play.

During the seventies, eighties and even at the outset of the nineties, the dynamic left-handers Jimmy Connors and John McEnroe were enormously successful and their impact was extraordinary. Connors was the consummate all-court player, going to the net on his own terms. His return of serve was one of the best ever. He finished five years in a row from 1974-78 at No. 1 in the world. And he won the U.S. Open on three different surfaces to set a record no one will ever break. McEnroe was the quintessential serve-and-volleyer. He concluded four years in a row at the top of the game from 1981-84, won seven majors in singles and established himself in the eyes of many as the best doubles player of all time.

In the era of Sampras, Agassi was the second best of a great American contingent, winning eight majors, becoming only the fifth man to take all four Grand Slam events in singles and setting the tennis world aflame with his personality, crackling groundstrokes and outstanding return of serve.

All of the aforementioned men were substantial figures in the history of American tennis. Meanwhile, many other formidable players came along in the Open Era which started in 1968. Some outstanding competitors did not make my top ten cut for the all-time historical ladder. They include the industrious Courier, four times a champion at the majors and one of the few men to reach all four finals at the "Big Four" events. Stan Smith was No. 1 in the world, a Wimbledon and U.S. Open champion and a Davis Cup stalwart in the early seventies. Had his career not been shortened by injuries, Smith would undoubtedly have collected more of the premier prizes. Vitas Gerulaitis took one Australian Open, made it to the finals of the French and U.S. Opens and was in back-to-back

Wimbledon semifinals during his heyday in the late seventies and early eighties. He was a versatile all surface player with a wide range of skills, excellent foot speed and anticipation and a deep affinity for the volley.

Both Michael Chang and Andy Roddick had celebrated Hall of Fame careers, securing a major apiece. Roddick was the world's top ranked player in 2003. He reached four other finals at the preeminent events. Chang was the youngest man ever to win at the French Open in 1989 at 17, and later got to three additional finals at the Grand Slam events. Roddick had one of the great serves of his or any era and Chang was among the fastest and fiercest competitors.

But the best American of them all across the Open Era and through all of time must be Sampras. In many ways, he was a fascinating blend of Kramer and Gonzales. His unimaginably smooth service motion was reminiscent of Gonzales and his temperament and attacking style were much like Kramer's. His six years in a row at No. 1 and 14 major crowns make him a strong candidate as the best player of all time from any country. But while the debate can linger about where Sampras belongs amidst the likes of Laver, Djokovic, Federer and Nadal, nearly all of the authorities believe that Pete Sampras is the best American ever to step out into the area of tennis.

## TOP 10 AMERICANS (ALL-TIME)

1. Pete Sampras
2. Jack Kramer
3. Bill Tilden
4. Don Budge
5. Pancho Gonzales
6. Jimmy Connors
7. Andre Agassi
8. John McEnroe
9. Ellsworth Vines
10. Tony Trabert

## TOP 10 AMERICANS (OPEN ERA)

1. Pete Sampras
2. Jimmy Connors
3. Andre Agassi
4. John McEnroe
5. Arthur Ashe
6. Jim Courier
7. Stan Smith
8. Vitas Gerulaitis
9. Michael Chang
10. Andy Roddick

In my view, Sampras at the top is non-negotiable. But determining who belonged highest among the rest of the players in both the all-time American and Open Era lists was more difficult. I placed Kramer at No. 2 in the best-ever category because he was virtually unbeatable at his zenith. Tilden was a genius of a match player and Budge took the game to a new level. Gonzales celebrated one of the longest ever runs at the loftiest levels of the game. But very little separated those four iconic performers. They all had the credentials to be No. 2.

Looking at the Open Era, Connors narrowly deserved the nod over Agassi and McEnroe for No. 2 in my estimation. McEnroe was the most gifted of that towering trio. He was better at his best on fast courts than either Connors or Agassi. But Connors set the highest standards of consistency over a long span and he was a singularly unwavering competitor. That settled it for me.

# CHAPTER 20

# PETE SAMPRAS POST-CAREER

After Sampras concluded his sterling career at the U.S. Open of 2002, he took some time to decompress. His first son, Christian Charles Sampras, was born on November 21, 2002. Nearly three years later, on July 29, 2005, his second son, Ryan Nikolaos, officially joined the Sampras family. Raised in Southern California, both kids were exposed to a variety of sports at their schools.

Sampras was, from the outset, a hands-on father who enjoyed being around on a daily basis to look after his children along with his wife. He took that parental role very seriously. He started playing some tennis exhibitions in 2006 along with World TeamTennis and the following year he played regularly on Courier's "Champions Series" senior tour. He continued playing some exhibitions and many senior events frequently through 2012 but much less after that. By his early forties, his body was not holding up as well as it had during his mid to late thirties.

Sampras was never gone for extended periods and thus was a modern-day family man. That fact was not lost on other players who admired his commitment to his two kids and his wife. As Wilander said in 2019, "I would love to hear him come out and share what he feels about today's game because I

Pete Sampras in action on the PowerShares Series "Champions" Tour organized by Jim Courier

think there is a lot we haven't gotten out of Pete Sampras about his knowledge of the game and his emotions on the game. I would love to hear that from him, but he is obviously going for 'Husband and Father of the Year.' You can never, ever respect that enough. He is taking care of the people around him and that is why he goes down as such a proper, stand-up guy with no frills. I respect a lot that he has never tried to be more than who he is."

Seles felt much the same way. Having followed Sampras admirably from afar, she said, "He has transitioned from his professional life to his personal life wonderfully. That is not an easy transition for athletes. He has prioritized very well what matters to him and that has been beautiful to watch."

Growing up, how much of a kick did the Sampras boys get out of having a well-known father? Sampras responded in 2019, "It is embarrassing. They put on those milk ads I did every now and then with my shirt off and watch them on the computer. They bust my chops."

Ryan Sampras—who like his father switched from a two-handed backhand to a one-hander—started playing some 14-and-under tennis tournaments in 2018. He developed a love of the sport. As Pete Sampras clarified in 2019, "I am giving him the best opportunity to be the best he can be, whether that is going to college and playing there, being a pro, or wherever his tennis takes him."

Pete Sampras and his younger son have had some amusing moments when they have gone on the court together to hit tennis balls. He said jovially in 2019, "If we had a tape of some of these conversations we have had on the court, you would be cracking up. I was working on his serve one time and giving him advice. He was frustrated. He said, 'Dad, you don't know what you are talking about.' That was hilarious.'"

Pete and Bridgette Sampras have complemented each other in a multitude of ways, bringing different attributes to their roles as parents. Sampras lauded his wife for her staunch character and fundamental decency as a parent. He said in 2019, "She is the most patient lady I have ever seen. She is all in with our kids. She is so nice and sweet and such a good communicator."

Sampras enjoyed returning to Indian Wells in both 2018 and 2019 with his family, particularly in the latter of those years. When Nadal had to default against Federer in the semifinals, Sampras was eating lunch on the grounds at Nobu with his older son Christian when tournament director Tommy Haas sent Pete a text asking him to play a brief doubles exhibition with Djokovic against Haas and John McEnroe.

As Sampras said, "I had just ordered some sushi with Christian when Tommy sent the text asking if I would be interested in playing with Novak. I looked at Christian and said, 'Oh my God.' Christian said, "What is it?" And I told him they were asking me to play in this doubles exhibition. I was in jeans and a tee-shirt with no rackets. I had not picked up a racket in months and I didn't have any gear. I was so unprepared. I was sitting there with Christian for ten or 15 minutes just debating, 'Do I want to do this? Do I not want to do this?' Christian knew

I was a little uptight about it and he said, 'Well, if you don't feel good, then don't do it.' But he also kind of wanted me to do it just to see me play. And so I ended up doing it. That was some nice interaction we had as a father and a son. He just pushed me a little bit to go out, have fun, get out of my own way and do it for my kids. It was a cool experience for me. I was stressing out and Christian helped me through it."

Nevertheless, Sampras was uncertain about his physical state as he walked on court. He said, "I thought I might pull a calf muscle. I ended up using Novak's racket and in twenty minutes I was on the court, kind of like a fish out of water. I felt a bit discombobulated and it was bizarre, but the fans seemed to like it and my wife and two kids all watched. I am a shadow of myself since I hardly play anymore. It was a weird situation to get thrown into, but I was just grateful I didn't get hurt and didn't totally embarrass myself. I told my kids I used to be a lot better than this."

When Sampras joined Djokovic for that doubles exhibition, it gave them the chance to catch up. Here was Sampras in his late forties, one of the sport's most celebrated citizens and the greatest of all American champions. And there was the eminent Djokovic, wanting to use that time to learn from his idol's vast range of experience.

As Djokovic said in his interview for this book in 2019, "We spoke prior to coming into the tunnel going out to the court and talked about the excitement and mentality of getting into a tennis match and what a player goes through. When I am next to Pete, I am always trying to ask questions and absorb his knowledge and experience because I always looked up to him. I value every word that comes out of his mouth. He was telling me to cover two thirds of the court and no excuse if I didn't. We had a lot of laughs."

After Sampras and Djokovic finished that exhibition against McEnroe and Haas, they spent some time together. As Djokovic said, "We really had a nice philosophical talk about tennis and life and the mental side of the game mostly, because at the end of the day everything comes down to what you project from your mind and how you deal with the circumstances in life, good and bad. He was the master at that so I can learn from him always."

Djokovic had enjoyed similar conversations with Sampras at other stages of his career dating back to when they met in 2010. They also had a 2011 dinner in California not long after Djokovic had first moved to No. 1 in the world. Djokovic said, "I think the difference in our characters is that throughout my life I tend to, when I am excited, focus on being happy and really enjoying what I do and sticking to the core emotion and feeling that got me into this sport. But I tend to be willing to do a lot of different things and to overthink and complicate my life on the court and off the court as well. So most of my questions to Pete when we had the private dinner in 2011 and other times like this year in 2019 are heading in that direction—how I should approach things. I ask Pete for his advice and to break it down for me clear and simple and basic. His message is that I should simplify things, stick to what I am good at and always prioritize tennis. He tells me to utilize the things that can benefit my tennis and don't get distracted."

Djokovic continued, "Pete was always so good at being focused on what he needed to do and simplifying things, while I am the kind of character who likes to explore different things off the court and go deep in trying to understand the essence of my tennis life. I am always trying to learn and to constantly evolve, but sometimes that gets me to a place where maybe I lose the ground under my feet. That is why that talk with Pete in 2011 showed me direction and reminded me of what matters most, and the same in 2019 at Indian Wells. Every time I speak with Pete, even if he doesn't say a word, just his being there, the message resonates because it is coming from him."

Addressing the conversation he had with Djokovic at Indian Wells in 2019, Sampras said, "Novak talked about motivation and how he has won so much and the distractions. He talked about his family life and how much that means to him. We were sitting there at Indian Wells with my wife and kids taking pictures after our exhibition and Novak just got right into it. He is a very conscientious guy and very thoughtful. I just gave him a bit of advice. I know he is heading up the Player Council for the ATP and how time consuming that is. I just told him the less distractions the better. You don't need to be dealing with any friction with other players or getting involved too much in the politics of the sport. I said, 'It is great that you care so much but just be aware that all of that stuff can take some energy out of you.'"

Another player Sampras spent a bit of time with at that Indian Wells 2019 event was Stefanos Tsitsipas. Like Sampras, Tsitsipas was born on August 12. And, of course, they have their Greek heritage in common. Tsitsipas is 27 years younger than Sampras. Paul Annacone arranged for the two men to meet and Sampras was impressed with the young player.

"He was a lot taller than I thought he was," said Sampras of the 6'4" Greek player in June of 2019. "This guy is an athlete who moves really well. He is going to be around for a while. He couldn't have been any nicer and we enjoyed talking about tennis. He has a great future. I like his attitude. He is one of the few guys who is really willing to come in. He moves well at the net. He has got good hands up there. I think he has got a great game. He can be top five for the rest of his career and he could very well potentially get to No. 1. He is going to get better and better. When he is 22 or 23, that is when things click in. He has got a great one-handed backhand and he can actually get on top of that high backhand. He will contend for and win some majors."

Not only did Sampras have fun with his family observing the BNP Paribas Open in California and catching up with some players, but he also had a blast watching the epic Djokovic-Federer 2019 Wimbledon final at home is Los Angeles with his two sons and his wife. The fan in Pete Sampras was evident as he discussed that experience.

As he recounted, "I watched bits and pieces of the match over the first four sets, but then saw the whole fifth set. Roger and Novak are two of the greatest players of all time and they were playing great at the same time in the biggest tournament in the world with so much at stake. It is rare in sports that everything aligns and this just aligned. Watching that match I am thinking, 'There is nothing that separates Roger and Novak. Nothing. It is just a little luck here or a bad break there.' It was one of the best matches I have ever seen. The level of tennis was through the roof and they both handled themselves great after the match, which they always do. It was a great moment not just in tennis but in all of sports to have a match like that. People were texting me during the match asking who was going to win and I was telling them I have no clue."

The Djokovic-Federer clash left Sampras drained. He reflected, "I would have been happy for either one of them to win and I was going to feel badly for whoever lost as well. I like them both a lot. I am more in contact with Roger than Novak, but they are both really good guys. For the rest of that day, I thought about the match and just the emotion of it for Roger and Novak."

Sampras found peace of mind and happiness as a family man after essentially curtailing competitive tennis of any kind in 2014 at 43. As he said in 2019, "I am very content. People ask me about commentating and I am not sure I would want to travel to do that. They ask about coaching and I am not sure that is what I want to do to get back to the sport. I am just content with my life in L.A. I work out every day, which makes me feel good and keeps me in shape. I play quite a bit of golf. I spend a lot of time with my wife and kids and we do things together as a family, going to Palm Desert—where I have a home—every now and then. I don't need to be at Wimbledon or the U.S. Open. If my kids want to go there, I am there. One of these years I might take my family to Wimbledon. I am just happy being where I am at. I miss tennis and a lot of those moments I have had, but I feel good every night. I am content. That is what matters to me."

He was always a private person thrust into the public arena as a renowned tennis player. There were parts of his fame that made him uncomfortable. That is why he has enjoyed being away from the limelight, simply living a quiet life on his own terms. When he was 47, he watched a special on the

Golf Channel about the great Ben Hogan and Sampras related to Hogan's desire to move almost completely away from the spotlight after so many years of competing in the upper regions of his sport.

"Hogan had this incredible career," said Sampras, "but when he went away, he went away. You really didn't see him again. And you don't see Sandy Koufax around much either. I am kind of made from that mold. I did my thing and played seniors and some exhibitions but now I am happy just doing what I am doing."

Speaking of parenthood, Sampras said, "It is the hardest job you can have. You have to stay checked in. I lived my life throughout my career keeping a lot of my emotions very close to the vest. So I encourage my kids to open up to me. I have told them it is okay to cry. I am reliving my youth through my kids. I have tried to reach out to the people close to me versus being very guarded and having a shield up as I did for a lot of my life. As a player I had to be self-centered but I am looking through a different set of glasses now. It has been a big transformation for me and a good one."

Pete Sampras was an outstanding champion who set the highest ethical standards on and off the court. Sampras will be celebrated forever as a master of his universe. He deservedly reaped the rewards of an unflagging dedication to his craft, turned himself into the game's ultimate professional, and was an exemplary ambassador everywhere he went over the course of a storied career. He was a craftsman through and through and an athlete who did things on a tennis court that could not be replicated by any of his peers. He transcended tennis and captured the imaginations of sports fans from every corner of the globe who appreciated his grit, dignity, graciousness and integrity. Pete Sampras always epitomized the notion that character is more easily kept than recovered.

# ALSO FROM
# NEW CHAPTER PRESS

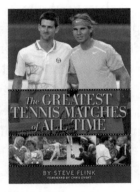

**The Greatest Tennis Matches of All Time**
*By Steve Flink*

Author and tennis historian Steve Flink profiles and ranks the greatest tennis matches in the history of the sport. Roger Federer, Billie Jean King, Rafael Nadal, Bjorn Borg, John McEnroe, Martina Navratilova, Rod Laver, Don Budge and Chris Evert are all featured in this book that breaks down, analyzes, and puts into historical context the most memorable matches ever played.

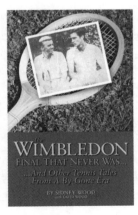

**The Wimbledon Final That Never Was… And Other Tennis Tales From A Bygone Era**
*By Sidney Wood with David Wood*

Sidney Wood tells the entertaining and fascinating tale of his Wimbledon title win 1931, capped with a strange default to his best friend, doubles partner, roommate and Davis Cup teammate Frank Shields ordered by the U.S. Tennis Association! Also included in this volume are a compilation of short stories that deliver fascinating anecdotes of old-school Hollywood and the styles of play of all 20th-century tennis legends.

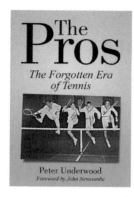

## The Pros: The Forgotten Era of Tennis
*By Peter Underwood*

To most modern day tennis fans, it was impossible to believe that until the late 1960s pro tennis players—that is those who played openly for prize money—were banned from competing in the world's major tournaments. Before this time, the great contests such as Wimbledon were exclusive to so-called amateurs. Amateur tennis players were meant to compete only for glory. Though this division arose the "pro tour" in the 1930s, and it endured for forty years. In *The Pros, The Forgotten Era of Tennis*, author Peter Underwood explains why professional players were forced into what was often called the traveling circus where these sporting outcasts played each other during long and rather tatty tours all over the world. Focusing on the eight champions who dominated the pro era beginning in 1930 with the ultimately tragic figure of "Big" Bill Tilden, this book follows each pro champion through the post-1962 Grand Slam pro career of Rod Laver, who then helped usher in the modern-era of pro tennis with the start of the "Open" Era in 1968.

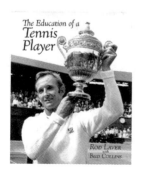

## The Education of a Tennis Player
*By Rod Laver with Bud Collins*

Rod Laver's historic 1969 Grand Slam sweep of all four major tennis titles is documented first-hand as it happened by Laver along with Hall of Fame journalist Bud Collins. This important tennis memoir details one of the famous years in tennis history while also documenting Laver's childhood, early career and his most important matches.